# IN
# A TIME
# OF TORMENT
### 1961–1967

By I. F. Stone

A NONCONFORMIST HISTORY OF OUR TIMES

# IN
# A TIME
# OF TORMENT
## 1961–1967

I. F. STONE

LITTLE, BROWN AND COMPANY

BOSTON          TORONTO          LONDON

*Library of Congress Cataloging-in-Publication Data*
Stone, I. F. (Isidor F.), 1907–
       In a time of torment, 1961–1967 / I. F. Stone.
          p.      cm. — (A nonconformist history of our times)
       Includes index.
       1. United States — Politics and government — 1963–1969.   2. United
States — Foreign relations — 1963–1969.   3. United States — Politics
and government — 1961–1963.   4. United States — Foreign
relations — 1961–1963.   I. Title.   II. Series: Stone, I. F. (Isidor
F.). 1907– Nonconformist history of our times.
E846.S76 1989
320.973 — dc 19                                                        88-39990

                                                                           CIP

MV-PA

*Published simultaneously in Canada*
*by Little, Brown & Company (Canada) Limited*

PRINTED IN THE UNITED STATES OF AMERICA

To my daughter, Celia

With acknowledgment to
Barbara K. Perlman
for her assistance
in the
selection and organization
of this collection

# CONTENTS

## X | A VISIT TO VIETNAM AND CAMBODIA

## XI | WE ALWAYS SEEM TO GUESS WRONG

**XIX** | **TRIBALISM'S TOLL: GERMAN, JEWS, ARABS**

    GOD'S "DEPUTY"                                           432
THE RACIST CHALLENGE IN ISRAEL                              435
THE HARDER BATTLE AND THE NOBLER
    VICTORY                                                 441
FOR A UNIVERSAL DAY OF ATONEMENT                            446


    INDEX                                                   449


    ABOUT THE AUTHOR                                        465

# AUTHOR'S PREFACE

## A WORD ABOUT MYSELF

I am, I suppose, an anachronism. In an age of corporation men, I have been an independent capitalist, the owner of my own enterprise, subject to neither mortgager nor broker, factor nor patron. In an age when young men, setting out on a career of journalism, must find their niche in some huge newspaper or magazine combine, I have been a wholly independent newspaperman, standing alone, without organizational or party backing, beholden to no one but my good readers. I am even one up on Benjamin Franklin — I have never accepted advertising.

The majority of the pieces collected in this volume are from a four-page miniature journal of news and opinion, on which I was a one-man editorial staff, from proofreader to publisher. This independence, like all else, had its price — the audience. My newspaper reached a relative handful, but the 5,000 readers with whom I started grew to more than 70,000 in nineteen years. I was in the black every one of those years and paid off the loans which helped me begin, without having to appeal to my readers or to wealthy friends to keep going. I paid my bills promptly, like a solid bourgeois, though in the eyes of many in the cold-war Washington where I operated I was regarded, I am sure, as a dangerous and subversive fellow.

I have been a newspaperman all my life. In the small town where I grew up, I published a paper at fourteen, worked for a country weekly and then as correspondent for a nearby city daily. I did this from my sophomore year in high school through college, until I quit in my junior year. I was a philosophy major and at one time thought of teaching philosophy, but the atmosphere of a college faculty repelled me. While going to college I was working ten hours afternoon and night doing combination rewrite and copy desk on the *Philadelphia Inquirer*, so I was already an experienced newspaperman making $40 a week — big pay in 1928. I have done everything on a newspaper except run a linotype machine.

I had become a radical in the twenties while in my teens, mostly through reading Jack London, Herbert Spencer, Kropotkin and Marx. I became a member of the Socialist Party and was elected to the New Jersey State Committee of the Socialist Party before I was old enough to vote. I did publicity for Norman Thomas in the 1928 campaign while a reporter on a small city daily, but soon drifted away from left-wing politics because of the sectarianism of the left. Moreover, I felt that party affiliation was incompatible with independent journalism, and I wanted to be free to help the unjustly treated, to defend everyone's civil liberty and to work for social reform without concern for leftist infighting.

I was fortunate in my employers. I rarely, if ever, felt compelled to compromise with my conscience; even as an anonymous editorial writer I never had to write something I thought untrue. I worked for a succession of newspaper people I remember with affection: J. David Stern and his editor Harry T. Saylor on the *Camden Courier-Post*, the *Philadelphia Record* and the *New York Post;* Freda Kirchwey of *The Nation;* Ralph Ingersoll and John P. Lewis of the newpaper *PM;* Bartley Crum and his editor Joseph Barnes of the short-lived New York *Star;* and Ted O. Thackrey of the *New York Post* and the New York *Daily Compass.* Working for them was a wonderfully rewarding experience and I learned much from all of them. From 1932 to 1939 I was an editorial writer on the *Philadelphia Record* and the *New York Post*, then strongly pro–New Deal papers. In 1940 I came to Washington as Washington Editor of *The Nation* and have been here ever since, working as reporter and columnist for *PM*, the New York *Star,* the *New York Post* (for a short interval) and the New York *Compass.* When the *Compass* closed in

November 1952 and no congenial job seemed likely to open up, I decided to launch a four-page weekly newsletter of my own.

I succeeded because it was what might be called a piggy-back launching. I had available the mailing lists of *PM*, the *Star* and the *Compass* and of people who had bought my books. For a remarkably small investment, in two advance mailings, I was able to get 5,000 subscribers at $5 each. I was my own biggest investor, but several friends helped me with loans and gifts. The existence of these highly selective mailing lists made it possible to reach what would otherwise appear to be needles in a haystack — a scattered tiny minority of liberals and radicals unafraid in McCarthy's heyday to support, and go on the mailing lists of, a new radical publication from Washington. I am deeply grateful to them.

It speaks well for the tradition of a free press in our country that even in the heyday of McCarthy it was possible for me to obtain my second-class mail permit without trouble. I had then been working in Washington for twelve years as correspondent for a succession of liberal and radical papers. I had supported Henry Wallace in 1948. I had fought for the civil liberties of Communists, and was for peace and coexistence with the Soviet Union. I had fought the loyalty purge, the FBI, the House Un-American Activities Committee, and McCarran as well as McCarthy. I had written the first magazine article against the Smith Act, when it was first used against the Trotskyites in 1940. There was nothing to the left of me but the *Daily Worker*.

Yet I was able to get second-class mail privilege without a single political question. I encountered old-fashioned civil service courtesy and political impartiality in the post office, and the second-class mail privilege when I started was my bread and butter. The difference between the second-class rate and the cheapest third-class rate was the equivalent of my salary.

My idea was to make the *Weekly* radical in viewpoint but conservative in format. I picked a beautiful type face, Garamond, for my main body type, and eschewed sensational headlines. I made no claim to inside stuff — obviously a radical reporter in those days had few pipelines into the government. I tried to give information which could be documented so the reader could check it for himself. I tried to dig the truth out of hearings, official transcripts and government documents, and to be as accurate as possible. I also sought to give the *Weekly* a personal flavor, to add humor, wit and good writing to the *Weekly* report. I felt that if one were able enough and had sufficient vision one could distill meaning, truth and even beauty from the swiftly flowing debris of the week's news. I sought in political reporting what Galsworthy in another context called "the significant trifle" — the bit of dialogue, the overlooked fact, the buried observation which illuminated the realities of the situation. These I often used in "boxes" to lighten up the otherwise solid pages of typography unrelieved either by picture or advertising. I tried in every issue to provide fact and opinion not available elsewhere in the press.

In the worst days of the witch hunt and cold war, I felt like a guerilla warrior, swooping down in surprise attack on a stuffy bureaucracy where it least expected independent inquiry. The reporter assigned to specific beats like the State Department or the Pentagon for a wire service or a big daily newspaper soon finds himself a captive. State and Pentagon have large press relations forces whose job it is to herd the press and shape the news. There are many ways to punish a reporter who gets out of line; if a big story breaks at 3 A.M., the press office may neglect to notify him while his rivals get the story. There are as many ways to flatter and take a reporter into camp — private off-the-record dinners with high officials, entertainment at the service clubs. Reporters tend to be absorbed by the bureaucracies they cover; they take on the habits, attitudes and even accents of the military or the diplomatic corps. Should a reporter resist the pressure, there are many ways to get rid of him. If his publisher is not particularly astute or independent, a little private talk, a hint that the reporter seems irresponsible — even a bit radical — "sometimes one could even mistake him for a Marxist" — will do the job of getting him replaced with a more malleable man.

But a reporter covering the whole capital on his own — particularly if he is his own employer — is immune from these pressures. Washington is full of news — if one story is denied him he can always get another. The bureaucracies put out so much that they cannot help letting the truth slip from time to time. The town is open. One can always ask questions, as one can see from one of my "coups" — forcing the Atomic Energy

Commission to admit that its first underground test was detected not 200 miles away — as it claimed — but 2600 miles away. This is the story of how I got that story — one example of what independent news gathering can be like.

The first underground test was held in the fall of 1957. The *New York Times* report from the test site in Nevada next morning said the results seemed to confirm the expectations of the experts: that it would not be detected more than 200 miles away. But the *Times* itself carried "shirttails" from Toronto, Rome and Tokyo saying that the shot had been detected there. Since the experts (viz. Dr. Edward Teller and his entourage at Livermore Laboratory, all opposed to a nuclear test ban agreement) were trying to prove that underground tests could not be detected at a distance, these reports from Toronto , Rome and Tokyo piqued my curiosity. I did not have the resources to check them by cable, so I filed the story away for future use.

Next spring, Stassen, then Eisenhower's chief disarmament negotiator, testified before the Humphrey Disarmament Sub-committee of the Senate that a network of stations a thousand kilometers (or 580 miles apart) could police a nuclear test ban agreement and detect any underground tests. Two days after his testimony the AEC issued its first official report on the Nevada explosion for publication the following Monday. This said that the Nevada underground explosion had not been detected more than 200 miles away. The effect was to undercut Stassen's testimony. If the Nevada blast could not be detected more than 200 miles away then a network of stations 580 miles apart would not be able to police an agreement. I recalled the *New York Times* report of the previous fall, dug it out of a basement file and telephoned the AEC press office. I asked how the AEC reconciled its statement in the report about to be released that the blast was not detected more than 200 miles away with the reports from Rome, Tokyo and Toronto the morning after that it had registered on seismographs there. The answer was that they didn't know but would try to find out.

In the meantime I decided to find me a seismologist. By telephoning around I learned there was a seismology branch in the Coast and Geodetic Survey, where I duly found a seismologist and asked him whether it was true that Tokyo, Rome and Toronto had detected the Nevada underground blast. He said that he did not believe the claims of these three foreign stations but he showed me a list of some twenty U.S. stations which he said had certainly detected it. One of these was 2600 miles north of the test site in Fairbanks, Alaska, another was 1200 miles east in Fayetteville, Arkansas. I copied the names and distances down. When he asked why I was so interested, I said the AEC was about to release a report for the following Monday claiming that the explosion was not detected more than 200 miles away. When he heard the AEC angle, he became less communicative. I had hardly got back to my office when the phone rang; it was the AEC press relations man. He said "We just heard from Coast and Geodetic. There must be some mistake. We'll reach Nevada by teletype in the morning and let you know." When the Joint Committee on Atomic Energy later investigated the incident, the AEC claimed it was an "inadvertent" error. No agency in Washington — not even State Department or Pentagon — has a worse record than the AEC for these little "errors."

No bureaucracy likes an independent newspaperman. Whether capitalist or communist, democratic or authoritarian, every regime does its best to color and control the flow of news in its favor. There *is* a difference here and I'm grateful for it. I could not operate in Moscow as I do in Washington. There is still freedom of fundamental dissent here, if only on the edges and in small publications.

For me, being a newspaperman has always seemed a cross between Galahad and William Randolph Hearst, a perpetual crusade. When the workers of Csespel and the 1956 Hungarian Revolution put a free press among their demands, I was thrilled. What Jefferson symbolized for me was being rediscovered in a socialist society as a necessity for good government.

I believe that no society is good and can be healthy without freedom for dissent and for creative independence. I have found among the Soviets kindred spirits in this regard and I watch their struggle for freedom against bureaucracy with deepest sympathy. I am sorry, when discussing our free press with them, to admit that our press is often almost as conformist as theirs. But I am happy that in my own small way I have been able to demonstrate that independence is possible, that a wholly free radical journalist can survive in our society. In the darkest days of McCarthy, when I often was made to feel a pariah, I was heartened by the thought that I was preserving and carrying forward the best in America's traditions, that in my humble way I stood in a line that reached back to Jefferson. These are the origins and the preconceptions, the hopes and the aspirations, from which sprang the pieces that follow.

I. F. STONE

# I

---

## KENNEDY: BRIGHT PROMISE BUT CONVENTIONAL PERFORMANCE

# AS IF THE PROPHET JEREMIAH
# WERE CAUGHT CHEERING

At the risk of alarming steady customers, inured to a weekly diet of apocalyptic pessimism, I must confess that I am becoming optimistic. This may seem in its way perverse. Just when a new President sends Congress a first message filled with perilous tidings at home and abroad, your Washington reporter suddenly begins to see hope ahead. I even feel a little embarrassed, like the prophet Jeremiah caught giving three lusty cheers. But ever since John F. Kennedy's first press conference, I haven't felt the same.

The swift movement of events here is bewildering; one would have to print morning, evening, noon and night to keep up with it. The appointments, the policy positions, have something in them for everybody. Mr. Kennedy's heroes are Churchill and the two Roosevelts, but his dazzling sleight-of-hand most resembles de Gaulle's—and de Gaulle, remember, for all the misgivings of the French left is pulling off the miracle of getting France and the French Army slowly to accept the idea of an independent Algeria. I believe Mr. Kennedy, by a similar dexterity, may succeed in bringing about a settlement, first with the Soviet Union and then with Peking, in ways and on terms some of us may find surprising and even unpalatable, but the result can pull us away from the brink.

Some readers may remember that back in the spring of 1953, we shocked some of them with a piece called "Challenge to the Left: Back Ike for Peace," which proposed that we circumvent the pall of McCarthyism and make Mr. Eisenhower's moves toward a Korean truce the rallying point for public support of a broader settlement; we asked the left to get rid of its stereotypes and see that the new Republican soldier President was a potential force for peace. So he would have been but for Chancellor Adenauer's skillful torpedoing of one constructive possibility after another on the way to the abortive summit last year, and the tragic accident of the U-2. The latter was due to Mr. Eisenhower's lazy slovenliness about his job; the former, to the pro-Bonn orientation which John Foster Dulles so long gave U.S. policy. The days of the Bonn-Washington axis are, I believe, over; Adenauer's sudden moves toward a settlement with Poland reflect his fear of being left high-and-dry by bilateral talks between Washington and Moscow; "not a word on Berlin" *Die Welt* of Hamburg complains of Mr. Kennedy's State of the Union message.

As for a new incident or provocation similar to the U-2, its possibility is not to be excluded. There are mountainous bureaucratic and corporate forces against a settlement, with huge funds and resources at their disposal. But they will no longer find a slack hand and an absent mind at the White House. I cannot tell you with what pleasure I watched the new President at his first press conference; his performance washed away a long-held and indeed cherished anti-Kennedy bias. Necessity may make his course tortuous but the direction is clearly toward peace. I feel that for the first time since Roosevelt we have a first-rater in the Presidency, a young man of energy, zest and ability. It is a post in which any man of any quality must grow, but when a man starts out with the gifts Mr. Kennedy so clearly has, we have the right to hope he will grow to greatness, and perform valiantly in the cause of mankind.

Many difficulties and disappointments lie ahead. The narrow victory in the House Rules fight will invigorate the coalition of Republicans and Southern Democrats, who see that Mr. Kennedy will have to pay dearly in concessions to get the precarious margins required for his domestic program, but it will also invigorate Mr. Kennedy, and I predict that his personal appeal over TV will give him a better margin in the next House elections two years hence. It is obvious that he loves nothing better than a hard fight; indeed he seems to have a weakness for seeing an Armageddon everywhere. In this respect, the State of

the Union message would have benefitted by a little under-
statement. This is neither Britain in September 1939 nor America in 1933, nor has Fort Sumter just been fired upon.

In one sense, of course, the crisis is greater and global, but
the hangover of fervent cold war clichés still impedes Mr. Kennedy's efforts to express it with a just sobriety. Much of what
the President will do in this connection, the peace movement
will find incomprehensible and distasteful, and we intend to
criticize watchfully but no longer in a tone of despair. In moving toward peace, Mr. Kennedy must carry with him somehow
a party and a labor movement strongly attached to the arms
race, and a country which would be startled if it too soon heard
an entirely different tune on Soviet-American relations. In this,
Mr. Kennedy's problem is much like Mr. Khrushchev's; both
must conciliate rigid fanatics in their ranks; both must make
co-existence appear as only another form of struggle to liberate
the other's sphere of influence; neither can afford to appear
"soft," the one on capitalism, the other on communism. But
both are master politicians, and both are well aware of the
crossroads to which history has brought them.

The immediate issue, the crucial main point, is the successful
negotiation of a nuclear test ban treaty and its ratification by
the Senate, which requires a two-thirds vote. This is a formidable hurdle. To achieve this arduous goal, the necessary first
step toward wider settlement and relaxation of tension, all the
contradictions and compromises plainly visible in the Kennedy
program and official family—and there will be more of them—
are justified. The President can be freed from these political
necessities only by a more aroused and better informed public
opinion. Never was there greater need for a broader peace
movement than now; never was there a President more open to
fresh ideas and more ready for flexible tactics. But the success
of such a movement in affecting the course of events will depend on its unconventionality, its freedom from pacifist and
party line stereotypes and a demonstrated independence of
Moscow. What we need is not an organization to sell any particular panacea but to draw more and more people into discussing the problems of foreign policy and of peace. What we
ourselves need most to lose are the chains of our old clichés.

Any President's power to act is limited by the people's power to understand. A whole series of unstable situations abroad may easily upset negotiations on critical wider issues. It would be good if public opinion understood that many of Mr. Kennedy's problems abroad are less the result of Soviet machinations than of the CIA's, the heritage of poor State Department policy and melodramatic thinking at home. It is silly to talk of Laos, the Congo and Cuba as tests of Soviet sincerity. Mr. Khrushchev cannot chase the Pathet Lao out of the jungle for us nor turn Mr. Lumumba into a willing tool of Belgian-American big business and he certainly cannot control Fidel Castro. If Dr. Castro were really a communist, he could be turned on or off like a party line spigot, but he is a real revolutionary and a handful. In Cuba, more than anywhere else, there is need for private negotiation; the alternative is bloody intervention direct or covert, which would enflame the hemisphere; it is by our attitude toward Cuba, not by new promises of new aid, *mañana*, that the Latin American masses will judge us. It is in this Lilliputian quarrel that I see the greatest danger.

FEBRUARY 6, 1961

# THE RAPID DETERIORATION IN OUR NATIONAL LEADERSHIP

Neither men nor nations can take the law into their own hands without paying a price. The price we are paying for our undercover war against Cuba is a rapid deterioration in our leadership, and in our moral standards. According to Chalmers Roberts in the *Washington Post* of April 23 the President made a significant remark at the National Security Council meeting called the day before to discuss the Cuban debacle and the world situation. He said of South Vietnam that the Vietminh does not have a *New York Times* reporting how many people it is sending south to assassinate officials of South Vietnam. "He had in mind," Mr. Roberts wrote, "the pre-invasion stories in the American press about the Cuban fiasco," and "what has come out of the Cuban affair has been a determination to meet the Communist para-military tactics of guerrilla warfare, infiltration, sabotage and so on." General Maxwell Taylor's assignment "now is going to try to figure out how to do it."

These remarks of the President, more cryptically reported in the *New York Times* of April 24, are alarming in their implications. In the first place they misconceive the situation in South Vietnam as seriously as our government does that in Cuba. The real causes of the disintegration in South Vietnam lie in the failure of the Diem regime to build a viable government in the seven years since the Geneva settlement; its corruption, its false elections, its concentration camps, its suppression of democratic liberties, its mistreatment of minorities, are the causes of the growing rebellion. In the second place, the President's animus seems to be directed not at the follies exposed in the Cuban fiasco but at the free press for exposing them. The *New York Times*, and particularly staff members Tad Szulc and James Reston, has acquitted itself in recent weeks in the best traditions of a free press. It has brought to light conditions of which the President himself seems to have been but dimly aware. In the third place, the President's remarks are disturbing because they indicate he is out, not to rid our foreign policy of the CIA's incubus, but merely to improve our cloak-and-dagger methods, and to go further along the path of adopting the worst practices attributed to the Soviet bloc, even to the point of wistfully eyeing the advantages he thinks it derives from the absence of a free press.

The failure of the attempted invasion of Cuba, like so many of our failures in the postwar period, had its roots in an inability to understand popular feeling. But in the briefings held at the State Department during the first two days of this week for visiting editors—a kind of mass brainwashing operation in

which no time was allowed for any but the official point of
view and little time for questions or discussion—there was no
evidence of a willingness to face up to this fact. From the con-
ceited Berle through the discombobulated Stevenson to the
smug Allen Dulles not a single official was willing to admit that
our intelligence was wrong in assessing the mood of the Cuban
people. Official Washington has learned nothing, on the contrary it has drawn all the wrong conclusions, from the failure
in Cuba. The Kennedy Administration's swift slide back to the
conventional viewpoint of the stuffed shirts who direct our intelligence, military and diplomatic bureaucracies is evident
from the men chosen by Kennedy to investigate the failure.
Only a few weeks ago, the President was enforcing a blue
pencil on the inflammatory remarks of Admiral Arleigh Burke,
one of the biggest windbags in the military establishment; now
the Admiral is to assist General Maxwell Taylor in the investigation. Admiral Burke is a member of the Joint Chiefs of Staff;
one of the points which ought to be investigated is the poor
advice given the President by them; how to get a real investigation with the Admiral at General Taylor's elbow? Just to make
sure that the inquiry will be equally impartial in assessing the
role of the CIA, Allen Dulles will also serve on this panel; he
too will be in the happy position of investigating himself. In
addition, Attorney General Robert Kennedy has been added to
the panel. Like his brother, he had been acting admirably until
the Cuban crisis came along. Now, in advance of the investigation, he has issued a disingenuous opinion which would so reduce the ambit of the Neutrality Act as to absolve the CIA and
big business paymasters of the Cuban counter revolution from
complicity. General Taylor himself is superior in intellectual
capacity to most of the Pentagon crowd, but as a professional
soldier he is concerned with military means for dealing with
social change; events have over and over again demonstrated
their futility. There is not a single man on this panel capable
of approaching the Cuban question and the broader problems
it illustrates with the independent mind and perceptive spirit
they require.

The clearest sign of deterioration in national leadership lay
in the tone, the implications and the deceptions of Mr. Kennedy's speech to the American Society of Newspaper Editors.

The tone in its arrogant and willful self-righteousness sounded like an echo of Bismarck and Teddy Roosevelt; this was the Monroe Doctrine nakedly restated as American domination of the hemisphere; here was exactly that doctrine of unilateral intervention Latin America so hates and fears. The implications were of a return to the worst days of the cold war, with a readiness to extend the use of cloak-and-dagger methods on a wider scale than ever before. The worst deception did not come out until several days later. Mr. Kennedy spoke that Thursday, April 20, of the Cuban affair as "a struggle of Cuban patriots against a Cuban dictator." But on Sunday, April 23, in both Washington and Miami many newspapermen heard but few dared to print the story of how the Cuban Revolutionary Council was taken into custody in New York on the eve of the Cuban invasion, kept in ignorance of it, shut off from all contact with their own forces, and held incommunicado at a supposedly abandoned air base in Florida while statements were drafted in its name by the CIA and issued through the Lem Jones advertising agency in New York. Despite White House orders to the contrary, Batista men were not weeded out of the invasion forces and the CIA's notorious Mr. Bender who is cordially hated by all but the extreme right-wingers still ran the show. Yet Mr. Dulles at the big private press briefing Tuesday (not having been invited we are not bound by secrecy) was brazen enough to claim that his intelligence estimates were correct and that failure was due solely to the poor Cuban exiles themselves!

Fidel Castro won in Cuba by provoking Batista into destroying himself; the dictator in his fear and frenzy set out on so brutal a course as to undermine all support for himself except among his partners in plunder. I have all along feared that if we allowed ourselves to be drawn into war with Castro, he would provoke us similarly to self-destruction. The chain reaction is already in motion, and all Americans of sense and devotion must speak up quickly while it can still be stopped. The bright promise of the new Administration is being quenched by its own panicky folly; the military and the right wingers have been strengthened within our own government. A moral obduracy like that of South Africa's is apparent in the unthinking clamor for get-tough policies. The danger of direct invasion seems to have passed for the moment, but the new emphasis on "para-military" methods has an ominous ring; "para-military" formations poisoned the life of the German Republic under Weimar, assassinated some of its best leaders, and paved the way for Nazism. We cannot set up government agencies empowered to act lawlessly without infecting the life of our own Republic. To fall back on the conspiracy theory of history, to assume that human convulsion and aspiration are but puppet movements on string from Moscow, to place our hopes in counter-conspiracy, is to misread man and history to our own ultimate undoing.

APRIL 26, 1961

# MR. KENNEDY'S SPEECH ON SPACE NATIONALISTIC SOAP AD HOOPLA

Mr. Kennedy's speech on the space challenge at Houston revealed more about Mr. Kennedy and his advisers than it did about the problems of space. The most important question he had to answer was why we were spending all those billions out there in space anyway. To this he gave two replies. One, which seems to reflect a family characteristic, might be called the touch-football-after-lunch explanation; the Kennedys love activity and competition for their own sake. As Mr. Kennedy said, "Why, some say, the moon? Why choose this as our goal? They may well ask why climb the highest mountain? Why thirty-five years ago fly the Atlantic? Why does Rice play Texas?" The race to the moon, from this vantage point, is a way to work off excess energy, a cosmic sporting event.

Mr. Kennedy's second explanation was a flag-waving appeal to nationalistic instincts. "We have vowed," he said, "that we shall not see it [space] governed by a hostile flag of conquest, but by a banner of freedom and peace." How can Mr. Kennedy say, as he did later in the speech, that "there is no strife, no prejudice, no national conflict in outer space," when he invites them?

Many serious questions are involved in the space race. One is the problem of preventing war in space while there is yet time. Here Mr. Kennedy managed to be his usual ambivalent self. At one point, he said "We have vowed that we shall not see space filled with weapons of mass destruction, but with instruments of knowledge and understanding." A few minutes later, as though with a reassuring nod to the Pentagon, he was adding, "I do not say that we should or will go unprotected against the hostile misuse of space any more than we go unprotected against the hostile misuse of land or sea." This promises that space will be kept "peaceful"—by adding a new space branch to the armed forces.

Mr. Kennedy's reference to "hostile misuse of space" was disturbingly *un*self-conscious. Up to now only one nation has misused space in a hostile manner, by creating a new radiation belt hazardous to astronauts and by sending up U-2s and "weather" satellites to spy on other nation's defenses. He implied a readiness to shoot down such activities by others. What if they shoot ours down? How can there be peace in space if our people's eyes are not opened by responsible leadership to see our actions as they look to others?

Mr. Kennedy dragged in the Pilgrim Fathers for inspiration. The Pilgrim Fathers didn't make a fortune selling their stories to a picture magazine even before they started. No vast industry sprang up to cash in on their venture. Space deserves treatment more sober than this kind of soap ad copy.

We are tackling the tasks of space, Mr. Kennedy said, with his weakness for the mock heroic, "not because they are easy but because they are hard." They are hard only for a handful of astronauts and scientists. For industry, this is a lush cost plus operation. For the leadership, it provides glamorous politics to be photographed with the heroes. For the rest of us it is only another, though fantastically expensive, form of spectator sports.

It could be arduous for both the leadership and the led. But Mr. Kennedy's speech on the space challenge left out the important challenge—that to man's obsolete tribal way of thinking. If space is not to bring final disaster, man must be forced to grow up, a painful business. To make him see space as a human adventure, to identify our efforts with nothing smaller than the race of man, to make our perspectives begin to match its distances, to see how ludicrous the little divisions of nations look from the moon or Venus—if Mr. Kennedy really wants a hard and worthy space age task, there it is.

SEPTEMBER 24, 1962

# WE ALL HAD A FINGER
# ON THAT TRIGGER

There was a fairy tale quality about the inaugural and there was a fairy tale quality about the funeral rites. One half expected that when the lovely princess knelt to kiss the casket for the last time, some winged godmother would wave her wand and restore the hero whole again in a final triumph over the dark forces which had slain him. There never was such a shining pageant of a Presidency before. We watched it as children do, raptly determined to believe but knowing all the time that it wasn't really true.

Of all the Presidents, this was the first to be a Prince Charming. To watch the President at press conference or at a private press briefing was to be delighted by his wit, his intelligence, his capacity and his youth. These made the terrible flash from Dallas incredible and painful. But perhaps the truth is that in some ways John Fitzgerald Kennedy died just in time. He died in time to be remembered as he would like to be remembered, as ever young, still victorious, struck down undefeated, with almost all the potentates and rulers of mankind, friend and foe, come to mourn at his bier.

For somehow one has the feeling that in the tangled dramaturgy of events, this sudden assassination was for the author the only satisfactory way out. The Kennedy Administration was approaching an impasse, certainly at home, quite possibly abroad, from which there seemed no escape. In Congress the President was faced with something worse than a filibuster. He was confronted with a shrewdly conceived and quietly staged sitdown strike by Southern committee chairmen determined to block civil rights even if it meant stopping the wheels of government altogether. The measure of their success is that we entered this final month of 1963 with nine of the thirteen basic appropriation bills as yet unpassed, though the fiscal year for which they were written began last July 1 and most of the government has been forced to live hand-to-mouth since. Never before in our history has the Senate so dragged its heels as this year; never before has the Southern oligarchy dared go so far in demonstrating its power in Washington. The President was caught between these old men, their faces set stubbornly toward their white supremacist past, and the advancing Negro masses, explosively demanding "freedom now." Mr. Kennedy's death, like those of the Birmingham children and of Medgar Evers, may some day seem the first drops portending a new storm which it was beyond his power to stay.

In foreign policy, the outlook was as unpromising. It was proving difficult to move toward co-existence a country so long conditioned to cold war. Even when Moscow offered gold for surplus wheat, it was hard to make a deal. The revolt in Congress against foreign aid illustrated how hard it was to carry on policy once tense fears of communism slackened even slightly. The President recognized the dangers of an unlimited arms race and the need for a modus vivendi if humanity was to survive but was afraid, even when the Sino-Soviet break offered the opportunity, to move at more than snail's pace toward agreement with Moscow. The word was that there could be no follow up to the nuclear test ban pact at least until after the next election; even so minor a step as a commercial airline agreement with the Soviets was in abeyance. The quarrel with Argentina over oil concessions lit up the dilemma of the Alliance for Progress; however much the President might speak of encouraging diversity, when it came to a showdown, Congress and the moneyed powers of our society insisted on "free enterprise." The anti-Castro movement our CIA covertly supports was still a spluttering fuse, and in Vietnam the stepping up of the war by the rebels was deflating all the romantic Kennedy notions about counter guerrillas, while in Europe the Germans still blocked every constructive move toward a settlement in Berlin.

Abroad, as at home, the problems were becoming too great for conventional leadership, and Kennedy, when the tinsel was stripped away, was a conventional leader, no more than an enlightened conservative, cautious as an old man for all his youth, with a basic distrust of the people and an astringent view of the evangelical as a tool of leadership. It is as well not to lose sight of these realities in the excitement of the funeral; funerals are always occasions for pious lying. A deep vein of superstition and a sudden touch of kindness always lead people to give the departed credit for more virtues than he possessed. This is particularly true when the dead man was the head of the richest and most powerful country in the world, its friendship courted, its enmity feared. Everybody is anxious to celebrate the dead leader and to court his successor. In the clouds of incense thus generated, it is easy to lose one's way, just when it becomes more important than ever to see where we really are.

The first problem that has to be faced is the murder itself: Whether it was done by a crackpot leftist on his own, or as the tool of some rightist plot, Van Der Lubbe style, the fact is that there are hundreds of thousands in the South who had murder in their hearts for the Kennedys, the President and his brother the Attorney General, because they sought in some degree to help the Negro. This potential for murder, which the

Negro community has felt for a long time, has become a national problem. But there are deeper realities to be faced.

Let us ask ourselves honest questions. How many Americans
have not assumed—with approval—that the CIA was probably trying to find a way to assassinate Castro? How many
would not applaud if the CIA succeeded? How many applauded when Lumumba was killed in the Congo, because
they assumed that he was dangerously neutralist or perhaps
pro-communist? Have we not become conditioned to the
notion that we should have a secret agency of government—the
CIA—with secret funds, to wield the dagger beneath the cloak
against leaders we dislike? Even some of our best young liberal
intellectuals can see nothing wrong in this picture except that
the "operational" functions of CIA should be kept separate
from its intelligence evaluations! How many of us—on the left
now—did not welcome the assassination of Diem and his
brother Nhu in South Vietnam? We all reach for the dagger, or
the gun, in our thinking when it suits our political view to do
so. We all believe the end justifies the means. We all favor
murder, when it reaches our own hated opponents. In this sense
we share the guilt with Oswald and Ruby and the rightist
crackpots. Where the right to kill is so universally accepted,
we should not be surprised if our young President was slain. It
is not just the ease in obtaining guns, it is the ease in obtaining
excuses, that fosters assassination. This is more urgently in need
of examination than who pulled the trigger. In this sense, as in
that multi-lateral nuclear monstrosity we are trying to sell Europe, we all had a finger on the trigger.

But if we are to dig out the evil, we must dig deeper yet,
into the way we have grown to accept the idea of murder on
the widest scale as the arbiter of controversy between nations.
In this connection, it would be wise to take a clear-sighted view
of the Kennedy Administration because it was the first U.S.
government in the nuclear age which acted on the belief that
it was possible to use war, or the threat of war, as an instrument of politics despite the possibility of annihilation. It was in
some ways a warlike administration. It seems to have been
ready, soon after taking office, to send troops into Vietnam to
crush the rebellion against Diem; fortunately both Diem and
our nearest Asian allies, notably the Filipinos, were against our

sending combat troops into the area. The Kennedy Administration, in violation of our own laws and international law, permitted that invasion from our shores which ended so ingloriously in the Bay of Pigs. It was the Kennedy Administration which met Khrushchev's demands for negotiations on Berlin by a partial mobilization and an alarming invitation to the country to dig backyard shelters against cataclysm.

Finally we come to the October crisis of a year ago. This set a bad precedent for his successors, who may not be as skillful as he was in finding a way out. What if the Russians had refused to back down and remove their missiles from Cuba? What if they had called our bluff and war had begun, and escalated? How would the historians of mankind, if a fragment survived, have regarded the events of October? Would they have thought us justified in blowing most of mankind to smithereens rather than negotiate, or appeal to the UN, or even to leave in Cuba the medium range missiles which were no different after all from those we had long aimed at the Russians from Turkey and England? When a whole people is in a state of mind where it is ready to risk extinction—its own and everybody else's—as a means of having its own way in an international dispute, the readiness for murder has become a way of life and a world menace. Since this is the kind of bluff that can easily be played once too often, and that his successors may feel urged to imitate, it would be well to think it over carefully before canonizing Kennedy as an apostle of peace.

DECEMBER 9, 1963

# II

---

# THE
# MISSILE
# CRISIS
# IN
# RETROSPECT

# WHAT IF KHRUSHCHEV HADN'T
# BACKED DOWN?

The essential, the terrifying, question about the missile crisis is what would have happened if Khrushchev had not backed down. It is extraordinary, in the welter of magazine articles and books dealing with the missile crisis, how rarely this question is raised. The story is told and retold as a test and triumph of the Kennedy brothers. But the deeper reaches of the story are avoided, as if we feared to look too closely into the larger implications of this successful first foray into nuclear brinkmanship. We may not be so lucky next time.

The public impression created by the government when the presence of the missiles in Cuba was verified is that they represented a direct threat to America's cities. For those a little more sophisticated it was said that they threatened the balance of power. Elie Abel's book on *The Missile Crisis*, like the earlier accounts by Sorensen and Schlesinger, shows that this was not the dominant view in the inner councils of the White House. Abel quotes McNamara as saying, "A missile is a missile. It makes no great difference whether you are killed by a missile fired from the Soviet Union or from Cuba." But in the week of argument, Abel relates, McNamara came to concede that even if the effect on the strategic balance was relatively small, "the political effect in Latin America and elsewhere would be large." As Sorensen wrote in his *Kennedy*, "To be sure, these Cuban missiles alone, in view of all the other megatonnage the Soviets were capable of unleashing upon us, did not substantially alter the strategic balance *in fact* . . . But that balance would have been substantially altered *in appearance* [italics in original]; and in matters of national will and world leadership, as the President said later, such appearances contribute to reality." The real stake was prestige.

The question was whether, with the whole world looking on, Kennedy would let Khrushchev get away with it. The world's first thermonuclear confrontation turned out to be a kind of ordeal by combat between two men to see which one would back down first. Schlesinger relates that in the earlier Berlin crisis, he wrote a memorandum to Kennedy protesting the tendency to define the issue as "Are you chicken or not?" But inescapably that's what the issue came around to. Schlesinger recounts an interview Kennedy gave James Wechsler of the *New York Post* in the Berlin crisis in which the President recognized that no one could win a nuclear war, that "the only alternatives were authentic negotiation or mutual annihilation," *but—*

> What worried him [Kennedy] was that Khrushchev might interpret his reluctance to wage nuclear war as a symptom of an American loss of nerve . . . "If Khrushchev wants to rub my nose in the dirt," he told Wechsler, "it's all over."

At a Book and Author lunch Abel recounted a story which should have been in his book. He told of a visit to the President in September, 1961, after the Bay of Pigs and the Berlin wall. Abel told Kennedy he wanted to write a book about the Administration's first year. "Who," the President asked despondently, "would want to read a book about disasters?" He felt that Khrushchev, after these two debacles, might think him a pushover. James Reston of the *New York Times*, who saw Kennedy emerge "shaken and angry" from his meeting with Khrushchev in Vienna, speculates that Khrushchev had studied the Bay of Pigs. "He would have understood if Kennedy had left Castro alone or destroyed him; but when Kennedy was rash enough to strike at Cuba but not bold enough to finish the job, Khrushchev decided he was dealing with an inexperienced young leader who could be intimidated and blackmailed." There was an intensely personal note in the Kennedy broadcast which announced the quarantine of Cuba. "This secret, swift and extraordinary buildup of communist missiles . . . is a deliberately provocative and unjustified change in the status quo which cannot be accepted by this country, if *our courage* [my italics] and our commitments are ever to be trusted again by either friend or foe." It was the courage of John F. Kennedy which was in question, the credibility of his readiness to go the whole way if the missiles were not removed. In the eyeball to eyeball confrontation, it was Khrushchev who was forced to blink first.

This was magnificent as drama. It was the best of therapies for Kennedy's nagging inferiority complex. Like any other showdown between the leaders of two contending hordes or tribes, it was also not without wider political significance. Certainly the fright it gave Khrushchev and the new sense of confidence it gave Kennedy were factors in the *détente* which followed. The look into the abyss made both men really feel in their bones the need for co-existence. But one may wonder how many Americans, consulted in a swift electronic plebiscite, would have cared to risk destruction to let John F. Kennedy prove himself.

A curious aspect of all three accounts, Sorensen's, Schlesinger's, and Abel's, is how they slide over Kennedy's immediate political situation. There might have been dispute as to whether those missiles in Cuba really represented any change in the balance of terror, any substantial new threat to the United States. There could have been no dispute that to face the November elections with these missiles intact would have been disastrous for Kennedy and the Democrats. The first alarms about missiles in Cuba, whether justified or not at the time, had been raised by the Republican Senator Keating. President Kennedy had assured the country on September 4 that the only missiles in Cuba were anti-aircraft with a twenty-five-mile range and on September 13 that new Soviet shipments to Cuba were not a "serious threat." The election was only three weeks off when the presence of nuclear missiles on the island was confirmed on October 15 by aerial photographs. There was no time for prolonged negotiations, summit conferences, or UN debates if the damage was to be undone before the election. Kennedy could not afford to wait. This gamble paid off when he was able on October 28 to "welcome" Khrushchev's "statesmanlike decision" to dismantle the missiles, and on November 2, four days before the election, to announce that they were being crated for removal. But what if the gamble had failed? What if Khrushchev, instead of backing down when he did, had engaged in a delaying action, offering to abide by the outcome of a United Nations debate? The Republicans would have accused Kennedy of gullibility and weakness; the nuclear menace from Cuba would certainly have cost the Democrats control of the House of Representatives. After the Bay of Pigs fiasco, the damage to Kennedy's reputation might have been irreparable even if ultimately some peaceful deal to get the missiles out of Cuba were achieved. Kennedy could not wait. But the country and the world could. Negotiations, however prolonged, would have been better than the risk of World War III. This is how the survivors would have felt. Here Kennedy's political interests and the country's safety diverged.

Could these political considerations have been as absent from the discussions and the minds of the Kennedy inner circle as the accounts of the two in-house historians, Sorensen and Schlesinger, and that of Abel would lead us to believe? Sorensen touches on the subject ever so tactfully at only one point. He relates that during the White House debates on what to do about the missiles, a Republican participant passed him a note saying:

> Ted—have you considered the very real possibility that if we allow Cuba to complete installation and operational readiness of missile bases, the next House of Representatives is likely to have a Republican majority? This would completely paralyze our ability to react sensibly and coherently to further Soviet advances.

Given the choice between the danger of a Republican majority in the House and the danger of a thermonuclear war, voters might conceivably have thought the former somewhat less frightening and irreversible.

Sorensen paints a sentimental, touching picture of Kennedy on the eve of the confrontation. "He spoke on the back porch on that Saturday before his speech not of his possible death but of all the innocent children of the world who had never had a chance or a voice." If Kennedy was so concerned he might have sacrificed his chances in the election to try and negotiate. It is difficult to reconcile this concern with the "consternation" Schlesinger reports when Radio Moscow broadcast a Khrushchev letter offering removal of its missiles from Cuba and a non-aggression pledge to Turkey if the U.S. would remove its missiles from Turkey and offer a non-aggression pledge to Cuba. This had been widely suggested at home and abroad, by Lippmann and many others, as a mutual face-saver. "But Kennedy," Schlesinger writes, "regarded the idea as unacceptable, and the swap was promptly rejected."

Abel recalls that early in 1961 the Joint Congressional Committee on Atomic Energy had recommended removal of these missiles from both Italy and Turkey as "unreliable, inaccurate, obsolete, and too easily sabotaged." He reveals that Kennedy in the late summer of 1961 gave orders for their removal. "It was therefore with a doubled sense of shock," Abel writes, "that Kennedy heard the news that Saturday morning. Not only were the missiles still in Turkey but they had just become pawns in a deadly chess game." Would it have been so unthinkable a sacrifice to have swapped those obsolete missiles, which Kennedy removed so soon afterward anyway?

Abel's account indicates that the Kennedy brothers were unwilling to be put in the position of paying any but the most minimal price for peace. Khrushchev's surrender had to be all but unconditional. Abel tells us that Adlai Stevenson at the White House conference on October 20 "forecast grave difficulties" at the UN "concerning the Jupiter bases in Turkey. People would certainly ask why it was right for the United States to have bases in Turkey but wrong for the Russians to have bases in Cuba." He also urged the President to consider offering to withdraw from Guantanamo as part of a plan to demilitarize, neutralize, and guarantee the territorial integrity of Cuba. Both ideas were rejected. "The bitter aftertaste of that Saturday afternoon in the Oval Room," Abel writes, "stayed with him [Stevenson] until his death. It was after this encounter that Robert Kennedy decided Stevenson lacked the toughness to deal effectively with the Russians at the UN" and suggested to the President "that John McCloy or Herman Phleger, the California Republican who had served as chief legal advisor to John Foster Dulles, be asked to help in the UN negotiations. McCloy got the job."

All these accounts are appallingly ethnocentric. Cuba's fate and interests are simply ignored. Neither Abel nor Schlesinger nor Sorensen mentions that two weeks earlier President Dorticos of Cuba in a speech to the General Assembly on October 8—before the presence of the missiles in Cuba had been verified—said his country was ready for demilitarization if the U.S. gave assurances "by word and by deed, that it would not commit acts of aggression against our country." This speech contained a cryptic reference to "our unavoidable weapons— weapons that we wish we did not need and that we do not want to use." This was ignored by the American press. Though Stevenson, we now learn from Abel, was soon to favor demilitarization of Cuba, his public reply on October 8 was the State Department line, "The maintenance of communism in the Americas is not negotiable."

All these possibilities for negotiating a way out indicate that the Cuban missile crisis was not one of those thermonuclear crises requiring instant response and leaving no time for negotiation and no time for consultation. The situation fits that described by George Kennan when he came back from Belgrade in August 1961 and said, "There is no presumption more terrifying than that of those who would blow up the world on the basis of their personal judgment of a transient situation. I do not propose to let the future of the world be settled, or ended, by a group of men operating on the basis of limited perspectives and short-run calculations." Schlesinger quotes Kennan's words to show the atmosphere of those "strange, moody days." He does not, of course, apply them to the missile crisis. Kennan's anguish may seem that of an outsider, without access to what the insiders alone know. But Sorensen says that at one time in the inner debate Kennedy and his circle "seriously considered" either doing nothing about the missiles or limiting our response to diplomatic action only. "As some (but not all) Pentagon advisors pointed out to the President," Sorensen reveals, "we had long lived within range of Soviet missiles, we expected Khrushchev to live with our missiles nearby, and by taking this addition calmly we would prevent him from inflating its importance."

There was fear in the inner circle that our Western allies might share this cool estimate. Perhaps this was one reason we did not consult them before deciding on a showdown. As Sorensen writes, "Most West Europeans cared nothing about Cuba and thought we were over-anxious about it. Would they support our risking a world war, or an attack on NATO member Turkey, or a move on West Berlin, because we now had a few dozen hostile missiles nearby?" Similarly Schlesinger reveals that Macmillan, when informed of Kennedy's plans, was troubled "because Europeans had grown so accustomed to living under the nuclear gun that they might wonder what all the fuss was about."

To consult was to invite advice we did not wish to hear. Abel reveals that when Acheson arrived as the President's special emissary to let De Gaulle know what was afoot, "De Gaulle raised his hand in a delaying gesture that the long departed kings of France might have envied," and asked, "Are you consulting or informing me?" When Acheson confessed that he was there to inform not consult, De Gaulle said dryly, "I am in favor of independent decisions." But three years later De Gaulle was to make an independent decision of his own and ask NATO to remove its bases in France. One reason for this was the Cuban missile crisis. As De Gaulle said at his last press conference February 21:

> . . . while the prospects of a world war breaking out on account of Europe are dissipating, conflicts in which America engages in other parts of the world—as the day before yesterday in Korea, yesterday in Cuba, today in Vietnam—risk, by virtue of that famous escalation, being extended so that the result would be a general conflagration. In that case Europe—whose strategy is, within NATO, that of America—would be automatically involved in the struggle, even when it would not have so desired . . . France's determination to dispose of herself . . . is incompatible with a defense organization in which she finds herself subordinate.

Had the Cuban missile crisis erupted into a thermonuclear exchange, NATO bases in France would automatically have been involved: They would have joined in the attack and been targets for the Russians. France, like the other NATO countries, might have been destroyed without ever being consulted.

It is not difficult to understand De Gaulle's distrust of an alliance in which the strongest member can plunge all the others into war without consulting them.

Kennedy no more consulted NATO before deciding to risk world war over Cuba than Khrushchev consulted his Warsaw Pact satellites before taking the risky step of placing missiles on the island. The objection to Khrushchev's course, as to Kennedy's, was primarily political rather than military. There is general agreement now that the Russians may have been tempted to put missiles in Cuba to redress in some small part the enormous missile gap against them which McNamara disclosed after Kennedy took office; for this view we can cite, among other studies, a Rand Corporation memorandum written for the Air Force by Arnold L. Horelick.[1] In retrospect the Air Force turned out to be the victim of its own ingenuity in developing the U-2. So long as the U.S. had to depend on surmise and normal intelligence, it was possible to inflate the estimates of Russian missile strength to support the demand for larger Air Force appropriations; hence first a bomber gap and then a missile gap, both of which turned out to be nonexistent. But when the U-2s began to bring back precise information, the nightmarish missile computations hawked by such Air Force mouthpieces as Stuart Symington and Joseph Alsop began to be deflated. Despite the sober warnings of Eisenhower and Allen Dulles that there was no missile gap, the Democrats used it in the 1960 campaign only to find on taking office that the gap was the other way. Militarily the missiles on Cuba didn't make too much difference. Even the Horelick study for the Air Force admits that these missiles "would presumably have been highly vulnerable to a U.S. first strike, even with conventional bombs," and their number was too small for a Soviet first strike. "Moreover," Horelick writes, "there would have been a problem, though perhaps not an insurmountable one, of coordinating salvoes from close-in and distant bases so as to avoid a ragged attack." (If missiles were fired at the same time from Cuba and Russia, the ones from nearby Cuba would have landed so far in advance as to give additional warning time.) Their deploy-

[1] See his "The Cuban Missile Crisis: An Analysis of Soviet Calculations and Behavior," an abridgement of the Rand memo published in the April 1964 issue of *World Politics*.

ment in Cuba bears all the earmarks of one of those febrile improvisations to which the impulsive Khrushchev was given, as in his proposals for a "troika" control of the United Nations.

Khrushchev was guilty of a foolish duplicity. Gromyko gave Kennedy a message from Khrushchev that he would suspend any action about Berlin until after the November election so as not to embarrass Kennedy. This and a Tass communique of September 11 made Kennedy and his advisers feel certain that the Russians would not upset the situation by secretly placing nuclear missiles in Cuba. Tass said the Soviet Union's nuclear weapons were so powerful and its rockets so wide-ranging "that there is no need to search for sites for them beyond the boundaries of the Soviet Union." How could Khrushchev hope to negotiate with Kennedy when the President discovered that he had been so grossly gulled? By first installing the missiles and then telling an easily detected lie about so serious a matter, Khrushchev shares responsibility with Kennedy for bringing the world to its first thermonuclear brink.

Because Kennedy succeeded and Khrushchev surrendered, the missile crisis is being held up as a model of how to run a confrontation in the thermonuclear age. In his February 17, 1966, statement advocating negotiations with the Vietcong, and offering them a place in a future government, Senator Robert F. Kennedy said Hanoi "must be given to understand as well that their present public demands are in fact for us to surrender a vital national interest—but that, as a far larger and more powerful nation learned in October of 1962, surrender of a vital interest of the United States is an objective which cannot be achieved." In the missile crisis the Kennedys played their dangerous game skillfully. They kept their means and aims sharply limited, resisting pressures to bomb the island and to demand the removal of Castro as well as the missiles. For this restraint we are indebted to the Kennedys. But all their skill would have been to no avail if in the end Khrushchev had preferred his prestige, as they preferred theirs, to the danger of a world war. In this respect we are all indebted to Khrushchev.

The missile crisis is a model of what to avoid. This is the lesson John F. Kennedy learned. "His feelings," Schlesinger writes in the finest passage of his *A Thousand Days*, "underwent a qualitative change after Cuba: A world in which nations threatened each other with nuclear weapons now seemed to him not just an irrational but an intolerable and impossible world. Cuba thus made vivid the sense that all humanity had a common interest in the prevention of nuclear war—an interest far above those national and ideological interests which had once seemed ultimate." This, and not the saga of a lucky hairbreadth balancing act on an abyss, is what most needs to be remembered about the missile crisis, if we are to avoid another.

APRIL 14, 1966

# III

---

## THE
## RIGHT
## FAILS
## TO
## TAKE
## OVER

# GOLDWATER RALLIES AN ODD
# TRIBE FOR A STRANGE WAR

The process of picking a presidential candidate bears only a distant relation to sober discussion of political issues. To see one in action is to see first of all that politics is a form of sports; the atmosphere in the crowded lobbies of the St. Francis and the Mark Hopkins in San Francisco, where each candidate had his rooters and his pennants, was much like that before a football game. At some of the most exciting moments, the convention seemed to call for coverage by an anthropologist. To descend from the galleries into the depths on the Cow Palace floor during one of the many demonstrations was to dive into a brightly lit jungle, a high forest of banners, with the horns blaring and the drums beating, as if for tribal war. At duller moments, during the long stretches of venerable clichés in the nominating speeches, the convention seemed to provide a psychic massage through semantic manipulation; all those familiar phrases about free enterprise began to seem like incantations, handed down from the past as sure formulas for the ills of the body politic. The platform could be read as ritual, as a form of verbal magic, the reassuring recitation of a secular mass.

We are familiar with the politics of insecurity when it exploits the insecurities of the poor. At the Republican convention one could see in action the politics which plays on the insecurity of the rich. The Goldwaterites made their appeal to people who were afraid—rich, powerful, fortunate beyond any dominant class in history, yet afraid. Some of the fears were obvious: fear of losing their property and power, fear lest the value of their dollars be diminished by the inflation which accompanies the welfare state. Above all they did not want to lose the old familiar devil of their neatly Manichean universe, the need for a devil being as deep as the need for a God. Communism as the devil had long been one of the main pillars in the edifice of their simple faith. Now it, too, was threatened by more sophisticated and pragmatic attitudes.

Goldwater expressed their alarm when he told the platform committee, "I was surprised, and am concerned, that during these platform hearings, mention even of the word 'communism' has been the exception rather than the rule." He complained that "even in the keynote address" it seemed to be taboo. "This Administration," he protested, "pretends that communism has so changed that we can now accommodate it. Our party cannot go the final and fatal step and pretend that it doesn't even exist." They didn't want to hear about the differences between Russia and China or the deviationist tendencies in Rumania or to be told that some communists were better than others. They wanted their old comfortable picture of a monolithic communism restored. A pragmatism without a devil frightened them more than a communism without a God. To realize that even at Republican platform hearings people had stopped speaking of communism seemed to them almost impious, if not evidence of the subtlest communist plot of all.

The Goldwaterite picture of themselves, as of their hero, is as distant from reality as the rest of the private universe they are defending. The frontier virtues they claim to embody are as synthetic as the frontier they inhabit. Their desert is air-conditioned and landscaped; their covered wagons are Cadillacs; their chaps are from Abercrombie & Fitch; their money, like their candidate's, is mostly inherited from grandpappy, or acquired with their wives. In their favorite compaign photos, on that horse and under that ten-gallon Stetson, looking into the setting sun, is no cowboy or even rancher but a Phoenix storekeeper. The Western trade he caters to, in business as in politics, is dude ranch.

This he-man's claim to fame in business is the development of "antsy-pants," men's underdrawers decorated with ants, a cute specialty item he advertised some years back in the wide open spaces of Manhattan through *The New Yorker* magazine. He roughs it in a $150,000 gadget-filled showplace of a home, designed, his architect said, as "a rough-hewn house for a rough-hewn guy," a sort of de luxe model log cabin to give one that authentic latter-day Lincoln decor. Low education and low intelligence, Goldwater once declared to the delight of his equally well-upholstered followers, are the real causes of poverty. One wonders what he, who did not last out more than one year of college, would have done if a family fortune and a family business did not await him back home. What he preaches is the same "rugged individualism" with which Herbert Hoover sought to combat the New Deal thirty years ago. Its essential phoniness could not have found a more perfect embodiment. The crowning touch is that this half-Jewish grandson of a Polish Jewish peddler who won acceptance for himself and his family on the tolerant frontier should emerge into politics as the hero of the racist forces in our society. It's enough to make one anti-Episcopalian.

This Mr. Conservative of 1964 is quite different from Taft, the Mr. Conservative of 1952. In foreign policy Taft was an isolationist; he wanted to keep the country out of trouble. Goldwater, though not an internationalist, is an ultra-nationalist, who's ready to get into trouble anywhere. Taft fought NATO; Goldwater wants to strengthen it with nuclear weapons. Taft was what used to be called a Republican standpatter but with progressive fringes; Scranton was right when he declared several times in San Francisco that on such specific issues as labor, education and housing, he was closer to Taft than was Goldwater. In the political spectrum Goldwater is half reactionary, half rightist European style. The same man who, in *The Conscience of a Conservative*, wrote that "our tendency to concentrate power in the hands of a few men deeply concerns me" could also say on ABC-TV's *Issues and Answers* (April 7, 1963), "I don't object to a dictatorship as violently as some people do because I realize that not all people in this world are ready for democratic processes. If they have to have a dictator in order to keep communism out, then I don't think we can object to that." It is no wonder that his nomination was regarded with dismay abroad everywhere but in Franco Spain and South Africa, and among the neo-fascists of Italy and Germany. For this has been one of the principal alibis for fascism ever since the March on Rome. Il Duce, too, only acted to save Italy from communism, and there are rightists who would emulate him here if they could.

The menace of the Goldwater movement, however, is not that its ranks are full of "kooks" but that on the contrary most of those who showed up at the convention were upper middle class solid citizens, no more (or less) looney than their fathers were thirty years ago when the American Liberty League and the Un-American Activities Committee under Martin Dies readily led them to believe the New Deal was a communist plot, and that American workers then, like Mississippi Negroes today, would be wholly content were it not for foreign agitators and conspirators. Even the Southern delegation, whose headquarters at the Jack Tar Hotel I visited, in no way matched the dangerously delusive picture of this movement as made up of little old ladies in tennis shoes. The one Texan I talked to there said Johnson would probably carry Texas. Every one of the half dozen Southern delegates I talked with put "fiscal responsibility" not civil rights as the No. 1 issue. Whether this was how they really felt I have no way of knowing, but I believe it was an accurate reflection of a major concern. The retired bulk large in the ranks of the Goldwaterites; the perpetual inflation with which we have been accustomed to financing the welfare state taxes them, like all others (including workers) on fixed incomes, unfairly. The declining value of the dollar haunts them, and as one nice lady from North Carolina explained to me sweetly, "money is one of the most important things in the country." Significantly another reporter told me he found hostility to Wallace among these Southern Republicans; they saw eye-to-eye with him, of course, on race but regarded him on non-racial issues as too much of a "liberal," i.e. a social welfare spender.

Goldwater's support shades off toward the right into a wide variety of offbeat organizations and stray woozy millionaires. Most of them were loosely united under "Independent Americans for Goldwater," which opened a headquarters at 1175 Mission Street in San Francisco during the convention. The organizers were Kent and Phoebe Courtney, authors of such works as "Disarmament—a Blueprint for Surrender" and editors of *The Independent American.* Books by Goldwater and Welch of the Birch Society were on sale along with a wide selection of pamphlets proving that Rockefeller was a tool of an international socialist conspiracy and that Nixon was soft on communism. The size of the movement may be indicated by the fact that a pre-convention rally drew only 700 people and the paid circulation Courtney claims for *The Independent American* is only 20,000. He turned out to be a blond, stout man with a high-powered salesman's manner. He said he was Minnesota born, but had lived in New Orleans since he was ten. He still has no trace of Southern accent. He said he was in marketing research before launching his publication and movement. He claimed to "pick up where the Birch Society leaves off." He said he was still a member of the Society but no longer an organizer for it. Courtney is also affiliated with the Citizens' Councils in Louisiana and told me that if the U.S. cut off relations with the Soviet Union "the whole civil rights movement would die on the vine." He claims to have sponsored the first Goldwater for President meeting in 1960 and thinks Goldwater will win unless, he hinted darkly, "we run into a contrived international crisis." He boasts of defeating Judd for re-election in Minnesota as "soft on communism," and regards the Council on Foreign Relations, a high-collar group which includes Allen Dulles and publishes *Foreign Affairs* quarterly, as the center of the Communist conspiracy in America. This is the kind of character Goldwater was asked to disavow by those who wanted a strong platform plank against extremists.

Several times Goldwater challenged his critics to define "extremism." I am convinced that in his mind the difficulty was a real one. The common denominator of these right-wing crackpot groups is that America is menaced by a worldwide communist conspiracy. But this is also a common article of belief in America. In Germany the way to Hitlerism was prepared by several generations of paranoid inculcation in the existence of a Jewish-Marxist conspiracy. So the emergence of rightists in control of the Republican Party was prepared by more than thirty years in which, first as part of the fight against the New Deal and then as part of the cold war, Americans have been led to believe in a communist conspiracy. The differences are in degree, but the effect is to push all of American politics rightward, so that groups which in any other country would be recognized as hopeless reactionaries or crypto-fascists can parade here as conservatives. While the left in this country has shriveled since 1948, rightism has flowered; it is almost impossible to tune in a car radio at any hour without hearing rightist speakers financed in part at public expense via some tax-exempt foundation or some oil millionaire grown rich on depletion allowances.

Interlocking with these civilian extremists is a broad band of military extremists to which Goldwater belongs. His affinity for the German militarists is instinctive; he belongs to the same breed as the right-wing German generals who thought they could use the Nazi riff-raff for their own purposes. Goldwater told *Der Spiegel* the German generals could have won the war but for interference by Hitler; the war itself might have been avoided if they, by interfering in politics, had not helped bring Hitler to power.[1] Goldwater's simple-minded ideas are precisely the kind the military has been spreading in this country through those "strategy for survival" conferences Fulbright attacked in 1961 and Goldwater and Strom Thurmond, both Air Force Reserve generals, defended. These reserve generals make up by the ferocity of their politics for the paucity of their combat records. They may not be as wacky as General Walker but they buy ideas from the same sources. Goldwater's speech writer, Karl Hess, the man who wrote those phrases about extremism in the defense of liberty never being a vice, is an example. He was a former editor of *Counterattack*, the vehicle of the entertainment blacklist; a contributing editor of the *American Mercury* during its worst years under the anti-Semitic Russell Maguire; a member of the anti-communist liaison set up by the evangelist Billy James Hargis in 1963 which included Birch Society members. Yet he was also made a consultant to the Advisory Committee to the Secretary of Defense on Non-Military Instruction set up in the wake of the famous Fulbright memorandum. From such sources does Goldwater obtain support, ideas and phrases. For him to condemn "extremism" would be to undercut his main political stock in trade.

[1] One reporter after hearing Goldwater's remark suggested a plank in the Republican platform condemning Hitler for having lost the war.

The Goldwater candidacy gives the nation a clear choice but it is not a choice between conservatism and liberalism. The Goldwaterites who shrieked like a lynch mob at Nelson Rockefeller and responded with the wildest enthusiasm of the convention when Eisenhower attacked "columnists" are in no real sense of the word conservatives. The true conservative is their pet hate; he disturbs their most cherished dreams and nightmares by insisting as Rockefeller and Lippmann do, that the Republicans must adapt themselves to the real world. The Goldwater movement is a merger of the worst Southern racists, the right wing military and the obsessed inveterate anti-Communists, with those elements which have never reconciled themselves to the New Deal. Their candidate is ready to dabble in any irresponsible demagogy if it promises votes. The man who is so strong for states' rights when it comes to civil rights spoke as if the federal government had police power to protect Northern cities from maurauders—(Negro, that is)—but not Mississippi Negroes from mobsters. I don't think he can win but to assume from the polls that his defeat is a foregone conclusion would be criminal folly especially after the Wallace withdrawal; popular majorities are in no event the same as electoral college majorities. The Harlem riots are a foretaste of what could happen elsewhere to magnify that "white backlash" on which Goldwater and the white supremacists count. We are fortunate that, as in the final censure and political destruction of McCarthy, the forces opposing Goldwater are headed by a conservative and represent a coalition of civilized forces, conservative and liberal. The anti-McCarthyites found a leader in the Midwestern conservative Watkins. The anti-Goldwater forces are lucky to be led by a moderate conservative Democrat from Texas. But the victory will not be easy, and no one should stand aside from the struggle for it. The peace of the country and of the world may be decided by the outcome.

JULY 27, 1964

# AN UNSOCIAL SCIENTIST

These works,[1] by Arizona's leading political scientist, seem to be a must this summer, though not for reading aloud at public meetings in Harlem. There they might unwittingly prove as unsettling as Malcolm X. Take the chapter in *The Conscience of a Conservative* which sets forth the evils created by the Welfare State. "One of the great evils of Welfarism," Senator Goldwater wrote, "is that it transforms the individual from a dignified, industrious, self-reliant *spiritual* [his italics] being into a dependent animal creature without his knowing it." This launches an original theory for the high incidence of juvenile delinquency and narcotics addiction in Negro ghettoes.

How much of the credit for all this should go to Senator Goldwater is not easy to determine. A Jefferson, a Lincoln, or a Wilson may be reconstructed from his writings. What a public figure today is supposed to have written may sometimes be less revealing than the men he picked to ghost-write it for him. In the Introduction to *Why Not Victory?* Senator Gold-

[1] *The Conscience of a Conservative* (1960) and *Why Not Victory?* (1962) by Barry M. Goldwater.

*Blue Cross and Private Health Insurance Coverage of Older Americans* [Medicare]. A Report by the Subcommittee on Health of the Elderly to the Special Committee on Aging, U. S. Senate, together with minority and individual views by Senators Dirksen, *Goldwater,* Carlson, and Fong (1964).

*Economic Opportunity Act of 1964, the War on Poverty Bill.* Report from the Senate Committee on Labor and Public Welfare, together with minority and individual views by Senators *Goldwater,* Tower, Javits, and Prouty (1964).

water admitted with engaging candor that Brent Bozell "was the guiding hand" in writing his earlier book, *The Conscience of a Conservative.* L. Brent Bozell was co-author with William F. Buckley, Jr., of *McCarthy and His Enemies,* the leading defense of the late Inquisitor. Bozell is the right wing of Buckley's right-wing weekly, *National Review.* He has moved down in recent years from an editor to a contributor. His enthusiasm for Franco Spain and his predilection for holy war and statism may have proven a little gamey even for the tastes of Buckley's "conservatives."

The introduction to *Why Not Victory?* gives credit for help on that book to a longer list, including Buckley, Russell Kirk, and Dr. Gerhart Niemeyer of the University of Notre Dame. Dr. Niemeyer fights the cold war as if he were reliving the bitterest controversies of medieval theology. He writes with the pedantic fury of a Thomist attacking William of Occam and Nominalism, with which he identifies modern Positivism and links the evils of Liberalism. It is hard to believe that Goldwater could follow Dr. Niemeyer's intricate polemics more than fifteen minutes without propping up his eyelids. But he writes that this dogged casuist's "views on the Communist War have proved an invaluable help in my research." At one point Goldwater refers to himself metaphorically as a cripple: "These are but a few of those who provided me with the crutches I so badly need . . . The fight for conservatism requires the thoughts and the efforts of many."

Goldwater's two books, and these two post-convention minority reports in which he opposes Medicare and the President's anti-poverty program, provide a comprehensive picture of the ideas on which he will campaign. They are, if the Senator will excuse the expression, the fruits of collective enterprise; to be read, by his own admissions, as a composite creation, the reflection as much of a movement as of a man. The man himself is curiously indistinct. His advisers try to discourage newspaper interviews because he has proved notoriously capable of expressing quite contradictory opinions on the same subject in the course of the same interview. His one press conference before the nomination at San Francisco was the only press conference of which no transcript was made; his aides handled the one tape recording as if top secret. After a long history of foot-in-mouth trouble, they would like him to campaign, if that were possible, not just from a front porch, like Warren Gamaliel Harding, with whom he shares many intellectual characteristics, but from a sound-proof room. Remarks which would seem sinister coming from any other man often have a quality of innocence when uttered by Goldwater; the man has an extraordinary gift for not realizing what he's saying.

To read these works after attending the Republican convention in San Francisco makes them more understandable and gives them a fresh interest. Most newspapermen, myself included, were surprised to find that the bulk of his supporters were solid citizens, unmistakably country club, suburbanite America. It would be a mistake to believe their views are uniformly belligerent, or necessarily sanguinary. But to a man they seem to see the world with the pristine purity of *Wagon Train*, where good and evil are sharply and unmistakably juxtaposed and the hero's six-shooter brings the triumph of justice at the end of each episode. Like Goldwater in *Why Not Victory?* they do not understand why a quick draw with the H-bomb cannot in the same way cow the wicked and pacify the world. The desire, not for war, but for a showdown with the communists, was evident in almost all my talks with the Goldwaterites at the convention.

Although Rockefeller was not warmly received, another liberal Republican was cheered, albeit posthumously. Abraham Lincoln's lack of moderation on the race issue threatened the party's hopes of carrying the South, but speaker after speaker resolutely acknowledged him as the father of the GOP. The candidate, too, refused to disown his humble origins. Goldwater risked loss of the Jewish vote by admitting he was half Episcopalian. The biased radical Eastern press never credited these courageous manifestations of conservative conscience. Not a single columnist or TV commentator considered the possibility that the booing of Rockefeller might only have been a vestigial outburst of Western Populism. One of those present, the Texas radical, H. L. Hunt, went so far as to suggest in a letter to the *San Francisco Chronicle* that Wall Street's moneyed oligarchy was stacking press and polls against Goldwater. We have indeed reached an odd pass when an oil multimillionaire is driven to adopt the language of William Jennings Bryan.

But these, more seriously speaking, were mere lapses of language. Judged by the sources from which the respective factions drew their funds, the party schism was a conflict between the new money of the oil fields, raw and impetuous, and the old money of the Eastern counting houses, which is sophisticated and wearily reconciled to the Welfare State. It bore no relation to Populism, except in geography. Goldwater's works show no kinship whatsoever with "the sons of the wild jackass," as Senate conservative Republicans a generation ago dubbed their maverick Populistic Republican colleagues from a West which was then not at all affluent. Nor does Goldwaterism derive from Lincoln, despite the pious tributes paid him at the convention. Lincoln's letter of 1859 gibing at the Democrats for abandoning Jefferson by putting property (in slaves) ahead of liberty and boasting that Republicans put "the man before the dollar" would be regarded as subversive by the Goldwaterites, for whom property comes first, a nose ahead of God.

Their objection to the Welfare State is that it takes from them and gives to the poor. Liberalism advocates Welfarism as the only effective way to combat Communism. But the Goldwaterites object to Liberalism as being liberal with *their* money. The ideological barricade thrown up by *The Conscience of a Conservative* is to deny "that a man's politics are determined by the amount of food in his belly." For them man is a spiritual being and therefore, presumably, can live on wind. "A man's politics are, primarily, the product of his mind," Goldwater writes in *The Conscience.* "Material wealth can help him further his political goals, but it will not change them." Hamilton and Madison in *The Federalist Papers* were more frank. "Those who hold and those who are without property," they wrote, "have ever formed distinct interests of society." The people, for Hamilton, were "a great beast" and government was to protect the propertied classes from them. Conservatism, whether Federalist or Whig, was openly anti-democratic down to Jackson's time when Chancellor Kent could still attack free public education and universal manhood suffrage as a menace because (as he argued) the poor if taught to know their interests and given the right to vote would vote themselves the property of the rich.

These are the authentic springs of Goldwaterism. They also help to explain the sinister alliance within it of those who want less government and crypto-fascists who want more. If the former can't dismantle the Welfare State, then many of them are prepared, with the latter, for a strong, harsh hand to protect them from the creeping socialism they see implicit in democracy.

Neither Goldwater nor most of his followers are fascist—yet just such solid but confused citizens were carried along by a strange tide in just such a direction in Italy and Germany. Their insecurities make them easy prospects for the wilder and wilier men in the Goldwater movement. Anti-democratic purposes cannot openly be avowed for fear of alienating not only votes outside but many within the movement. So extremism in the defense of property is cloaked as zeal in the defense of liberty. The most recent antecedent of Goldwaterism was the American Liberty League; in the 1936 campaign it sold the same line of anti-Welfarism in the name of anti-Communism. When Goldwater argues, with Dirksen and Carlson in their minority report against Medicare, that public health insurance would interfere with "the desire of older people to live independently and with maximum freedom of choice" it sounds like a cracked record of that earlier oratory against the New Deal. So does the Goldwater-Tower minority report against the President's War on Poverty program. They protest that taking youngsters from the slums and putting them into a Job Corps would "consciously weaken the family relationship which has been the backbone of our free society for hundreds of years."

In 1936, only Vermont and Maine bought this sanctimonious nonsense from the Republicans. The GOP might do better this time. They count on exploiting racism at home and frustration abroad. They are helped by thirty years of steady indoctrination in the belief that the Marxists are wizards. It is sometimes hard to tell in our country where the solid citizenry's belief in a worldwide communist conspiracy ends and paranoia begins. Goldwater himself sees plots at home and plots abroad; the graduated income tax is a plot and disarmament is a plot. One of the most diabolic in his opinion, as an Air Force Reserve major general, is the plot to muzzle those "cold war seminars" jointly run by rightists and military men which Fulbright attacked in 1961. The Goldwater books faithfully follow the line of those seminars, particularly in denouncing that "craven fear of war" which has lamentably emerged in the wake of Hiroshima. Goldwater devotes an angry chapter to this in *Why Not Victory?* He blames the scientists and scolds them for their "guilt complex," "their humanitarian distaste for the bomb," and their "presumptuousness and conceit" in telling the generals what to do.

Goldwater thinks world victory would be relatively easy. First we must "persuade the enemy that we would rather follow the world to Kingdom Come than to consign it to Hell under Communism." Then we should, he believes (like the Birchites), use the methods of the communists against them. "I would suggest," he writes in *Why Not Victory?*, "that we analyze and copy the strategy of the enemy; theirs has worked and ours has not." To advocate communism-in-reverse is a novel form of conservatism. Goldwater's effort to sell it in the coming campaign will test the country's sanity. I believe that despite "backlash," white and black, the truly conservative and the more civilized will prove the majority, as they did in the Senate when McCarthy was censured, over Goldwater's protest.

AUGUST 20, 1964

# IV

---

ALL

THE

WAY

(DOWNHILL)

WITH

LBJ

# FAR BELOW JFK

The scramble for positions of influence with the new Johnson Administration makes it almost impossible to get an objective view of the man; everybody from the politicians to the Washington correspondents are, with few exceptions,[1] outdoing themselves in flattery of the new monarch. His vanity, his thin skin and his vindictiveness make even the mildest criticism, or approach to objectivity, dangerous.

The negative aspects of Johnson are these. In sophistication, education and taste, he is a sharp drop from Kennedy. He has hardly read a book in years; never reads when he can help it; prefers to get information by ear, but rarely listens. He is one of the most long-winded men in Washington; a Babbit, with a remarkably small stock of basic ideas; these consist of a few clichés about freedom, which he translates largely into the freedom of the entrepreneur to make a buck. Money and power have been the motivating passions of his life. He was a New Dealer when that was the road to power, he became a conservative when that was the way to stay in. He is the perfect extrovert, with no convictions and a passion for "getting things done," anything. He rose as rapidly as he did in the House and

---

[1] The only exception we have noted is James Reston who dared write in his column (*New York Times*, Nov. 27) that Johnson was "tyrannical with his personal staff, disorderly about administration and apoplectic about characters who write sentences like this . . . more thin-skinned about press criticism than anybody . . . since the last President Johnson . . . he has tended to regard dissent as perversity . . . as if criticism were not a duty in a free society but a crime." For a bureau chief, for whom access to the White House is a necessity, this took courage.

later the Senate by endless sitting-at-the-feet, after hours, of
Sam Rayburn and later Senator Russell. *Then* he listened, the
respectful and flattering young man; he had a genius for ingra-
tiating himself with the old men of the Southern oligarchy. But
he kept his lines open to the liberals, in order to deal with them,
too, and he likes to picture himself as a Westerner rather than
a Southerner.

Johnson's skill as a legislative manipulator may be overestimated. In the Eisenhower period, he was an effective middle
man between the Republican and Democratic conservatives. In
the special session of 1960, after the election, however, he and
Kennedy together found it impossible to put through a moder-
ately liberal program. Johnson is not a racist or a reactionary;
he once told a visiting civil rights group that he had learned
all he knew on the subject from Aubrey Williams (of the Southern Conference Educational Fund, once Johnson's boss in the
New Deal's National Youth Administration) and Mary McLeod
Bethune. As a shrewd politician, he knows he must move
slightly leftward and make civil rights his No. 1 issue if he is to
change the view of him as a Southern politician, with a basically standpat philosophy. In Texas the liberals distrust him
deeply for running out on them and his New Deal past; the
conservatives hate him for having been a more than loyal
Kennedy lieutenant on civil rights.

The Republicans suddenly feel a chance to win the next election and he will have a very short honeymoon. The Kennedy
assassination has not softened the hearts of the Southern oli-
garchs and their coalition with the Republicans may easily and
quickly be resumed. The vulnerable point of the new President
is his old protégé, Bobby Baker, a mercenary corkscrew of a
character whose extraordinary influence in the Senate throws a
horrifying light on the decayed underside of that august institution, and on Johnson's own aesthetic standards. The Republicans may have trouble in exploiting the Baker case, however,
because it probably links up with as many ugly deals on their
side of the aisle as on the Democratic side. It will take all Johnson's skill and energy to hush up this scandal and get action out
of Congress. Men like Fulbright and Benjamin V. Cohen will
be good influences in this Administration, but on the whole
Johnson like Truman will bring a lot of rather unseemly cronies

to town and its level of literacy and civilization will fall again, as it did after FDR.

The hope is that men change and grow. The sense of role, the maturing effect of responsibility, the consciousness of duty and love of country, the sense of humanity and history, all have their effect. Tom Clark, a one-time Texas lobbyist, not much of a lawyer, but a decent human being and never a racist, has made an honorable record and grown in stature on the U. S. Supreme Court. There may be surprises in Johnson, and we wish the new President luck. The manner and energy of his debut stir hope.

DECEMBER 9, 1963

# BIOGRAPHY AS FACIAL SURGERY

Whatever William S. White [1] lacks as a biographer he more than makes up as a plastic surgeon. His most striking operation occurs in his chapter on civil rights. There he says that "as early as March of 1949, as the very new and junior Senator from Texas with a plurality of less than a hundred votes in his pocket," Johnson went on record against racial discrimination. "Perhaps no prejudice," he quotes Johnson as saying, "is so contagious or so unreasoning as the unreasoning prejudice against men because of their birth, the color of their skin or their ancestral background . . ." White does not tell the reader that the quotation is taken from a speech *against* civil rights legislation, and in defense of the filibuster. "I say frankly," Johnson

[1] *The Professional: Lyndon B. Johnson* (1964).

had declared in the same speech, "that the Negro . . . has more to lose by the adoption of any resolution outlawing free debate in the Senate than he stands to gain by the enactment of the civil rights bills." He had pictured Fair Employment Practices legislation as if it would repeal the Emancipation Proclamation. "If the law can compel me to employ a Negro," Johnson then argued, "it can compel that Negro to work for me."

Another example of White's face-lifting occurs when he tries to explain Johnson's vote for the Taft-Hartley Act. White says Johnson had become convinced that labor had moved "from a place of too great weakness to a place of too great power." So "in 1935 he had voted, without a qualm, for the Wagner Act, Labor's 'Magna Carta.' In 1946, while his career in the House was drawing toward its close, he voted, again without a qualm, for the Taft-Hartley Act—sometimes called, though most unfairly so, 'the slave labor bill.'" Johnson never voted for the Wagner Act. If the reader turns back from this glowing portrait of the perfect moderate on page 155 to page 136, he will see that Johnson was not elected to Congress until 1937, two years after the Wagner Act was passed.

Marx once wrote that history is a form of politics; White seems to be taking this maxim literally. He rearranges even the dates. The fact is that though elected in 1937 as a 100 per cent New Dealer, Johnson soon joined forces with the anti-labor Southerners. When they finally achieved their objective in the Smith-Connally Act of 1943, Johnson voted to override FDR's veto as four years later he voted to override Truman's veto of Taft-Hartley. This anti-labor record was so pronounced that when Johnson first ran for the Senate in 1948, Texas labor for the first time in a half-century endorsed a candidate for the Democratic nomination, picking his right-wing opponent, "Coke" Stevenson. White pictures his hero as the aggrieved victim of what White calls an "Orwellian" plot to represent Johnson "as the tool of reactionary employers." He does not mention that Johnson by his program and his sponsorship left Texas labor nowhere else to go. Johnson opened his campaign by advocating right-to-work laws. One of the most reactionary employers in Texas, Herman Brown of Brown & Root of Houston, sat approvingly on the platform behind him in Austin when he did so. White mentions the brothers Herman and

George Brown only as the old friends to whose country home in Virginia Johnson was motoring when stricken by his heart attack in 1955. They deserve fuller treatment. Their contracting firm was long one of the biggest non-union employers in the country. They are among Johnson's oldest backers and he has reciprocated their devotion, notably in his first term as Senate majority leader when he knocked out of an $8 billion highway bill a provision requiring fair labor standards.

White calls labor's opposition to Johnson in the 1948 campaign "a towering absurdity." But his record in the Senate proved little different from that in the House. In August 1959, Johnson was still boasting to employer constituents in Texas [2] that he had always favored "strong, effective regulatory legislation to protect Americans from improper labor practices."

The biggest scoop of the White biography is that it was Johnson who "engaged McCarthy and defeated him." White says McCarthy's downfall "was Johnson's achievement, personally, to an almost incredible degree." The incredibility is undeniable. This, if true, was the most successfully guarded secret of the McCarthy era. It comes as a surprise to all of us who covered his heyday and downfall. It appears in none of the books on McCarthy, not even in White's own 1956 book on the U. S. Senate (*Citadel*) which discusses the affair at some length. It appears to be one of those happy tricks of memory—like Johnson's vote for the Wagner Act. On the other hand, while Johnson now remembers defeating McCarthy, he and White seem completely to have forgotten Johnson's successful use of McCarthyite tactics to smear and defeat the late Leland Olds for reappointment to a third term as chairman of the Federal Power Commission. The oversight is odd, since this was Johnson's biggest exploit as a freshman Senator. Johnson was chairman of a special subcommittee which rehashed stale red charges to drive Olds from public life. He was a man whose integrity had earned him the enmity of the utilities and the oil and gas industry.

The White book must be read in broader context. The swiftness with which Johnson changed his "image" within a short few months of taking office as President is a triumph of razzle-

---

[2] In a letter which leaked to the *United Mine Workers Journal* and was reprinted in the *New York Times* January 6, 1960.

dazzle unequaled in the annals of Madison Avenue. The press and opinion-makers of all kinds were wooed at a temperature and tempo no office-holder has ever achieved before; one famous columnist even heard the maid announce one day that the President, unexpected, was at the door. White's is one of five (four new and one reissued) campaign biographies [3] tailored to the man's enormous vanity and to his need for a new liberal look.

This personality cult chorus is a pity, for Lyndon B. Johnson's true story is fascinating, the rough-and-tumble rise of a poor boy to the Presidency by hard work, an innocence of all scruples, and a sure instinct for which way the wind was blowing. It should be written by a Dreiser; it belongs beside *The Titan* and *The Financier;* its robust realities are far superior to the anemic falsities dished up by his hangers-on. All kinds of marvelous characters are smuggled out of the story in their expurgated versions. One is Roy Miller, the legendary lobbyist for Texas Gulf Sulphur, who helped Johnson get his first job in politics and guided him on his way upward. Another is the unrepentantly feudal George Parr, boss of those *latifundista* regions along the Mexican border which turned in the fantastically one-sided returns that finally gave Johnson his 87-vote victory over "Coke" Stevenson in 1948, and the sobriquet of Landslide Lyndon. These figure in the stories LBJ himself must tell to his innermost circle over the bourbon-and-branch-water.

All five of these pseudo biographies are remarkable for the complete absence of any mention of Bobby Baker, Johnson's right-hand man in the Senate since 1951, his lieutenant in the fight for the nomination in 1960. White in his earlier book on the U. S. Senate thought it cute that Democratic Senators as august as George of Georgia consulted the then twenty-seven-year-old Baker on matters as momentous as Quemoy-Matsu in

[3] The others are Clarke Newlon's *LBJ: The Man from Johnson City;* Harry Provence's *Lyndon B. Johnson;* Kurt Singer and Jane Sherrod's *Johnson, Man of Reason,* the silliest of the lot—it confuses Carl Vinson of Georgia, who helped Johnson's rise, with Fred Vinson of Kentucky; and Booth Mooney's *The Lyndon Johnson Story,* the revised edition of a 1956 campaign biography by an LBJ employee now working for H. L. Hunt, the right-wing oil man. Laurence Stern in the *Washington Post* last February 16 analyzed the amusing changes in the two editions, especially the omission of earlier slurring references to the "left-wing ADA."

1955.[4] But Baker becomes an un-person in White's biography, though a writer as close to Johnson as Helen Fuller only two years ago in her book *Year of Trial* respectfully included "Robert G. Baker, Secretary to the Senate Policy Committee" in the most intimate circle of advisers to whom Johnson turned when asked to run for Vice President. Never was a major scandal buried with greater dispatch. Yet it might have been wiser to air at least a little of the painful story to lessen the risk of its rising to haunt Johnson in the coming campaign.

Biographies like White's do him a disservice altogether. They create a reaction so sharp as to overlook his virtues. In the highest offices a man's past is not always a clue to his future; the Presidency and the Supreme Court are full of surprises. The White House is LBJ's last chapter, and he wants desperately to make it a great one. His awe-inspiring energy has been put behind the search for peace, an attack on poverty, and civil rights. The means may be inadequate and the commercials flamboyant; the Far Eastern brink a dizzy place to search for peace. But the Grand Design is there. The trouble with disguising this crafty moderate conservative as a liberal and taking the liberals into camp is that this deprives his program of the push that an opposition to the left of him would give it. He will be callous toward Latin America, tricky in handling the regulatory commisisons, and determined that the big interests are protected in the control of basic resources and in the tax structure. But he also knows the forward motions that the times require. It is an asset to have so able and persuasive a Southerner in the White House at so crucial a moment in the history of American race relations. De Gaulle's genius at flim-flam enabled him to free Algeria against the wishes of those who brought him to power. Johnson's may reconcile the South to equality for the Negro.

JULY 30, 1964

[4] In case the reader is curious, what Baker said was, "Senator, I can tell you this: I for one haven't lost a single damned thing on Quemoy or Matsu." Baker was cautious about his investments.

# LBJ'S GREAT SOCIETY—AND
# MRS. FANNIE HAMER'S

The first full Johnson Administration has made an auspicious start. Even before the inaugural, there were reassuring portents for better international relations: the deflation of the campaign for an MLF,[1] the discouragement of plans for widening the Vietnamese war, the announcement that we would negotiate a new treaty with Panama. The inaugural set a useful precedent in picking prime TV time for the President's message; there is no reason why that communications wasteland should not be commandeered more often. The President's diction and delivery have improved, as has the style, though it dragged a little toward the end with repetition. The one sentence which reached a truly high level was "We seek the unity of man with the world he has built." The passage which was most revealing and touching, amid so much that was corn, came when Mr. Johnson said the President's hardest task was not to do what was right but to know what was right. "Yet," he added sadly, "the Presidency brings no special gift of prophecy or foresight." This was the man himself speaking.

In the sphere of foreign policy, the inaugural recalled the cautious Eisenhower more than the combative Kennedy. Mr. Johnson is taking up where Eisenhower left off with the U-2 incident. His invitation to the new Russian leaders to visit here, communicated in advance of delivery to the Soviet Embassy, opens the door to that first Presidential visit to Russia which

[1] Multilateral nuclear force.

Ike originally discussed with Khrushchev at Camp David. The communist menace, that standby of the past two decades, was subtly subordinated at least in Eastern Europe to "older and deeper sources" of world unrest. "In Asia," Mr. Johnson said, "communism wears a more aggressive face." We hope the time will come when U.S. policy recognizes that the more aggressive face we see in the Far East is in substantial degree the mirror image of the aggressive face we steadily turn toward it. The friendlier face in Eastern Europe is largely a reflection of our own. The discussion of Vietnam continued the sham that we are only there to help a friendly nation against outside aggression, but mercifully it was brief and left the door open for more flexible policy in the future. The one distressing and perhaps historic omission was the absence of any reference to the arms race; we have settled down comfortably to our annual $50 billion pump-priming war expenditures and Mr. Johnson is not one to disturb the comforts of the status quo. His is a prudent and peripheral idealism.

This was evident in his domestic program. He recalled—in his buoyant optimism about U.S. business—the inaugural of Herbert Hoover, which promised two cars in every garage and two chickens in every pot. There was the same naive confidence that our business civilization is the best of all possible worlds, which needs only to be cleaned up around the edges to become the Great Society. The most revealing passage was the President's call for "a new and substantial effort . . . to landscape highways"—those highways onto which General Motors and Ford can pour ever more cars at the fabulous 20 per cent or more they earn on net worth. But what happens to prosperity when these roads are hopelessly clogged? There was no recognition in the inaugural of those tougher problems before us if full employment is to be achieved in the shadow of automation and profit-maximizing administered prices in our basic industries. Mr. Johnson spoke of "relentlessly" pursuing "the conquest of space." This makes new millionaires in Houston but there is still nothing "relentless" about the magnitude of his war on poverty. Even doubled, as promised, it will hardly mean a billion dollars a year in new money. This is the program of a moderate conservative Democrat, offering fringe benefits to the less privileged sectors of society. In the politics of consensus a little for the poor makes it easier to go on giving a lot to the rich.

The most important promise here is the beginnings of Medicare. The huge Democratic majority now makes this possible. The vote in the House against shelving the rules reform showed that the coalition of Republicans and Southern Democrats has lost control. Though only 16 Republicans voted for the new rules, and the South was solid for the old, the vote was 224 to 201 for the change. This vote is the true index to the shift of power, and clears the way for the President's moderate social reform program. The rules changes themselves were in keeping with this program; the reform was minimal. It gave the Speaker power, through the twenty-one-day rule and two lesser changes, to override recalcitrant committee chairmen, especially in the Rules committee. But it does not give greater power to the *hoi polloi* on the floor. It is the Speaker and the party leadership which decides when to utilize these devices.

That there is a potential for more drastic action in the rank-and-file membership was indicated when two dozen rose with Congressman William Ryan of New York to challenge the election of the Mississippi delegation and 148 voted not to seat them, an extraordinary vote for the Negro and the Mississippi Freedom Party. This should stimulate the taking of depositions on how white supremacy procedures prevent honest elections in the deep South, and the size of the vote will make it harder for the privileges and elections committee to bury the challenge. For the first time since Reconstruction, the Negro from the deep South made his appearance on Capitol Hill, still outside the door but definitely on his way in.

To watch the Mississippi Negroes arrive in their rickety buses, chilled but eager, in the darkness before a downtown church the night before was to see an oppressed people pressing at last for justice. The most disappointing thing in the inaugural was the absence of any appeal against the spirit of racism; the few meager words about the right to vote were no substitute. In such great challenges lie the birth of great societies, and Mr. Johnson's failure to give this the lofty word it deserved made his own vision of a Great Society seem little more than a middle class suburbanite dream. The whole world would have applauded if America had opened the doors of Congress, at least for opening day, to the three women from Mississippi. An ugly Nazi clown, insulting the Negro, was able to get through the strict security, but not the three women challengers. Of all that was said on opening day, history may best remember Mrs. Fannie Hamer's bitter words outside the door. "Mississippi Negroes are excluded from everything except hanging," she said as she was turned away. "Someday we want to be able to teach our children that this really is a democracy." Here is the real blueprint for that greater society.

JANUARY 11, 1965

# A MAN THE WHOLE WORLD HAS BEGUN TO DISTRUST

After a year and a half with Lyndon Johnson as President, one thing can be said about him with certainty. It is dangerous to trust anything he says. His favorite stance on the platform is that of a country preacher, brimful of Gospel. Events have shown that beneath his corny brand of idealism is a hard-boiled operator who believes in force. The difference between him and Goldwater is that the latter candidly espoused what the former covertly practices. The Arizonian lost because he was more honest and less clever. But there is a limit to cleverness, and Johnson has about reached the limit.

The good will built up by Kennedy for our country in every section of the world except East Asia has been dissipated by his successor. It is no exaggeration to say that Johnson is today distrusted everywhere: in Latin America, where he has destroyed the hopes aroused by the Alliance for Progress; in Western Europe, where he is regarded as impulsive and high-handed; in India, where he affronted Shastri by cancelling his visit rather than risk hearing an Asian dissent on our Vietnamese war; and in Eastern Europe, where the Russians had expected a continuation of the detente begun under Kennedy and the satellites had hoped for a continued thaw in the cold war as their one sure means of liberation. Rarely has one man blasted so many hopes so quickly.

In Mr. Johnson's recent VE day address to Europe, he touched on "the dramatic contrast between this twenty years and the twenty years which followed World War I" and said that November 11, 1938, "Munich was just six weeks old and war less than a year away." Perhaps he spoke too quickly. Many of his listeners must have wondered whether a general war might not again be only another year away. Others must have recalled that it was behind the Pied Piper banner of anti-communism that the Japanese began their incursions into China in the thirties and the Germans their mobilization for their second attempt in a generation to rule the world. The League of Nations was destroyed in the process as the United Nations is being destroyed by our own policy of unilateral military intervention. Humanity has long feared that some day a reckless man would have his finger on the H-bomb. Johnson has himself to blame if people are beginning to fear that maybe he is that man.

In a flurry of recent speeches and press conferences, Mr. Johnson has shown himself on the defensive. He is finding his critics much less ready than they were in the campaign to be taken in by sweet-talk. He has tried first of all to counteract the widespread resentment in the press corps and in the colleges over his inability to take criticism and his effort to stifle independent reporting and foreign policy debate. He is trying to sound like Jefferson in public while he sounds more like McCarthy in private. He told an entourage of reporters at the White House recently that he knew that communists were behind the teach-ins. He said he had instructed J. Edgar Hoover to root them out. "How rare is the land and extraordinary the people," he said at the National Cathedral school

May 31, "who freely allow, and encourage as I have on many occasions, citizens to debate their nation's policies in time of danger." But after so warmly patting himself on the back, he refused to answer at press conference next day when asked whether this meant that he approved "university teach-in techniques." Even a pretended magnanimity is beyond him. The real Lyndon Johnson is reflected in *U.S. News & World Report* (June 7) which says, "The White House is known to be concerned about the number of extreme 'left-wingers' getting across their views in newspapers and on television and adding to U.S. troubles." This will be news even to moderate "left-wingers" accustomed to being sealed off from access to major communication media. Apparently any criticism is regarded in the White House as "extreme" left-wing.

The teach-in on the campuses has been paralleled by something which might be described as a stall-in in the Organization of American States. Here again Mr. Johnson is on the defensive, and trying to hide the truth about our isolation in the hemisphere. A long-winded filibuster-style reply at press conference was an attempt to hide the political bankruptcy of his Dominican policy. Even as he was talking he was encountering great difficulty in getting the OAS to send an ad hoc advisory committee to Santo Domingo. The revealing blow came when Gonzalo Facio, the Costa Rican Ambassador to the OAS and the only democratic representative suggested for this three-man body, declined to serve on it. He said he could not serve because of his country's policies against military dictatorship and military participation in politics. The OAS meetings, characteristically, are held behind closed doors, but Facio made a public statement (*Washington Star,* June 1). When the three-man mission was finally approved after a debate which lasted into the morning hours, the Ambassador of the rightist military dictatorship in El Salvador had to be substituted for Costa Rica. The other two members will be the U.S. and the Brazilian military dictatorship. The biggest and most democratic regimes in the hemisphere either voted "no" (Uruguay and Mexico) or abstained (Argentina, Venezuela and Chile).

Mr. Johnson said at press conference that the other countries in the hemisphere had long ago declared communism incompatible with the inter-American system. This does not mean they agreed that the U.S. Marines could march in whenever and wherever we thought a government leaned too far left. Just how far off base we are in Santo Domingo is indicated by the fact that two well-known anti-communist Latin American experts, both strongly anti-Castro, have attacked Johnson's red-scare excuse for intervening in the Dominican Republic: Theodore Draper in the May 24 issue of *The New Leader* and Robert J. Alexander in the May 20 issue of *New America,* organ of the Socialist Party. The Administration's Dominican intervention was not made to look less silly by Secretary Rusk's defense of it at press conference May 26. "There was a time," Mr. Rusk said, to demonstrate the power of a handful, "when Hitler sat in a beer hall in Munich with seven people." The Washington correspondent of the *London Times* (May 27) commented tartly, "Apparently, however, tens of thousands of American troops are not to be deployed whenever eight suspicious men gather together over glasses of beer."

What we found most repulsive in the press conference was Mr. Johnson's unctuous call for plastic surgeons to go to Vietnam. An easier way to meet that need would be to stop dropping napalm on its people.

JUNE 7, 1965

# LYNDON JOHNSON LETS THE OFFICE BOY DECLARE WAR

There seems to be a peculiar division of labor here in Washington. The President makes peace speeches and the Pentagon makes foreign policy but the unpleasant task of declaring war is left to the poor State Department. The news that U.S. troops in Vietnam have been authorized to engage in full combat is the news that we are embarking on a new war. Article I, Section 8, of the Constitution, that half-forgotten document, put the power to declare war in the hands of Congress. Its members might insist at least that they have the right to hear declarations of war from some official higher up than the press officer of the State Department. It is hard to find any Constitutional or administrative reason to explain why Robert J. McCloskey, the press officer, should have been pushed suddenly into the pages of history by being assigned the task of announcing at his daily, usually routine and almost always boring, noon press briefing that we were no longer advising or patrolling or defensively shooting back in Vietnam but going full-scale into war. As a major decision, it should have been announced at the White House. As a change in military orders, it might have been made public at the Pentagon. As a hot potato, both seem to have passed it on to the State Department. There in turn it was passed on down from the Secretary through the many Assistant Secretaries to the lowest echelon available. Maybe the higher-ups are hoping it will be called not Johnson's or McNamara's but Bob McCloskey's war.

Nothing better attests the slim popular support for the war than the care thus exercised by Lyndon Johnson not to be photographed marching at the head of the troops straight into it. The White House acted as if it couldn't be bothered by such trivial matters. "The White House," *The Washington Post* reported June 9, "declined to comment on the State Department announcement. Informed officials sought to play down the significance of the announcement, arguing that American forces already are patrolling vigorously and that the commander should not be inhibited in making the best use of his troops." This genius at obfuscation was evident in the very form of the announcement given McCloskey to read: the U.S. commander in Saigon had been authorized to commit U.S. troops to "combat support" of South Vietnam units *if* asked to do so by the South Vietnamese government. This would seem to put the power to declare America at war in the hands of whoever happened to be on top in Saigon's Ferris wheel changes of government and military command. This is quite a departure from the tight centralization of powers characteristic of the Johnson Administration. Here in Washington minor officials can hardly announce a new post office for Chilicothe, Ohio, without clearing it with the White House. But whether or not our troops move into full combat will be decided by someone 9000 miles away whose name the papers can't even spell properly. Delegation of powers has never been so distant. It looks as if while the rest of us may be plunged into war, Lyndon Johnson wants to keep as far away from it as possible. Maybe he can blame it on Dirksen, who was foolish enough to say plainly that he feared this new move would "transform this into a conventional war." That's the kind of candor that lost Republicans the last election.

The truth is that the South Vietnamese army is out of reserves, though the expected Viet Cong monsoon offensive is only just getting underway. The urgent problem at the moment is to supply from U.S. combat forces the extra 160,000 men McNamara was so confident a few months ago he could mobilize from among Saigon's idle but indifferent youth; the men who couldn't be drafted there will soon have to be drafted here. The political situation is as precarious as the military. The Quat government, which has no real popular base, is tottering under attack by Catholic extremists who will be satisfied by nothing short of an Asian anti-communist Armaggedon. The shaky government and its shakier military needed the shot in the arm of a public announcement that they were being given a blank check to draw as they pleased on American manpower. But worse is in the offing. Military planners here must be prepared to deal with the possibility that the Viet Cong may soon inflict so heavy a blow as to demoralize the South Vietnamese forces and make impossible the maintenance of any governmental façade in beleaguered Saigon. Very shortly the problem may be more serious than providing mobile reserves to rescue South Vietnamese forces from unexpected attacks. The problem soon may be that if resistance is to go on, the U.S. will have to take over the government and the war altogether.

So we will do what we swore after the Korean war we would never do again—commit American troops to an Asian land war. Militarily and politically, McCloskey's war is folly. It will tie down a major portion of U.S. military power in a minor theatre of conflict, and create an image made to order for hostile propaganda. White men will be fighting colored men in an effort to put down a rebellion so deeply rooted that it has gone on for two decades, and extended its power steadily during the four years in which we trained, directed and supplied a satellite native army. We are worse off politically than the French were a decade ago: they at least had a puppet Emperor, Bao Dai, to cover the nakedness of imperial rule. Once again, as against the Japanese and the French, the communists can muster wide support as leaders of a resistance to alien domination. We have again made Ho Chi Minh a national leader.

It would be hazardous to comfort ourselves by expecting no more than another Korea, a distant limited conflict, relatively minor in casualties and rich in business stimulation. Vietnam is not Korea. Korea was a civil war between North and South; there were few communist guerrillas behind South Korea's lines. South Korea had a real government and it was headed by a national hero. Syngman Rhee, for all his failings, was a man who had devoted his life to his country's liberation from Japanese rule. There is no such figure to head a South Vietnamese government; the guerrillas hold most of its territory and can at will shut off road and rail supply to the besieged cities. It is doubly a civil war, within the South as well as between South and North. It therefore does not lend itself to the kind of neat settlement arrived at in the Korean war. That war could be ended when Chinese "volunteers" pushed our forces back to the 38th parallel and reconstituted the status quo ante. It was also relatively easy to limit the Korean war on the understanding that our side would not bomb the privileged sanctuary in China from which the "volunteers" were supplied and their side would not bomb the privileged sanctuary in Japan from which our troops operated. It will be more difficult to keep this war contained.

If our troops meet serious reverses in the South, it will be hard to resist the clamor for a tougher bombing policy in the North. If Hanoi and Haiphong are bombed, the North will have nothing to lose and will escalate the war by moving its army south. Those elements in our military itching for a preventive war against China will press for bombing the roads and railroads which connect it with Vietnam. Whether and how China will react, what Russia will do, are unknowns, perhaps as much in Peking and Moscow as in Washington. To go to war is to leave oneself at the mercy of the unexpected. How far it will spread and how many lives it will cost depends on the capricious roulette of war. One thing alone is certain. The further we get in, the harder it will be to get out.

JUNE 9, 1965

# A LOUIS XIV—IN ALL BUT STYLE

Theodore H. White has become the poet laureate of American presidential campaigns. The occupational hazard of poets laureate, judging by the experience of royal courts, is a declining ratio of flattery to poetry. White's first book in this genre, *The Making of the President: 1960,* holds up amazingly well. It is written with unflagging narrative tension and is full of rewarding insights; I think it will last as a minor masterpiece of political reporting. Its successor, *The Making of the President: 1964,* is on a lower level. The wonder and zest of the first often decline into a schoolgirlish gushiness in the second. The first is muscular, the second mawkish.

Looking back into the 1960 volume, one can see the faults of the second prefigured. Even in the earlier volume, White sometimes laid his paeans on a little profusely. "To a Rockefeller," he wrote, on a favorite subject, "all things are possible. This is a family . . . that examines a rotting tenement area . . . and begins there to realize such a dream as the Lincoln Center of the Performing Arts, designed to be the most fantastic monument of man's spirit since Athens." Already in the first book White showed himself almost incapable of saying a harsh word about anyone and prepared to scatter certificates of genius wholesale. Senator Symington, whom the Washington press corps had long regarded as a leading lightweight, was pictured as a human IBM machine. "Over each subject," White wrote of a long lunch with Symington, "the same executive mind cut with the same bold stroke of action." A writer who can be so universally admiring need never lunch alone.

These occasional patches of overly warm fellowship in the first book spread out into marshes of goo in the second. As we near the climax of *The Making of the President: 1964*, White tells us that "Abundance and Peace" were the legacies Kennedy left Johnson. Then White takes off. "It is as if Kennedy, a younger Moses, had led an elderly Joshua to the height of Mount Nebo," White writes, "and there shown him the promised land which he himself would never enter but which Joshua would make his own." This schmaltz should go far to heal the wounds left by the unfortunate fact that the only candidate treated just a little roughly in the book on the 1960 campaign turned out to be the President in the 1964 campaign. Even Nixon was handled tenderly in the first. "If Nixon won his first major campaign [against Helen Gahagen Douglas] as a 'Red-baiter,'" White explained, in a gem of apologetics, "it was because that was the ethos of the time and place where he campaigned." This was perhaps the highest point ever reached in White's determined effort to love every candidate. But White faltered a little with Lyndon Johnson: ". . . essentially provincial . . . 'cornball' . . . the Senate has become almost a monomania with him," can be sifted out from amid the compliments in which they were encased.

In the 1964 book White allows himself only two directly and strongly disapproving remarks. He calls Dirksen's speech nominating Goldwater "the most tasteless" ever made and he terms Johnson's acceptance speech "the poorest he made in the campaign." But he hastens to soften the blow by turning it into a compliment. He says the acceptance speech was "a consensus of the worst thinking of the best thinkers" at the White House—Willard Wirtz, Richard Goodwin, McGeorge Bundy, Horace Busby, and Bill Moyers are named—and "not half so good as the speeches he could and later *did* deliver of his own composition." This picture of Johnson writing his own speeches, like another Lincoln, and outdoing his own best ghost-writers in the process, is a Texas-size helping of flattery. If this wasn't enough to win White admission into LBJ's inner sanctum, it was more than earned early in the book by the resounding osculation, "as he [Johnson] slept, it could well be stated that no man would ever waken to his first full day of the Presidency of the United States better educated in the meaning of that office, better trained in its mechanics, more artistically interested in its execution than Lyndon Baines Johnson." The cult of personality hasn't been so assiduously cultivated since Stalin's heyday, except in Peking where Mao, too, likes to be hailed as a universal genius. This indicates hopefully that we are already One World, at least when it comes to reassuring touchy rulers.

White is a genuinely, an overwhelmingly, friendly man. The eye of kindness may often see what the critical, by its very relentlessness, misses. But friendliness is not the only reason for the basic approach of White's books on the presidential campaigns. This is his second; he is under contract to do one every four years until 1980. Ready access to the candidates, and the inside information which give the books much of their value and interest, are obtainable only if the candidates feel that they will be handled gently, and not seen through a harsh, ironic, or maverick eye. White's journalistic bedside manner is an important stock in trade. No one could feel a candidate's pulse more sympathetically. For the same reason he shies away from too close an examination of the issues, and focuses attention on political techniques. To be able to write these books, and to get them serialized in *Life* magazine, White had to join the Establishment and to be circumspect about the deeper insights of which he is capable. He has moved a long way from his first book, *Thunder Out of China*, which appeared in 1946 just before the cold war began and angered Chiang Kai-shek. Its tone of indignation has now gone out of fashion. In his new book he can write of the Tonkin Bay reprisal raids in August, 1964, that "The deft response of American planes to the jabbing of North Vietnam's torpedo boats had been carried out with the nicest balance between boldness and precision." What was bold about an attack by the world's greatest naval power on a mosquito boat flotilla? What was precise about the heavy reprisals we took for two attacks so slight that we had great difficulty proving they had actually occurred? Was this not, instead, a warning that under fire, real, suspected, or feigned, Johnson, despite all his campaign talk about Isaiah, would shoot from the hip?

The last two American presidential campaigns could be seen as ironic comedy. White treats them as soap opera. In his Foreword to the 1964 volume, White begins by saying that every man who writes of politics "shapes unknowingly in his mind some fanciful metaphor to embrace all the wild, apparently erratic events and personalities in the process he tries to describe." He says that for him the image that has taken shape is "of an immense journey—the panorama of an endless wagon train." Unconsciously he picked his metaphor from a TV Western. The truth with which a Mark Twain or a Will Rogers would have begun is barely touched on in White's pages. "Rarely in American history," he admitted in the first book, "has there been a political campaign that discussed issues less or clarified them less." But this was no more than a discreet aside. In his new book White says that in 1960 either Nixon or Kennedy could have campaigned under the other's chief slogan: "Nixon could easily have bannered his campaign with 'Let's Get America Moving Again' and Kennedy could easily have accepted 'Keep the Peace Without Surrender.'" White says it was "an inner music of the soul which separated them." He feels that in 1964 on the contrary, "The gap between Johnson and Goldwater was total. Though as masculine Southwest types they used the same language, the same profanities, shared the same drinking style, indulged in the same homespun metaphors, these similarities were meaningless when compared to the philosophies that separated them." White, like many of us, was taken in. Events that occurred since his book had gone to press in February have changed the picture drastically. Since the escalation of the war in North Vietnam, the landing of the Marines in Santo Domingo, and Johnson's cold speech on the twentieth anniversary of the United Nations, the inner music of Johnson's soul begins to sound astonishingly like Goldwater's.

White is a master of the courtly circumlocution. In his first book, discussing how Nixon managed to make himself distrusted by both Southern white and Northern Negro, White could write, "This is one of Nixon's characteristic and fatal flaws—that he presents too often a split image." In plain language, it would be said that Nixon was two-faced. In this new book, writing of Rockefeller, White says, "His enemies called him, quite simply, the most ruthless man in politics. But what in other men would be simply arrogance was in Rockefeller the direct and abrupt expression of motives which, since he knew them to be good, he expected all other men to accept as good also." Even after this explanation, it is hard to see how arrogance in a Rockefeller differs from arrogance in other men. Amid the pages of sentimentalizing White devotes to Goldwater, it is refreshing to come across the plain statement from an unnamed Republican in the stop-Goldwater camp, "What we were looking for was something that would put the nation and the rank and file of the Party on the alert to the fact that our leading candidate was impetuous, irresponsible and slightly stupid."

A good example of White's technique is in the pages he devotes to Johnson's vanity, no small matter. White says "This was not a vanity of person so much as an obsession with self . . ." This leaves me a little glassy-eyed: how does one distinguish vanity from obsession with self? Then he goes on to say "and an obsession with self and self-performance so deep as to recall all the insecurities and awkwardnesses he had first brought with him to Washington from the hardship and reaching of his past." This romanticizes the picture, down to that touch about the "reaching of his past," a phrase which evokes an almost Pre-Raphaelite haze of yearning, until one remembers that other kind of "reaching" brought to light in the Bobby Baker case. Johnson during the New Deal is described as "one of the best, most vigorous and earthiest conversationalists of the younger thinkers who were then remaking America." I knew the Brain Trust crowd in those days; this is the first time I have ever heard Johnson mentioned as one of those "younger thinkers." Anyway it soon appears that even in those days he was not so much a conversationalist as a monologist; for "when the conversation passed to someone else" he would "droop his head" and doze off.

After all this flattery, White offers one of those revealing reportorial nuggets he so often digs up. It appears that a correspondent who had known Johnson well before the war was visiting in Sam Rayburn's office after the war when Lyndon Johnson dropped in. After Johnson left, the correspondent observed, according to White, how Johnson had changed. "Mr.

Rayburn said, 'Lyndon ain't been the same since he started buying two hundred dollar suits.'" There follow accounts of Johnson's anger because an old friend had written about the huge gold cuff links he wore; of how, the night after Kennedy's funeral, Walter Jenkins phoned the State Department to make sure that at an international reception to be held that night the camera took only Johnson's left profile; and of a tantrum with government press officers because they had not been getting him on the front pages enough. A few pages later White is describing Johnson as "performing flawlessly as President, though less well as a human being." Flattery and revelation follow each other almost contrapuntally.

Yet the skillful courtier in White never swallows the superlative reporter. "When he thought of America," White says of Johnson in one of his sharpest observations, "he thought of it either in primitive terms of Fourth-of-July patriotism or else as groups of people, forces, individuals, leaders, lobbies, pressures that he had spent his life in intermeshing. He was ill at ease with the broad phraseologies, purposes and meanings of civilization." This, though White does not say so, is the portrait of an intellectually quite limited man. It raises the question of whether the kind of man most likely to become President is really best qualified for the job. To become President today requires money, gobs of it, either one's own or that of rich friends; it requires, as does success in any other calling, abnormal energy, drive, and concentration; it requires shrewdness in manipulating men, and it requires luck. These qualities are not necessarily those which make for success in the Presidency itself, where unprecedented power and unprecedented circumstance may call for fresh thought and a willingness to risk popularity in order to lead in new directions.

The biggest missing ingredient in Johnson is magnanimity. The man whose lineaments appear in White's book, after all the flattery is peeled away, is not a very engaging person. The cruelty to those closest to him, hired help and faithful aides alike, when coupled with his enormous vanity, recalls Saint-Simon's memoirs of Louis XIV, whom Johnson sometimes resembles, though not in elegance of style. Like Louis, Johnson feels that he is the State. He shows the same exhausting and sometimes ludicrous passion for detail. How Louis would have loved to "bug" the humiliation of a younger rival as Johnson did in tape-recording the conversation in which, with a delicious sadism, he told Bobby Kennedy that "he wasn't going to ask him to run for Vice President with him this time." The White House, like Versailles, is also reputed to have a circle of petty informers like those who served Le Grand Monarque—"this jealous and despotic master [as Saint-Simon described him] who wanted to command and conduct everything himself and who made up for the contempt in which he was held abroad by doubling the terror through which he ruled at home." Let us hope the latter part of this description does not prove prophetic.

AUGUST 15, 1965

# HO CHI JOHNSON MOBILIZES
# LITTLE OLD NEW ASIA

Honolulu was dreamed up to distract attention from the Fulbright hearings; Manila, to get Johnson off the hook of that exuberant promise last July to campaign in all fifty states. Too many Democratic candidates had suggested that they might do better if he stayed away. How keep Johnson on the front pages and the TV screens in the meantime? The Republicans provided the idea for an Asia peace conference. So we have had this magnificent Madison Avenue charade; Johnson, crossing the Pacific with giant strides in the search for peace, high above partisan politics, and even turning up for the camera men with his troops in Vietnam on the Frontiers of Freedom. The trip has been a public relations man's dream, an immensely successful travelling rodeo.

True, Manila has not exactly been a peace conference. How, as Goldwater, that innocent, asked on TV last Monday, do you have a peace conference when the other side isn't there? Nor has it been a war conference. It is hard to see what kind of a conference it has been, except a conference to get Johnson's picture with all those Asian potentates. The schedule is indicative. Of seventeen days allotted to the trip, barely two were devoted to the conference itself. There was hardly time to read, much less debate, the 3,000 words of the triple pronunciamentoes prefabricated for it: The Goals of Freedom, the Communique, and the Declaration on Peace and Progress in Asia and the Pacific. The verbiage was familiar State Department prose garnished with Johnsonian evangelism about "men and nations" having "no choice but to live together like brothers." There's nothing like a little old-time religion while Cain bombs the hell out of Abel.

The heart of the three documents, the signal—as diplomats say—is "former enemies are asked only to lay down their weapons." This is our friend from World War II, unconditional surrender. No peace conference, no negotiations, are necessary. If North Vietnam stops helping the rebels and the rebels give up, we are willing to stop fighting, too. To this magnificent offer to let them surrender, there was added—"for dramatic effect," as one U.S. official explained to the press—a promise that six months after, our troops will be withdrawn. If the other side does not accept this, we step up the bombings and pour in more troops. As Johnson said at Canberra, "we cannot tire of sacrifice until peace comes to Vietnam." LBJ is the world's most indefatigable pacifist.

There is hardly a phrase in the creamy prose of the Manila documents which is not an affront. Asia, the Continent of the Coolie, where the poor have been miserable and despised since human time began, is described as having "a rich heritage of the intrinsic worth and dignity of every man"! The signers are symbols of everything Asia's poor have been rebelling against: Australia and New Zealand, which bar the brown and yellow man from their empty spaces to keep them white men's preserves; the military dictators of three small Asian countries where the rich landowners and merchants look to U.S. support to keep them going a little longer; the leader of the fantastically corrupt Filipino oligarchy, whose islands are another U.S. military outpost. These peripheral pygmies precariously poised on the edges of a giant continent in eruption are orchestrated by a Texan as the voice of the New Asia. Only in America could anybody get away with such cosmic nonsense.

OCTOBER 31, 1966

# WILL DEFEAT SOBER
# UP ROCK JOHNSON?

Goldwaterism has now lost two elections—for the Republicans in 1964 and the Democrats in 1966. This is a sweeping over-simplification. But the element of truth in it is essential if the Republicans are not to win in 1968. It is not easy to sum up the last election. In one way it was lifeless; it could make one despair to see a free country hold an election in which the main issues were hardly mentioned. How does one sum up results so diverse that Goldwater's heir apparent could win the Governorship in California and his leading Republican opponent be re-elected Governor of New York, in which racially moderate Republicans won over Democrats in Arkansas and Tennessee while both parties competed in racism in Alabama and Georgia, and the Auto Workers machine went down to defeat in Michigan? In which white backlash unseated Douglas in Illinois but a Negro Senator was elected in Massachusetts? After a campaign in which Eastland and Hale Boggs were attacked by Republicans in Mississippi and Louisiana as leftists while the GOP's foremost dove won a Senate seat from Oregon in the only contest where Vietnam was *the* issue? If ever there was a political crazy quilt, this is it.

The issue few mentioned, on which most people are confused, was nevertheless crucial. Almost everything which ailed the Democratic party in this election and caused its shattering defeat, can be traced back to the war, *Johnson's war*. If Johnson had not done what Goldwater advocated and stepped up the whole scale of the conflict by launching an air war against the North and a major invasion by American land forces in Asia, there would have been no inflation, no disruption of the home building market, no loss of business confidence so great that the stock market plummeted while the price level rose. There would have been no split in Democratic ranks, no alienation of the peace-minded like that which helped swamp Brown in California and has brought Johnson the hatred of many who would otherwise applaud his domestic program. There would be few doves and there would be few hawks if the war were still a distant conflict simmering away in Southeast Asia. It is Johnson's war which was Johnson's undoing.

This might be dismissed as largely the wishful thinking of one who is deeply opposed to the war if it were not the opinion of others as deeply committed to it. Nixon, who has wanted large-scale American intervention in Vietnam since 1954, the man who emerged from the campaign with the best record for sizing up its cross-currents in advance, was expressing his fears not his hopes when he said that if the war is still going on in 1968 "there is no power on earth" which can keep his own party "from trying to outbid the Democrats for the peace vote." It was not wishful thinking which made the pro-war *U.S. News & World Report* report, "Politicians in both parties are saying Mr. Johnson will need to get the war ended by or before mid-1968, or he'll have a hard time getting elected." Even the hawks are unhawklike in that they have no enthusiasm for the war; they want it over as quickly as possible. This is very different from the jingoism of the British in the comparable Boer war or the ethnocentric militarism of the Germans. It is the impatience of a people who regard war as an unfortunate interruption of their main business which is *business*. If Johnson does not heed this message, the Republicans will. Many of us will see a Republican victory again—as in 1952—the only way to end an Asian war. The price will be the end of that progress on the home front which began under Kennedy and took on real momentum under Johnson before he made his error in February, 1965, in the skies over North Vietnam. Even another interlude of social stagnation and lackluster leadership would not be too high a price to pay for peace if Johnson does not change course.

NOVEMBER 21, 1966

# A STRATEGY ONLY FELLOW CON-MEN CAN APPRECIATE

The State of the Union message was a half-hearted affair, delivered to a half-hearted audience. The warmest applause greeted the reference to lower interest rates and revival of the home building market. This touched the profit nerve in a Congress dominated by small town business men and their lawyers, many of them engaged in real estate speculations dependent on cheap money. The most revealing reaction was the tepid applause when the President quoted General Westmoreland as saying the enemy could no longer succeed on the battlefield. Congress has heard too many predictions by too many generals in this war.

Something more deadly than unpopularity has overtaken this conflict—it has become a bore. Congress is tired of it. It wasn't particularly thrilling anyway to hear that the world's most powerful military machine, and certainly the most costly and the most boastful, couldn't be knocked out on the battlefield by a ragged army of underfed coolies. If that negative proposition was the Pentagon's best sales talk, the war was a poor buy. Westmoreland may yet go down in history as the first general to be saluted by a yawn.

Nothing in the Johnson program has dimension. The tax boost is too small to end the deficit. The social program is too small to do more than provoke the poor. The old age pension increase is too small to save the elderly from slow starvation. The war is too small to enthuse the hawks. Johnson is like a speaker who has begun to lose his audience. The audience senses that he knows it. This is the moment when people begin to feel around for their overshoes and to nudge their way out to the aisles. Johnson's strategy is too slick to talk about and so subtle that only a few fellow con-men can appreciate it. Johnson must keep his European flank quiet when so much of his military force is bogged down in his fifth-rate colonial war. This dictates friendly overtures to Moscow and the East European communists lest they stir up some new Berlin-type crisis. The overtures have the virtue of intensifying suspicion between Moscow and Peking. They undermine guerrilla morale and seek to buy communist acquiescence in the crushing of the South Vietnamese revolt. Johnson makes overtures even to Peking and Hanoi. He wants to isolate the Viet Cong. If he had the nerve to stop the bombing of North Vietnam, he might even succeed, for it is the bombing of another "socialist country" not the uprising on the other side of the containment line which really has upset the bloc and led it to pour supplies into Vietnam.

Johnson's Grand Design is too corkscrew. It is to end the cold war while fighting a hot one. This is too complicated a strategy for either side. Most people are too simple-minded for such crafty tactics. The guerrillas ask themselves how Moscow can make deals with Washington while American napalm burns them up. The ordinary American asks why he should give trade and other concessions to Moscow and Warsaw and Prague when they are supplying the planes and radar and the guns to shoot down American fliers. One side asks—if imperialism is so black an enemy, why compromise with it? The other side substitutes communism for imperialism and asks the very same question. If communism is so total an enemy that it must be burned out in Vietnam, why strengthen it in Europe? Or, some may ask, if we can get along with it in Europe, why not in Vietnam?

Truman had a much easier way to sell his limited war in Korea. He could argue, as he did through General Bradley, that to let that war widen into a war with China would be the wrong war, at the wrong place, at the wrong time and "with the wrong enemy." We had to keep our nuclear powder dry for the Soviet Union. Truman's little hot war fit quite easily into his global cold war. Johnson's proposition is far different: to try and end the global cold war with communism while mercilessly bombing a communist country in Asia. Those on the other side must ask: If we let the Americans get away with this in North Vietnam, what is to stop them from handing out the same treatment to us next time? The rest of the world must ask: Who is this mountebank who talks of relaxing world tension while he pours death and destruction on a tiny country?

How can Johnson talk of slowing down the world's arms race while he shows how helpless a country is which has no means of retaliating? How can we blame China for spending its bread on nuclear arms when we demonstrate on its borders what we can do to them, too, if they have no means of hitting back? The inner logic of the Vietnamese war for our military-industrial complex is to let the desperate, the hopeless and the hungry elsewhere in Asia, Africa and Latin America know what we can do to them if they dare to rise against their privileged oligarchies and our investments. The Pax America is at stake in the Mekong Delta. This effort to impose our will by blood and fire wherever we chose to do so is hardly calculated to make the rest of the world feel relaxed.

JANUARY 16, 1967

# V

---

A

NEW

CAUSE

FOR

MANKIND

# "TO LIVE AS ONE FAMILY"

A cultivated Roman from the better days of the Antonines, come suddenly back to life, would be delighted by the Pope's "Pacem in Terris." He would be enchanted to find that this obscure neo-Jewish Gnostic cult of the Christians, with their familiar myth of the God re-arisen each spring, had preserved for two millennia the humane traditions of Roman Stoic philosophy and, best of all, the great creative idea of Roman law: a universal empire, enforcing the peace throughout the civilized world, on the basis of a common citizenship open to all from Gibraltar to the Black Sea, in Rome, the mystic city which became a world and gave it several centuries of tranquillity. A kind of new Pax Romana is the Pope's plea.

The rich and crowded pages of this great document contain much that is revolutionary for Catholic doctrine, notably its abandonment of talk about "just war" and "unjust war" for the rejection altogether of nuclear war, and the new tolerance it breathes for other sects, abandoning the older Catholic idea (so like the communist) that "error has no rights." The encyclical must also have a massive impact on Italian and world politics by its new attitude toward co-existence, in the former supporting that "opening to the left" which can alone give Italy a firm majority and a sure course of social reform, in the latter pointing the way to a modus vivendi for East and West.

But none of these momentous shifts, not even the Pope's call for disarmament and a nuclear test ban, equal in importance his healing proposal for a new world community. Technology, the Pope says, is more and more forcing men "to

work together and live as one family." In this context the
nation-state system is obsolete. The problems of security and
peace have grown too complex to be solved within it. Not lack
of good will, the Pope sees, but "structural defects" in the
existing order hinder their solution. "Today," His Holiness
pleads, "the universal common good poses problems of worldwide dimensions, which cannot be adequately tackled or solved
except by the efforts of public authorities . . . in a position to
operate in an effective manner on a worldwide basis." This
would not supersede but supplement existing political struc-
tures, creating law in their relations. Otherwise, as he quotes
from St. Augustine, "What are kingdoms without justice but
bands of robbers?" And those bands of robbers are now armed
with the nuclear thunderbolt. . . .

This is the Vision which can alone save us: the conception
of one family, one race, one planet, one universal creed of
human brotherhood broad enough to encompass us all, based
on a Declaration of Human Rights enforceable everywhere.
Within this framework of law, all is possible: a nuclear test
ban, disarmament, reunification of divided countries from
Germany to Korea, a new era of creative co-existence without
fear or hatred which must lead ultimately to a common human
society, both socialistic and spiritually free. Otherwise we are
all on a dead-end street.

The Pope says that the same moral law "which covers relations between individual human beings serves also to regulate
the relations of political communities with one another." This,
unfortunately, describes what should be, not what is. Between
man and man, resort to murder is not allowed. Not so among
Nation States, where murder is the final sanction, and preparation for it the main business of the State.

To kill or be killed is the higher law of nations, and this
makes them moral monsters. "It would be absurd," the Roman
Pontiff says, "even to imagine that men could surrender their
own human attributes, or be compelled to do so, by the very
fact of their appointment to public office." It may be absurd,
but it is true. This is exactly what appointment to the highest
office does in the existing international jungle. The No. 1 man
in the White House or the Kremlin is put into a position where
he may feel compelled to do what he would never do as a moral

individual, give the signal to consign hundreds of millions of human beings to a final hell—as could have happened last October over Cuba, if one man hadn't backed down and another had pressed the button. Power to murder, not morality, determined the outcome.

The Nation State system dehumanizes the ruler and the ruled. To make us feel morally absolved for preparing mass cremation, we create caricatures of our adversaries. They are made to appear not our brothers but less-than-human, there "reds," here "capitalists." In this lawless world we bear the mark of our ancestor Cain and are compelled to go on killing our brother. The Bomb forces a new answer, and His Holiness offers us a new one, which is an old one, but with a new urgency and in a new form.

APRIL 23, 1963

# WHAT SHOULD THE PEACE MOVEMENT DO?

Roughly speaking, the peace movement may be divided into three groups. One wants to persuade, to win public support for an end to the war in Vietnam and to intervention in the Dominican Republic. These might be termed the democratic forces. A second group is not so much concerned with persuasion as with *testifying,* in the sense that the word has in the Gospels. The term martyr in Greek meant a witness; the Christian martyrs *testified* to their faith. These people want to demonstrate their moral disapproval of war by disobeying the law—by refusing to pay taxes or to serve in the armed forces; by obstructing the draft or tearing up their draft cards; or urging others to do so. These may be termed the religious forces, though many among them are not religious in a conventional sense. The third group are those who want to express their solidarity with the Viet Cong and the rebels in the Dominican Republic by doing all they can to obstruct the war effort in this country. These may be termed the revolutionary forces; many among them believe peace can only be won by getting rid of the capitalist order.

It is obvious that these three groups, though often present in the same demonstrations, would lead the peace movement in very different directions. Those who want to work for peace may find it useful first to determine to which of these three groups they belong. Only one of them, the first, can change public opinion for the better. The revolutionaries, in the context of present political realities, can fulfill little more than the role of *agents provocateurs,* giving the government an excuse for repression. Their curious melange of Maoism and Stalinism with Negro nationalism may win a few converts on the left but only at the expense of strengthening the widespread mania about a communist conspiracy. Their tactics would have meaning only in a revolutionary situation; in as prosperous a country as this with a conservatively organized labor movement, they couldn't marshal enough men for a *putsch;* they'd be lucky to seize one post office. If the cause of world peace depends on the overthrow of American capitalism, there isn't much hope for the world. This is a recipe for holocaust, an apocalyptic Marxist-Leninist version of the old belief in a Second Coming. In any event, the intra-communist feuds of recent years, from Tito's to Mao's, should be enough to demonstrate that wars will not end with capitalism, that the problem is deeper than social systems.

As for the religious, we sympathize with them but have little faith in their efficacy. They cannot accomplish in a few crucial months what Isaiah, Buddha, Jesus, St. Francis, Tolstoy and Gandhi could not do in 2500 years. If all hope of stopping a wider conflict disappears, they will perform a moral duty by resistance and abstention. But though this will ease their consciences, it will not affect the course of events. I watched the devoted pacifist handful who held a speak-in at the Pentagon the other day under the admirable Rev. A. J. Muste. Their demonstration had publicity value for the peace movement, but I did not think their speeches at all effective. One speaker several times addressed the curious listeners as "fellow workers of the Pentagon," an archaic echo of the Thirties unlikely to do anything but bolster the stereotype of *peaceniks* as out of this world. Secretary McNamara, once an ACLU-er in Detroit, allowed them to speak on the steps and in the Concourse and gave them a half hour interview. I don't think they said anything that touched him. I suspect they really had nothing to say which was relevant to the necessities imposed upon him by his position.

Only the first group, in our opinion, can have some impact on American public opinion and thus perhaps put some brake on the war machine. We will not create a "pause for reflection" by adding from our own side to hate and hysteria. War is the greatest of human sports, and it is a spectator sport. As in football or baseball, those who cheer for their team from the grandstand enjoy the catharsis of vicarious conflict. Even the peace movement in times of rising tension often becomes a disguised vehicle for aggression and hatred. We're not going to calm our fellow citizens by jumping up and down, screaming. We're not going to aid the cause of peaceful co-existence by demonstrating that we cannot even co-exist peacefully with our own fellow citizens. So long as we can still speak and write and preach and march and demonstrate, it is our duty to our country and the world to try and do so in a way which will persuade, not provoke. We must appeal to kindness and to reason. These, though slim, are our only hope.

We hope the student movement will not be led astray by stunt-mongers and suicide tactics. We believe the teach-ins have made extraordinary progress. The Washington teach-in was too diffuse, the TV discussion with Bundy was too concerned with abstractions. But debate has been opened up. The Administration has been put on the defensive. The polls show that while the majority is prepared to support Johnson wherever he leads, in the sheeplike way that human herds always move toward war, the educated minority question his course.

Our job is by the widening of debate to increase their number. Add their dissent to a general anxiety and we have leverage for peace. If the teach-ins can be taken from the campuses to the communities, if we can have teach-ins in every town or city, we can build up formidable pressure for peace.

But this demands a real effort to reach and teach, to speak in a tone not of desperation but of faith in the power to touch the hearts and minds of our fellow Americans. The wonderful students I have seen at various teach-ins, from Washington to Berkeley, have achieved more than any one dreamed was possible a few months ago. They must widen their efforts. Their task is not to express alienation, or to bring about estrangement, but to make free institutions work in foreign policy. Their duty is to help humanity by furthering the reconciliation on which our survival depends, reconciliation with our communist rivals abroad, reconciliation in equality between white and black men at home, the consciousness of common heritage and of common danger as human beings, the urgent necessity of brotherhood. Religious faith and revolutionary zeal could make a contribution if they joined in this healing task.

JUNE 23, 1965

# A SEVEN-POINT PROGRAM
# FOR WORLD PEACE

*It is clear now to everyone that the suicide of civilization is in progress . . . Wherever there is lost the consciousness that every man is an object of concern for us just because he is man, civilization and morals are shaken, and the advance to fully developed inhumanity is only a question of time . . . We have talked for decades with ever increasing light-mindedness about war and conquest, as if these were merely operations on a chessboard; how was this possible save as the result of a tone of mind which no longer pictured to itself the fate of individuals, but thought of them only as figures or objects belonging to the material world? . . . Only such thinking as establishes the sway of the mental attitude of reverence for life can bring to mankind perpetual peace.*

    —ALBERT SCHWEITZER: "THE PHILOSOPHY OF CIVILIZATION"
                                           (1923)

Only a few hours before, the world's statesmen had been paying tribute to Albert Schweitzer, and to his philosophy of reverence for life. But when war broke out full scale between India and Pakistan, what appeared uppermost in their calculations was reverence for strategy. It was not what the war would do to the peasant on both sides, his wife and children, his cow or goat and his hopes, which stirred concern, but what it might do to the balance of power. The world was seen just as Schweitzer described it four decades ago, as a chess-board.

Britain feared the end of its Commonwealth; Russia, the end of its friendly ties with neutralist India; America, the effect on its effort to contain China.

This unconcern with the human factor was as evident in the area of conflict. To listen to the propaganda from New Delhi and Rawalpindi, their struggle was an effort to preserve the freedom of the Kashmir peasant, just as our aim in Vietnam is supposed to be the freedom of the Vietnamese peasant. As a practical matter, his wishes, his comfort and his life are of the least concern in either arena to his self-appointed liberators. This is what Schweitzer meant when he warned against treating individual human beings as objects. It is here that he saw the suicide of civilization. Within two decades of his warning, the Nazis set up crematoria for the mass incineration of races they disliked. Now all of us live in the shadow of nuclear incineration any time our leaders deem this unavoidable as a matter of honor or interest. Inhumanity is so taken for granted, we expect it even for ourselves.

Whatever the immediate outcome in India or Vietnam, sooner or later one of these lesser conflicts may escalate out of control into the big conflict we all fear. The time has come to recognize the general character which marks most of them, and the need for general solutions in advance. The war between India and Pakistan arose out of much the same circumstances to be found in Vietnam, in Germany, in Korea, in China and in Palestine. In each of these situations, cease-fire lines long ago established have never been turned into firm boundaries by peace treaties. War can erupt over these precarious lines at any time as in Kashmir. All are divided countries, kept apart by deep religious or ideological differences. Their Lilliputian divisions have become the symbols and the consequences of larger East-West divisions. They can best be solved in the framework of a world settlement. Without a world settlement, rival great powers will always have some interest in exacerbating them. In each case specific solutions may be beyond the political power of local leaders.

In the framework of a general solution, dangerous big power animosities can also be more easily resolved. Above all what the smaller countries need is not preachment but example. The feeling that the U.S. or Russia want to patch up the

Indian-Pakistan quarrel only in order to further their own three-cornered struggle among themselves and China is conducive to cynicism. This is why we believe the time has come to offer a general program for the cementing of a new world order. The U.S. as the world's greatest power must take the lead in abnegation. It must show that it, too, is prepared to sacrifice politics-as-usual and thereby evoke a similar response from other nations. So we suggest a seven-point program for world peace:

1. Settle territorial disputes by election. This would mean a plebiscite in Kashmir to give its people a choice of joining Pakistan or India or independence. It would mean a free election in South Vietnam. In both cases all foreign troops would be withdrawn, including our own.

2. Federal systems, even if on a very limited basis to start with, for all divided countries. This would mean that Kashmir, Pakistan and India, North and South Vietnam, Formosa and mainland China, North and South Korea, West and East Germany, Israel and Arab Palestine would be encouraged to set up limited federal institutions for such common problems as trade and cultural relations, widening and deepening these ties later as tension between the two parts relaxed.

3. Universal membership in the United Nations for all existing governments, representing the actual territories they control; the U.S. as a corollary to adopt the French system of relations with countries rather than governments, thus permanently ending the poisonous practice of awarding recognition as a kind of certificate of morality and merit.

4. A universal declaration that no government will henceforth play politics with hunger, as we have done by refusing to sell food to, or to trade with, nations of which we disapprove. This would entail an end of our wheat sale discrimination against the Soviet Union and our embargoes against China and Cuba. It would establish trade for peace in place of trade embargoes for political punishment.

5. A universal declaration that no government will henceforth give or sell military equipment to another, but that this will be diverted to economic development instead.

6. A world freeze on all arms budgets and an end of all

nuclear tests, above ground or below. We would give up our fetish about inspection as our contribution. These first dramatic steps ought to be followed by a world conference for arms reduction by stages with the savings diverted to development in the poorer areas of the earth.

7. Expand the World Court into a larger and more flexible agency for conciliation, mediation and arbitration, and pledge all nations to submit disputes to the Court.

The United States could also make a dramatic contribution to ending world lawlessness by liquidating two activities which create world suspicion. One are our spy-in-the-sky satellites; their main function is to map the targets in other countries for our bombers and missiles in the event of war. These satellites offend our allies as well as our rivals. The other is the CIA, which is widely regarded as a source of constant interference by the U.S. in other people's affairs, a mechanism for bribery and corruption, sometimes for the overthrow of governments and even the assassination of their rulers. Greece is the latest country where people suspect justly or unjustly that their political life has been poisoned and their democratic institutions endangered by CIA operations. To abolish this cloak-and-dagger agency would enhance our reputation and improve world stability.

SEPTEMBER 13, 1965

# VI

---

## TWO
## SHAKY
## LIBERALS
## AND
## A
## BOMBER
## GENERAL

# HUMPHREY: A VIEW THAT
# PROVED TOO HOPEFUL

Two new books by Senator Humphrey [1] are models of non-abrasive liberalism. During the Democratic convention they could be read in rolling chairs on Atlantic City's boardwalk, by big business men, without their suffering the slightest ill-effect. In *The Cause is Mankind* Humphrey allows business to share his exuberant affection for organized labor. "Two of the mainstays of our remarkable economic system," Humphrey writes, throwing in a kind word for capitalism, "also seem to be two of our pet scapegoats—big business and organized labor." Absolution could hardly be more sweeping. "'Bigness' per se can be bad," Humphrey concedes, "and I have made my past criticism of it." Having made this stalwart admission of past radicalism, he proceeds to deliver what amounts to a eulogy.

"I do not think that we have many real grievances," he writes, "to be urged against bigness in business today." There are some Americans, he admits, who "hark back to the days before the managerial revolution, back to the days of the 'robber barons.' But this country and its economy have matured spectacularly since the trust-busting days . . ." "This is not," Humphrey continues, "to minimize the evils of the past . . . The big businesses of bygone generations did, indeed, act in a pattern of savage repression of competition." At this moment the perverse reader may vaguely recall the Westinghouse case.

[1] *The Cause Is Mankind* and *War on Poverty.*

Weren't its executives convicted recently of taking the government for millions of dollars through secret price conspiracies with other manufacturers of electrical equipment? Humphrey is ready to deal with such queasy recollections. "Current revelations of price-fixing and other price-holding practices," he observes, with a delicacy of which he has never been accused before, "do not help to ease a strong historical suspicion of the motives of great corporations on the part of government leaders, small business men and others." This tact, worthy of a senior public relations account executive, prepares us for his final plea on the subject. It is "high time that the traditional hostility between the intellectuals on the one hand and management on the other was ended." Only an ebullient idealist like Humphrey could show such extremism in the pursuit of moderation.

These two books indicate that Lyndon Johnson picked a running mate almost his equal in the art of sweet-talking. The Johnson-Humphrey ticket is not just a balanced ticket; balanced tickets are an old story. This is a more wondrous contraption. It's not just that the rich like Lyndon and the poor like Hubert. It's that they're turning into Siamese twins. Johnson, the faithful Janissary of the oil depletion millionaires, is crusading against poverty while Humphrey, the darling of Americans for Democratic Action, is chucking chairmen of the board under their double chins. While the twin on the left moves right, the twin on the right moves left. How can poor Goldwater outmaneuver this dazzling political choreography?

Liberalism, as Humphrey presents it, is as unassailable as motherhood. For those who might consider him merely a salesman of social reform, he adds a little muscle-flexing: "Free government cannot stand," he declares, "unless it is prepared to defeat aggression from without or within. Liberalism becomes a mockery when it is spineless and cowardly. No slogans, no long-range policies offering economic and social progress can defeat the threat of immediate naked force . . . only force itself—and the willingness to use it swiftly, powerfully and courageously—can maintain a free government in power when subversion and terrorism are used against it." Air Force Reserve Generals like Goldwater and Thurmond will be hard put to read that without snapping to attention.

Of all the Senate's outstanding liberals in recent years, Humphrey clearly is the one that best fits the Lyndon Johnson format. Douglas, the foremost intellectual of them all, would be poison ivy to the rich, especially of Texas: his main fight has been for tax reform, particularly of depletion allowances. Not a word on these subjects in Humphrey's books. Clark's specialty has been rules reform, which attacks the Senate Establishment at its most vital point; he was barely called off from his dogged pursuit of the Bobby Baker case. These matters are also among the missing in Humphrey's "liberal program for America." Morse, the bravest of the lot, has fought military aid and foreign adventure, casting with Gruening the only two votes in Congress against Johnson's blank check for war in Southeast Asia. The best Humphrey offers on South Vietnam is that our military effort must be accompanied by social reforms to give its people "the will to fight." This chestnut is a Pentagon staple, too. No other people in the world has shown so much will to fight, albeit on the other side, first against the Japanese, then the French, and now us. On military and foreign policy, Humphrey provides a compote of safe clichés and a truly Johnsonian agility at reconciling the irreconcilable. Thus Humphrey, the hero of the National Committee for a Sane Nuclear Policy, can praise George Meany's "leadership in the international struggle for freedom," a leadership which won him a medal from Adenauer for undercutting not only Kennedy's but Eisenhower's moves away from cold war.

The liberal Senator least imaginable as a running mate for Johnson would have been the late Estes Kefauver. That proud and incisive Tennessean not only treated the worshipful Pashas of the Senate, Byrd and Russell, with disdain but drew blood from big business by his campaigns against drug abuses and monopoly practices. His findings came to mind when I read Humphrey's *War on Poverty*, a better book than *The Cause Is Mankind*, which is little more than an orgy of liberal platitudes. But even when discussing poverty Humphrey stays with the inspirational and avoids not only hard words but the hard problems. Humphrey finds it "astonishing" in the latter book that we are "the only major power with such a high rate of unemployment," and that the U.S., "the epitome of free enterprise, the center of world capitalism" continues to tolerate the idleness of more than 5 per cent of its manpower and 16 per cent of its plant capacity. It is not so astonishing if we recall Kefauver's revelations of the part that administrative pricing plays in maximizing profit for such basic industries as steel and autos. The profitable planned underemployment of resources has its counterpart in the underemployment of manpower, helping to create the wide human wasteland in which the colored, the unskilled, and the youth of our society wander in despair. If the war on poverty is to become more than a campaign slogan and a grab-bag of assorted welfare measures, some politically difficult problems will have to be tackled sooner or later.

When that time comes Humphrey will be ready for them, for he's better than his books; indeed, his facility for these painless platitudes is the secret of his success. In the Senate he has made friends without making enemies, and it is this which has drawn Johnson to him despite their diversity of outlook. No liberal in the Senate has been more effective than Humphrey. None has been knocked down more often, only to rise and fight again. Much of what was best in the New Frontier came from measures Humphrey launched long before it. Medicare, the Peace Corps, the National Education Act, began with Humphrey. More than any other American, he paved the way for the nuclear test ban treaty. He had the nerve to make the politically dangerous issue of disarmament his own. No man in the Senate has been a firmer champion of the Negro; none worked harder to make the new Civil Rights Act the legislative triumph that it is. None has done more through Food for Peace to infuse a larger component of idealism into our foreign policy. Humphrey has known how to play the game and get results. No Democrat more deserved the Vice-Presidential nomination. The defects of these campaign volumes are more than compensated for by the genuine concern and the unquenchable optimism that shine through them. It is to Johnson's credit that he picked him as running mate, despite his strong association with civil rights and the ADA. What this team of glad-handers may lack in intellectual subtlety they more than make up in political finesse. It will be tantalizing in the months ahead to watch how they finesse each other.

SEPTEMBER 24, 1964

# LEMAY: CAVE MAN
# IN A JET BOMBER

One of General Curtis LeMay's earliest memories [1]—he thinks it must have been at four or five in the winter of 1910–11 or the next—was the sight of his first plane. He ran as fast as he could to try to catch it. He felt when it vanished that "I had lost something unique and in a way Divine." At least this is the recollection, after a lifetime of bomber command, as he told it to the writer of his story, MacKinlay Kantor. The general is not a religious man; this early feeling for the plane is the one note of piety in the account he helped prepare of his life. Nor is he a man ordinarily moved by beauty. It is the memory of the first plane he saw close-up on the ground that evokes the one moment of aesthetic enthusiasm in the book; what he remembers is "the appealing gush of its engine—the energy and beauty of the brute." He went from Ohio State with an engineering degree to the old Army Air Corps in 1928. In 1937 at Langley Field, he met the plane which was to be linked with the most heroic episodes of his life—the B-17. There he saw "seven of the Flying Fortresses squatting on the ramp." Of these he writes "I fell in love with the 17 at first sight." Six years later he led an entire Air Division of these bombers over the European continent. It was not until 1944, when he began the first fire raids over Japan, that he switched to the bigger B-29. He can remember the smell of the B-17 as different from

[1] In *Mission with LeMay.*

the smell of any other plane. This ability to differentiate these mighty metallic monsters by his animal sense of smell is even more impressive than the love and worship that so closely linked this man to his machines. He emerges in this story as much their instrument as they were his. LeMay's later, long and stubborn rear-guard action to keep the bombers flying in the age of the missile begins to seem touching, like any attempt to maintain the vanishing familiar in a world of change without pity. So, unexpectedly, on the bomber, too, Vergil's *lacrimae rerum* fall.

Unlike Mao Tse-tung and Ho Chi Minh, the targets of whom LeMay has dreamed voluptuously in recent years, our bomber general was of impeccably proletarian origin. His father began as a railroad worker but was soon reduced to all kinds of handyman jobs to support his family of seven children, a task at which he never fully succeeded. LeMay as the eldest began selling papers during high school to help the family budget, and sent money home while he worked his way through college. Poverty and insecurity no more led him to question the economic system than the weather. Indeed he speaks of his father's struggles as if they were a meteorological phenomenon. "Like many men in his category [not—let us notice—class] and time, he was subject," LeMay relates, "to whims and pressures of regional and national economy." The Depression years, when he was a fledgling aviator, were hard for him and his family, but his only reference to them is "Depression or no Depression, they were opening up airports all over the country." Neither these early struggles nor his later experience in military service with plane manufacturers notorious for overcharges, led him to take a critical view of free enterprise. His nearest approach to an unfriendly remark about the capitalist system is an angry comment in his account of how the Air Corps flew the mails in 1934 under Roosevelt. "The public bought the idea (and still retains it)," he comments sourly, "that scores of Air Corps pilots lost their lives in an heroic but absurd attempt to emulate the superb performance of the commercial airlines." It is only in the bitterness of his feud with McNamara, that he allows himself to reflect by implication on the Business Man. "I hadn't spent the bulk of the years since World War II," he says, "in reorganizing any vast business for the purpose of pulling it from the red side of the ledger to the black . . . I had reorganized and built up a vast business, the Strategic Air Command, but its mission was not to make a profit for stockholders . . . I had not been in the financial and organizational side of the automobile business . . . Thus it may be believed that Secretary McNamara and I would hold different views on the matter of manned aircraft."

This might be described as a *non sequitur de profundis*, since it is difficult to see why McNamara's experience in the (manned) automobile business should predispose him against the manned plane. LeMay's record otherwise is spotless. Though he did a tour of duty in Research and Development, the experience did not lead him (as it did General Gavin) to protest big business practices in dealing with the armed services, nor (like Admiral Rickover) to acid comment on performance and profits. The military-industrial complex never had an officer more loyally blinkered.

His reflexes were already exemplary when he joined the ROTC his first week at Ohio State. He recounts with relish being part of an ROTC mob on its way to "clean out" a bunch of campus pacifists until stopped by a First Lieutenant with more sense. He reveals that in those days on the same campus Milt Caniff, whose Steve Canyon is the Air Force's pride and joy, was then painting anti-military posters. No such ideological wild oats were sown by LeMay. Even in his youth he was no deviator.

LeMay's own story, as told by himself and prettied up by MacKinlay Kantor, is hardly a candid portrait. It reads like the glossy fiction at which Kantor is so adept. To separate the truth from the treacle is a sticky task. But the ferocious prejudices which brought LeMay and Goldwater together in a mutual admiration society break through: ". . . in a day when labor unions howl for a twenty-four-hour week, and God knows what fringe benefits besides" . . . "some newly emergent so-called Republic in darkest Africa" . . . "the Whiz Kid liberal of today" . . . "the intellectuals, the inveterate pacifists, the dreamers and idealists . . . who believed firmly that the soft answer turned away wrath." In recalling the San Francisco Fair of 1915 to celebrate the opening of the Panama Canal, the prose turns apoplectic at the thought that if any man had said then that some day we would agree not to fly the U.S. flag over the Canal "unless the Panamanian flag floated beside it, on the same level" we would have "suspected that man to be a traitor." Since it was LBJ who agreed to this traitorous concession, it is not hard to believe that the President was glad to "press the flesh" with LeMay in farewell last January 31 after the shortest extension of service ever given a Chief of Staff—ten months from the previous April, or just long enough to keep LeMay from campaigning for Goldwater.

LeMay's attitude toward his bomber command exploits are of a piece with these ripe reflections. He says defensively in his Foreword that his bombings were of "military targets" on which attack was "justified morally." But he can't resist adding a sneer, "I've tried to stay away from hospitals, prison camps, orphan asylums, nunneries and dog kennels." He says, "I have sought to slaughter as few civilians as possible." But a few pages later he is boasting that in the great fire raids on Japan, "We burned up nearly sixteen square miles of Tokyo." He quotes with relish General Power, who led that raid and later succeeded him as head of the Strategic Air Command, as saying that this one attack on Tokyo produced "more casualties than in any other military action in the history of the world, greater than those of Hiroshima and Nagasaki put together.

These were civilian casualties. For all his businesslike attitude toward bombings, a touch of unseemly zest colors LeMay's jubilant description, "Enemy cities were pulverized or fried to a crisp." Secretary of War Stimson, we now know, was horrified by these fire raids, and called in General Arnold to protest that the Air Force had promised there would be only precision bombing in Japan. In the autobiography Stimson wrote after the war with McGeorge Bundy, he admitted that "in the conflagration bombings by massed B-29s" he had found himself permitting "the kind of war he had always hated." Stimson later told Robert Oppenheimer [2] he was appalled by the lack of public protest and thought "there was something wrong with a country where no one questioned" such raids. Even more appalling is the inability of men in the highest

[2] This and the two previous references are from Giovannitti and Freed's fascinating recent account, *The Decision to Drop the Bomb*.

offices to control their instruments once war breaks out. This is a lesson to be ignored at our peril.

The excuse General Arnold gave Secretary Stimson is the same excuse LeMay offers at a later point in his story, that the wide dispersion of Japanese industry made the fire raids necessary. He claimed with what seems obvious and characteristic exaggeration that in the ruins one could see "a drill press sticking up through the wreckage of every home." "We knew we were going to kill a lot of women and kids when we burned that town," he now says. "Had to be done." But there were other reasons for indiscriminate urban bombing. As so often happens, the Air Force changed doctrine to suit its weapons. The B-29s, as Giovannitti and Freed explain, "had been designed for daylight precision bombing" but the effects had proven disappointing. The Air Force then decided that incendiary bombing against the cities of Japan, with their crowded quarters and wooden construction "would be more effective." LeMay in a message to Norstad, then Chief of Staff of the 20th Air Force, felt the air war against Japan presented "the AAF for the first time with an opportunity of proving the power of the strategic air arm" (Giovannitti-Freed). The fire raids were the greatest advertisement yet for strategic air power. But they were only made possible because naval blockade had strangled the Japanese economy. The Japanese air force in the homeland had become almost non-existent so that low-level fire raids could be staged with little resistance and few losses. These raids were dramatic but were they necessary? A passage in the U. S. Strategic Bombing Survey study of the effects on Japan's war economy (p. 38) indicates that LeMay does not tell the whole story when he claims that widespread killing of women and children was unavoidable. "Although an effort was made," this report says of the fire raids, "to direct these attacks toward targets the destruction of which would do damage to industrial production, *the preponderant purpose appears to have been to secure the heaviest possible morale and shock effect by widespread attack upon the Japanese civilian population.*"

No matter how you choose to disguise it, the essence of the victory-by-airpower thesis is victory by terror against the civilian population. The ideas of the Italian Douhet and of the American Billy Mitchell grew out of the doctrine of the Prussian military writers of the nineteenth century. "The moment a national war breaks out," General Julius von Hartman wrote in 1877, "terrorism becomes a necessary military principle." This was the origin of *Schrecklichkeit*, the doctrine of frightfulness applied by the Germans in the First World War. Military airpower, as Douhet and Mitchell envisaged it, was to give the doctrine a new dimension. The rationalization they offered is that all-out bombardment would shorten the war and be more humane in the long run.

Hindenburg once wrote in the same spirit during World War I while he was commander in Poland, "Lodz is starving. That is deplorable, but it ought to be so. The more pitiless the conduct of the war the more humane it is in reality, for it will run its course all the sooner." The date of the utterance is enough to demonstrate the fallacy of the proposition. It was November 20, 1914, and the war was to last four years more despite these frightful beginnings.[3] Yet men like LeMay, Nixon, and Goldwater peddle the same fallacies when they urge us to "save lives" and "shorten the war" by mass bombings of North Vietnam and, if necessary, of China.

Just as the First World War proved that frightfulness would not bring victory, so the Second World War proved that Douhet and Mitchell were wrong about aerial bombardment. "The result of warfare by air," Mitchell wrote in 1930 (*Skyways*, p. 256), "will be to bring about quick decisions. Superior air power will cause such havoc, or the threat of such havoc, in the opposing country that a long drawn-out campaign will be impossible." But the Second World War lasted two years longer than the First despite aerial bombardment of unparalleled weight and horror. Strategic bombing failed to break Britain's will to resist. Germany's war production rose steadily until the summer of 1944; the Nazis did not capitulate until Allied and Russian ground armies met on the Elbe. Japan was defeated by blockade. "World War II proved in every instance," Marshall Andrews wrote in his incisive little book, *Disaster Through Airpower*, a decade ago, "that strategic bombing was costly all out of proportion to whatever results it obtained."

[3] Marshall Andrews, *Disaster Through Air Power*, p. 39.

LeMay regards terror from the skies as the one sure remedy for all political ills. He reveals that for three years—that is since 1962—he had been urging in the Joint Chiefs of Staff that the way to end the war in Vietnam was to let them know that "we're going to bomb them back into the Stone Age." This is one of his favorite phrases; in World War II he boasted that the Japanese air raids "were driving them back to the Stone Age." [4] The Stone Age is a metaphor for the days when brute force reigned supreme; instinctively LeMay harks back to it. He is as simple minded in prescribing strategic bombing for small wars with underdeveloped peoples as in big wars with industrialized societies. He reminds us that in the Korean war his "immediate suggestion" was to "go up north and burn the principal cities." But he does not frankly admit how ineffective airpower proved in the Korean war. One has only to compare his account with that in the Air Force's own official history of the Korean war,[5] to see how dubious his advice was. Strategic bombing, aerial reconnaissance, and interdiction bombing all failed in the Korean war. LeMay does not tell us how quickly his advice about going north and burning down its cities was taken. Between August 10, 1950, one month after the war began, and September 25, the Far East Air Forces Bomber Command leveled every urban and industrial target above the 38th parallel except some naval oil storage tanks too close to the Russian border to be bombed without risk. But the war went on for three more years. Aerial reconnaissance also failed to detect the Chinese intervention that followed this massive devastation on their border. "According to Chinese Communist records captured much later," the official AF history reveals (p. 16), "the Chinese had begun to slip troops across the Yalu as early as 14 October" or just four days before MacArthur announced that the Korean war was "definitely" coming to an end. By then major portions of the Chinese Fourth Field Army were in North Korea. Interdiction was no more successful. Though "Operation Strangle" and "Operation Saturate" made sensational headlines in the U.S. press, as do current "interdic-

[4] Gar Alperovitz's *Atomic Diplomacy: Hiroshima and Potsdam*, p. 106.
[5] *The U. S. Air Force in Korea, 1950–53*, by Futrell, Moseley, and Simpson.

tion raids" on North Vietnam, they no more succeeded then than now in interdicting supply lines. Our troops were pushed back to the 38th parallel. Despite bombardment so lavish that one Air Force officer said "we were trading B-26s for trucks," the communists were able to fire 102,000 rounds against Allied positions in May, 1952 as compared with 8000 the previous July and they soon built up enough anti-aircraft, as the official Air Force history admits, "to take an unacceptable toll" of our bomber planes.

One explanation lamely offered by LeMay in his autobiography is that bombardment failed because of an "undying Oriental philosophy and fanaticism." He says, "Human attrition means nothing to such people," that their lives are so miserable on earth that they look forward with delight to a death which promises them "everything from tea-parties with long dead grandfathers down to their pick of all the golden little dancing girls in Paradise." Anyone capable of such silliness is a poor guide to Asian military policy. Neither Buddhism nor Confucianism nor communism offers life after death of any kind, much less "golden little dancing girls in Paradise"—he has them mixed up with Mohammedanism. The notion that poor people care less for their own lives and those of their children belongs to Kipling-era colonialism. Was it Oriental fatalism that maintained London's spirits during the blitz?

LeMay's other explanation, of course, is the MacArthurite complaint that the communists were allowed to have a bomb-free sanctuary in Manchuria. One answer to this is that we had a bomb-free sanctuary ourselves in Japan which we used as the Reds did Manchuria for rest and supply. There is also another answer. LeMay concedes the little-known fact that the communists also allowed us a bomb-free sanctuary in Korea itself. LeMay says we learned later that the Migs in Manchuria had the range to reach the front lines in Korea. "If I had been working for the other side," he writes, "and had all those Migs in Manchuria that the Chinese had, I would have run General MacArthur right out of Korea . . . With that Mig force, any energetic commander could have cleaned out all the airfields we had in Korea, and mighty soon . . . then they could have started working on the troops. Why they didn't do it I'll never know." In this revealing conjecture LeMay unwittingly provides his own explanation for the restriction against bombing Manchuria of which he so bitterly complains.

Despite this experience, LeMay nowhere soberly discusses the question of what to do if the Chinese react to the devastation of North Vietnam as they did to that of North Korea. The early predictions of the victory-by-airpower people have proven ludicrously wrong in the Vietnamese war. General Thomas S. Power, retired, who was LeMay's successor as Chief of the Strategic Air Command, wrote two years ago in his book *Design for Survival* that an aerial ultimatum and selected bombing of military depots would force the North to surrender "within a few days." Almost a year has now passed since Johnson adopted the LeMay-Goldwater-Power-Nixon thesis and began to bomb the North, but the only visible result has been increased infiltration. Instead of a slow trickle of Southerners heading home for guerrilla war, full North Vietnamese regiments now appear in the South. Blackmail by bombardment—the new euphemism for it, in the words of our current U. S. Air Force Chief of Staff General McConnell, is "strategic persuasion" [6]—has failed. Instead of giving the President "a heavily flexible tool," as General McConnell blandly phrases it, "in inducing North Vietnam eventually to accept his offer of unconditional discussions," strategic bombardment has galvanized North Vietnam into greater and more open aid to the Southern insurgents. Strategic bombing in the South—the use of sledgehammers against gnats—has also proved a failure, as shown by the mounting number and size of Vietcong attacks. Though General McConnell is still calling these B-52 saturation bombings "highly effective" they run counter to anti-guerrilla experience in the Philippines, Malaya, and Algeria. The Air Force's own most experienced anti-guerrilla expert, General Lansdale—reputedly the Quiet American of Graham Greene's novel about Indochina, and now an advisor to Ambassador Lodge—has protested in vain that indiscriminate area bombing only increases a civilian bitterness which facilitates Vietcong recruitment. The reader of LeMay's story would never guess such vital problems are raised by his brutal quickie proposals.

[6] Speech to the Detroit Economics Club, December 6, 1965.

What if our escalating military action against North Vietnam, like invasion of North Korea, is followed by Chinese intervention? Will LeMay, Nixon, and Goldwater then advocate the bombing of China—and of Russia if it aids China—in a giddy logical progression that Herblock, in a recent cartoon, brilliantly called "Total Peace Through Total Victory Through Total World Blowup"? Here again *Mission with LeMay* is far from candid. No one would guess from it how basic to Air Force thinking is the idea of the first strike and of preventive war. The first explicit though hitherto almost unnoticed formulation of these strategies may be found as early as 1947 in *Air Campaigns of the Pacific War*, a book the Air Force published because it did not like the U. S. Strategic Bombing Survey with its downgrading of airpower.[7] A section of this book is called "Keeping the American Public Informed With Respect to the Danger of Accepting the First Blow in a Future War." This sets forth a new definition of what constitutes an act of war:

> We must recognize [it says] that an overt act of war has been committed by an enemy when that enemy builds a military force intended for our eventual destruction, and that the destruction of that force before it can be launched or employed is defensive action and not aggression . . . As a nation we must understand that an overt act of war has been committed long before the delivery of that first blow and that the earlier such an overt act is recognized the more effective the defense can be.

Then U. S. Army Infantry Major, now Colonel Lawrence J. Legere, Jr., to whose unpublished 1950 Ph.D. thesis we owe this revealing quotation, comments, "Whatever this unique concept is, it is not international law. It may be an example of the kind of reasoning Hitler used to justify his wars of aggression." It is also the rationale for the kind of "preventive" blow at China and its nuclear installations LeMay and the Air Force favor. McNamara's warnings to last December's meeting of the NATO Council about China's coming nuclear power may give them new support. McNamara, like Stimson, could find his military instruments running away with him.

The pages in *Mission with LeMay* which discuss preventive

[7] The U. S. Strategic Bombing Survey was established by Stimson in 1944. Franklin D'Olier was the chairman; George Ball, J. K. Galbraith and Paul Nitze served as officers.

war against Russia verge on self-caricature in their light-minded shallowness. LeMay says that there was a time in the period before the Russians got the Bomb and their achievement of a stockpile, when we could have destroyed all of Russia "without losing a man to their defenses. The only losses incurred would have been the normal accident rate for the number of flying hours which would have been flown to do the job." This assurance that we would not have lost a *single* plane begins to sound like something out of *Doctor Strangelove.* So does LeMay's idea that America could then have said to Russia, " 'Here's a blueprint for your immediate future. We'll give you a deadline of five or six months'—something like that—'to pull out of the satellite countries, and effect a complete change of conduct. You will behave your damn selves from this moment forth.' " It is hard to believe that this is not satirical fiction: General Turgidson at work and play.

All through the years to which LeMay refers, he was sounding the alarms on Capitol Hill; we were in danger of being overrun by Russian hordes; we were woefully short of bombers and later of missiles. He and his supporters were the ultimate source of the imaginary bomber gap and the equally imaginary missile gap. Now he tells us we could have smashed all Russia even before the missile age without losing a single plane. He even says one "might argue whether it would be desirable to present such a challenge to the Russians, even at this [1965] stage." Obviously he thinks we have enough now to put Russia in the reformatory by ultimatum.

The strangest aspect of LeMay's story is his detachment. While he is ready to bomb almost anybody, he really seems to hate almost nobody—nobody, that is, among America's national enemies, past, present, or future. Their destruction is his job, the occasion for demonstrating his abilities. This is no winged warrior, with blood-lust in his veins, as in the ancient Sagas; no young Mussolini thrilling to the red flowers that spring from the Ethiopian earth as the bombs fall from his plane. He even has words of praise for Mao Tse-tung and his ready co-operation in helping U.S. fliers downed over Chinese Communist territory during World War II. If he ever gets his chance to blow Mao to Kingdom Come, it will be with no hard feelings whatsoever.

What LeMay really hates, with an abiding and never slaked passion, is first and above all the U. S. Navy. If war were the product only of hate and not of institutional patterns, it is the Navy the Strategic Air Command would strike some black night in swift preventive action before those "web-footed" (a favorite phrase of LeMay's) so-and-so's could get more money out of Congress for contraptions the Air Force regards as useless and competitive. Russia is a necessary anti-hero in the Air Force's dramaturgy, but the Navy is Enemy No. 1 from of old. This sibling feud began with the bomber vs. battleship controversy; one of its earliest episodes was the trial "bombing" of the battleship *Utah* three years before World War II. LeMay's account hints darkly at "perfidious tactics" in the War Department through which enemy spies, naval spies that is, obtained advance information on the Air Force's plans in that test. Hate and suspicion of the Navy appear and reappear as the darkest thread in his story. This is because, short of abolishing the Navy altogether, it has to have its own aircraft in support of its traditional functions. Planes must protect surface ships, provide them with reconnaissance, supply them with firepower in battles against other ships, hunt out submarines and lay mines. The Army, too, could use its own tactical air forces; both the Russians and the Germans, in different ways, effectively provided close support planes under the direction of the ground commander. But the U. S. Army gave up its fight to control its own tactical arm long ago and clings only to its helicopters. The Navy, on the other hand, not only refused to throw in the sponge but hit the Air Force an unforgivable blow in developing the carrier, a floating air base with its own planes. This ended the Air Force dream of controlling all military aviation, and made peaceful coexistence between Air Force and Navy unthinkable.

LeMay's other unforgivable enemy is McNamara. For LeMay no ideological difference could be deeper than their dispute over the manned bomber. But the inexorable logic of industrial society and the airpower it spawned are against LeMay. The rise of airpower has from the beginning injected the idea into warfare that the machine was more important than the man. And the supersonic speed and enormous complexity of modern combat airplanes have reduced the pilot to a relatively minor cog in a machine. As McNamara said in giving the death blow three years ago to LeMay's last great bomber project, the B-70, the bomber has become a manned missile with "none of the advantages or flexibility generally attributed to manned bombers." Their flight has to be directed from the ground in "pre-planned attack against previously known targets," a mission better performed by the swifter and simpler unmanned missile. LeMay, by the strange reversal of events, has come to seem a Don Quixote in his old age, as he has seen more and more of his airmen go underground like moles to tend missiles. Billy Mitchell envisaged pilots as a new chivalric order of the air; they have instead become sitters for panels of pushbuttons. Yet while LeMay despises McNamara as a factory manager, he himself reveals throughout his story the attitudes not so much of a warrior as of a great industrial expert, albeit in demolition. The machine molded him and the machine threatens to replace him—and the machine, like the policies he advocates, lacks mind and heart.

But this tough old troglodyte is not through yet. The whole Air Force drive in Vietnam is to transform the war we can't win to a war we might; from a war for the loyalties of the Vietnamese people into a war to destroy them; this is giving the obsolete B-52 its last murderous gasp over South Vietnam's jungles and rice paddies. There is also China, weak and with only a few atom bombs. The Air Force recognizes the mutual stand-off in its relations with the Soviet Union, but its Strategic Air Command hungers for a last chance against China. LeMay in retirement, unmuzzled, could be more dangerous than when he was Air Force Chief of Staff. The delusion of an easy victory-by-airpower may yet bog us down like the Japanese in endless land war with mankind's most numerous and enduring people. This is the danger.

JANUARY 20, 1966

# WHILE OTHERS DODGE THE DRAFT, BOBBY DODGES THE WAR

Robert F. Kennedy is not setting a good example for American youth. To be a trimmer, to put career ahead of duty, to be all but silent on the greatest moral and political issue of our time is to be no different from the other politicians. We are sure that if a young man went to the Senator and asked his advice on how best to dodge military service in Vietnam, Kennedy would regard him as a coward and unpatriotic. But we are also sure that if we had the Senator's confidence and asked him privately why he was not speaking out on the war, he would explain it was too risky, that he had already established a position slightly to the left of the Administration in his Vietnam speech of February 19, 1966, that this was sufficient to hold his liberal constituency and that anything more would be politically dangerous, and might put him in the isolated position of a Morse or Gruening. To die for your country is one thing. To put your political future in jeopardy for it is another.

These are roles we take for granted in the ancient dramaturgy of human conflict. Honor requires the soldier to kill or be killed, whatever his scruples. But it is not regarded as dishonorable for the politician to swallow his misgivings and allow the young to go out to die without protest. Kennedy in the U. S. Senate has at his disposal a forum second only to that of the Presidency. But he hasn't said a word about the war in the Senate since his one speech last February. A wistful committee has been organized for a Kennedy-Fulbright ticket in

1968 but Fulbright has been speaking out while Kennedy has been falling silent. Kennedy did not support his effort to rescind the Tonkin Bay resolution nor to alert the country on the danger in Thailand. He even achieved the feat of delivering a speech on peace in New York (October 11, 1966) without mentioning Vietnam!

Kennedy thinks of himself as a moral man. He proclaims it in South Africa and in Latin America but at home, where thousands are being drafted every month, he says as little as he can about the one issue that matters most. It is only in response to questions that he occasionally speaks of the war, often with a remarkable complacency. "We have to realize," he told a questioner in Iowa (*New York Times,* October 10, 1966), "that the casualties are going to continue to be large." Shouldn't he, who sees himself as the candidate of youth, do something to stop them? He has a small army of ghost writers turning out speeches and hunting up apt quotations. Why not on the war?

At Hunter College in New York recently he confined himself, as Brother Teddy does, to the safe topic of aid to Vietnamese refugees. He met "all questions on the propriety of the war in Vietnam," the *New York Times* reported October 8, 1966 "with an appeal for the students to acknowledge that was a subject separate from providing relief for noncombatants hurt by the war." It is indecent to talk of helping the refugees while keeping silent about the napalm and the saturation bombings that make a hell of their lives. He would go no further than to say, coyly, "You are aware that I have some reservations about our role in Vietnam." This drew the biggest applause of the evening, but it is time Kennedy stopped getting cheers for such tepid observations. The students cheered because they were hungry for a word against the war and because they had faith in Kennedy. But he betrays their faith, by playing skillful politics on the issue that may mean life or death for them. We are glad to see that he was heckled in Chicago and met with signs saying, "Kennedy and Douglas Support Mass Murderers in Vietnam." There, too, in the same equivocal vein as at Hunter, he said he "happened to have some disagreements with President Johnson on Vietnam." (*Washington Post,* October 16, 1966). Is he saving them for his memoirs?

William Shannon in *Harper's* for October (1966) says he is

out for the Vice-Presidency in 1968. "With skillful publicity," Shannon writes, "this could be made to appear not as an act of bold usurpation and impatient ambition by Kennedy but a reluctant rescue mission to prop up an aging wartime President whose popularity is sagging." Just as Johnson moved left to outflank Goldwater, with whom he had been allied in the Senate, so Kennedy moved left to outflank Humphrey and take over the latter's liberal constituency. But he is careful not to get so far out as to break his ties with the White House.

We do not mean to imply that Kennedy is insincere. We only note that the liberal views he has adopted also serve his political purposes. Nor do we mean to say that he is not troubled by the war. We believe he is. But he is not troubled enough to risk a confrontation with Johnson. In a *Wall Street Journal* (October 17, 1966) survey of Bobby's campaign activities one can see how little he deals with any concrete issues in those tours which have the bobby-soxers squealing. As for the war, that paper noted "Actually Mr. Kennedy has been careful of late to avoid sharp attacks on the President. When he expressed doubts about Vietnam policy, he always stresses that 'these are very complex problems, with no simple solutions.'" Johnson was for peace, too, before he won election. What guarantee that Kennedy would prove any better, under the enormous pressure of the military bureaucracy, if his convictions are already so feeble, his mind so divided?

OCTOBER 24, 1966

# VII

---

## A
## RACE
## IN
## REVOLT

# THE PILGRIMAGE OF MALCOLM X

Malcolm X was born into Black Nationalism. His father was a follower of Marcus Garvey, the West Indian who launched a "Back to Africa" movement in the Twenties. Malcolm's first clash with white men took place when his mother was pregnant with him; a mob of Klansmen in Omaha, Nebraska, waving shotguns and rifles, warned her one night to move out of town because her husband was spreading trouble among the "good" Negroes with Garvey's teachings. One of his earliest memories was of seeing their home burned down in Lansing, Michigan, in 1929, because the Black Legion, a white fascist organization, considered his father an "uppity" Negro. The body of his father, a tall, powerful black man from Georgia, soon afterwards was found literally cut to pieces in one of those mysterious accidents that often veil a racial killing.

His mother was a West Indian who looked like a white woman. Her unknown father was white. She slowly went to pieces mentally under the burden of raising eight children. When the family was broken up, Malcolm was sent to a detention home, from which he attended a white school. He must have been a bright and attractive lad, for he was at the top of his class and was elected class president in the seventh grade. Many years later, in a speech on the Black Revolution which is included in the collection, *Malcolm X Speaks*, he was able to boast bitterly, "I grew up with white people. I was integrated before they even invented the word." The reason for the bitterness was an incident that changed his life. His English teacher told him he ought to begin thinking about his career. Malcolm said he would like to be a lawyer. His teacher suggested carpentry instead. "We all here like you, you know that," the teacher said, "but you've got to be realistic about being a nigger."

Malcolm X left Lansing deeply alienated and in the slums of Boston and New York he became a "hustler," selling numbers, women, and dope. "All of us," he says, in his *Autobiography,* of his friends in the human jungle, "who might have probed space or cured cancer or built industries, were instead black victims of the white man's American social system." Insofar as he was concerned, this was no exaggeration. He was an extraordinary man. Had he been wholly white, instead of irretrievably "Negro" by American standards, he might easily have become a leader of the bar. In the underworld he went from marijuana to cocaine. To meet the cost he took up burglary. He was arrested with a white mistress who had become his look-out woman. In February 1946, not quite twenty-one, he was sentenced to ten years in prison in Massachusetts. The heavy sentence reflected the revulsion created in the judge by the discovery that Malcolm had made a white woman his "love slave." In prison, he went on nutmeg, reefers, Nembutal, and benzedrine in a desperate effort to replace the drugs. He was a vicious prisoner, often in solitary. The other prisoners nicknamed him "Satan." But the prison had an unusually well stocked library to which he was introduced by a fellow prisoner, an old-time burglar named Bimbi. Through him, Malcolm first encountered Thoreau. Prison became his university; there also he was converted to the Nation of Islam, the sect the press calls Black Muslims.

The important word here is conversion. To understand Malcolm's experience, one must go to the literature of conversion. "Were we writing the history of the mind from the purely natural history point of view," William James concludes in his *Varieties of Religious Experience,* "we would still have to write down man's liability to sudden and complete conversion as one of his most curious peculiarities." The convert's sense of being born anew, the sudden change from despair to elation, bears an obvious resemblance to the manic-depressive cycle, except that the change in the personality is often permanent. But those who experience it must first—to borrow Gospel language—be brought low. James quotes the theological maxim, "Man's extremity is God's opportunity." It is only out of the depths that men on occasion experience this phenomenon of renewal. The success of the Black Muslims in converting and rehabilitating criminals and dope addicts like Malcolm X recalls the mighty phrases James quotes from Luther. "God," he preached, "is the God . . . of those that are brought even to nothing . . . and his nature is . . . to save the very desperate and damned." Malcolm had been brought to nothing, he was one of those very desperate and damned, when he was "saved" by Elijah Muhammad, the self-proclaimed Messenger of Allah to the lost Black Nation of that imaginary Islam he preaches.

The tendency is to dismiss Elijah Muhammad's weird doctrine as another example of the superstitions, old and new, that thrive in the Negro ghetto. It is not really any more absurd than the Virgin Birth or the Sacrifice of Isaac. The rational absurdity does not detract from the psychic therapy. Indeed the therapy may lie in the absurdity. Converts to any creed talk of the joy in complete surrender; a rape of the mind occurs. "Credo quia absurdum," Tertullian, the first really cultivated apologist for Christianity, is said to have exulted, "I believe because it is absurd." Tertullian was himself a convert. Black Nationalists may even claim him as an African, for his home was Carthage.

There is a special reason for the efficacy of the Black Muslims in reaching the Negro damned. The sickness of the Negro in America is that he has been made to feel a nigger; the genocide is psychic. The Negro must rid himself of this feeling if he is to stand erect again. He can do so in two ways. He can change the outer world of white supremacy, or he can change his inner world by "conversion." The teachings of the Black Muslims may be fantastic but they are superbly suited to the task of shaking off the feeling of nigger-ness. Elijah Muhammad teaches that the original man was black, that Caucasians are "white devils" created almost 6,000 years ago by a black genius named Yakub. He bleached a number of blacks by a process of mutation into pale-faced blue-eyed devils in order to test the mettle of the Black Nation. This inferior breed has ruled by deviltry but their time will soon be up, at the end of the sixth millenium, which may be by 1970 or thereabouts. To explain the white man as a devil is, as Malcolm X says in the *Autobiography,* to strike "a nerve center in the American black man" for "when he thinks about his own life, he is going to see where, to him personally, the white man sure has acted like a devil." To see the white man this way is, in Gospel imagery, to cast out the devil. With him go his values, as he has impressed them on the Black Man, above all the inner feeling of being a nigger. To lose that feeling is to be fully emancipated. For the poor Negro no drug could be a stronger opiate than this black religion.

With rejection of the white man's values goes rejection of the white man's God. "We're worshipping a Jesus," Malcolm protested in one of his sermons after he became a Black Muslim Minister, "who doesn't even *look* like us." The white man, he declared, "has brainwashed us black people to fasten our gaze upon a blond-haired, blue-eyed Jesus." This Black Muslim doctrine may seem a blasphemous joke until one makes the effort to imagine how whites would feel if taught to worship a black God with thick African lips. Men prefer to create a God in their own image. "The Ethiopians," one of the pre-Socratic Greek philosophers [1] observed a half millennium before Christ, "assert that their gods are snub-nosed and black" while the "Nordic" Thracians said theirs were "blue-eyed and red-haired." When Marcus Garvey, the first apostle of Pan-Africanism, toured Africa, urging expulsion of the white man, he called for a Negro religion with a Negro Christ. Just as Malcolm Little, in accordance with Black Muslim practice, rejected his "slave name" and became Malcolm X, so Malcolm X, son of a Baptist preacher, rejected Christianity as a slave religion. His teacher, Elijah Muhammad, did not have to read Nietszche to discover that Christianity was admirably suited to make Rome's slaves submissive. In our ante-bellum South the value of Christian teaching in making slaves tractable was widely recognized even by slaveholders themselves agnostic.[2] The Negro converted to Christianity was cut off from the disturbing memory of his own gods and of his lost freedom, and reconciled to his lot in the

---

[1] Xenophon of Kolophon, Fragment No. 16 in Diels: *Die Fragmente der Vorsokratiker.*

[2] See Stampp's *The Peculiar Institution,* pps. 158–60.

white man's chains. Here again the primitivistic fantasies of the Black Muslims unerringly focus on a crucial point. It is in the Christian mission that what Malcolm X called the "brainwashing" of the blacks began.

Racism and nationalism are poisons. Sometimes a poison may be prescribed as a medicine, and Negroes have found in racism a way to restore their self-respect. But black racism is still racism, with all its primitive irrationality and danger. There are passages in the *Autobiography* in which Malcolm, recounting some of his Black Muslim sermons, sounds like a Southern white supremacist in reverse, vibrating with anger and sexual obsession over the horrors of race pollution. There is the same preoccupation with rape, the same revulsion about mixed breeds. "Why," he cried out, "the white man's raping of the black race's woman began right on those slave ships!" A psychoanalyst might see in his fury the feeling of rejection by the race of his white grandfather. A biologist might see in the achievements of this tall sandy-complexioned Negro—his friends called him "Red"—an example of the possibilities of successful racial mixture. But Malcolm's feelings on the subject were as outraged as those of a Daughter of the Confederacy. He returned revulsion for revulsion and hate for hate. He named his first child, a daughter, Attilah, and explained that he named her for the Hun who sacked Rome.

But hidden under the surface of the Black Nationalist creed to which he was won there lay a peculiar anti-Negroism. The true nationalist loves his people and their peculiarities; he wants to preserve them; he is filled with filial piety. But there is in Elijah Muhammad's Black Muslim creed none of the love for the Negro one finds in W. E. B. du Bois, or of that yearning for the ancestral Africa which obsessed Garvey. Elijah Muhammad—who himself looks more Chinese than Negro—teaches his people that they are Asians, not Africans; that their original tongue is Arabic. He turns his people into middle-class Americans. Their clothes are conservative, almost Ivy League. Their religious services eschew that rich antiphony between preacher and congregation which one finds in Negro churches. The Nigerian, E. U. Essien-Udom, whose *Black Nationalism* is the best book on the Black Muslims, was struck by their middle-class attitudes and coldness to Africa and African ways. In

Black Muslim homes, when jazz was played, he writes that he was "often tempted to tap his feet to the tune of jazz" but was inhibited because his Black Muslim hosts "listened to it without ostensible response to the rhythm." In their own way the Black Muslims are as much in flight from Negritude as was Booker T. Washington. Indeed Elijah Muhammad's stress on Negro private business and his hostility to trade unionism in his own dealings with Negroes are very much in the Booker T. Washington pattern. The virtues of bourgeois America are what Elijah Muhammad seeks to recreate in his separate Black Nation. This is the banal reality which lies behind all his hocus-pocus about the Koran, and here lie the roots of his split with Malcolm X.

For Elijah Muhammad practices separation not only from American life but from the American Negro community, and from its concrete struggles for racial justice. Malcolm X was drawn more and more to engagement in that struggle. In the midst of describing in the *Autobiography* his happy and successful years as a Black Muslim organizer, Malcolm X says:

> If I harbored any personal disappointment, whatsoever, it was that privately I was convinced that our Nation of Islam could be an even greater force in the American black man's overall struggle—if we engaged in more *action*. By that I mean I thought privately that we should have amended or relaxed, our general non-engagement policy. I felt that, wherever black people committed themselves, in the Little Rocks and Birminghams and other places, militantly disciplined Muslims should also be there —for all the world to see, and respect and discuss. It could be heard increasingly in the Negro communities: "Those Muslims *talk* tough, but they never *do* anything, unless somebody bothers Muslims." [Italics in original.]

This alone was bound to divide the prophet and disciple. But there were also personal factors. Elijah Muhammad won Malcolm's devotion by his kindness in corresponding with the young convict when Malcolm was still in prison. But Malcolm's intellectual horizons were already far wider than those of the rather narrow, ill-educated, and suspicious Messenger of Allah. In the prison library Malcolm X was finding substantiation for the Black Muslim creed in *Paradise Lost* and in Herodotus; this passionate curiosity and voracious reading were bound to make

him outgrow Elijah's dream-book theology. On the one side
envy and on the other disillusion were to drive the two men
apart. The crowds drawn by Malcolm and his very organizing
success made Elijah Muhammad and his family jealous. On the
other hand, Malcolm, who had kept the sect's vows of chastity,
was shocked when former secretaries of Elijah Muhammad filed
paternity suits against the prophet. Malcolm had nothing but
a small salary and the house the sect had provided for him.
Elijah Muhammad's cars (two Cadillacs and a Lincoln Continental), his $200 pin-striped banker-style suits, his elegantly
furnished eighteen-room house in one of the better sections of
Chicago's Hyde Park, began to make a sour impression on
Malcolm. The hierarchy lives well in practically all religions,
and their worldly affluence fosters schism. Malcolm was too
big, too smart, too able, to fit into the confines of this little sect
and remain submissive to its family oligarchy. He began to
open up a larger world, and this endangered Elijah Muhammad's hold on the little band of unsophisticated faithful he had
recruited.

*Muhammad Speaks,* the weekly organ of the Black Muslims,
had begun to play down Malcolm's activities. The break came
over Malcolm's comment on Kennedy's assassination. Within
hours after the President's killing, Elijah Muhammad sent out
a directive ordering the cult's ministers to make no comment
on the murder. Malcolm, speaking at Manhattan Center a few
days afterward, was asked in the question period what he
thought of the assassination. He answered it was a case of "the
chickens coming home to roost." Malcolm explains in the *Autobiography,* "I said that the hate in white men had not stopped
with the killing of defenseless black people but . . . finally had
struck down the President." He complains that "some of the
world's most important personages were saying in various ways,
and in far stronger ways that I did, that America's climate of
hate had been responsible for the President's death. But when
Malcolm X said the same thing it was ominous." Elijah Muhammad called him in. "That was a very bad statement," he said.
"The country loved this man." He ordered Malcolm silenced
for ninety days so that the Black Muslims could be "disasso-
ciated from the blunder." Malcolm agreed and submitted. But
three days later he heard that a Mosque official was suggesting

his own assassination. Soon after, another Black Muslim told him of a plan to wire his car so that it would explode when he turned the ignition key. Malcolm decided to build a Muslim Mosque of his own, and open its doors to black men of all faiths for common action. To prepare himself he decided to make the pilgrimage to Mecca.

This visit to Mecca was a turning-point for Malcolm. His warm reception in the Arabic world, the sight of white men in equal fraternity with black and brown, marked a second conversion in his life. "For the past week," Malcolm wrote home, "I have been utterly speechless and spellbound by the graciousness I see displayed all around me by people *of all colors*." The italics were his. The man who made the seven circuits around the Ka'ba and drank the waters of Zem-Zem emerged from his pilgrimage no longer a racist or a Black Muslim. He took the title of El Hajj earned by his visit to Mecca and called himself henceforth El-Hajj Malik El-Shabazz. He turned Muslim in the true sense of the word. How indelibly he also remained an American go-getter is deliciously reflected in a passage of the *Autobiography* where he says that while in Mecca:

> I saw that Islam's conversions around the world could double and triple if the colorfulness and the true spiritualness of the Hajj pilgrimage were properly advertised and communicated to the outside world. I saw that the Arabs are poor at understanding the psychology of non-Arabs and the importance of public relations. The Arabs said inshālla ("God willing")—then they waited for converts, but I knew that with improved public relations methods the new converts turning to Allah could be turned into millions.

He had become a Hajj but remained in some way a Babbitt, the salesman, archetype of our American society. A creed was something to *sell*. Allah, the Merciful, needed better merchandising.

Malcolm returned from abroad May 21, 1964. Several attempts were made on his life. On February 21, 1965, he was killed by gunmen when he got up to speak at a meeting in New York's Audubon Ballroom. He was not quite forty when he died. The most revealing tribute paid him was the complaint by Elijah Muhammad after Malcolm was killed. "He came back preaching that we should not hate the enemy . . . He was a star who went astray." What nobler way to go astray? In Africa and in America there was almost unanimous recognition that the Negro race had lost a gifted son; only the then head of the U. S. Information Agency, Carl Rowan, immortalized himself with a monumental Uncle Tomism. "All this about an ex-convict, ex-dope peddler who became a racial fanatic," was Rowan's obtuse and ugly comment; it ranks with his discovery, as USIA Director, of what he called the public's "right *not* to know."

From tape-recorded conversations, a Negro writer, Alex Haley, put together the *Autobiography;* he did his job with sensitivity and with devotion. Here one may read, in the agony of this brilliant Negro's self-creation, the agony of an entire people in their search for identity. But more fully to understand this remarkable man, one must turn to *Malcolm X Speaks,* which supplements the *Autobiography.* All but one of the speeches were made in those last eight tumultuous months of his life after his break with the Black Muslims when he was seeking a new path. In their pages one can begin to understand his power as a speaker and to see, more clearly than in the *Autobiography,* the political legacy he left his people in its struggle for full emancipation.

Over and over again in simple imagery, savagely uncompromising, he drove home the real truth about the Negro's position in America. It may not be pleasant but it must be faced. "Those Hunkies that just got off the boat," he said in one of his favorite comparisons, "they're already Americans. Polacks are already Americans; the Italian refugees are already Americans. Everything that comes out of Europe, every blue-eyed thing, is already an American. And as long as you and I have been over here, we aren't Americans yet. They don't have to pass civil rights legislation to make a Polack an American." In a favorite metaphor, he said "I'm not going to sit at your table and watch you eat, with nothing on my plate, and call myself a diner. Sitting at the table doesn't make you a diner, unless you eat some of what's on the plate. Being here in America doesn't make you an American. Being born here in America doesn't make you an American." He often said, "Don't be shocked when I say that I was in prison. You're still in prison. That's what America means—prison." Who can deny that this is true for the black man? No matter how high he rises, he never loses consciousness of the invisible bars which hem him in. "We didn't land on Plymouth Rock," Malcolm was fond of saying, "It landed on us."

He counselled violence but he defended this as an answer to white violence. "If they make the Klan non-violent," he said over and over again, "I'll be non-violent." In another speech he said, "If violence is wrong in America, violence is wrong abroad. If it is wrong to be violent defending black women and black children and black babies and black men, then it is wrong for America to draft us and make us violent abroad in defense of her." He taunted his people in the same speech, "As long as the white man sent you to Korea, you bled . . . You bleed for white people, but when it comes to seeing your own churches being bombed and little black girls murdered, you haven't any blood." In a speech he made about the brutal beating of Fannie Lou Hamer of Mississippi, he said of the white man, "if he only understands the language of a rifle, get a rifle. If he only understands the language of a rope, get a rope. But don't waste time talking the wrong language to a man if you really want to communicate with him." In preaching Pan-Africanism, he reached down into the aching roots of Negro self-hatred as few men have ever done. "You can't hate Africa and not hate yourself," he said in one speech. "This is what the white man knows. So they make you and me hate our African identity . . . We hated our heads, we hated the shape of our nose, we wanted one of those long dove-like noses, you know; we hated the color of our skin, hated the blood of Africa that was in our veins. And in hating our features and our skin and our blood, we had to end up hating ourselves." No man has better expressed his people's trapped anguish.

Malcolm's most important message to his people is muted in the *Autobiography*, perhaps because Alex Haley, its writer, is politically conventional, but it comes out sharply in *Malcolm X Speaks* which was edited and published by a group of Trotsky-ists. This was the idea that while the Negro is a minority in this country, he is part of a majority if he thinks of common action with the rest of the world's colored peoples. "The first thing the American power structure doesn't want any Negroes

to start," he says in the *Autobiography*, "is thinking internationally." In a speech at Ibadan University in Nigeria, he relates in
the *Autobiography*, he urged the Africans to bring the American Negro's plight before the United Nations: "I said that just
as the American Jew is in political, cultural, and economic
harmony with world Jewry, I was convinced that it was time
for all Afro-Americans to join the world's Pan-Africanists."
Malcolm persuaded the Organization of African Unity at its
Cairo conference to pass a resolution saying that discrimination
against Negroes in the United States was "a matter of deep
concern" to the Africans, and the *New York Times* in August
1964 reported that the State and Justice Departments had
begun "to take an interest in Malcolm's campaign because it
might create 'a touchy problem' for the U.S. if raised at the
UN." In the UN debate over U.S. intervention to save white
lives in the Congo, African delegates at the UN for the first
time accused the U.S. of being indifferent to similar atrocities
against blacks in Mississippi. This is what Malcolm wanted
when he spoke of putting the Negro struggle in a world context.

An Italian writer, Vittorio Lanternari, published a remarkable book five years ago, which appeared here in 1963 as *The
Religions of the Oppressed: A Study of Modern Messianic
Cults*. It suggests that wherever white men have driven out or
subdued colored men, whether in the case of the American Indians, or in Africa, or in that of the Maoris in New Zealand,
the Tai-Pings in China and the Cao Dai in Vietnam or among
the uprooted blacks and harried Indians in the Caribbean and
Latin America, Messianic cults have arisen, rejecting white
men's values and seeking the restoration of shattered cultural
identities as the first step toward political freedom. He did not
include in his survey the cults which thrive in our Negro ghettoes though they are of the same character. One striking common bond among all these sects of the oppressed has been their
effort to free their people from drinking the white man's "fire-
water" or (in China) smoking his opium. To see the Black
Muslims and Malcolm's life in this perspective is to begin to
understand the psychic havoc wrought around the world by
white imperialism in the centuries since America was discovered and Afro-Asia opened up to white penetration. There are
few places on earth where whites have not grown rich robbing

the colored races. It was Malcolm's great contribution to help make us all aware of this.

His assassination was a loss to the country as well as to his race. These two books will have a permanent place in the literature of the Afro-American struggle. It is tantalizing to speculate on what he might have become had he lived. What makes his life so moving a story was his capacity to learn and grow. New disillusions, and a richer view of the human condition, lay ahead for the man who could say, as he did in one of his last speeches, when discussing the first Bandung conference, "Once they excluded the white man, they found they could get together." Since then India and Pakistan, Singapore and Malaysia, the rebellion against the Arabs in Zanzibar and the splits in Black Africa itself have demonstrated that fratricide does not end with the eviction of the white devil. Various left sects, Maoist and Trotskyist and communist, sought to recruit him, but he was trying to build a movement of his own. He was shopping around for new political ideas. He was also becoming active in the South instead of merely talking about a Dixie Mau-Mau from the relative safety of Harlem. I believe there was in him a readiness painfully to find and face new truths which might have made him one of the great Negroes, and Americans, of our time.

NOVEMBER 11, 1965

# THE MARCH ON WASHINGTON

The March is over, but it will never be forgotten. Every one who was there had his own special moment. Mine was to stand in the early morning inside the Union Terminal and watch the thousands pouring in from New York and Pittsburgh and Chicago, and suddenly to feel no longer alone in this hot-house capital but as if out in the country people did care. Of the Marchers themselves, I along with almost every other observer was impressed with their gentle sweetness, a tribute to the Negro people, who have managed by humor and faith, amid so much suffering, not to be soured.

For me the heroes of the March, or heroines, were the gnarled old colored ladies on tired feet and comfortably broken shoes, the kind who walked into history in Montgomery. Amid the well dressed middle class Negroes and their white sympathizers were many black folk misshapen by malnutrition and hard work. They carried upon them a story more plainly writ than any banner. These were, literally, the downtrodden and the treadmarks of oppression were visible upon their faces. They sang, "We shall not be moved." But those who saw them—and what life had done to them—were moved.

Then it was a pleasure to see amid the Marchers so many old-time radicals, the unquenchables of so many vanished movements, many of them long ago forced out of jobs and pulpits, now joyously turning up again, with the feeling that they were at last part of a mass upsurge, no longer lonely relics.

With Lincoln behind them, and those eager thousands before them, the speakers at the Memorial were inevitably dwarfed and on the whole disappointing. None—not even Martin Luther King, who is a little too saccharine for my taste—broke through to the kind of simple purity of utterance the place and the occasion called for. The price of having so many respectables on the bandwagon was to mute Negro militancy—John Lewis of SNCC had to tone down his speech under pressure from Archbishop O'Boyle—and the rally turned into one of support for the Kennedy civil rights program. Somehow on that lovely day, in that picnic atmosphere, the Negro's anguish never found full expression.

Far superior to anything at the Monument were the discussions I heard next day at a civil rights conference called by the Socialist Party. On that dismal rainy morning-after, in a dark union hall in the Negro section, I heard A. Philip Randolph speak with an eloquence and a humanity few can achieve. When he spoke of the abolitionists, and of the heroes of the Reconstruction, it was with a filial piety and an immediacy that made them live again. One felt the presence of a great American. He reminded the black nationalists gently that "we must not forget that the civil rights revolution was begun by white people as well as black at a time when the winds of hate were sweeping the country." He reminded the moderates that political equality was not enough. "The white sharecroppers of the South," he pointed out, "have full civil rights but live in bleakest poverty." One began to understand what was meant by a march for "*jobs* and freedom." For most Negroes, civil rights alone will only be the right to join the underprivileged whites. "We must liberate not only ourselves," Mr. Randolph said, "but our white brothers and sisters."

The direction in which full emancipation lies was indicated when Mr. Randolph spoke of the need to extend the public sector of the economy. His brilliant assistant on the March, Bayard Rustin, urged an economic Master Plan to deal with the technological unemployment that weighs so heavily on the Negro and threatens to create a permanently depressed class of whites and blacks living precariously on the edges of an otherwise affluent society. It was clear from the discussion that neither tax cuts nor public works nor job training (for what jobs?) would solve the problem while automation with giant steps made so many workers obsolete. The civil rights movement, Mr. Rustin said, could not get beyond a certain level unless it merged into a broader plan of social change.

In that ill-lighted hall, amid the assorted young students and venerables like Norman Thomas, socialism took on fresh meaning and revived urgency. It was not accidental that so many of those who ran the March turned out to be members or fellow travellers of the Socialist Party. One saw that for the lower third of our society, white as well as black, the search for answers must lead them back—though Americans still start nervously at the very word—toward socialism.

SEPTEMBER 16, 1963

# THE WASTELAND IN THE
# WHITE MAN'S HEART

It's not so much the killings as the lack of contrition. The morning after the Birmingham bombing, the Senate in its expansive fashion filled thirty-five pages of the *Congressional Record* with remarks on diverse matters before resuming debate on the nuclear test ban treaty. But the speeches on the bombing in Birmingham filled barely a single page. Of a hundred ordinarily loquacious Senators, only four felt moved to speak. Javits of New York and Kuchel of California expressed outrage. The Majority Leader, Mansfield, also spoke up, but half his time was devoted to defending J. Edgar Hoover from charges of indifference to racial bombings. His speech was remarkable only for its inane phrasing. "There can be no excuse for an occurrence of that kind," Mansfield said of the bombing, in which four little girls at Sunday school were killed, "under any possible circumstances." Negroes might otherwise have supposed that states' rights or the doctrine of interposition or the failure of the minister that morning to say "sir" to a passing white man might be regarded as a mitigating circumstance. Even so Mansfield's proposition was too radical for his Southern colleagues. Only Fulbright rose to associate himself with Mansfield's remarks and to express condemnation. There was more indignation in the Senate over Nhu's pagoda raids in Saigon.

If four children had been killed in the bombing of a Berlin church by communists, the country would be on the verge of war. But when four Senators (Hart, Kuchel, Humphrey and Javits) framed a resolution asking that the Sunday after the Birmingham bombing be set aside as a national day of mourning, they knew their fellow Senators too well even to introduce it. They sent it on to the White House where it was lost in the shuffle. Despite the formal expressions of regret, the sermons, the editorials and the marches, neither white America nor its leadership was really moved. When Martin Luther King and six other Negro leaders finally saw the President four days after the bombing, it was to find that he had already appointed a two-man committee to represent him "personally" in Birmingham, but that both men were white. This hardly set a precedent for bi-racial action. If Mr. Kennedy could take a judge off the Supreme Court to settle a labor dispute, he could have taken one of the country's two Negro judges off the Court of Appeals to dignify a mission of mediation. He might have insisted, for once, after so terrible a crime, on seeing white and Negro leaders together, instead of giving a separate audience four days later to a white delegation from Birmingham. It is as if, even in the White House, there are equal but separate facilities.

The Negro leaders, facing the TV cameras outside the Executive Offices that Thursday afternoon, looked like men pursued by despair, afraid that at the slightest misstep they might be trampled under by the hopeless fury in the ranks behind them. The white delegation, the following Monday, had underling written all over it. The President of the United States could take time out to hear white Birmingham, but the mayor was too busy and sent his secretary. With him were neither the Big Mules nor their Northern capitalist overlords; it is as if they had assigned their office boys to see the President. If what they told the press afterward was a sample of what they told the President, he too must have despaired of finding a solution. Even these supposed moderates could not shake loose from the mythology of white supremacy: if only outside agitators like Martin Luther King would stay away peace and quiet could be restored; many Negroes favored segregation, but apparently were afraid to say so except privately to their white friends. Hire a Negro policeman? That was a "profoundly difficult," "almost impossible," problem. Just why was never explained; perhaps Negroes do not look good in blue, with brass buttons.

Four centuries of white supremacy have left their indelible mark in the double standard we whites instinctively apply to race relations. The Attorney General rejecting a Negro appeal for federal troops, said hearts could not be changed by bayonets. But few stop to think that the alternative is to leave the Negro community of Birmingham to the bayonets of the state troopers. Gene Grove in the *New York Post* vividly pictured how the Negro community is ruled. When one reporter approached Colonel Al Lingo of the state police "with a question, the only reply was a shotgun in the belly. Wednesday night the troopers beat an aged man in the Negro district of East Thomas and a young boy in the Negro district of Parker Heights, both for failing to move off the street fast enough. Yesterday morning they rode down the street with carbines perking from every window, shouting at Negroes sitting on their porches to 'get back in the house, niggers, get your ass the hell off the street.'" The mayor's secretary looked surprised when a reporter asked him if he thought the manners of the state troops toward the Negroes were not provocative. He found no fault with it. Such ways and language, after all, are accepted institutions in the South, the way "peace and quiet" have been preserved.

When I was in Germany, I felt the empty wasteland of the German heart. I feel the same way about the hearts of my fellow white men in America, where the Negro is concerned. The good people there as here are in the minority and weak. Just as many Germans feel it was somehow the fault of the Jews that they got themselves cremated, so many whites here, North and South, feel that the bombing wouldn't have happened if the Negroes weren't so pushy. As a white housewife in a Birmingham supermarket told Robert Baker of the *Washington Post*, it was "terrible" but "that's what they get for trying to force their way where they're not wanted." Worse than the bombing is this inhuman chill.

SEPTEMBER 30, 1963

# JUDICIAL SUSTENANCE FOR
# THE SOUTHERN RACIST

Justices Black, Harlan and White have done the country a double injury by their dissent in the sit-in cases. The majority decisions, by one device or another, found it possible to reverse or remand the convictions without passing upon the fundamental issue, which is whether the States may under the 14th Amendment *in any way* enforce racial discrimination in public accommodations. The case which Black, Harlan and White made their main battle ground was *Bell v. Maryland,* which involved twelve Negro students convicted of criminal trespass for a restaurant sit-in in Baltimore in 1960. Since that time both the City of Baltimore and the State of Maryland have passed public accommodations laws. Under these laws what the students did is no longer a crime. The majority, speaking through

Mr. Justice Brennan, therefore vacated the judgments against them and remanded to the State courts for such action as may now seem justifiable under the State law as changed.

At this moment in our national history, when Congress is in the final stage of passing the first public accommodations law since the Civil Rights Act of 1875, there was good grounds for restraint in the Court. If it could not muster a majority clearly to affirm the right to equality then it was wiser to postpone the issue, especially when there were sound legal grounds for doing so. The risk otherwise was to throw doubt in advance on the constitutionality of the new statute by a split within the high Court itself and thus to cast a baneful influence into the scales wherever public opinion is precariously poised between resistance and compliance. It was mischievous of Black, Harlan and White to open the question up and to open it in such a way as inevitably to give emotional support to mass resistance. "We fully recognize," Black wrote apologetically for the dissenters, "the salutary general judicial practice of not unnecessarily reaching out to decide constitutional questions. But this is neither," he quickly added, "a constitutional nor a statutory requirement." So off they went, in an opinion which sounded as if it were written by David Lawrence.

They protected themselves in the small print, of course. They said they were not passing on the constitutionality "of any existing or proposed state or federal legislation." In his oral, as in his written text, Mr. Justice Black was careful to say that he meant only that the 14th Amendment did not *of itself* and without Congressional legislation, prohibit denial of public accommodations to Negroes. These fine points will not protect the country from the bigots who will now say, "Why even Black. . . ." The whole emotional coloration of the Black dissent is on the side of the aggrieved white Southerner, not his Negro victim. He waded in with joyous abandon on the side of Harlan and White, with whom he otherwise rarely agrees. For Harlan property rights have always been a No. 1 consideration; he has always subordinated civil rights to them. But this was a new stance for Black.

The 13th, 14th and 15th Amendments were intended to free the Negro from slavery and give him first class citizenship. The Southern states sought to circumvent them first by the

Black Codes and then by Jim Crowism. In this they were aided by Supreme Court decisions which read the 14th amendment so narrowly as to take the heart out of the first Civil Rights Act. Their spirit lives on in the Black-Harlan-White dissent. Here is a sample of its question-begging formulations. The 14th Amendment, it says, "does not forbid a State to prosecute for crimes committed against a person or his property, however prejudiced or narrow the victim's views may be." Of course not. But is it a crime for a Negro to try and buy a meal at a lunch counter which otherwise serves the public? "Nor," they go on, "can whatever prejudice and bigotry the victim of a crime may have be automatically attributed to the State that prosecutes." Not automatically, of course. But the records of these cases is full of testimony that restaurant and hotel owners refuse service to Negroes not because of their own prejudices but because they fear those "local customs" the Southern states foster.

The Solicitor General, in a brilliant supplemental brief *amicus*, argued that "a State which has drawn a color line may not suddenly assert that it is color blind." Black argues that if this were accepted "we would have one 14th Amendment for the South and quite a different and more lenient one for other parts of the country." It is not the 14th Amendment which is more "lenient" in the North. It is the North which is far less harsh and brazen than the South about defying the Amendment. Black complains that to infer state responsibility where there is racial bias in public accommodations would leave constitutional rights to be "governed by past history in the South— by present conduct in the North and West." Surely these Justices do not think racial discrimination in the South is merely a matter of "past history?"

It is the standard Southern answer to say, as the dissenters do, that "the 14th Amendment of itself does not compel either a black man or a white man running his own private business to trade with anyone against his will." This is a tissue of invidious misstatement. The 14th Amendment can and should be read as part of the public policy of this country, which is against racial discrimination. What a man does in his "private business" may be his own affair. But where he has a business which opens its doors to all comers then he cannot deny entrance or service to some solely because of their race. When he does so, he cannot under the 14th Amendment have state support in the shape of police and judicial action to enforce the discrimination via "criminal trespass." Nor can states which have done all they could to maintain the Negro in subjection then come into court and claim that they are merely enforcing property rights. This was the argument of the Solicitor General and of counsel for the sit-in demonstrators.

Of course it is not easy, in this as in other basic questions of constitutional law, to find clear answers to present problems in the debates and intentions of its framers. But Black in other cases has not hesitated to pour new wine into the old bottles. However obscure the details may be, the main lines are clear. The South has been engaged for a century in attempting to nullify the Negro's emancipation. It has done its best, in the vivid phrase of the first Mr. Justice Harlan, this one's grandfather, to turn the 13th, 14th and 15th Amendments into "splendid baubles, thrown out to delude those who deserved fair and generous treatment at the hands of the nation." Those words are from a dissent in 1883 which at last is being made the law by the Civil Rights Act of 1964. Congress is thereby reversing the Supreme Court. Goldberg, Warren and Douglas would have had the Court, too, reverse that 1883 decision on public accommodations. Mr. Justice Douglas felt that the Court dodged its duty in not doing so. He asked scornfully, "how is a 'personal' right infringed when a corporate chain store, for example, is forced to open its lunch counters to people of all races?" He put the issue unanswerably when he wrote:

> Segregation of Negroes in the restaurants and lunch counters of parts of America is a relic of slavery. It is a badge of second class citizenship. It is a denial of a privilege and immunity of national citizenship and of the Equal Protection guaranteed by the 14th Amendment against abridgement by the States. When the state police, the state prosecutor and the state courts unite to convict Negroes for renouncing that relic of slavery, the "state" violates the 14th Amendment.

It is tragic at this moment, when the strongest kind of stand is necessary to avoid bloodshed, that the Supreme Court did not do its duty and take that unequivocal position.

# THE FERMENT AND THE FURY IN NEW YORK'S NEGRO GHETTOES

I spent several days in New York last week trying to learn more about the racial situation there, on which so much may depend. To see the great city again after the Harlem and Bedford-Stuyvesant riots is to see it with eyes freshly opened. Driving in from Long Island, over the Tri-Borough bridge, into 125th Street, I saw the Negro ghetto looking as dingy as ever, but relaxed and somnolent, as if its fury was spent. Downtown, walking on opulent Fifth Avenue, amid all the new steel and glass skyscrapers, one noticed with a new sharpness the almost complete absence of black or brown faces. Except for an occasional poorly dressed messenger boy, one saw only whites, and one felt that this wonder city, with its towering and majestic beauty, rested like ancient Athens on a slave class, kept out of sight in a menial quarter of its own. I went to the theater and saw three plays on the race question, two by Negroes: James Baldwin's *Blues for Mister Charlie*, Le Roi Jones's *Dutchman* and Martin Duberman's *In White America*. The message of the first is hate; the second, loathing; the third, the only one by a white man, compassion. Even at these performances, though the audiences were responsive, it was as if the stories told were of another world, far removed from these well-dressed and educated white and Negro intellectuals, some of them mixed couples, but otherwise moving about racially separate to talk and smoke during intermission.

I began my exploration of this other world at the downtown

headquarters of the Congress for Racial Equality in a rundown loft building on Park Row just across the little park that fronts on City Hall. It was a hectic morning. The papers that day carried the text of the statement by the leaders of major Negro organizations calling for a temporary suspension of mass demonstrations until after election day because the defeat of Goldwater was more important "than any local or state condition." My talk with the white press officer was constantly interrupted by angry phone calls from branches of CORE as far away as California protesting any such moratorium. James Farmer of CORE and John Lewis of SNCC did not sign the statement with Roy Wilkins of NAACP, Martin Luther King of the Southern Christian Leadership Conference, Whitney M. Young, Jr., of the National Urban League, and A. Philip Randolph, chairman of the Negro American Labor Council. But Wilkins told the press both Farmer and Lewis agreed with suspension of mass demonstrations and withheld their signatures until meetings of their steering committees. The press officer vehemently denied over and over again that Farmer had made any such statement; he said Farmer agreed with the estimate of the Goldwater danger, but not with the call to suspend mass demonstrations. It was soon clear from the tone of these phone conversations that the black backlash against any suggestion for halting militancy was as strong as the white backlash on the other side.

During the phone calls I had a chance to look around the loft, jammed with battered desks and old typewriters on which a whole corps of volunteers were working. I ran into oldtimers like Jim Peck, the pacifist-anarchist, who has been beaten up on more picket lines for more good causes since the 1930s than any other man in the country; here he was back on the firing line, after a bout with tuberculosis, as diffident and devoted as ever. While I was looking around a more dramatic telephone call came in from the sheriff's office in Jonesboro, La., where a CORE volunteer, Danny Mitchell, a young Ph.D. from Syracuse, had been arrested on the usual charge of "contributing to the delinquency of a minor" presumably for recruiting some local Negro into the voter registration drive. Carl Rachlin, another old-timer, of the Workers Defense League, now general counsel for CORE, got on the other extension. "We won't forget you," he assured the caller. "We'll get right on it." The words suddenly evoked the terrifying scene a thousand miles away in the Deep South. The phone was no sooner hung up than another call reached lawyer volunteers in the area and sent them speeding to the sheriff's office. Rachlin told me of a similar frightening night call a few weeks earlier when another volunteer worker, Ronny Moore of Southern University, was shot at while crossing the Mississippi at St. Francisville. He took refuge in a Negro home at Jonesboro only to have it surrounded by a mob of whites threatening to burn the house down. A frantic phone call to the Justice Department in Washington for help elicited no response. In desperation a call was put through to FBI headquarters in New Orleans. It had stayed open all night. The alert FBI man who took the call phoned the local police in Jonesboro. On his urgent demand, the local police dispersed the mob and prevented a tragedy.

With a telephoned introduction from the downtown office I went next to the CORE office in Harlem at 307 W. 125th St. This turned out to be on the second floor of a decayed business property. The office had one old desk and typewriter. The walls were decorated with tattered signs and photos. One said, "Please report all injuries caused by stick happy police to CORE." George Johnson, the CORE official in charge, is a Negro from a small town near Cincinnati, with a master's degree in education from the University of Michigan. He taught special children's classes in the Cincinnati schools before going full time into the civil rights movement. He himself lives in the Bronx and said he found Harlem "very depressing."

"The only people who stay in Harlem," Johnson told me, "are those who have no alternative. As in the South, all who can get away, do so. We perform all kinds of social and civic services. People come to us in desperation because they have nothing to eat or no place to sleep and we try to do what we can. We try to awaken people to their responsibilities, to teach them why civil rights are important and why, being black, they should be in the movement. We tell them they have two main weapons—the ballot and selective buying. Registration is low. During the riot we operated a first aid station and won twenty new recruits. People could see we were doing a service. We had spotters out and whenever they saw a knot of tension they would phone in and we would send somebody out to calm the people and asked them to go home. What does Harlem need? Vast mass preferential assistance for better education, employment and housing. We in CORE have about exhausted moral persuasion. Do we reach down to the grass roots? We have about a thousand members in a community of close to half a million. The No. 1 influence is the churches. Then come the Black Muslims, the Malcolm X people and Nationalists of various kinds. We come next, but far below them in influence."

A middle-aged woman came in to consult Johnson. She said her white employer had accused her thirteen-year-old daughter of taking $20 from the white woman's purse. She declared her daughter was innocent. Johnson interrupted her to phone the Malcolm X headquarters and the Black Nationalist bookstore at 125th Street and Seventh Avenue to ask that someone there talk with me. A young Negro college student from Philadelphia had been hanging sadly around the office, waiting for something to do; he was assigned to accompany me. A white man is safer in the streets of Harlem if walking with a Negro. Our first stop was the Malcolm X headquarters on the second floor of the Hotel Theresa on Lenox Avenue which I had last visited when a reception was given there for Fidel Castro several years ago. Room 128, the Muslim Mosque of Malcolm X, turned out to be a large meeting hall with a big blackboard at one end. Malcolm X was in Egypt but one of his chief aides, James 67X was explaining the essentials of Islam to a young snub-nosed Negro girl while a light brown secretary at the reception desk looked on adoringly. A placard behind the door advertised a Pan African Students "High Life" dance. James 67X was a neatly dressed young man with a thin fuzz of beard on an intense brown face. He used a ruler to make his points and he addressed the one young convert on the five basic duties of Islam with the passion he might have used in speaking to a multitude. I found myself listening with rapt attention as I waited.

"Islam," James 67X explained, "is Arabic. It means to submit, to surrender. A Muslim is one who surrenders his will to God's. His first duty is prayer. The Koran says men must pray five times a day. Every living thing is an act of prayer. When a rose grows, it is a prayer. You must practice charity. Two and a half percent of all you make, give to the poor. Anything you give, you must get back in return, that is the law of the universe. Whatever you plant in earth shall come back seven-fold. A kind word is an act of charity. To feed pigeons is an act of charity. To help a blind man across the street is an act of charity. Every act of charity brings the planet to a greater state of perfection. After prayer and charity comes fasting, for there is nothing like hunger to let you know that all men are alike; in Ramadan all hunger together. The fourth duty of Islam is pilgrimage, so that one may see men of all colors join in Mecca in the praise of God, all wearing the same white cloth, so there is no distinction between prince and peasant, rich and poor. The fifth and last of the basic duties is Jihad, holy war, which Westerners have confused with war. But Islam's greatest achievements have been accomplished not by bullets or the sword but by the conquest of intelligence. Spain was conquered by intelligence and when Islam left, Spain slipped backward. Jihad is using any method that is worthy to bring any form of life that is not in submission to the will of God into submission and into a state of tranquility and peace. There will never be peace on earth until all men submit to the will of God. This is Jihad."

This is a shortened but verbally faithful version of what James 67X said. It seemed to me, in its humanity, on a level with Islam as interpreted by its own greatest mystics and poets. There was not a word of hate in anything he said. In an off the record talk afterward, he was wary and distrustful. I was interested in his background. He was Harlem born, largely self-educated, and had left the Black Muslim movement of Elijah Mohammed before Malcolm X did. He would say nothing in the slightest derogatory, even by implication, of Elijah. After leaving the latter's movement he spent weeks alone reading and meditating on the roof of a Harlem tenement. His Islamic creed is far more sophisticated and humane than Elijah's mixture of black racism and superstitious hate of "white devils." He winced when I said that Muslim Arab traders had sold his people into bondage. He insisted that a slave could free himself by accepting Islam while slavery was accepted and institutionalized under Christianity, for which he feels a deep repugnance, though brought up by Baptist parents. One felt

in talking with this gifted young Negro that finding himself
alienated from American society he was drawn to as distant
and alien a creed as he could find, that of Islam, and had
created a dream world in fraternity with those distant pilgrims
in Mecca. He had gone into an internal spiritual exile as a
refuge from the miseries of the Negro ghetto in white America.

I encountered an older, more conventional, form of Negro
retreat from white realities in Michaux's Black Nationalist
bookstore on the other side of Seventh Avenue. This is the bookstore made famous in countless pictures with the placard in
front advertising the book, "The God Damned White Man."
The walls, tables and even parts of the floor overflow with
books, mostly on Negro problems and Africa. I was ushered
through a back door on which hung a large portrait of Nasser
into a back room crowded with more books and mementoes.
There at an ancient roll-top desk sat a thin elderly Negro in his
seventies. This was the proprietor Lewis Michaux, a lifetime
follower of Black Nationalism. He burst into speech like a
volcano, stopping only from time to time to show me another
cherished memento from a long table full of African carvings
and oddities. His special joys were products from Ghana. He
showed me a bottle of lager beer brewed in Ghana, a can of
lemon squash made in Ghana, a jar of peppers put up in
Ghana, as if these were precious relics. He had visited on
cocoa ships in New York harbor from Ghana, and it was Ghana
of which he thought first when he spoke of "back to Africa."
He was like an old Zionist longing for Eretz Israel, and despite
the Black Nationalist fervor a gentle humor and a human kindness were evident as he talked with me.

"No Negro is a citizen," Michaux burst forth. "Otherwise
there would be no need for a Civil Rights Act. Dr. King is not
a citizen. Dr. Bunche is not a citizen. Russians can become
citizens. Germans can become citizens. But not Negroes. Neither the pulpit nor the politicians give our people leadership.
In the last uprising [his term for the riot] no preacher and no
politician could venture into the streets. The people organized
themselves block by block. You ask who does speak for the
Negro masses? Nobody speaks for the grass roots. Those Negroes who claim to speak for them don't even associate with
the Negro masses they claim to represent. They all live up in

penthouses and they never come down to the henhouses,"
Michaux chuckled, "until they want some eggs. But the chickens are no longer laying eggs. The classes never meet the
masses till trouble starts. There are two elements of Negroes—
one integrationist, the other separationist. The class Negro is
integrationist. The mass Negro is separationist, that is, Nationalist. Aren't they suffering from too much separation already,
you ask. Well, they're born sufferers. To enjoy anything else
but a life of suffering would kill them quicker. The white man's
heart will never change. If his heart hasn't changed in four hundred years, we don't think he has a heart. What could be done
for Harlem now? Take that money that's going to the moon and
put it into Harlem, and set an example for all the Harlems of
the USA. Give people jobs and there will be no muggings.
Men don't steal when they have enough to eat. Give people
proper ideas and there will be no difference between white and
black. Till then nothing will happen."

I went next day to another of New York's Negro ghettoes,
one not yet in the news. On McKinley Square in the East
Bronx, I talked with Herbert Callendar, chairman of Bronx
CORE. I last saw this section of the Bronx more than thirty
years ago when it was a Jewish neighborhood; today it is a rundown Negro slum, almost as grimy as Harlem. I found Callendar in a huge warehouse-like second floor lined with banners
bearing the names of Medgar Evers and other martyrs in the
civil rights struggle. He turned out to be a big, slim, brown
young man of thirty, who gives the impression of quiet patience
and great strength, and of complete devotion without fanaticism or hate. He is New York born, went to high school in Manhattan, and was in the Army two years, part of them in Japan.
He went to work on his return in the Ford works at Mahwah,
N.J. His ability soon made him an organizer for the UAW. "I
had a Lincoln and a house in the upper Bronx," Callendar said
of those days. But then he went on a Freedom Ride through
the South in 1961 and came back a changed man. "I came back
with my eyes open," he said, "and dedicated to civil rights. I
was arrested down there for the first time but I realized that it
was not so different for the Negro up here. I saw that only the
lowest and hardest and poorest paid jobs were open to the Negroes in the Ford shops and I began to use the grievance

machinery to advance the Negro. I became a thorn in the side of management and I got fired." He found that in his own local there were racists and even Birchites, mostly from rural New York and New Jersey, typical of the kind of union members swept up by compulsory union shop contracts instead of by persuasion and the hard lessons of experience. He lost his fight for reinstatement and went into CORE instead. I asked him how many of Bronx CORE were white and he said about 30 per cent, some Italians, a few Irish and Puerto Ricans but mostly Jewish. He was setting up car pools and block captains to get out the vote this year; he told me only about 40 per cent of the Negroes in his area were registered. "But we're going to register them as independents," he said. "We can't afford to be in anybody's hip pocket." He had teaching teams out helping people to pass their literacy tests. He objected strongly to any moratorium on demonstrations.

"The NAACP's had a moratorium on demonstrations for fif-teen years," Callendar said. "Negroes are losing faith in civil rights organizations. We need demonstrations on specific issues if we are to keep unrest channeled in a responsible non-violent peaceful way. We've scheduled demonstrations against Jim Crow in the building trades, and against slum landlords—some parts of the East Bronx are as rat-ridden as Harlem—and against police brutality. We have one case where police spread-eagled a Puerto Rican in his cell as if he were being crucified. This community can blow up as easily as Harlem if we can't show them accomplishments. The most important task of all here is to save our youth. We need job opportunities for them and above all we need to save them from narcotics. The rate of addiction in the East Bronx is tremendous, and it will be worse in the next generation unless we take steps to stop it now. We need a hospital for rehabilitation, a training center where addicts can go after they've been cured and learn a trade. Otherwise they'll soon be back on the drug out of hope-lessness. A big portion of all the crime in our Negro sections is linked to dope addiction. Wiping it out would be the biggest single step forward."

Of all the people with whom I talked in New York the most extraordinary was Callendar's youth coordinator, Judy Howell, a young girl of seventeen, who has worked six years for CORE.

Her beautiful brown African face, her sharp intelligent eyes, her trim person, radiated energy, purposefulness and capacity. While I interviewed her, we were constantly being interrupted by youngsters in white sweat shirts with CORE in blue letters on them and she handled these subordinates with an almost Napoleonic speed and decisiveness. "Let the kids fix up the place themselves," she told one subordinate worried about a new branch headquarters. "Then they'll consider it their own and keep it in good shape." She told me how she was organizing the youth of the East Bronx, gang fashion, for constructive purposes. The teams, with their block and field leaders, are to be set up in the same hierarchical semi-military fashion as juvenile gangs, with ages from eleven to twenty-one, the older boys and girls in the leadership positions.

"These teams will be used to distribute leaflets, to help get out a community paper, to organize block parties for civil rights, to join in getting out the vote, to run clean-up campaigns in each block, and to arrange trips," she said. "There will be competition between the various blocks. Boston Road might get an award for getting out the biggest voter registration. Freeman Street might be first in the clean block contest. Each block will try to win in some activity. Here at headquarters we're setting up a field staff, a secretarial staff, a newspaper staff—we hope to publish a weekly—and an education staff, which will take care of complaints from parents and various school problems."

Judy is in her last year at high school and hopes afterward to enter Hunter College and then make a career in stage management and production. When I asked her how the youth drive originated she said it was her idea and that she sold it to the adults in CORE. "They didn't realize," she said, "that young people had to be handled differently and needed special organization." As she spoke, the phone rang. Callendar answered and then shouted across the room that Bedford-Stuyvesant had just got a special grant for its youth work. "Maybe we'd better have a riot here, too," Judy said laughingly. "Those people downtown didn't have a dime for young people till the riots broke out in Harlem and Bedford-Stuyvesant. Now the churches have come up with $100,000 and the city with

$200,000. We here in the Bronx have managed on less than $60 so far this summer."

Judy herself was one of the leaders of the youth demonstration which led to the Harlem riot and gave me her own account of how it happened. The purpose was to protest the slaying of fifteen-year-old James Powell by Police Lieutenant Gilligan, to urge the latter's suspension and to ask Police Commissioner Murphy to come to Harlem and speak with the people. She said that when the demonstrators marched to Police Precinct 28 on 123rd Street, Inspector Pendergast would not let any of the youth leaders speak but instead received Rev. Nelson C. Dukes, a Negro Baptist minister, who tried to take over the leadership of the demonstration. "They didn't know who Reverend Dukes was and were suspicious of the report he made when he came out of the police station," Judy related. "Inspector Pendergast wouldn't listen to any of us and the crowd wouldn't listen to him. Finally he yelled, 'To hell with the niggers, get them out of here any way you can.' Then the police arrested me and the other fifteen youth leaders and began pushing the crowd back. That's when trouble began. We could have stopped it in a minute if they had just let us use the bull horn. Instead they rushed all of us youth leaders into the police station. The police aren't popular in the neighborhood anyway and cans and bottles began to fly. I was the only girl arrested and a policewoman took me away after I had been kicked and hit over the head. The others were given a beating and the crowd outside could hear their screams. We didn't know a riot had started until we got out of night court at 2 A.M. The man to be blamed is Inspector Pendergast who is supposed to be experienced and to have a reputation for fairness. If it wasn't for his stupid handling of the affair, there would have been no riot."

AUGUST 10, 1964

# THE NEGRO, THE FBI AND
# POLICE BRUTALITY

We turn aside this week from more resounding events to devote this letter to the report on "Justice" by the U. S. Commission on Civil Rights. The Berlin crisis will be with us for many months, Latin American convulsions for many years. But this newly released study of police brutality, particularly to Negroes, offers an opportunity that may not occur again for a long time. The report seeks to turn attention to a dark corner of our national life, where the poor and the defenseless suffer; many months of patient investigation went into it; it had the unanimous approval of six Commissioners, two of them white Southerners and one a Negro; it offers some thoughtful recommendations and it dares even to imply some criticism of that sacred cow, the FBI. It is heart-breaking to see how meagerly it has been covered by most papers, how quickly it is being brushed under the rug. No phrase carries more opprobrium in the United States than "police state practices," none brings forth more firmly conditioned reflexes from editorial writers and commentators. But no burst of indignation has greeted this report on police state practices in our own country, behind that other iron curtain which shuts off from view the realities under which the Negro lives in the rural South and in Northern slums.

Eleven "typical cases of police brutality" are reported by the commission and there are many others in the extensive footnotes. Plutarch tells us how the Spartans terrorized and humiliated their Helots, weeding out the spirited, to keep their slaves in line; the "uppity" Negro is a target in the South for the same reasons. The police brutality is not "senseless." There is a cold racial logic behind it: to maintain the Negro in subservient status as a source of cheap labor. As Sheriff Z. T. Mathews of Terrell County, Georgia, told reporter Robert Baker of the *Washington Post* after the fatal beating of James Brazier, a Negro, by two police officers in 1958, "there's nothing like fear to keep niggers in line." In the beating to death of Bobby Hall by Sheriff Claude M. Screws of Baker County, Georgia, an FBI agent testified at the sheriff's trial, "Mr. Screws . . . told me that he had had trouble with Bobby Hall, that he seemed to be a leader . . . when a Negro got in trouble with the law that he, Bobby Hall, would advise him." So in the case of Brazier, fatally beaten before his wife and four children, it was said that he was "uppity." A year after the killing Sheriff Mathews told his widow, "I oughta slap your damn brains out. A nigger like you I feel like slapping them out. You niggers set around here and look at television and go up North and come back and do to white folks here like the niggers up North do, but you ain't gonna do it. I'm going to carry the South's orders out like it oughta be done."

Since the brutality serves the purposes of the dominant race, it is not surprising that the police are rarely punished and often promoted. One of the two officers who beat Brazier to death was promoted to Chief of Police in Dawson City, Georgia; no state or local action was ever taken against the killers and a federal grand jury refused to indict. In the Bobby Hall killing, white eye-witnesses made it possible to convict Sheriff Screws in a federal prosecution but the Supreme Court reversed the conviction in a landmark decision which must fill Negroes with despair. In it a badly split Court held in effect that police officers who kill Negroes are guilty of violating the federal Civil Rights Act only if there was "specific intent" to deprive the Negro of his constitutional rights. If the killing was done in hate, meanness, spite or just plain fun, it doesn't count, at least not in the federal courts. In a new trial Sheriff Screws was then acquitted and in 1958 he was elected to the State Senate of Georgia.

The Department of Justice has not been too energetic in civil rights cases, for these bring it into conflict with the Southern oligarchy in Congress. Frank Murphy, who cared deeply about basic rights, established the first Civil Rights Section of the Department in 1939 and Congress elevated it to a Division in 1957. The new report says "The Truman Committee wrote of the Civil Rights Section in 1947 that 'the total picture . . . is that of a sincere, hard-working, but perhaps over-cautious agency.' This same statement would fairly characterize the Civil Rights Division today in its efforts against unlawful official violence." This is putting it gently. Since its establishment, the report points out, the division has obtained convictions or *nolo contendere* pleas in only six police brutality cases, "not," the report comments, "an impressive statistical record for a period of over three years." Inquiry by this writer disclosed that only one of these six successful cases was racial, involving the brutal beating of an Indian in Idaho. Though four of the six cases were in the South, none involved Negroes. As a matter of fact no police officer has been convicted of brutality to Negroes since two sheriffs, one from Texas and the other from Alabama, pleaded guilty after indictment in 1955. There has not been a conviction in a police brutality case, white or colored, for more than two years, since October 30, 1959, though more than 1300 complaints were received and 52 prosecutions authorized in the two and a half years from January, 1958 to July, 1960. This is not much of a record.

A major reason for the poor record lies in the attitude of the FBI on which the department depends for investigation of civil rights complaints. One of the virtues of this report is that it lifts the curtain, however cautiously, on this untold aspect of the story. The first hint of this appeared in a footnote to the report of Truman's Committee on Civil Rights in 1947 which said there was "evidence" that the FBI considered civil rights investigations "burdensome." Footnotes [1] on pages 213–15 of this new report gives excerpts from an exchange of letters between J. Edgar Hoover and Attorney General Tom Clark which Civil Rights Commission staff members dug up in the Harry S. Truman Library in Independence, Missouri. In a letter dated September 24, 1946, Mr. Hoover complained to the

[1] It is indicative of the FBI's untouchability and the timidity of its critics that such crucial matters are relegated to the obscurity of footnotes.

Attorney General that "as a result of the aggressiveness of pressure groups or as a result of newspaper stories" the FBI was being forced to expend "a considerable amount of manpower investigating murders, lynchings and assaults, particularly in the Southern States" where it was improbable that violations of federal laws had occurred. Mr. Hoover felt this hurt the "prestige" of his bureau. Attorney General Clark replied the same day (the fusillade of formal letters seemed to reflect frigid relations between them on the subject) that while many such investigations proved fruitless, "If we do not investigate, we are placed in the position of having received the complaint of a violation and of having failed to satisfy ourselves that it is or is not such a violation." The commission's investigators failed to notice that this exchange occurred just two months after four Negroes were lynched by a mob in Monroe, Georgia, and one month before Attorney General Clark announced that he was ordering a federal grand jury investigation. Had Mr. Hoover been opposing an FBI inquiry into the Monroe, Georgia, lynchings? The new report leaves the question unanswered. It says only (footnote 134, page 215), "Such discussions between the incumbent Attorney General and the Director of the FBI regarding Bureau investigation procedure in civil rights cases continued into subsequent years."

This delicate subject is treated in the text of the new report with the tactful and apologetic circumspection accorded the lamentable weakness of a reigning monarch. "It has been reported, from time to time," the Civil Rights Commission says (at p. 61),

> that the Bureau has little enthusiasm for its task of investigating complaints of police brutality. If the contention is accurate, the fact is, to some degree, understandable. The Director has used the strongest language to stress the need for cooperation between the Bureau and law enforcement officials at all levels. Apparently without this cooperation the FBI could not maintain the excellent record it now enjoys in the enforcement of a long list of Federal criminal statutes. Although the Bureau states that it "has not experienced any particular difficulty or embarrassment in connection with investigation of police brutality," there is evidence that investigations of such offenses may jeopardize that working relationship. The very purpose of these investigations is to ascertain

whether or not State or local officials have committed a Federal offense. Even though the allegations may later prove groundless, the investigation of them may place the FBI in a delicate position.

The plain meaning of this is that the civil rights statutes, like the Negro they were supposed to protect, are relegated to secondary status, expendable items in the chase for bank robbers and stolen cars.

A careful reading of the report and the footnotes shows that the FBI's procedure in handling civil rights complaints is hardly zealous. In most cases the FBI field office forwards the complaint without preliminary investigation in so bare a form that it "frequently lacks those minimal facts required to determine if a violation occurred or even if there is a need for a preliminary investigation." The complaint goes to the Civil Rights Division and is assigned to an attorney. If he wants a preliminary investigation "this must be cleared through his section chief, a higher Division official, and Bureau headquarters in Washington." This leads to "time-consuming" delays; here another of those footnotes whispers, "It has been claimed that delays have afforded guilty officials the opportunity to intimidate complainants and witnesses." If a preliminary investigation is ordered, "At the outset, the FBI contacts the head of the agency and advises him of the complaint which has been received and that investigation is being ordered." This advance notice, the Civil Rights Commission objects, "can jeopardize a section 242 [Civil Rights] case. Police force superiors may adopt an unduly protective attitude toward their officers. They may share the racial prejudices of their subordinates and of their communities."

So exquisite is the FBI's empathy for peculiar regional mores that "In 1959 a case of an allegedly unjustified killing of a Negro by a State policeman was closed because of the [Civil Rights] Division's reluctance to have the Bureau [FBI] notify the Arkansas Governor of a civil rights investigation during the tense school situation in Little Rock." Apparently the FBI would have refused to investigate the case without first notifying Governor Faubus. There are even, the report notes, "some victims of violence who distrust FBI agents, believing them to be in league with local officers." But, the report goes on to say staunchly, "the Bureau cannot, on their account, resign its heavy responsibilities in those fields of Federal law enforcement that requires its close association with local officials." This sounds as if it was revised by the FBI before publication.

The report recommends three main reforms: a change in Section 242 of the Civil Rights Act to remove the stumbling block of the "specific intent" requirement set up by the Screws case; another change to make it possible to sue cities and counties for damages in police brutality cases; and grants-in-aid to improve police training. But the man who could do most in this situation is J. Edgar Hoover. Three federal inquiries in the past generation have shown that police brutality is widespread, and not confined to Negroes, Mexicans and Indians: the Wickersham Commission report in 1931, the Truman Committee in 1947 and now this commission in 1961. In all these years Mr. Hoover has been head of the FBI, in charge of police training programs through the FBI's National Academy. The FBI, whatever its faults, has been trained to avoid rough stuff. Its example and Mr. Hoover's admonitions, if they were forthcoming, could do a great deal to make the brutal cop a shunned exception. But though the magazines and newspapers are full of articles in which he holds forth on juvenile delinquency, smutty books, communism, hitchhikers and other of his favorite menaces, we do not ever remember his speaking out on the dangers of racism or the disgrace of police brutality. Commission attorneys reviewed the FBI Law Enforcement Bulletin from January 1956 through August 1961 and found only one item dealing with civil rights, a piece by Roscoe Drummond flattering to the FBI.

The commission might have found it useful to study Mr. Hoover's annual appearances before the House Appropriations Committee. The hearings during the last ten years show not a single occasion on which Mr. Hoover has spoken against police brutality or for civil rights. On the contrary his presentation has been calculated to curry favor with the Southerners and reactionaries on the committee. On one occasion he warned against communist exploitation of the sitdown movement; on another he assured the committee that civil rights cases are handled only "by mature special agents" (1959 hearing on the 1960 budget). The figures he gave on three occasions showed how very few complaints against police officers result even in prosecution. Mr. Hoover has made it clear that the FBI acts in civil rights cases only because ordered to. Finally it is a pity that the commission, in recommending prosecution by information where federal grand juries refuse to indict in Section 242 cases, fails to mention the biggest obstacle to this approach. It would require the FBI to sign the supporting affidavit. This the FBI does not want to do, for it would make it look like a crusader on civil rights. It prefers to crusade on safer subjects and against easier menaces.

NOVEMBER 27, 1961

# IF WE ACTED IN SELMA
# AS WE ACT IN SAIGON

Senator Eastland of Mississippi made a speech in the Senate February 3. It was entitled "Communist Forces Behind Negro Revolution in This Country." It was the second major speech of its kind by Eastland. He made an earlier one last July 22 on "Communist Infiltration into the So-called Civil Rights Movement," the latter remarkable because of its suggestion that the murder of the three civil rights workers last summer in Mississippi might be a hoax. It is instructive, and it may be therapeutic, to notice that Senator Eastland's theory of why there is trouble in our South is exactly the same as the theory propounded by Secretary of State Rusk as to why there is trouble in South Vietnam. The theory in both cases is that all would be well if only the North let its neighbors alone.

Like the State Department, Eastland sees not rebellion but an invasion, a "mass invasion of Mississippi," as he said last July, "by demonstrators, agitators, agents of provocation and inciters to mass violence, under the cover of the so-called civil rights movements." Just as the Pentagon and State put out figures recently show "Troop Flow from Hanoi up Sharply" so Eastland provided the names, the subversive records and the border crossing dates of infiltration from the North. Eastland even cited the same alarmist journalistic sources. "By April of this year," Eastland told the Senate last July, "so much evidence had piled up of Communist infiltration and Communist influence in racial agitations that Mr. Joseph Alsop devoted one of his columns to what he called 'the unhappy secret' of Communist success in infiltrating the civil rights movement." To read the two speeches of Eastland and the supporting remarks of his Mississippi colleague, Stennis, is like reading the speeches of Rusk and McNamara about South Vietnam before Diem was overthrown—in both cases the picture is of a happy land and a contented people menaced by outside agitators. One would never guess the misery, the beatings, the killings, the violations of elementary rights, the exploitation, which are the roots of the rebellions. No high born Mandarin from Hué could be more sorrowful than Stennis when he told the Senate February 3 it was these communist agitators "who flouted all the customs and traditions of a social order to which people had been accustomed and had lived under for almost two centuries." Eastland told the Senate the same day that 95 per cent of the Negroes in his area had "spurned any association" with the invaders and Stennis said he found "the same pattern" in his area. But somehow by esoteric means these infiltrators managed nevertheless here and there to disrupt "the spiritual life of both races . . . the peace and harmony of the people." This is how the South felt a century ago about the abolitionists: snakes in a patriarchal paradise.

The sickness of the South is the sickness of every ruling class in history. These always see conspiracy rather than suffering as the mainspring of every upsurge by the oppressed. Eastland buttressed his speech with quotations from J. Edgar Hoover and ideological police records from the files of the Un-

American Activities Committee and his own Internal Security Committee just as the State Department's "Blue Book" in 1961 justified our intervention in South Vietnam by citing evidence of communist conspiracy against Diem. In one colloquy on the Senate floor February 3, Eastland and Stennis agreed that South Vietnam and our own South were both confronted by the same universal conspiracy. They are as indignant about Washington's aid to the civil rights movement as Washington is indignant about Moscow's and Peking's encouragement to the guerrilla fighters in South Vietnam. One almost expects to hear Eastland and Stennis ask how Washington can claim to be for peaceful co-existence and yet insist on supporting "wars of liberation" in the South. Or accuse old Ho Chi Johnson of persisting in his dastardly ambition to reunify the country.

There are even the same contradictions in both areas. Just as our government in South Vietnam oscillates between treating the uprising as a rebellion and calling for social reforms to conciliate the people, so Stennis the day after Eastland's speech last week put into the *Congressional Record* the resolution passed by the Mississippi Economic Council, calling for law and order in the state. That resolution, the expression of Mississippi's better conscience, abandoned conspiracy theory and urged compliance with the civil rights laws. Stennis, to his credit, praised the council for taking a "stand out front" for that "obedience to law" which is the foundation of "true liberty." It is difficult to reconcile what Stennis said to the Senate on February 3 with what he said on February 4.

Can we not learn something from the two situations? We see the idealism of the volunteers who go south here. Can we not see that in Vietnam we fight the same liberating zeal? In this double mirror, costly fallacies quickly show their face. If the federal government handled Negro aspiration as it handles the revolt in South Vietnam, we would be sending "counter-insurgency" teams from Fort Bragg into the South to kill civil rights agitators. We would be burning out with napalm the Negro neighborhoods in which we suspected that CORE or SNCC workers were hiding.

Conversely, if the South had an Air Force at its disposal, we would be hearing a clamor in Mississippi for escalation of the war by bombarding the source of all the trouble. Since Wash-

ington persists in giving aid and comfort to the civil rights
rebels, why not bomb the supply lines and the source?

FEBRUARY 15, 1965

# FROM THE BLACK MAN'S
# POINT OF VIEW

From the black man's point of view, the world picture is not a
pleasant one. In England, despite the promise of a multi-racial
Commonwealth, the unwelcome sign is up for colored peoples.
The Labor Party, long the champion of the colored man and of
anti-colonialism, has passed the first legislation restricting colored immigration, and done so under clear pressure from white
prejudice. While in England colored men are not wanted even
in a precarious minority status, white minorities still rule the
south of Africa. Rhodesia is following the path of South Africa,
which means keeping the black man an outcast in his own continent. Portugal holds vast neighboring territories on the same
basis.

This was supposed to be the century that would see the end
of colonialism. The five centuries since the discovery of America were a period during which white men, thanks to superior
firepower and technology, disrupted and plundered colored
men's empires and societies from Mexico and Peru to India
and China. In this century the white Europeans, weakened by
two civil wars which we call World Wars, have been forced to

give up most of their colonial possessions. But now again superior firepower and technology seem to be giving the white presence in Asia, Africa and Latin America a comeback. In this perspective, the vast deployment of firepower in Vietnam is a foretaste of what American capitalism can do wherever its power is challenged. Already in Peru, where 2,000,000 whites rule and exploit 12,000,000 miserable mestizos and Indians, the helicopters and napalm we supply the Latin military have been used to burn up rebellious Indian mountain villages and guerrillas. Our junior partner, Britain, is imposing naked military rule on Aden at the tip of the Arabian peninsula in order to maintain a "lifeline of empire" across the Indian Ocean to Singapore. We let the British know that the price of dollar aid for the pound is that Britain shall hold up its end of keeping these vast waters a white imperialist sea.

A neo-colonialist American Century is taking shape. The signs of it are clear in Latin America. There our alliance with the Brazilian military is seen as a menace by democratic elements. The recent gubernatorial elections were a defeat for the military and for the banker-led conservatives who sought fiscal stability at the expense of Brazil's poorer classes. The military must now move with our help to more repressive measures or see the return of reformist elements to power. The Brazilian military are our only major ally in our drive for an inter-American force which can be used elsewhere as it was in the Dominican Republic. The extent to which this is feared is little realized in our own country. In Santiago, Chile, last week the Latin American Parliament, composed of legislators from Argentina, Brazil, Colombia, Chile, El Salvador, Uruguay and Peru, rejected the Selden resolution thesis that we have a right to intervene in the hemisphere against governments we consider too leftist. This means the attempt to perpetuate the privileged position of small white oligarchies and foreign white investors over Negro and Indian mixed peoples, hardly risen above serfdom.

At home the black man must wonder why he must be sent to safeguard the right of self-determination in Vietnam. There are jungles closer home. The South has become a jungle in which the Negro and his white sympathizers are fair game for any white hunter. The Haynesville, Alabama, trial in which the slayer of Jonathan Daniels was acquitted is only the latest in such denials of justice. More offensive than the crass injustice was the complacency of Attorney General Katzenbach in commenting on the acquittal, "This is the price you have to pay for the jury system, but I don't think it is too high a price to pay." The jury system is supposed to represent the community. These lily-white Southern juries merely represent the white supremacists. More than 75 per cent of the people in Lowndes County, where the trial took place, are Negroes, but Negroes rarely serve on juries there. How can the Attorney General be so smug?

The Justice Department is dragging its heels on voter registrars while the Department of Health, Education and Welfare is dragging its heels on the power given it to enforce school desegregation by cutting off school funds. Where white racists in the North, as in Chicago, put on the heat, the Department quickly caves in. But all over the South it has ignored Negro protests and accepted not only "tokenism" but "freedom of choice" plans that continue segregation. This is what lies behind the Crawfordsville, Georgia, demonstrations. There the whites have "freedom of choice" to attend all-white schools outside the county while the Negroes have "freedom of choice" to go on attending rundown Negro schools. But HEW is still "studying" the situation. The Department announced with fanfare that all but eighty of the 5,000 Southern school districts had begun desegregation. But a detailed study by SNCC shows that 92 per cent of all Negro children in the eleven Southern states are still attending segregated schools. Negroes are being shot at, losing jobs and beaten up for trying to attend white schools, as they are for trying to register, yet somehow HEW and Justice do little more than "study" these situations. The black man can study, too. He knows from a century of experience the capacity of white supremacists to nullify equal rights legislation. A volcanic bitterness is building up. U.S. troops, instead of being in Vietnam, ought to be protecting Negroes trying to register and to attend integrated schools. This would really be enforcing self-determination.

OCTOBER 18, 1965

# PEOPLE WITHOUT A COUNTRY

Some truths are too terrible to be uttered. They lead nowhere but to despair. They subvert hope, the ultimate pillar of the social order. We prefer to cast about for assuaging myths. One such truth, which goes back to Heraclitus, the founder of the dialectic, is that conflict is the essence of life, that "war"—in his own dark phrase—is "the father of all things." It is not a maxim on which to found a society for eternal peace. Another such truth casts its shadow over the civil rights movement. All kinds of insights, concepts, and hypotheses are trotted out and tested in the 750 pages of the huge symposium, *The Negro American,* except the one which seems to me the most fundamental of all. The confusion, frustration, and despair of the civil rights movement become comprehensible if one looks at the American Negro (a less hopeful but more accurate description) simply as a people without a country.

The Negro is the second oldest imported stock in our country. Only the white Anglo-Saxon Protestant predates him, and that only by a few years. The distinguished Negro historian, John Hope Franklin, in his contribution to this symposium, reminds us that the first Negro indentured servants were brought here in 1619. That was a year before the Pilgrims landed at Plymouth Rock. After three-and-a-half centuries of living in America, the Negro is still a race apart. Ours is the world's oldest and most successful experiment in *apartheid*. The South Carolina code of 1712 set up special laws for Negroes to "restrain the disorders, rapines and inhumanity to which they are naturally prone and inclined." This is still the white stereotype of the Negro. In 1964 it was heartbreakingly possible for the White Citizens Council to place in newspaper advertising a declaration of Negro inequality made one hundred years earlier at Peoria by Lincoln, his reluctant Emancipator. "In a fundamental sense," Philip M. Hauser writes in this same symposium, "the Negro really did not enter white American society until World War I." And even after World War I Negro soldiers returning from their segregated regiments were lynched, sometimes in their military uniforms, while the renascent Klan warned them to respect the rights of the white race "in whose country they are permitted to reside." Even now, in our enlightened time, Congress is queasy about passing a civil rights bill with an "open housing" provision because most whites don't want to have Negroes as neighbors. After three-and-a-half-centuries in residence, the Negro still does not feel at home.

All these problems of open housing, educational standards, and different ways of life, would disappear, of course, if the American Negro, like other Negroes, had a territorial base in which he was the irrepressible majority instead of an unwanted minority. The American Negro may not yet be ready to compete on equal terms with the white man, but he is far more advanced than most of the darker peoples who have won their independence since World War II, and taken seats, in all their exotic splendor, in the United Nations. Neither in Africa nor in the Caribbean nor in Latin America is there any group of Negroes so prepared for self-government as our twenty million American Negroes. No other Negro group has so high a level of literacy, so wide an educated stratum, so large an elite, so much experience with politics, as the American Negro. But he alone of all these Negro or mulatto nations has no territory of his own.

Such cries as "Freedom Now" or "Black Power" reflect the repressed recognition of this bitter anomaly. As slogans or political programs they may make little sense in a country where he is little more than a tenth of the population, and where he is fenced off by taboo as racially untouchable in marriage. What does "Freedom Now" mean? Freedom from what? It really means freedom from the white man's presence, just as "Black Power" really means the end of white man's power. If America's twenty million Negroes were concentrated in an African territory under white rule, or even concentrated in a Black Belt here, these cries clearly would make political sense. They would mean the end of white rule and the beginning of black rule. It might be less competent, and even more corrupt, but it would restore racial self-respect, as the end of white domination has done in Africa. This is the deep string these phrases pluck in black American hearts. This is what they cannot achieve in a white man's country and this is why you have leaders floundering around in despair, one day fighting segregation and the next day fighting integration. The basic emotion is hatred of "Whitey" and this is why Black Nationalism of one variety or another strikes so deeply into the apathetic, disillusioned, and despairing black masses. Of the conventional leaders only Martin Luther King sways them, and he does so for reasons that have little to do with the creed he preaches. They see him as a Moses, but they have no Promised Land.

*The Negro American* is the most comprehensive survey of its kind since Myrdal's *An American Dilemma* was published twenty-two years ago. There is hardly one of its thirty essays which does not provide some fresh insight. But its viewpoints are limited to the establishment, as was to be expected from a work under the auspices of the American Academy of Arts and Sciences. Of the Negro leadership, only Whitney M. Young, Jr., of the National Urban League, appears in these pages; his organization might best be described as lily-black. His essay with John B. Turner is the least rewarding in the whole volume, though it does have one illuminating sentence, "At least until now the Negro has not been so much trying to change the American system as attempting to become a part of it." None of the newer organizations, CORE or SNCC or Mississippi Freedom Democratic Party, which seek to change the system as well as join it, are represented among the contributors; even the NAACP and Martin Luther King are absent. No Negro nationalist, no radical Marxist, or moderate socialist analysis is included, though there is a free enterprise approach in a vigorous essay by James Tobin which calls for changes in attitude and policy hardly less drastic. Tobin, Sterling Professor of Economics at Yale, sees the maintenance of full employment as "the single most important step" the nation could take to help the Negro. He is for a guaranteed basic income in the form of "a negative income tax" which would provide basic family allowances for the poor in a form which avoids the demeaning and degrading characteristics of the welfare system. He would revolutionize agricultural policy "to give income support to people rather than price support to crops and to take people off the land rather than to take land out of cultivation." He believes we are "paying much too high a social price for avoiding creeping inflation and for protecting our gold stock and 'the dollar.'" He sees the interests of "the unemployed, the poor and the Negroes" under-represented in "the comfortable consensus" behind policies which stress monetary stability more than full employment. He urges organizations of the poor and the Negro to study the relation between their plight and fiscal policy.

The nearest approach to a radical evaluation of the civil rights movement itself is Kenneth B. Clark's essay on it. His criticism of Martin Luther King's Gandhian philosophy anticipates the reaction against non-violence which has broken out in the civil rights movement since this symposium was written. "In Hitler's Germany," Dr. Clark writes, "the Jews suffered non-violently without stirring Nazi repentance; the early Christians who were eaten by lions seem to have stimulated not guilt but greed in the watching multitudes." The non-violent oppressed cannot twinge the conscience of the oppressor unless he has one. In addition the whole approach becomes irrelevant where the Negro is up against not cruelty, as in the South, but an impersonal system masked by benign attitudes as in the North. "What do you do," Dr. Clark asks, "in a situation in which you have laws on your side, where whites smile and say to you that they are your friends, but where your white 'friends' move to the suburbs . . . How can you demonstrate a philosophy of love in response to this? . . . One can be hailed justifiably as a Nobel Prize hero by the Mayor of New York, but this will not in itself change a single aspect of the total pattern of pathology which dominates the lives of the prisoners of the ghettoes of New York."

The most striking gap in the area covered is the absence of any essay on the political leadership developed in the Negro community; perhaps no respectable writer could be found sufficiently intrepid to take on the phenomena of Adam Clayton Powell and William L. Dawson. We only have the sobering observation in an astringent essay by Oscar Handlin,

> Nor is it to be expected that these people [i.e., the Negroes] will be more enlightened in the use of power than their predecessors. Politics is not the cure-all that some naive observers consider it to be.

There is still an eighteenth-century naiveté under the surface of radical agitation about the Negro; he is unconsciously regarded by many leftists as the Noble Savage who will rejuvenate our politics, and give white radicalism a chance to re-enter with him the mainstream of American politics from which it has so long been shut off. In the so-called New Politics, these lost causes are to be the Black Man's Burden. We have found ourselves an American proletariat.

But ours is an age in which, in a manner late Victorian liberal and Marxist optimists had thought obsolete, the ancient divisive forces of nationalism and tribalism have demonstrated a furious vitality. It would be a mistake to dismiss their recurrence among American Negroes as a passing aberration. In an age of decolonization, it may be fruitful to regard the problem of the American Negro as a unique case of colonialism, an instance of internal imperialism, an underdeveloped people in our very midst. A clue is afforded by the demographic characteristics of the American Negro, which turn out to be like those of other under-developed peoples in our time. "The Negro," Hauser writes in the discussion of demographic factors he contributed to this volume,

> like the inhabitant of the developing regions in Asia, Latin America, and Africa, in his exposure to the amenities of twentieth century living, is experiencing rapidly declining mortality while fertility rates either remain high or, as in urban areas, actually increase.

The high birth rate and the youthful age structure which mark the Negro community are characteristic of the under-developed world today. Unlike external colonies, however, the Negro community has not been a source of cheap raw materials; all it could offer was cheap labor, and the need for cheap labor has been declining on the farm, where most Negroes used to live, and in the cities to which he has moved. The American Negro is condemned to live in Egypt, but it is an Egypt which has already built its Pyramids and no longer needs slaves. Mechanization on the farm and automation in industry have at last set him free, but now freedom turns out to be joblessness.

The most important Negro revolution of our time may be his transformation from a rural to an urban dweller; and to an increasing extent a dweller in idleness. In less than half a century the predominantly rural Negro has become more urban even than the white man. In 1960 the Negro was already 73 per cent urban as compared with 70 per cent for whites. At the same time, as Daniel P. Moynihan observes in his essay on "Employment, Income and the Ordeal of the Negro Family," the rate of Negro unemployment, "from being rather less than that of whites, has steadily moved to the point where it is now regularly more than twice as great." It is no wonder the Negro feels unwanted.

This is only true, however, of the Negro masses. The success of the civil rights movement has deepened the gap between the Negro elite and the Negro mass. "Anyone with eyes to see," Moynihan writes, "can observe the emergence of a Negro middle class that is on the whole doing very well. This group has, if anything, a preferred position in the job market. A nation catching up with centuries of discrimination has rather sharply raised the demand for a group on short supply. One would be hard put to describe a person with better job opportunities than a newly minted Negro Ph. D. . . . At the same time there would also seem to be no question that opportunities for a large mass of Negro workers in the lower ranges of training and education have not been improving, that in many ways the circumstances of these workers relative to the white work force have grown worse." The anarchist, Max Nomad, helped to popularize the theory that revolutions, national or social, are made by déclassé intellectuals seeking their place in the sun or, to switch metaphors, at the public trough. Our Negro Revolution, too, has so far primarily benefitted the Negro elite. The masses have a long wait ahead for "Black Power" but the trained minority is snapped up by government agencies and business firms anxious to acquire their own token Negroes.

A footnote to the Moynihan article points out that in 1964 "the number of corporation personnel representatives visiting the campus of Lincoln University in Pennsylvania was twice that of the graduating class." No one is more revolutionary than idle intellectuals; the Negroes are, in effect, being bought off.

As educational standards and technological requirements rise, it may become harder rather than easier for the Negro to join the ranks of the happy few. Rashi Fein in his essay, "An Economic and Social Profile of the Negro American," quotes from a 1962 Census Bureau report which said:

> It thus appears that not only is the nonwhite population more poorly educated than the white population, but the net gain of nonwhites at higher levels of education, as calculated from the educational differences in the fathers' and sons' generations, has not been as great as for whites.

Fein's analysis shows that while the Negro like the white shows improvement in education, health, and welfare, white progress has been so much swifter than Negro that the differential between them is greater than a generation ago. Fein turns up some fascinating statistics:

> In 1940, for example, the absolute difference between the white and nonwhite infant mortality rate was 31 per 1,000 live births, while in 1962 the difference had declined to 19 per 1,000. Yet in 1940 nonwhite infant mortality was 70 per cent greater than that of whites and in 1962 it was 90 per cent greater.

The lag in rate of progress feeds Negro discontent.

Some of Fein's statistics starkly light up the background of that situation which gave us the "Black Panther" party.

> Even as late as 1952 [Fein writes] the chances were barely 50–50 that a Negro baby born in Mississippi was born in a hospital, but the chances were 99 to 100 for white Mississippi-born babies. And for Negro residents of Dallas County and Lowndes County, Alabama, the rates in 1962 were 27 and 9 per 1,000 (while rates for white residents were 99 and 96 respectively).

This disparity of nine Negro babies per hundred and ninety-six white babies per hundred born in hospitals in Lowndes County may help us to understand the context from which the cry of Black Power originated. The discrimination against the over-whelming black majority in counties like Lowndes is almost genocidal.

The picture which emerges from this symposium, however, has its more hopeful aspects. Lee Rainwater, in his essay on "The Crucible of Identity," throws doubt on the view that slavery, by destroying the Negro family, has created charac-teristics which make it difficult for the Negro to shake off "nigger-ness." Rainwater points out that "in the hundred years since Emancipation, Negroes in rural areas have been able to maintain full nuclear families almost as well as similarly situ-ated whites." The slum and the decline in the need for unskilled labor have more to do with the psychically crippling family conditions of the Negro than the heritage of slavery. Given half a chance, the Negro can respond as quickly as the white to the means for his own improvement. Adelaide Cromwell and Frederick S. Jaffe in their study of "Negro Fertility and Family Size Preferences" show how responsive Negroes are to the birth control which is an essential step to the climb out of poverty. "Privately organized Planned Parenthood centers in some 120 communities," they write, "are still the main birth-control clinics available to low-income families in the U.S.; among the 282,000 patients served in their clinics in 1964, the largest single clinic group—47 per cent—was Negro." A wider availability of contraceptive knowledge for mothers and jobs for fathers would transform the Negro in a generation.

But there is no reason why this transformation must change the Negro merely into a darker version of the white man. The new emphasis on "blackness" in the civil rights movement reflects a healthy instinct. The Negro has two basic needs. One is more jobs and the other is the restoration of self-respect. But how is self-respect to be restored if he rejects himself as Negro and aspires to be something else? Assimilation may come some day to the Negro, as it has to other ethnic groups in our Ameri-can melting pot; the forces making for homogeneity may prove irresistible for him too. But on the way the Negro can only wipe out the self-contempt imposed upon him by three cen-turies of white supremacy by accepting and affirming and intensifying his negritude. A man must absorb, face, and not reject his past in order to stand fully erect, and that past includes the past of the people to which he belongs. To abandon part of one's self is by implication to accept that part's inferiority. The current revulsion against integration is made more understandable by Erik H. Erikson's essay on "The Concept of Identity."

Dr. Erikson, who is lecturer on psychiatry at Harvard, shows us that the Negro is often asked to accept "an unsure outer integration" at the cost of giving up that "inner integration" in which he had learned to accept himself as a Negro. He quotes a young Negro woman student as exclaiming, "What am I supposed to be integrated *out* of? I laugh like my grandmother—and I would rather die than not laugh like that." Dr. Erikson remarks: "Desegregation, compensation, balance, reconciliation—do they all sometimes seem to save the Negro at the cost of an absorption which he is not sure will leave much of himself behind?"

This has implications for the Negro collectively as well as individually. Oscar Handlin's essay on "The Goals of Integration" is not so far from the sharp new turn in the civil rights movement signaled by Stokely Carmichael.

> It is the ultimate illogic of integration [Handlin writes] to deny the separateness of the Negro and therefore to inhibit him from creating the communal institutions which can help him cope with his problem . . . To confuse segregation, the function of which is to establish Negro inferiority, with the awareness of separate identity, the function of which is to generate the power for voluntary action, hopelessly confuses the struggle for equality.

Handlin restates calmly what the Negro radicals cry out in their anguish:

> As long as common memories, experience and interests make the Negroes a group, they will find it advantageous to organize and act as such. And the society will better be able to accommodate them as equals on those terms than it could under the pretense that integration could wipe out the past.

This is the logic of "black power," though devoid of those semantic, psychological, and mystical overtones that have spread it so swiftly through the Negro community, as if it were

an incantation to the forgotten tribal gods long torn away from
them.

The Negro requires and deserves the fullest measure of patience and understanding in his agony, for this is the agony of
his rebirth. His racism, answering ours, is a necessary step
toward our ultimate reconciliation. The riots—and they will
become worse—have a logic of their own: Can we deny that
only the fear of race war can force us finally to gird for Negro
rehabilitation and reconstruction as we gird for war abroad, on
a giant scale and with a generous hand? Of all I read in *The
Negro American* what I liked best is a remark Robert Coles
records from an unnamed Negro in Mississippi. "Negroes don't
have it so bad," he said, "they can recover mighty fast, if we
only get a chance." There lies the hope for him and for us and
for what must become, in the fullest sense, our common
country.

AUGUST 18, 1966

# THE EARLY DISTANT WARNING
# OUT OF THE CONGO

It is a pity more Americans could not have seen the events of
the past week through African and Negro eyes from the vantage point of the UN debate on the Congo. The summary dis-
missal of charges against the accused killers of the three civil
rights workers in Mississippi, the refusal to hear the confession
by one of the accused, could not have come at a more terrible

moment. Mr. Botsio of Ghana, on the opening day of the Congo debate, had already told the Security Council that under international law the U.S. was no more entitled to intervene in the Congo than Ghana in the American South where "Afro-American inhabitants" are "from time to time tortured and murdered for asserting their legitimate rights." Next day came the news from Meridian, like a flash of lightning before a storm, revealing sharply the true lineaments of the racial landscape, with the colored man everywhere a creature of lesser concern, even to white men of good will.

Nothing could be more unwise for our country than to treat the Congo debate as another inning in the cold war, calculating its effects on the UN dues quarrel and China membership issue, as if following a familiar sporting event on a score-card. The protests to the Security Council were downgraded in our press as coming from "left-leaning" African states, the implication being that ideology explained it all. This is dangerous self-delusion. The common bond that unites Negro and Arab, African and Asian, Hindu and Chinese, and the whole underworld of mixed blood in Latin America, is the all too fresh recollection of humiliation at the hands of the white man. This is what the Congo episode stirred up and this is something they do not need to read about in pamphlets from Peking. There never was a sharper cleavage at the UN between white and colored than on the Congo question. Intervention to protect lives and property—gunboat diplomacy—has too long been the traditional excuse of imperialism in Latin America and Eurasia. The Western plea of humanitarianism created solidarity among those accustomed to being regarded as not quite human. Suddenly Africa was talking about Mississippi and Cuba, as if in a worldwide colonial and racial upsurge.

Mr. Beovagui of Guinea protested to the Security Council that the U.S. and Belgium had tried for weeks before the rescue at Stanleyville to impose a military solution on the Congo while the African States were seeking to bring about a political reconciliation. He complained that white mercenaries "under the protection of U.S. military planes piloted by Cubans recruited and financed by the U.S.—soldiers of fortune trying to redeem their fiasco in the Bay of Pigs" had massacred Congolese civilians and "bombarded cities held by the forces of the

National Liberation Front . . . as in Albertville and Bakavu" without stirring any indignation in the West. "Was it," he asked, "because the thousands of Congolese citizens murdered by the South Africans, the Rhodesians, the Belgians and the Cuban refugee adventurers had dark skins just like the colored U.S. citizens murdered in Mississippi?" This is a bitterness we would do well to heed. The debate was a Distant Early Warning Line on which we may hear in time the approach of a conflict more serious than the anti-communist cold war with which we continue to be obsessed. Mississippi, Rhodesia, South Africa and Brazil each in their own time and their own way may bring about a new polarization between white and colored, rich and poor, threatening a war in which our ICBM's would stand impotent, a war from which all mankind would lose.

We exaggerate the divisions among the African States. Senegal, with Liberia and Nigeria, is counted "on our side." The speech made by Mr. Thiam of Senegal to the General Assembly a week earlier should put us on guard against such over-simplifications. Mr. Thiam did indeed address some perceptive advice to his fellow Africans. "Very often," he pointed out, "it is we ourselves who start the cold war in our countries. Because of internal rivalries between men and different political tendencies, we invite others to interfere in our domestic affairs." He said interventions are approved or condemned, depending on whether they were from Washington or Moscow, without concern for the principle of non-intervention, "bringing into question our independence and our sovereignty." But Senegal's spokesman is no Western mouthpiece. He opposed expulsion of the Soviets on the debt issue. He warned that the chaos in the Congo was a preview of what would happen in Angola unless Portugal, unlike Belgium, began to train native cadres to take over. He ended by touching on issues more fundamental than color: the continued fall in the raw material prices on which the ex-colonial countries depend; the damage done them by the one-crop economies imposed under imperialism; "the elementary duty of justice and humanity" which requires the ex-colonizers "not to go away and leave us to pay the bill"; the need for "a new organization of our planet based on a new ethics." This was man's better conscience speaking through Africa.

Mr. Spaak of Belgium defended his country with eloquence. He said he would not attempt to give lessons to black men because after Buchenwald and Auschwitz the white man had no right to give lessons in humanity. He said that in the Nairobi talks, the representative of the rebels had demanded a cease-fire, which Belgium and the U.S. could not obtain because the Leopoldville government opposed it. But Tshombe was put into power by Belgium and the U.S. They could have put pressure on him if they were not themselves opposed to a peaceful settlement which would bring the rebels into the government. Spaak was on stronger ground when he discussed the people Belgium had rescued. He said these were the technical assistants, the professors, the veterinarians, the doctors for whose services the Congo had asked. "They went to the Congo at our request," he said, "and it was because we had a special responsibility toward them that we had to make a special effort in their behalf." How could Africa get the white technical aid it needed if they were to become the hostages of internal struggle?

But one felt that the quarrel had reached that blind stage where neither side hears the other, and each is more occupied with his own grievances than in squarely meeting the issue. The Belgians felt aggrieved that after being asked to come back they were being mistreated and denounced. The Africans remembered Leopold and the horrors of his Congo Free State; this is but yesterday for them. They recalled how the CIA had connived in the overthrow of Lumumba, the Congo's one national leader, and picked that clown, Mobutu, as our strong man. They regard Tshombe as Lumumba's murderer and our puppet and feel as a slight on all of them the headlines about a cannibalism that never occurred. In their rage they forgot that their own savagery to each other in the Congo was worse than anything the white man had done to them.

There never was greater need for the voice of reason. The debate may cost Africa aid it badly needs from the U. S. Congress. The news from the Congo will not make it easy to recruit the technicians it requires. Che Guevara in his green fatigues, symbol of the guerrilla fighters against whom the

West has proven powerless, suited the mood of the moment and was given an ovation by the Afro-Asians after a revolutionary speech even the Chinese might have thought a bit sweeping. He was escorted out of the hall by a throng of admiring blacks. Mr. Stevenson could not have made a more foolish reply than calling Guevara "a man with a long communist and revolutionary record in Latin America." In that atmosphere it sounded to the Europeans like a feeble echo of McCarthy and to the embittered Afro-Asians like a positive accolade.

DECEMBER 13, 1964

# WHY THEY CRY BLACK POWER

There is a hopeful side to the riots and picketing in the slums. They indicate that the poor are no longer poor in spirit. This is the spark that hope has kindled, the real achievement of the poverty program, the beginning of rehabilitation. The negative side is the spread of race war. The Negro, the Puerto Rican and the Mexican-American will no longer wait humbly at the back door of our society. For them its shiny affirmation of equality is a taunt. Either we make it real or see our country torn apart. A race is on between the constructive capacity of our society and an ugly white backlash with fascist overtones. The crossroads of America's future is not far off.

Our country is the last hope of multiracialism. The French, for all their civilizing gift, were unable to create that multiracial community Ho Chi Minh was once willing to enter. The

British Commonwealth is splitting up over British unwillingness to act against the dictatorship of white minorities in
Rhodesia and South Africa. Racialism and tribalism are the
curse of mankind, anachronistic contemporaries of the astro-
naut. Where white supremacy is gone forever, Arab and Negro
slaughter each other in the Sudan; Malay and Chinese riot in
Singapore; tribalism is breaking up Black Africa's most promising nation in Nigeria.

Racism here is only another example of a universal human
disease. The cry of "black power" is less a program than an
incantation to deal with the crippling effects of white supremacy. The "black" affirms a lost racial pride and the "power" the
virility of which the Negro has been robbed by generations of
humiliation. Its swift spread testifies to the deep feelings it
satisfies. It is not practical politics; it is psychological therapy.
Stokely Carmichael's burning explanation of it in the September 22 issue of the *New York Review* is to be read as the
poetry of despair. The United States is not Mr. Carmichael's
cherished model, Lowndes County; there are few other counties which have its overwhelming black majority. And it is
typical New Left *narodnik* mysticism, albeit in Negro form,
to call for "the coming together of black people" to pick their
own representatives and at the same time to reject "most of the
black politicians we see around the country today." Who picked
Adam Clayton Powell, Harlem's absentee political landlord?

But rational argument will not meet the appeal of "black
power." It affirms separation because it has met rejection.
When Senators go out on the golf links to forestall a quorum
rather than vote on "open occupancy," when hateful faces in
the North greet Negro demonstrators with cries of "kill the
jungle bunnies," when whites flee the cities as if the Negro
were some kind of rodent, how else salvage pride except by
counter-rejection? It is the taking of white supremacy for
granted that is the danger, not the cry of "black power," which
is as pathetic as a locked-out child's agony. Nothing could be
more disastrous than to divert attention from the real problems
of our society by setting off on a witch hunt against SNCC. In
Atlanta, as in Watts, trouble began not because of SNCC but
because the cops are trigger-happy when dealing with black
men.

Without extremists to prod us into action, we will not take the giant steps required to rehabilitate the colored and the poor. The Negro still wants in; he cannot go back to Africa; his only future is here. Not black power or white but a sense of belonging to one human family can alone save this planet. But the time is short before hate shuts the doors. The time is coming when we will regret the billions wasted in Vietnam. The time is coming when we may regret the number of Negroes we have trained there in guerrilla war. There is hardly a city where the Negroes do not already dominate the strategic areas through which the affluent commuter passes on his way to the inner core. SNCC's hostility to the war is not disloyalty but wisdom. We cannot rebuild that sense of community so essential to our beloved country's future by engaging in a white man's war in Asia while a black man's revolt rises at home.

SEPTEMBER 19, 1966

# VIII

---

## THE
## GREEN
## BERET:
## SILLY
## AND
## SINISTER

# WHEN BRASS HATS BEGIN TO READ
# MAO TSE-TUNG, BEWARE!

The most important lesson for Washington in the recently attempted Army revolt in Algeria has gone unnoticed in the American press. Yet that lesson could hardly be more timely. The core of the revolt lay in a strange group of offbeat colonels. These are the colonels who started the fad for reading Mao Tse-tung and the emphasis, suddenly fashionable in Washington, on using "para-military," "guerrilla" and "revolutionary war" tactics against the communists. This is the same group of colonels who helped bring de Gaulle to power in 1958 and whom he began quietly transferring out of Algeria as soon as he could. The lesson de Gaulle understood but Kennedy hasn't yet grasped is that when military men read Mao (and Che Guevara) and seek to turn their tactics to counter-revolutionary purposes, they also turn, often without knowing it, into communists-in-reverse, i.e. to put it bluntly, into fascists. And sooner or later they will be tempted to use at home, against their own people and government, the psychological warfare, the brainwashings, the cloak-and-dagger methods and the "dirty tricks" they are allowed to utilize in colonial areas.

The distinguished journalist and historian, Alexander Werth, in his book *The De Gaulle Revolution* which has just appeared in England, describes this group and its origins in a passage which sounds like a preview of military ideas now bubbling in the Pentagon. "Ever since returning from Indo-China, and particularly in 1957–58," Mr. Werth writes, "it was fascinating among French officers in Algeria to talk about Mao Tse-tung, and about the primary importance in modern warfare of 'psychological action.' " Then he goes on to describe the next stage, which we have not yet reached publicly. "This psychological action," Mr. Werth continues, "was primarily to be applied to the 'natives,' and to colonial peoples in revolt; but gradually the idea also gained ground that a parallel psychological action could be exercised on the French in Algeria, and ultimately on France itself." Mr. Werth quotes one of this group, the notorious Colonel Trinquier, a veteran of Indochina, who recently tried to join the foreign mercenaries in Katanga, as telling a newspaperman in Algeria in 1958, "What we have to do is to organize the population from top to bottom. I don't care if you call me a fascist; but we must have a docile population, every gesture of which shall be subject to our control."

The traditional American principle of subordinating the military to civilian control takes on new meaning when seen against the background of the putsch these colonels staged to put de Gaulle into power in 1958 and to try and replace him with a military junta a few weeks ago. This background also lends heightened significance to a passage in an anonymous report on "Special Warfare" which Lieutenant General Arthur G. Trudeau, the Army's research and development chief, has been circulating among senior officers at the Pentagon. The document leaked to the *Army Navy Air Force Journal*, which published the full text April 8. "The U.S. still maintains a wall of separation between politics and the military," said this anonymous military expert. "This is fine for our domestic problems, but it does not work against communist-supported guerrillas where political and military action are one." But if you use cloak-and-dagger forces abroad on the assumption that you are dealing with a vast communist conspiracy, how prevent these methods from being used again suspected radicals at home? To break down the wall between politics and the military, to invite the military into the sphere of politics is to undermine the Republic. France learned that lesson again a few weeks ago. We should benefit from it while there is still time.

There is a close corollary of this proposition. Jean Planchais in *Le Monde* (April 24), discussing the different ideological currents in the Algerian military rebellion, noted two points of danger. One was the colonels, who had drawn from their Indochinese contacts with Marxism fuzzy ideas about regenerating their homeland with a "national socialist" and "national communist" revolution which recall the National Socialism of Hitler. The other was the extent to which they leaned for support not only on special cadres of professional soldiers and elite elements, like the parachutists, but on Foreign Legion units largely composed of Germans. We are recruiting similar adventurers from Central and Eastern Europe for service in the so-called Special Warfare units. They seem to come chiefly from right-wing elements. I was told that there were many former *Chetniks* among them; these were the Royal Yugoslav partisans under Mihailovitch, who collaborated during certain periods with the Nazis. The anonymous memorandum in the *Army Navy Air Force Journal* ends by saying "the two names . . . who are most mentionable in this field are Colonel Ed Lansdale, OSO, and Slavko N. Bjelajac, Special Warfare." When I reached Mr. Bjelajac by phone at the Pentagon, he admitted he had served with the Yugoslav Partisan forces under Mihailovitch.[1]

It is no wonder the revolting French officers thought they had American sympathizers. I found at the Pentagon that ACSI (Assistant Chief of Staff for Intelligence) had translated and circulated widely among senior officers the leading "ideological" work of these French colonels. This was put together by a Colonel Lacheroy under the pen name of Ximenès in a special double issue (February-March, 1957) of the *Revue Militaire d'Information*. Mr. Werth calls it "amateurish and even childish in its starry-eyed discovery of the 'revolutionary war tactics' of Bolshevism," but it seems to have been regarded as hot stuff indeed at the Pentagon, where it fit neatly into the Birch Society-style views all too prevalent among some officers. A British writer who served in American Combat Intelligence during the last war criticized these French military ideologists

[1] It is interesting to notice that the Cuban exiles who told Sam Pope Brewer (*New York Times,* May 7) that they had been imprisoned and mistreated for objecting to the presence of Batista men in the Guatemalan training camps, described some of the supposed CIA men in charge as speaking English with an accent, "perhaps of Central European origin."

for a "comic strip concept of history" which tended to see a communist plot behind all colonial insurrectionist movements, whether left or nationalist.[2] The Steve Canyon comic strip mentality is even stronger at the Pentagon.

MAY 15, 1961

# ANTI-GUERRILLA WAR—THE DAZZLING NEW MILITARY TOOTHPASTE FOR SOCIAL DECAY

In reading the military literature on guerrilla warfare now so fashionable at the Pentagon,[1] one feels that these writers are like men watching a dance from outside through heavy plate glass windows. They see the motions but they can't hear the music. They put the mechanical gestures down on paper with pedantic fidelity. But what rarely comes through to them are the injured racial feelings, the misery, the rankling slights, the

[2] Paret: "The French Army and *La Guerre Revolutionnaire*," *Journal of the Royal United Service Institution*, February 1959, reprinted by the British Institute for Strategic Studies in the March-April, 1959, issue of its organ, *Survival*.

[1] This is based on a reading of the special double issue (February-March 1957) of the *Revue Militaire d'Information* which ACSI (Assistant Chief of Staff for Intelligence) has been circulating in translation at the Pentagon. This issue was edited by Colonel Lacheroy, right hand man to General Salan in the coup which brought de Gaulle to power in 1958.

hatred, the devotion, the inspiration and the desperation. So they do not really understand what leads men to abandon wife, children, home, career and friends; to take to the bush and live gun in hand like a hunted animal; to challenge overwhelming military odds rather than acquiesce any longer in humiliation, injustice or poverty. These military theoreticians, astounded by the success that such handfuls of men can achieve under a Castro or a Ho Chi Minh against huge and well-equipped armies, think their tactics can be duplicated mechanically, in reverse, like a drill, if only their recruits can be taught to go through the same motions.

The armed services are oriented to battle on the field of public relations, where higher appropriations are won. They have to deal with a gimmick-minded public, which is used to mechanical devices and looks for some new pushbutton solution whenever confronted by a new problem. So the dazzling latest military toothpaste for social decay is this idea of our using guerrilla methods, too. Nobody notices that the chief theoreticians on our side are a group of French colonels who not only failed to win by these methods in Algeria but have had to be scattered and suppressed by the French government because they began turning their "dirty tricks" against the French Republic. Nor does anyone stop to consider that these tactics and the men who would be in charge of them here have just had an opportunity in nearby Cuba, and failed dismally. The same Joint Chiefs of Staff which lacked the competence to stage an invasion of Cuba, and the same intelligence agents who could not correctly evaluate the mood of the Cuban people—can they be expected to do better, let us say, in far-away North Vietnam? Against an older regime, right on the border of Communist China?

It is time we realized that the brutal surgery of military and para-military methods cannot cure complex social and economic problems. The CIA got rid of a popular reformer, Mossadegh, in Iran, but the makeshift corrupt regime with which he was replaced is now collapsing. Guatemala, where the CIA got rid of Arbenz, is ripe for new trouble. These counter-conspiracies only postpone crises which burst forth again with redoubled force. If the hundreds of millions we have squandered in Laos and South Vietnam had gone into public improvements during the past decade, both countries would be models of stability. As it is, the only stable country in the area is Cambodia, where the CIA tried to overthrow Prince Sihanouk because of his neutralism and failed.

It is said, and some of the liberals around the President seem to believe it, that these methods can be combined with economic and social reform. But experience is against them. We never succeeded in getting Chiang or Syngman Rhee to make reforms; our support merely strengthened their heavy hand. Can we do better with Diem in South Vietnam? One of the tasks of counter guerrilla forces will be to eliminate suspected subversive influences in the villages. Can this be done without eliminating the very men who want reform and leaving the dull and acquiescent? Military methods of this kind weaken the reform elements at the bottom of the pyramid, or drive them into the arms of the communists, and at the same time strengthen the rulers and ruling classes who are the principal enemy of reform. This new course is a dead-end street. If followed, it not only will fail to spread democracy abroad but will poison it at home.

MAY 22, 1961

# IX

---

IN
THE
QUICKSAND
OF
SOUTHEAST
ASIA

# LOST CHANCES FOR PEACE
# IN INDOCHINA

The history of Indochina since the war has been a history of lost opportunities. Ho Chi Minh's Vietminh worked closely with the OSS during the Second World War, and took FDR's promises of colonial liberation seriously. So pro-American was its orientation at one time that, as Oliver E. Clubb, Jr., writes in his *The U.S. and the Sino-Soviet Bloc in South East Asia* (Brookings, 1962), "Vietnam's declaration of independence began with lines from America's own Declaration of Independence and its first constitution more closely resembled that of the U.S. than that of the Soviet Union." Hopes of American support were dashed when the Truman Administration acquiesced in France's effort to restore colonial rule. Ellen J. Hammer in her book, *The Struggle for Indochina* (Stanford, 1952) tells the story of another blasted Vietminh hope. Ho Chi Minh risked his political leadership to reach a moderate agreement with the French on March 6, 1946, accepting a limited independence within the French Union. Because of this agreement the Vietminh permitted the French to reoccupy Hanoi without a shot being fired. The French troops "fresh from the liberation of Paris" were hailed "as the incarnation of Free France." But French promises were broken, and a war began that was to cost France $5 billion and the blood of many of her best young professional soldiers before Dien Bien Phu and the Geneva agreement marked her defeat eight years later.

Another of these opportunities is now being lost. The international situation makes this a favorable moment to negotiate an end of the war with China and North Vietnam. The latter would like resumption of its normal trade relations with the South; it fears expansion of the war would risk destruction of its resources by American bombardment and end its precarious independence of China. The most important revelation in Bernard B. Fall's forthcoming book *The Two Viet-Nams* (Praeger, 1963) is that the North Vietnamese leaders in three interviews given Westerners last year (the London *Daily Express* in March, Dr. Fall in July and Colonel Jules Roy of *L'Express* in December) made it obvious to all three that North Vietnam "had backed away from outright conquest of South Vietnam and was veering toward a negotiated solution embodying the existence of a neutral South Vietnamese state that would not be reunited with the North for a long time to come."

A representative of the National Liberation Front of South Vietnam in a clandestine interview with Georges Chaffard of *Le Monde* (August 24) during his visit to Saigon last summer also set forth a program for an independent South Vietnam to be established in free elections. "We have not fought all these years, in the worst conditions," he told M. Chaffard, "to end by replacing one dictatorship with another. None of us can accept a relation of dependence on the North." The domestic program outlined was a moderate one, with a friendly attitude toward foreign investments. "We wish to be realists," M. Chaffard was told. "We know the difficulties of our compatriots in the North, and we have also studied the example of the states of Black Africa. There is no question of wishing to install systematically a Popular Democracy in the South . . ." The desire is for a neutral regime which can deal with both sides in economic development. Both Peking and Hanoi last year called for reconvening the Geneva Conference to make peace in South Vietnam. For North Vietnam a neutral regime in the South would enable it again to exchange its coal and industrial products for the rice of the South. If East and West Germany can do an enormous trade, despite sharp political differences, why not North and South Vietnam, especially since such trade would go a long way toward ending the trade deficits of both? For China, looking for new ties in the West to fight off the isolation imposed on her by Russia, the ending of the war in

South Vietnam would remove one major obstacle to better trade relations with the West. This is an ideal time for the West to negotiate.

Unfortunately we still have two basic policies for dealing with communist regimes. In Eastern Europe we seem to have given up containment for conciliation. We reward the Kadar government in Hungary for liberalization at home by resuming relations. We continue to give support to Gomulka in Poland as a means of encouraging some independence of Russia. Ever since Tito's break with Stalin, we have moved away from the notion that the communist world is a faceless monolith run from Moscow, and sought to foster centrifugal forces within it. But in the Far East, as in our dealings with Cuba, we still cling to the older view that the only way to deal with a revolutionary movement is to do all in our power to starve it out. If we were treating East Asia as we treat East Europe, we would be actively exploring the differences between China and Russia, and those between North Vietnam and China, for leverage with which to end the costly uprising in South Vietnam. But we still think of China and of North Vietnam, as we did in the twenties of Russia, as untouchable regimes.

The lack of a constructive policy in East Asia becomes more understandable when one looks back and sees that the change in our policy toward Eastern Europe was a reaction to events in that area rather than the result of any diplomatic initiatives on our part. Churchill, after Stalin died, flew to Washington and urged us to negotiate with Malenkov, but the State Department insisted nothing had changed. It was not until the 20th Congress and the upsurges to which it gave rise in Hungary and Poland that we began to recognize belatedly that something was happening in the Soviet world. The policy of détente in recent months was largely made in Moscow, and our continued freeze in the Far East also shares the made in Moscow label. For suddenly the conflict between the Chinese and Russian ruling bureaucracies has led the latter to seek the isolation of China. Thus Russian policy and the policy imposed on us by our China lobby converged. The path of least resistance was to accept Russian overtures in the West—while pursuing the old rigid cold war policy in the Far East.

It should be obvious by now that problems arising in territories contiguous to China can no more be settled without her than Caribbean problems can be settled without the United States. The Chinese taught us a lesson at the 38th parallel in Korea which we seem unwilling to acknowledge at the 17th parallel in Vietnam. China in effect warned us that if we crossed the 38th parallel it would intervene; its "volunteers" forced us back to the parallel. To end the Korean war, we had to negotiate with China. The West had to negotiate with China to settle the Laotian conflict. There will have to be negotiations with China again to end the South Vietnamese war.

The primary obstacle to the negotiation of such a settlement lies in Washington. Kennedy cannot afford to go into the campaign next year and face a Republican cry that under the Democrats we "lost" Vietnam, whether by withdrawal or negotiation. The politically safest course is to "stand firm," i.e. to follow the line of least resistance, though this means continuation of a war that most observers agree cannot be won, and could at any time expand dangerously. As in France, the national interest is to be subordinated to the convenience of the political leadership; we will go on pouring out blood and treasure; we have already sunk some $5 billions in the Indo-chinese quagmire. The Administration hopes that by a little pressure on Diem, at least for some face-saving reforms, and by a lot of flim-flam at home, it can keep this tragic comedy going at least until after the 1964 elections. The political realities of Washington, not the military realities in Saigon, explain the October 2 White House statement that General Taylor and Secretary McNamara had "reported their judgment that the major part of the U.S. military task" in South Vietnam "can be completed by the end of 1965," i.e. a year after the elections. Never was a crystal ball more clearly clouded by politics.

The outcry about Diem diverts attention from the policies of Kennedy. The inhumanity which has made a world scandal of South Vietnam has its origin as much in Washington as in Saigon. The uprooting of the rural population and its incarceration in stockaded villages, the spraying of poisons from the air on crops and cattle in violation of the Geneva convention, the use of napalm for attack on villages suspected of harboring rebels—these policies were all formulated and directed out of Washington. The familiar belief that the end justifies the means in any conflict with communism was enough to wipe out qualms, if any, about the mistreatment of the Vietnamese. It was only the unexpected clash with the Buddhists which brought relations between Washington and Saigon to a crisis. The spectacle of a U.S. supported Catholic family dictatorship oppressing the majority creed, the international repercussions in the Buddhist world and Kennedy's own Catholicism made this most embarrassing. Above all, in the cant of the cold war, religion is sacred, God being regarded as safely on our side in the struggle against "atheistic communism." Religious persecution could not be reconciled with holy war. So Mr. Kennedy in his interview with Walter Cronkite on CBS September 2 ventured the opinion that "in the last two months the government" of Diem "has gotten out of touch with the people." This ranks with the best understatements of our time; Diem quite obviously has been out of touch with his people a good deal longer than two months.[1] Mr. Kennedy condemned the repression of the Buddhists but again his choice of words was tepid; he called it "very unwise." The words reflect neither moral revulsion nor human sympathy but only cool calculation. At a press conference a week later he summed up his policy. The test of official action in our government or Diem's was to be whether it might "handicap the winning of the war." This, and not justice for the people of South Vietnam or the establishment of a decent regime there, is our No. 1 aim. All else is subordinate to it. When the main objective is thus military, our main reliance is on the Pentagon and on cloak-and-dagger operations. The government becomes a prisoner of the end and the means it chooses. The type of men, mentality and institution brought into play determines the course of events and constricts the choice of alternatives.

The CIA's dominant outlook, even more under McCone than

[1] Diem seems to be out of touch altogether. The Australian newspaperman, Denis Warner, in his new book, *The Last Confucian*, writes, "Diem talks but never listens; he looks but never sees. Any Ambassador who can get in 500 words in a four-hour conversation with him feels that he is just about hitting par for the course. Diem talks monotonously and repetitively, rambling from one subject to another and never talking a problem through . . . never does he spark with humor. Twin threads of thought provide the only continuity. One is the assumption that he is right and knows best; the other that he is the victim of lies and calumny."

under Dulles, sees communist conspiracy in every type of colonial struggle and gravitates instinctively to repressive measures for dealing with it. The alliance between the CIA and Ngo Dinh Nhu, whose special forces—his Storm Troopers—have been getting $3,000,000 a year from CIA, is not accidental but reflects a kinship of spirit; McCone's religious and apocalyptic views are much like those of Vietnam's ruling family. The President has recalled John H. Richardson, the CIA chief in Saigon, under pressure from Ambassador Lodge, but there is no way of knowing what if any changes in CIA policy will be made. A cloak-and-dagger organization is by its very nature hard to control. It is difficult enough for the White House to keep a firm rein on the State Department a few blocks away; it is almost impossible to control a distant underground operation attracting a local entourage of informers eager to jump on the gravy train. The intelligence supplied by such a network is probably a good deal less reliable and perceptive than that which the careful reader can get for himself from the American, British and French press. Certainly no one following the press reports would have been as silly as was Secretary McNamara when he told a Congressional committee that there were three times as many Catholics as Buddhists in South Vietnam, and that the latter constituted only about 10 per cent of the population! This was a real scoop, comparable to the discovery that Ireland is largely populated by Protestants.

Whether Secretary McNamara was the victim in this of the CIA or of military intelligence no one knows. But the latter, too, must be a rich source of misinformation. Louis R. Rukeyser in the last of a revealing six-part series from Saigon in the *Baltimore Sun* October 18 wrote that at the military headquarters of General Paul D. Harkins, "all is sweetness and light. The Viet Cong guerrillas are being licked, one is told, and it is only a matter of time before the assisting Americans can go home victorious." The French had a whole series of such generals in Indochina; victory was always just around the corner.

The Kennedy Administration, like Eisenhower's and Truman's before it, has carried on its Indochinese policies behind a thick smokescreen of official falsification. The contrast between propaganda and reality is visible in Eisenhower's forthcoming memoirs (*Mandate for Change*, Doubleday) where Ike begins his part of this story by describing the Vietminh in the customary way as "so-called 'patriots' " and "Chinese supported rebels." He recalls with approval the NATO resolution of December 17, 1952, on the basis of which the Truman Administration next day launched its program of military aid to the French. This resolution said the war "was essential to the defense of liberty" and "in harmony with the ideals and aims of NATO." But Ike himself could not have taken these ringing phrases very seriously. For he confesses that he did not want to intervene in 1954 without at least token forces from other nations to "lend real moral standing to a venture that otherwise could be made to appear as a brutal example of imperialism." This need "was particularly acute," Ike adds, "because there was no incontrovertible evidence of overt Red Chinese participation in the Indochinese conflict." Later in the story Ike makes another admission that the government did its best at the time to keep from the American people. "I have never talked or corresponded with a person knowledgeable in Indochinese affairs," Ike now discloses, "who did not agree that had elections been held as of the time of the fighting, possibly 80 per cent of the population would have voted for Ho Chi Minh." What the government said in public was very different from what it knew in private. The truth then and since has been that we were financing a war to impose on the Vietnamese a regime they did not want, first that of the French and then that of Diem.

An elaborate mythology has been built up by the Kennedy Administration to cloak our role in what the French are calling the second Indochinese war. The first article of faith in this mythology is that the war broke out not because of Diem's failure to satisfy his people's aspirations in South Vietnam but because of his success. As Kennedy wrote Diem on October 26, 1961, "The Communist response to the growing strength and prosperity of your people was to send terror into your villages, to burn your new schools and to make ambushes of your new roads." This myth was further amplified in the two-volume "Blue Book" on the war put out by the State Department a few weeks later, "A Threat to the Peace: North Vietnam's Effort to Conquer South Vietnam." Here the genesis of the war was spelled out even more glamorously, "The years

1956 to 1960 produced something close to an economic miracle in South Vietnam . . . The economic and social advances scored by the South Vietnamese up to last year made it plain that Hanoi's program for peaceful takeover had little or no chance of success. If they were to win the Communists had to resort to force . . . South Vietnam was outstripping the North in the same fashion that West Germany had exceeded the achievements of the 'socialist' East. The leaders in Hanoi apparently could not accept that prospect. They decided on a course of violence . . ." The State Department has never tried to sell more obvious nonsense. Guerrilla war cannot be stirred up among a contented people. Yet this has been the official line ever since.

In part this myth was made necessary by the position Kennedy took on Vietnam in the 1960 campaign. The book of foreign policy speeches edited by the distinguished historian Allan Nevins for the campaign as Kennedy's *Strategy of Peace* also hailed, and virtually took credit for, "a near miracle" in South Vietnam. One of the speeches was made in 1956 to Diem's sounding board in this country, the American Friends of Vietnam. Nevins said "exceptional interest" attached to this speech because despite fears at the time—

> the faith of friends like Senator Kennedy was actually well founded. The U.S. had the wisdom to grant South Vietnam about $500 million in various forms of assistance . . . The little republic truly became what Mr. Kennedy calls it, a proving ground of democracy. It has produced in its President, Ngo Dinh Diem, one of the true statesmen of the new Asia . . . Vietnam is a country of which the West may feel proud.

It would have been embarrassing to admit so soon that our statesman friend was a bust. A second reason for the myth that the revolt against Diem was fomented from outside was to marshal international support against it. In his speech to the UN General Assembly in New York on September 25, 1961, Kennedy cited South Vietnam as a threat to the peace. "South Vietnam," the President said, "is already under attack— sometimes by a single assassin, sometimes by a band of guerrillas, recently by full battalions . . . No one can call these 'wars of liberation.' For these are free countries living under their own governments."

But this picture of a peaceful and democratic regime attacked from outside soon became difficult to reconcile with Kennedy's own troubles with the Diem regime. Two months later (November 29) he was questioned at a press conference about the bitter attacks suddenly launched against the U.S. by "the government controlled press in Vietnam, apparently because we are asking for political reforms in exchange for our military and economic assistance." Kennedy in a rather fumbling reply said the U.S. was trying to get the Diem government to take "steps which will increase the sense of commitment by the people of Vietnam to the struggle." If Vietnam was a prosperous and democratic state, why this worry about an inadequate sense of commitment to the struggle by its people?

The truth is that the problem was not one of "inadequate commitment" by the people to the Diem regime but of positive hostility. To go through a pile of books and articles on the revolt against Diem as I have been doing in the past few weeks and to compare these unofficial accounts with the official pronouncements of the Kennedy Administration is a disturbing experience. On every major aspect of the war the Kennedy Administration has sought to deceive the country. To bolster up these myths, it has cooperated with the Diem regime in making it as difficult as possible for independent American journalists to get the truth. Only a few weeks ago the Moss subcommittee on government information of the House of Representatives reported (September 26) that

> In recent weeks the American public has been surprised by developments in Vietnam—developments which have been many months in the making but which the American people are just now discovering. The restrictive U.S. press policy in Vietnam— drafted in the State Department's public relations office by an official with an admitted distrust for the people's right to know —unquestionably contributed to the lack of information about conditions in Vietnam which created an international crisis. Instead of hiding the facts from the American public, the State Department should have done everything possible to expose the true situation to full view.

The final sentence is incredibly naive. In thirty years' experience, the writer has never yet known the State Department to expose any true situation to full view. "Papa knows best" has always been its basic attitude. The official criticized, perhaps unfairly, since he was only conforming to the department's traditional press policy, is Carl T. Rowan, now Ambassador to Finland, then Deputy Assistant Secretary of State for Public Affairs. The Moss subcommittee called attention to a speech in which Rowan talked of the public's "right *not* to know." He said that "in a period of undeclared war, we constantly must decide how far we can go in providing the well-informed populace without which a 'free society' becomes a mockery without violating our oath to protect this country" and complained that too few newspapers "are willing to weigh their stories against the national interest." But the Moss subcommittee did not mention that Rowan was only developing ideas put forward a few months earlier after the Cuban debacle by Kennedy in his speech before the American Newspaper Publishers Association. The purport of that speech was that if and when the government decided on a policy of undeclared war, the press ought not to publish matters which would let the public know what was going on. The effort to manage the news has never been more blatant than on Vietnam.

In some military circles suspicion of the press seems to have reached Birchite dimensions. Thus Dr. Fall, in his book, *The Two Viet-Nams*, discloses that the U. S. Army's most respected publication, the *Military Review* of the U. S. Army Command and Staff College, ran an article in its May 1962 issue by Suzanne Labin, "a French socialist with extreme right wing leanings." The article, according to Dr. Fall, "flatly accuses anyone who does not support Ngo Dinh Diem . . . of being a participant in an immense campaign . . . launched by the Communists and their dupes." A milder variant of the same conspiracy charge was made by Joseph Alsop, always a faithful satellite of the military, in a column of September 23. While generously absolving his colleagues in Saigon of being under communist influence, Alsop accuses them of engaging in a deliberate campaign to discredit and unnerve Diem. This may help to explain why Alsop seems to be Mme. Nhu's favorite correspondent: Dr. Fall in his book recalls that even *Time* once poked fun at her for suggesting creation of a committee of foreign correspondents, preferably headed by Alsop, to hammer out a general line to which they would all adhere, just like the boys on *Pravda*. This was another glimpse of the mentality Robert Guillian described in *Le Monde* (April 16, 1961). "One sees South Vietnam," he wrote from Saigon, which has since barred him, "by a strange and fascinating mimicry, borrow part of its methods from North Vietnam and China, and transform itself more and more into a bad copy of a Communist totalitarian regime." The desperate attempt to hide the truth about this hopeless but savage war is pulling our government in the same direction, toward the rewriting of history in an attempt to impose a party line myth on the press and public. Unless there is a counter campaign of pressure to bring home the truth, the war will drag on, poisoning the air of freedom at home, imposing misery on the bewildered people of South Vietnam and risking a wider conflagration.

OCTOBER 28, 1963

# WHAT IF THE PEOPLE, AFTER DIEM'S OVERTHROW, VOTE FOR PEACE?

The state of mind in Washington in the wake of Diem's overthrow was neatly mirrored in two statements, one before and one after the coup, by Congressman Zablocki (D. Wis.), just back from Vietnam as chairman of a Special Study Mission to Southeast Asia. The day before the coup Zablocki warned against an attempt to get rid of Diem. "The lesson of Cuba

must not be forgotten," he reported. "Batista was bad but
Castro is worse." After the coup Zablocki told the House the
U.S. should demand definite commitments for free elections
and vigorous prosecution of the war. But what if, in free
elections, the people were to vote for peace? Or for reunification with the North under Ho Chi Minh? Would we risk such
a verdict by allowing neutralist, anti-war or pro-communist
candidates?

The answer seemed obvious to the victorious generals. On
the one hand they said they would not set up a dictatorship
because they were "well aware that the best weapon to fight
communism is democracy and liberty." But in the very next
breath they also said that they would not allow "a disorderly
democratic regime." In Saigon a street rally calling for a neutralist government was forbidden and its banners torn down.
Censorship continues. Only prisoners the military regard as
non-communist are being released; only parties they regard as
non-communist will be allowed. In practice this means that if
there is to be a choice between democracy and continuance of
the war, it is democracy that will go.

This is the reality the pro-Kennedy liberals will not allow
themselves to see. Saigon is like Paris after the liberation; the
people dance in the streets. But the *Washington Post* (November 5) in a leading editorial thinks "the cause of freedom need
not sink with the passing of the old government!" This is Or-
wellianism with a vengeance. "The cause of freedom" is not
the Vietnamese desire for freedom from a U.S. supported
tyranny; "the cause of freedom" is soap advertising lingo for
continuation of cold and hot war. Yet the *Washington Post*
goes on sanctimoniously to say that Diem "refused to respond
to the feelings of his own people." The conservative *Washington Star's* editorial (November 4) was more honest. If the
people turn on a new government "force may have to be
used . . . we cannot be too squeamish." If the Vietnamese don't
want strategic hamlets, prison for those who oppose the war,
napalm on suspect villages, we'll back a new dictatorship. This
cabal of generals headed by a weak turncoat who has served
any and every regime foreign and domestic will bring neither
peace nor freedom to Vietnam.

In the case of Vietnam, as in that of Cuba, we need a Com-

mittee to agitate for a truly democratic foreign policy: peace
in Vietnam, lifting of the embargo that strangles hurricane-
ravaged Cuba. Can America's better conscience be mobilized?

NOVEMBER 11, 1963

# UNTESTED IN WAR BUT ALREADY
# A GENIUS AT FINANCE

A charming note of self-sacrifice was struck by South Vietnam's
new dictator, General Khanh, on his first visit to the countryside
to give out candy to the children, GI style, and establish his
"image" as just folks. He told junior officers in Ben Cat that
the men he overthrew were "unworthy" leaders "who spent
their time in night clubs flirting with girls!" He, on the other
hand "is now in a position to flee South Vietnam with $10
million and 'live an easy life—but I have chosen this one'." We
saw this account in the *New York Herald-Tribune* February 3.
All the other papers we read seem to have omitted this charming on-the-scene report. It may make readers wonder how a
minor general in a country like South Vietnam could spare
enough time from the task of fighting guerrillas night and day
to amass $10 million. Our new strong man may or may not turn
out to be much of a general, but he is already a success as a financier. Perhaps our psychological warfare corps can make good
use of this. We can see the posters going up in the most remote
villages, with the story: South Vietnam as a land of opportunity
under free enterprise, where the humblest village boy may

aspire to become a general and amass ten million bucks. We can safely double-dare Ho Chi Minh to try and match that one.

While this Horatio Alger hero was busy building up morale in the villages, we were happy to see that the *New York Times* led off its editorial page February 1 with a plea to utilize de Gaulle's initiative for a neutral solution in Vietnam like that originally intended (until Dulles upset it) by the 1954 Geneva settlement. The *Times* said there were few responsible officials in Washington "who, privately, would not be delighted to do just that." That same day, President Johnson at press conference indicated that if de Gaulle's proposal were to neutralize North as well as South Vietnam it would be "considered sympathetically." De Gaulle's proposal *is* to neutralize North as well as South Vietnam. Edgar Snow in a recent interview raised this question with Chou En-Lai without eliciting a direct refusal.[1] We believe the path to peace lies through a conference on Cambodia in which the two sides can feel each other out unofficially on Vietnam. The Vietnamese war is a blind alley which is destroying faith in our government not only there but at home. One day McNamara says the situation is grave; next day that we're making progress. The day after, in its weekly Vietnam report, the Pentagon's statistics show that the war is going worse than ever, while the latest news is that for the first time since 1959 the Viet Cong were bold enough to raid and bomb a U.S. military compound.

The biggest obstacle to a settlement is the myth that the South Vietnamese war is an invasion, not a rebellion. Secretary Rusk in his speech January 22 at the seventy-fifth anniversary of Barnard College trotted out this same stale official version. The dangerous corollary of the view that it was all a plot from outside is the reckless proposition that the way to end the fighting around Saigon is to bomb Hanoi. That way lies a new Korea or worse. Short of occupation by a major U.S. army, which the guerrillas can bog down for years as they did the French, there is no alternative to negotiation and neutralization. It is a pity more opinion-makers do not have the courage to say this aloud as did the *New York Times*.

FEBRUARY 10, 1964

[1] Complete text, *Washington Post*, February 3, 1964.

# WHEN A NATION'S LEADERS
# FEAR TO TELL THE TRUTH

Our emissary to Saigon, Secretary McNamara, seems to be as confused as he is confusing on the subject of the war in Vietnam. In January he made a statement which led people to believe that the U.S. was committed to total victory at any cost in that area. In his annual military posture statement January 27 to House Armed Services Committee he said "the survival of an independent government in South Vietnam is so important to the security of all Southeast Asia and to the free world that I can conceive of no alternative other than to take all necessary measures within our capability to prevent a communist victory." This led many to believe that the U.S. was ready to extend the war in order to win.

But under questioning by the committee in closed session, he took a very different position. Unfortunately this was not released until February 18 and was buried in more than 1,000 pages of testimony. The first time the matter came up was when Congressman Stratton (D., N.Y.) asked him, "Wouldn't you say that in the event that things do not go as well as you hope they will, that unquestionably we can't continue to withdraw any more of our forces?" This elicited a surprising answer. "No, sir; I would not," McNamara replied, "I don't believe that we as a nation should assume the primary responsibility for the war in South Vietnam. It is a counter-guerrilla war, it is a war that can only be won by the Vietnamese themselves." When Congressman Cohelan (D., Cal.) said he wanted to be sure "we are very conscious of other options that we might have to exercise if things were not going quite the way we want it," the Secretary answered, "It is the unsatisfactory character of most of those other options that leads me personally to conclude we should continue our program in South Vietnam." Among the other "options" of course is to widen the war by an attack on North Vietnam which might bring the Chinese in.

Later Congressman Pike (D., N.Y.) said he was "concerned with what I think to be a conflict between what we say about the importance of this area and what we actually propose to do about it." McNamara replied, "Well, I think they are in agreement and it goes back to the point I made earlier, that only the Vietnamese can win this war." He said it wasn't "artillery shells but the confidence of the peasants" that would "ultimately determine the outcome of the war" and he added that "doubling our military aid would not, in my opinion, substantially increase the effectiveness of their military operations." The question was raised again and elicited an even clearer answer later in these closed hearings:

> *Mr. Long (D. Md.):* If the Vietnamese war goes very badly, do you contemplate another Korean war from our point of view, our pouring in hundreds of thousands of troops?
> *Secretary McNamara:* No, sir.
> *Mr. Long:* You mentioned before that this is an area we must hold at all costs?
> *Secretary McNamara:* I don't believe that pouring in hundreds of thousands of troops is the solution to the problem in Vietnam.

These answers were supplemented by an even more sober reply from Army Chief of Staff General Wheeler to Mr. Becker (R., N.Y.). "It would seem to me," Mr. Becker said, "that in South Vietnam, and through North Vietnam and these other areas they [the Chinese] can *keep sending them in for years* (italics added), and eventually the South Vietnamese, no matter how much they may desire to save their own country, eventually are going to be weakened to the point where they can no longer do it." The basic fallacy here lies in the words we have italicized. It is that the South Vietnamese war is an invasion, somehow run by the Chinese, when it is actually a rebellion by the South Vietnamese themselves. The contrary was implied in General Wheeler's reply:

> If we can ever get the Government leaders of South Vietnam in control of their territory and their own people—that is if the Government leaders identify themselves to the people as being the protectors of the population, advancing their interests politically, economically, sociologically and every other way—there won't be any way for the enemy to infiltrate, because guerrillas have to live among the people. Guerrillas can't survive unless the people hide them. Mao Tse-tung has a thesis that goes something like this—guerrillas hide among the population as the fish hide in the sea. This is a very true adage. Now, as I say, if the South Vietnamese government can ever achieve this degree of control of their own territory and people, you will have no guerrilla problem. There will be a threat and this will be the threat of the regular North Vietnamese forces, backed by the Chinese. However this is an entirely different problem than the one we are faced with today.

This clear-sighted view is characteristic of the Army. General Wheeler's predecessor as Chief of Staff, General Ridgeway, threw his weight on similar grounds against intervention in the same area when it was advocated by Dulles, Nixon and Radford in 1954. Unfortunately this realistic estimate was given in closed hearings and is buried in a voluminous record. It is out of harmony with the demonological views impressed on American thinking by cold war propaganda. This has led us to see the Vietnamese uprising simply as a communist plot, and communism as an occult conspiracy with magical powers whereby a handful of infiltrating agitators can "infect" a whole population with Marxism-Leninism though these same natives can barely read the directions on a can of soup. It then seems logical to infer that this infection (like witchcraft) can only be stopped by burning out its source in Peking whence these diabolic subversives fan out like a corps of Fausts to seduce all these maiden minds.

The basic problem is not in Vietnam but in the USA. So long as these melodramatic nightmares color so much of American political thinking, there will be demands for extension of the war, though we can smash all North Vietnam and China with nuclear bombs without making the peasants in the

Mekong Valley any more content with the corrupt and repressive governments we have maintained in power over them. This is no doubt what Secretary Rusk meant when he said cryptically February 27 that "no miracle" in the North would solve the problem in the South. But such remarks are made *sotto voce*. Into the headlines which mold the public mind Rusk and McNamara continue to pour a picture of the conflict as an invasion from the North, supplied by arms from China. So long as they fear to tell the truth about the war, they cannot free themselves from the undertow pulling them toward its suicidal extension.

MARCH 16, 1964

# WHAT FEW KNOW ABOUT THE
# TONKIN BAY INCIDENTS

The American government and the American press have kept the full truth about the Tonkin Bay incidents from the American public. Let us begin with the retaliatory bombing raids on North Vietnam. When I went to New York to cover the UN Security Council debate on the affair, UN correspondents at lunch recalled cynically that four months earlier Adlai Stevenson told the Security Council the U.S. had "repeatedly expressed" its emphatic disapproval "of retaliatory raids, wherever they occur and by whomever they are committed." But none mentioned this in their dispatches.

On that occasion, last April, the complaint was brought by

Yemen against Britain. The British, in retaliation for attacks from Yemen into the British protectorate of Aden, decided to strike at the "privileged sanctuary" from which the raids were coming. The debate then might have been a preview of the Vietnamese affair. The British argued that their reprisal raid was justified because the fort they attacked at Harib was "a center for subversive and aggressive activities across the border." The Yemeni Republicans in turn accused the British of supporting raids into Yemen by the Yemeni Royalists. "Obviously," Stevenson said, "it is most difficult to determine precisely what has been happening on the remote frontiers of Southern Arabia." But he thought all UN members could "join in expressing our disapproval of the use of force by either side as a means of solving disputes, a principle that is enshrined in the Charter," especially when such "attacks across borders" could "quickly escalate into full-scale wars." The outcome was a resolution condemning "reprisals as incompatible with the purposes and principles of the United Nations." That resolution and Stevenson's words are as applicable to Southeast Asia as to Southern Arabia. Though the Czech delegate cited them in his speech to the Council on August 7 about the Vietnamese affair, no word of this appeared in the papers next day.

In the August 7 debate, only Nationalist China and Britain supported the U.S. reprisal raids. The French privately recalled the international uproar over the raid they had made under similar circumstances in February, 1958, into the "privileged sanctuary" afforded the Algerian rebels by Tunisia. They struck at the Sakiet-Sidi-Youssef camp just across the border. Senators Kennedy, Humphrey, Morse and Knowland denounced the raid and Eisenhower warned the French the U.S. would not be able to defend their action in the Security Council.

Reprisals in peacetime were supposed to have been outlawed by the League of Nations Covenant, the Kellogg Pact and the United Nations Charter. All of them pledged peaceful settlement of disputes. Between nations, as between men, reprisals are lynch law. Some White House ghost writer deserves a literary booby prize for the mindless jingle he turned out to defend ours in Vietnam. "The world remembers, the world must never forget," were the words he supplied for Johnson's speech at Syracuse, "that aggression unchallenged is aggression unleashed." This gem of prose is a pretty babble. What the world (and particularly the White House) needs to remember is that aggression is unleashed and escalated when one party to a dispute decides for itself who is guilty and how he is to be punished. This is what is happening in Cyprus, where we have been begging Greeks and Turks to desist from the murderous escalation of reprisal and counter-reprisal. Johnson practices in Southeast Asia what he deplores in the Mediterranean.

Public awareness of this is essential because the tide is running strongly toward more reprisal raids in the Far East. The first was the raid by U.S. Navy planes in June on Pathet Lao headquarters in Laos in retaliation for shooting down two reconnaissance planes. We would not hesitate to shoot down reconnaissance planes over our own territory; such overflights are a clear violation of international law. But the U.S. now seems to operate on the principle that invasion of other people's skies is our right, and efforts to interfere with it (at least by weaker powers) punishable by reprisal. This is pure "might is right" doctrine.

The very day we took the Vietnamese affair to the Security Council, Cambodia illustrated a sardonic point to be found in Schwarzenberger's *Manual of International Law*—"military reprisals are open only to the strong against the weak." The UN distributed to Security Council members the latest in a series of complaints from Cambodia that U.S. and South Vietnamese forces had been violating its borders. It alleged that at dawn on July 31 "elements of the armed forces of the Republic of Vietnam, among them Americans in uniform," opened fire "with automatic weapons and mortars," seriously wounding a peasant and killing a bull. If Cambodia could only afford a fleet large enough, we suppose it would be justified by Johnsonian standards in lobbing a few shells into the U.S.A.

Even in wartime, reprisals are supposed to be kept within narrow limits. Hackworth's *Digest*, the State Department's huge Talmud of international law, quotes an old War Department manual, *Rules of Land Warfare*, as authoritative on the subject. This says reprisals are never to be taken "merely for revenge" but "only as an unavoidable last resort" to "enforce the recognized rules of civilized warfare." Even then reprisals "should not be excessive or exceed the degree of violence committed by the enemy." These were the principles we applied at the Nuremberg trials. Our reprisal raids on North Vietnam hardly conformed to these standards. By our own account, in self-defense, we had already sunk three or four attacking torpedo boats in two incidents. In neither were our ships damaged nor any of our men hurt; indeed, one bullet imbedded in one destroyer hull is the only proof we have been able to muster that the second of the attacks even took place. To fly sixty-four bombing sorties in reprisal over four North Vietnamese bases and an oil depot, destroying or damaging twenty-five North Vietnamese PT boats, a major part of that tiny navy, was hardly punishment to fit the crime. What was our hurry? Why did we have to shoot from the hip and then go to the Security Council? Who was Johnson trying to impress? Ho Chi Minh? Or Barry Goldwater?

This is how it looks on the basis of our own public accounts. It looks worse if one probes behind them. Here we come to the questions raised by Morse of Oregon on the Senate floor August 5 and 6 during debate on the resolution giving Johnson a pre-dated declaration of war in Southeast Asia. Morse was speaking on the basis of information given in executive session by Secretaries Rusk and McNamara to a joint session of the Senate Committee on Foreign Relations and Armed Services. Morse said he was not justifying the attacks on U.S. ships in the Bay of Tonkin but "as in domestic criminal law," he added, "crimes are sometimes committed under provocation" and this "is taken into account by a wise judge in imposing sentence."

Morse revealed that U.S. warships were on patrol in Tonkin Bay nearby during the shelling of two islands off the North Vietnamese coast on Friday, July 31, by South Vietnamese vessels. Morse said our warships were within three to eleven miles of North Vietnamese territory, at the time, although North Vietnam claims a twelve-mile limit. Morse declared that the U.S. "knew that the bombing was going to take place." He noted that General Khanh had been demanding escalation of the war to the North and said that with this shelling of the islands it was escalated. Morse declared the attack was made "by South Vietnamese naval vessels—not by junks but by armed vessels of the PT boat type" given to South Vietnam as part of U.S. military aid. Morse said it was not just another attempt to infiltrate agents but "a well thought-out military operation." Morse charged that the presence of our warships in the proximity "where they could have given protection, if it became necessary" was "bound to be looked upon by our enemies as an act of provocation." The press, which dropped an Iron Curtain weeks ago on the anti-war speeches of Morse and Gruening, ignored this one, too.

Yet a reading of the debate will show that Fulbright and Russell, the chairmen of the two committees Rusk and McNamara had briefed in secret session, did not deny Morse's facts in their defense of the Administration and did not meet the issue he raised. Fulbright's replies to questions were hardly a model of frankness. When Ellender of Louisiana asked him at whose request we were patrolling in the Bay of Tonkin, Fulbright replied:

> These are international waters. Our assistance to South Vietnam is at the request of the South Vietnamese government. The particular measures we may take in connection with that request is our own responsibility.

Senator Nelson of Wisconsin wanted to know how close to the shore our ships had been patrolling:

> *Mr. Fulbright:* It was testified that they went in at least eleven miles in order to show that we do not recognize a twelve-mile limit, which I believe North Vietnam has asserted.
>
> *Mr. Nelson:* The patrolling was for the purpose of demonstrating to the North Vietnamese that we did not recognize a twelve-mile limit?
>
> *Mr. Fulbright:* That was one reason given . . .
>
> *Mr. Nelson:* It would be mighty risky if Cuban PT boats were firing on Florida, for Russian armed ships or destroyers to be patrolling between us and Cuba, eleven miles out.

When Ellender asked whether our warships were there to protect the South Vietnamese vessels shelling the islands, Fulbright replied:

> The ships were not assigned to protect anyone. They were conducting patrol duty. The question was asked specifically of the highest authority, the Secretary of Defense and the Secretary of State. They stated without equivocation that these ships, the

*Maddox* and the *C. Turner Joy*, were not on convoy duty. They had no connection whatever with any Vietnamese ships that might have been operating in the same general area.

Fulbright did not deny that both destroyers were in the area at the time of the July 31 shelling and inside the territorial limits claimed by North Vietnam. He did not deny Morse's charge that the U.S. knew about the shelling of the islands before it took place. He merely denied that the warships were there to cover the operation in any way. Our warships, according to the official account, just happened to be hanging around. Morse's point—which neither Fulbright nor Russell challenged—was that they had no business to be in an area where an attack was about to take place, that this was bound to appear provocative. Indeed the only rational explanation for their presence at the time was that the Navy was looking for trouble, daring the North Vietnamese to do something about it.

Morse made another disclosure. "I think I violate no privilege or secrecy," he declared, "if I say that subsequent to the bombing, and apparently because there was some concern about the intelligence that we were getting, our ships took out to sea." Was this intelligence that the ships were about to be attacked within the territorial waters claimed by North Vietnam? Morse said our warships went out to sea and "finally, on Sunday, the PT boats were close enough for the first engagement to take place." This dovetails with a curious answer given by Senator Russell at another point in the debate to Senator Scott of Pennsylvania when the latter asked whether Communist China had not published a series of warnings (as required by international law) against violations of the twelve-mile limit. Russell confirmed this but said, "I might add that our vessels had turned away from the North Vietnamese shore and were making for the middle of the gulf, *where there could be no question,* at the time they were attacked."

The italics are ours and call attention to an evident uneasiness about our legal position. The uneasiness is justified. A great many questions of international law are raised by the presence of our warships within an area claimed by another country as its territorial waters while its shores were being shelled by ships we supplied to a satellite power. There is, first of all, some doubt as to whether warships have a right of "innocent passage" through territorial waters even under peaceful circumstances. There is, secondly, the whole question of territorial limits. The three-mile limit was set some centuries ago by the range of a cannon shot. It has long been obsolete but is favored by nations with large navies. We make the three-mile limit the norm when it suits our purposes but widen it when we need to. We claim another 9 miles as "contiguous waters" in which we can enforce our laws on foreign ships. While our planes on reconnaissance operate three miles off other people's shores, we enforce an Air Defense Identification Zone on our own coasts, requiring all planes to identify themselves when two hours out. In any case, defense actions may be taken beyond territorial limits. The law as cited in the U. S. Naval Academy's handbook, *International Law for Sea-Going Officers*, is that "the right of a nation to protect itself from injury" is "not restrained to territorial limits . . . It may watch its coast and seize ships that are approaching it with an intention to violate its laws. It is not obliged to wait until the offense is consummated before it can act."

More important in this case is the doctrine of "hot pursuit." The North Vietnamese radio claims that in the first attack it chased the U.S. warships away from its shores. "The right of hot pursuit," says Schwarzenberger's *Manual of International Law*, "is the right to continue the pursuit of a ship from the territorial sea into the high sea." The logic of this, our Naval Academy handbook explains, is that "the offender should not go free simply because of the proximity of the high seas." It is easy to imagine how fully these questions would be aired if we spotted Russian ships hanging around in our waters while Cuban PT boats shelled Key West. Our actions hardly fit Johnson's description of himself to the American Bar Association as a champion of world law.

There are reasons to believe that the raids at the end of July marked a new step-up in the scale of South Vietnamese operations against the North. These have been going on for some time. In fact, a detailed account in *Le Monde* (August 7) says they began three years before the rebellion broke out in South Vietnam. Ever since January of this year the U.S. press has been full of reports that we were planning to move from infiltration and commando operations to overt attacks against the North. *Newsweek* (March 9) discussed a "Rostow Plan No. 6" for a naval blockade of Haiphong, North Vietnam's main port, to be followed by PT boat raids on North Vietnamese coastal installations and then by strategic bombing raids. In the middle of July the North Vietnamese radio reported that the U.S. had given South Vietnam 500 "river landing ships" and four small warships from our mine sweeping fleet. A dispatch from Hong Kong in the *New York Times* (August 14) quoted an "informed source" as saying that the North Vietnamese had concealed the fact "that the shelling of the islands" on July 31 "had been directed at a sensitive radar installation." The shelling of radar installations would look from the other side like a prelude to a landing attempt.

These circumstances cast a very different light on the *Maddox* affair, but very few Americans are aware of them. The process of brain-washing the public starts with off-the-record briefings for newspapermen in which all sorts of far-fetched theories are suggested to explain why the tiny North Vietnamese navy would be mad enough to venture an attack on the Seventh Fleet, one of the world's most powerful. *Everything is discussed except the possibility that the attack might have been provoked.* In this case the "information agencies," i.e. the propaganda apparatus of the government, handed out two versions, one for domestic, the other for foreign consumption. The image created at home was that the U.S. had manfully hit back at an unprovoked attack—no paper tiger we. On the other hand, friendly foreign diplomats were told that the South Vietnamese had pulled a raid on the coast and we had been forced to back them up. As some of the truth began to trickle out, the information agencies fell back on the theory that maybe the North Vietnamese had "miscalculated." That our warships may have been providing cover for an escalation in raiding activities never got through to public consciousness at all.

The two attacks themselves are still shrouded in mystery. The *Maddox* claims to have fired three warning shots across the bow of her pursuers; three warning shots are used to make a merchantman heave-to for inspection. A warship would take this as the opening of fire, not as a warning signal. The North Vietnamese radio admitted the first encounter but claimed its patrol boats chased the *Maddox* out of territorial waters. The second alleged attack North Vietnam calls a fabrication. It is strange that though we claim three boats sunk, we picked up no flotsam and jetsam as proof from the wreckage. Nor have any pictures been provided. Whatever the true story, the second incident seems to have triggered off a long planned attack of our own. There are some reasons to doubt that it was merely that "measured response" against PT bases it was advertised to be. Bernard Fall, author of *The Two Viet-Nams*, who knows the area well, pointed out in the *Washington Post* August 9 that "none of the targets attacked" in the reprisal raids "was previously known as a regular port or base area. Hon-Gay, for example, was one of the largest open-pit coal mining operations in Asia, if not the world." Was this one of the strategic industrial targets in Rostow's "Plan No. 6"?

AUGUST 24, 1964

# LIKE A BAR-ROOM BRAWL
# WITH THE LIGHTS OUT

It is not surprising that Secretary McNamara abruptly shut off his press conference on the latest Tonkin Bay incident so he would not have to answer questions. The U.S. has never engaged in a more obscure bit of brinkmanship. The *Washington Post* (September 20) in reporting the White House reactions said President Johnson "believes that history might have turned out differently if Kaiser Wilhelm and Chancellor Adolf Hitler had not made miscalculations about the U.S." The parallel is doubly unfortunate. Germany twice precipitated world wars by a "right is might" policy ours has begun to resemble. The Germans did indeed miscalculate U.S. reaction, but that miscalculation was a simple affair. Then Berlin did not know what Washington would do. Here we have a situation in which Washington itself does not know what it's doing. Neither Washington nor Moscow nor Peking nor Hanoi can calculate clearly because none of them seem sure of what happened. We say we shot at some blips on a radar screen; Peking and Hanoi say, in substance, that nothing at all happened; and Moscow says we sank three ships. Now Washington says it thinks maybe we did. This is beginning to resemble a barroom brawl with the lights out.

Last time our Navy at least claimed to have heard and seen gun flashes. This time the whole encounter took place on the radar screens. We don't seem to know what the hostile blips were, or what happened to them. According to Mr. Johnson's press conference of September 21, when the early reports came in some persons had urged rapid retaliation again, as after the alleged attack on August 5, which Peking and Hanoi also say never happened. Fortunately Mr. Johnson said he preferred to wait until daylight when the situation could be better understood and evaluated. One more swift reprisal raid like the last one, and it would have been hard to tell from the blips on the political radar screen whether that was Johnson or Goldwater shooting from the hip again. McNamara may have fled that press conference because answers to, or unwillingness to answer, certain questions might have been embarrassing. He might also have fled lest the press discover that he, too, didn't know the answers. It's not news that the American people long ago lost touch with what is really happening in Vietnam. It's painful to discover that their leaders aren't sure either.

In the last Tonkin Bay incidents the alibi was that while the CIA knew, it failed to let the Navy know, that attacks were being made on the North Vietnamese coast while our destroyers cruised nearby. After that incident, it was announced that our patrols were being removed from the Bay of Tonkin but that we reserved the right to resume them later. Now again the AP from Washington (*Baltimore Sun,* September 22) carries the news, "The two-destroyer patrol involved in last Friday's shooting incident has been withdrawn from the Gulf of Tonkin, informed sources said tonight. The patrol was finished on schedule, they said, and it is indefinite when another will go into the gulf . . ." Was this the first patrol since the August 5 affair? [1] Were any covert operations scheduled at the same time by the South Vietnamese, using the naval vessels we have given them? How does North Vietnamese radar distinguish U.S. naval vessels when under U.S. command from the same vessels when under South Vietnamese control? Do U.S. patrols engage in reconnaissance which pinpoints radar and coastal defense installations along the North Vietnamese coast and is this information then turned over to the South Vietnamese to help them in raiding activities? If Russian or Chinese destroyers prowled the Florida coast while ships they supplied Castro engaged in coastal raids, what would we do? Send hampers of Florida grapefruit to their skippers?

We may have double electronic locks on our nuclear weapons but we seem to have less and less control over our own and our puppet forces in Vietnam though these could spark off a wider war. The situation in South Vietnam is falling apart so quickly that one suspects it is too fast for the Vietcong as well as ourselves. Divisional capitals are left unguarded—and yet are not taken over—as commanding generals move their troops on Saigon to see if they can emerge as the new "strong men" or at least get themselves another star on their shoulder straps as consolation prizes. The indifference of the populace in Saigon was the most striking feature of the abortive coup. The country is sick of war and sick of us, especially of our habit of napalming and machine-gunning whole villages to get at a few suspected guerrillas. Behind the Catholic-Buddhist feud is a division between Catholic extremists anxious to carry on the war at any cost and Buddhists who want restoration of civilian gov-

[1] "Navy chiefs," said the Washington wire of the *Wall Street Journal* September 4, "plan to send another sea patrol into the Gulf of Tonkin soon. It will resemble the force that encountered North Vietnamese attacks in early August. Officers talk of the plan as just another reconnaissance mission. But it could test Red belligerency afresh." Was this advance leak part of a war of nerves?

ernment and a cease-fire. The most dangerous element in the situation are those military men who see a widening of the war as the only way to prevent a negotiated peace. One of these is the young Air Force Commander and playboy, Nguyen Cao Ky, to whom Khanh owes his survival. In an interview with *Le Monde* (September 17) Ky advocated extension of the war to the North and when asked whether the Americans would permit this declared angrily, "I can order and carry out these operations at any time," and cut off the interview. This is the new power behind the collapsing throne in Saigon.

Our puppets have a way of making us dance to their strings. It would be well to be on guard against provocations or phony news stories designed to provoke or excuse what these light-headed desperadoes want. In this category is the story from Saigon in the *New York Times* (September 22) quoting "reliable military sources" as saying that South Vietnamese forces had inflicted heavy casualties on two companies of North Vietnamese who had crossed over the demilitarized zone that separates the two parts of Vietnam. The AP (*Baltimore Sun*, September 22) treated this more circumspectly as a "possibility" that U.S. authorities were investigating. Why should North Vietnam risk an invasion and a U.S. attack when the collapse of the South Vietnamese government and a negotiated peace may be in sight?

SEPTEMBER 28, 1964

# WHAT A LITTLE LANOLIN D CAN
# DO FOR THAT WAR IN VIETNAM

We sat in at our TV the evening of September 10 on the beginning of a new ABC series called *Letters from Vietnam* about
"The Daring American." The program, if not the war, seemed
to be self-sustaining. It was sponsored by Purex, the cleanser
with the woman's touch; Instant Fels, with that built-in fabric
softener; Trend, with the tiny suds, so much better than the big
bubbles; and Sweetheart Soap, which makes elegance afford-
able today. Part of the hour long program permitted us to
listen in as a U. S. Army lieutenant talked into a dictaphone for
his absent wife those "letters from Vietnam" which gave the
program its name. Part of the program permitted us to sit in on
battle scenes which lived up to the advance billing, "Specially
mounted cameras on combat helicopters take you into battle,
show you what it's like to come within a hair of being shot
down on a rescue mission." It's a new sensation in warfare to
know that you're going into battle with TV cameras trained on
you for the folks back home, and that if you're wounded the
whole country will see it, unless you have the misfortune of
being hit during the commercial.

It was nice to be assured that our soldiers don't take the war
as personal. The lieutenant explained to his wife on the dictaphone that to our fighting men the Viet Cong are "vermin,
they're not human, so you don't worry about it as you shoot
them up." The finer feelings, like the finer hands in washing
with Purex, are not calloused. In another memorable scene we

could watch a village being shot up from the air. The announcer explained, "the VC got his back a thousand fold—a return designed to make VC even more unpopular in the countryside." Without this explanation, shooting up a whole village because we suspected a few guerrillas were hidden in it might be regarded as making us a little unpopular in the countryside, too. "We may sometimes kill women and children inadvertently," the lieutenant wrote his wife that night, "but never on purpose." Then he added what seemed to us a dangerous thought, that he supposed the VC have a family, too. A later sequence, to demonstrate his kindly feelings, showed the lieutenant visiting an orphanage in Saigon. As the orphans waved good-bye, the painful scene merged into a happy commercial, with American children playing about their mother, her hands protected against dryness by Gentle Fels soap, which contains Lanolin D, "nature's own skin conditioner to make your work easier." We hope the Vietnamese war can be kept going until this series is completed. It shows how smoothly a war can be fought, with a little Lanolin D.

The war may not be going as well as we would like it from a military point of view, but with this series we have hit our stride when it comes to merchandising it. The war is at last being packaged properly, and it's the package which makes the sale. The U. S. Army has achieved a break-through.

SEPTEMBER 21, 1964

# A WORD OF GOOD ADVICE
# FROM MAO TSE-TUNG

At the Special Warfare school in Fort Bragg, Mao's manual on guerrilla warfare is regarded as an indispensable handbook for combatting "wars of liberation," almost as if it were a captured secret document, which discloses the plans and tactics of the other side. If the military find Mao so rewarding, we poor civilians may hardly be blamed for taking him seriously, too, and we are glad that the *New Republic* in its issue of February 27 [1] is printing the full text of Edgar Snow's interview with the leader of the Chinese Revolution. The most important word of advice in it is the one most likely to go unheeded.

The bit of caution to which we refer comes at a timely moment. The most important casualty of the reprisal raids after Pleiku is the collapse of the hopes that our military, and certain New Frontier intellectuals like W. W. Rostow, had attached to counter-guerrilla warfare. The decision to bomb North Vietnam confessed that after four years of try-out in South Vietnam, their counter-guerrilla theories had failed; the guerrillas were stronger, better armed, enjoyed more popular support and controlled more territory than when our intervention began in 1961. The reprisal bombings marked a shift back

[1] A substantial but incomplete text was published by the *Washington Post* Feb. 14. Abroad it appeared in West Germany's *Stern* (Feb. 21), the *London Sunday Times* (Feb. 14) and *Le Nouveau Candide* in Paris (Feb. 18). The last provided an uncut version. It is a pity it got wider circulation abroad than in the United States where an understanding of the Chinese viewpoint is most needed.

to the simplistic theory that "wars of revolution" are operated by remote control from Hanoi, Moscow or Peking. We are now prepared to escalate back to John Foster Dulles's "massive retaliation" if these distant sorcerers do not call off their annoying apprentices. Mao told Snow that he had read General Maxwell Taylor's book, *The Uncertain Trumpet,* and some of the U.S. anti-guerrilla manuals which sought to apply Mao's ideas in reverse. Their weakness, Mao told Snow, is that they ignore "the decisive political fact that . . . governments cut off from the masses could not win against wars of liberation."

Reprisal raids are no substitute for popular support; they merely deepen the revulsion and widen the area of conflict. What would we do with the "Pleiku doctrine" in the Congolese civil war, Dr. Bernard Fall, the author of *The Two Viet-Nams,* asked the other day. Will we bomb Algeria and Egypt for supplying the rebels? Latin America, where we have been training the local military and gendarmerie in "special warfare," may soon provide a reductio ad absurdum of the reprisal doctrine. What if a revolt breaks out in Brazil against the military dictatorship we helped to impose on that huge country? Will we threaten to bomb Havana, Moscow or Peking unless the desperate peasants of the Northeast march back to the plantations with their hungry bellies rumbling?

The failure to grasp Mao's point in South Vietnam does not arise from any special stupidity. The trouble is that the situation there has degenerated to the point where any government which was *not* cut off from the masses would respond to their war-weariness. It would open negotiations with the rebels and ask our troops to leave. It has proven so hard to form a new government because it becomes ever harder to find political figures willing to continue the war. In our latest effort to provide some cover for a naked military dictatorship we have had to fall back on men to the right of the late Ngo Dinh Diem. Diem's earlier reputation was based on his refusal to serve as a puppet for the French. The three leading figures in the latest regime in Saigon were all collaborators in the years when Diem preferred an honorable exile in America. The new Prime Minister, Pham Huy Quat, was Minister of National Defense in the Bao Dai regime from 1950 until the French defeat in 1954. This is hardly a testimonial to his prowess or his patriotism. Of the three Vice Premiers, two of them were also Ministers in the Bao Dai regime.[2] The Dai Viet party to which the new Premier belongs is a party of the far right, expansionist and fascistic. The day he took office troops fired on demonstrators demanding peace. We can empty every bomb load in the Seventh Fleet on North Vietnam but it won't make this regime any more popular in the South. This is the dead-end street of which Mao's words would warn us.

Snow's interview with Mao is given additional interest by another casualty of the Pleiku reprisal raids. They killed the hope, perceptible in some quarters of the Administration, that the Russians would get us off the hook in South Vietnam without our having to negotiate with the Chinese. In the long run, in any case, no stable settlement is possible in an area so close to China without taking Peking's wishes into account. It is as if the Chinese and Russians between them were to try and determine the destiny of Mexico without consulting Washington. The U.S. has a Monroe Doctrine; the Russians insist on friendly neighbors; neither can logically deny similar geographical spheres of influence to Peking. But can we negotiate with China? Snow interviewed Mao on January 9, just about the time Washington was full of inspired stories that an attempt to sound out the Chinese had evoked only an arrogant reply: first the U.S. must withdraw its troops and then China would see what could be done. Just where these stories originated is not known but they are hardly borne out by what Mao said to Snow. The Chinese leader was neither bellicose nor dogmatic; he expressed the hope of improved relations with the U.S. He said peace could be negotiated before an American withdrawal or after "or a conference might be held but U.S. troops might stay around Saigon, as in the case of South Korea." The U.S. would be better off *out*, but this at least offers face-saving possibilities (how Oriental we are all becoming!) which would seem to be worth exploring. It's easier to drop bombs than talk peace, but LBJ's favorite Biblical admonition, if we recall correctly, is not "come and let us throw bombs together."

FEBRUARY 16, 1965

[2] Paris *Figaro*, February 15, 1965.

# A REPLY TO THE WHITE PAPER

That North Vietnam supports the guerrillas in South Vietnam is no more a secret than that the United States supports the South Vietnamese government against them. The striking thing about the State Department's new White Paper is how little support it can prove. "Incontrovertible evidence of Hanoi's elaborate program to supply its forces in the South with weapons, ammunition and other supplies," the White Paper says, "has accumulated over the years." A detailed presentation of this evidence is in Appendix D; unfortunately few will see the appendices since even the *New York Times* did not reprint them, though these are more revealing than the report. Appendix D provides a list of weapons, ammunition and other supplies of Chinese Communist, Soviet, Czech and North Vietnamese manufacture, with the dates and place of capture from the Viet Cong guerrillas, over the eighteen-month period from June, 1962, to January 29 last year, when it was presented to the International Control Commission. The commission was set up by the Geneva agreement of 1954. This list provides a good point at which to begin an analysis of the White Paper.

To put the figures in perspective, we called the Pentagon press office and obtained some figures the White Paper does not supply—the number of weapons captured from the guerrillas and the number lost to them in recent years:

| | Captured From Guerrillas | Lost to Them |
|---|---|---|
| 1962 | 4,800 | 5,200 |
| 1963 | 5,400 | 8,500 |
| 1964 | 4,900 | 13,700 |
| 3-Year Total | 15,100 | 27,400 |

In three years, the guerrillas captured from our side 12,300 more weapons than they lost to us.

What interests us at the moment is not this favorable balance but the number of guerrilla weapons our side captured during the past three years. The grand total was 15,100. If Hanoi has indeed engaged in an "elaborate program" to supply the Viet Cong, one would expect a substantial number of enemy-produced weapons to turn up. Here is the sum total of enemy-produced weapons and supplies in that eighteen-month tally to the Control Commission—

```
 72 rifles (46 Soviet, 26 Czech)
 64 submachine guns (40 Czech, 24 French but "modified"
      in North Vietnam)
 15 carbines (Soviet)
  8 machine guns (6 Chinese, 2 North Vietnamese)
  5 pistols (4 Soviet, 1 Czech)
  4 mortars (Chinese)
  3 recoilless 75 mm. rifles (Chinese)
  3 recoilless 57 mm. guns (Chinese)
  2 bazookas (1 Chinese, 1 Czech)
  2 rocket launchers (Chinese)
  1 grenade launcher (Czech)
179 total
```

This is not a very impressive total. According to the Pentagon figures, we captured on the average 7,500 weapons each eighteen months in the past three years. If only 179 communist-made weapons turned up in eighteen months, that is less than 2½ per cent of the total. Judging by these White Paper figures, our military are wrong in estimating, as they have in recent months, that 80 per cent of the weapons used by the guerrillas are captured from us. It looks as if the proportion is considerably higher. The material of North Vietnamese origin included only those twenty-four French sub-machine guns "modified" in North Vietnam, two machine guns made in North Vietnam, sixteen helmets, a uniform and an undisclosed number of mess kits, belts, sweaters and socks. Judging by this tally, the main retaliatory blow should be at North Vietnam's clothing factories.

There is another way to judge this tally of captured communist weapons. A communist battalion has about 450 men. It needs 500 rifles, four 80 mm. mortars, eight 60 mm. mortars and at least four recoilless rifles. The weapons of communist origin captured in eighteen months would not adequately outfit one battalion. The figures in the appendix on ammunition captured provides another index. We captured 183 (Chinese) shells for a 60 mm. mortar. This fires about twenty shells a minute, so that was hardly enough ammunition for ten minutes of firing. There were 100,000 (Chinese) cartridges for 7.26 mm. machine guns. That looks impressive until one discovers on checking with knowledgeable military sources that these machine guns fire 600 rounds a minute. A machine gun platoon normally has four machine guns. This was enough ammunition for about forty minutes of firing by one platoon. Indeed, if the ratio of communist-made weapons captured is the same for weapons used, then only twelve and a half days of those eighteen months were fought by the guerrillas on the basis of communist-made supplies.

If these figures were being presented in a court of law, they would run up against a further difficulty: one would have to prove the arms actually came from the communist side. There is a worldwide market in second-hand weapons. One can buy Soviet, Czech and Chinese Communist weapons of all kinds only two miles or so from the Pentagon at Interarmco, Ltd., 7 Prince Street, Alexandria, Virginia. Interarmco, one of the world's foremost dealers, can provide more communist weapons than we picked up in eighteen months on Vietnamese battlefields. Interarmco's East European Communist weapons come in large part from the huge stocks of Soviet and Czech arms captured by the Israelis in the Suez campaign. It has Chinese Communist weapons captured by our side in the

Korean war. It also has, of course, a wide selection of our own military surplus. This has turned up in strange places.

For example, a book on the Algerian war, *Les Algeriens en guerre,* by Dominique Darbois and Phillippe Vingneau, was published in Milan in 1960 by Feltrinelli. It shows pictures of FLN (National Liberation Front) Algerian rebels wearing U.S. Marine Corps uniforms from which the "USM" and the eagle and globe insignia have not even been removed. It shows Algerians carry U.S. 80 mm. mortars and U.S. .50 calibre machine guns. Such photos could have been used by France to accuse the U.S. of supplying the Algerian rebels.

The State Department's White Paper says "dramatic new proof was exposed just as this report was being completed" in the discovery of a suspected Viet Cong arms cargo ship on February 16. The *New York Times* commented astringently on this in an editorial February 28—

> Apparently, the major new evidence of a need for escalating the war, with all the hazard that this entails, was provided by the sinking in a South Vietnamese cove earlier this month of a 100-ton cargo ship loaded with Communist-made small arms and ammunition. A ship of that size is not much above the Oriental junk class. The standard Liberty or Victory ship of World War II had a capacity of 7,150 to 7,650 tons.

The affair of the cargo ship is curious. Until now there has been little evidence of arms coming in by ship. A huge fleet of small vessels patrols the coast and there have been glowing stories in the past of its efficiency. "About 12,000 vessels," the AP reported from Saigon (*New York Times,* February 22), "are searched each month by the South Vietnamese coastal junk patrol force but arrests are rare and no significant amounts of incriminating goods or weapons ever have been found." This lone case of a whole shipload of arms is puzzling.

The White Paper's story on the influx of men from the North also deserves a closer analysis than the newspapers have given it. Appendix C provides an elaborate table from 1959–60 to 1964 inclusive, showing the number of "confirmed" military infiltrees per year from the North. The total is given as 19,550. One way to measure this number is against that of the military we have assigned to South Vietnam in the same years. These now total 23,500, or 25 per cent more, and 1,000 are to be added in the near future. The number of North Vietnamese infiltrees is "based on information . . . from at least two independent sources." *Nowhere are we told how many men who infiltrated from the North have actually been captured.* There is reason to wonder whether the count of infiltrees may be as bloated as the count of Viet Cong dead; in both cases the numbers used are estimates rather than actual bodies.

The White Paper calls the war an invasion and claims "that as many as 75 per cent of the more than 4400 Viet Cong who are known to have entered the South in the first eight months of 1964 were natives of North Vietnam." But a careful reading of the text and the appendices turns up the names of only six North Vietnamese infiltrees. In Part I of the White Paper, Section B gives "individual case histories of North Vietnamese soldiers" sent South by Hanoi but all nine of these are of South Vietnamese origin. The next Section, C, is headed "Infiltration of Native North Vietnamese." It names five infiltrees but one of these is also from the South. That leaves four North Vietnamese natives. Then, in Appendix C, we are given the case histories and photographs of nine other Viet Cong sent South by Hanoi. The report does not explain which ones were originally from the South but it does give the names of the provinces in which they were born. When these are checked, it turns out that only two of the nine were born in North Vietnam. This gives us a total of six Northern infiltrees. It is strange that after five years of fighting, the White Paper can cite so few.

None of this is discussed frankly in the White Paper. To do so would be to bring the war into focus as a rebellion in the South, which may owe some men and materiel to the North but is largely dependent on popular indigenous support for its manpower, as it is on captured U.S. weapons for its supply. The White Paper withholds all evidence which points to a civil war. It also fails to tell the full story of the July 1962 Special Report by the International Control Commission. Appendix A quotes that portion in which the commission 2-to-1 (Poland dissenting) declared that the North had in specific instances sent men and material south in violation of the Geneva accords. But nowhere does the State Department mention that the same report also condemned South Vietnam and the U.S., declaring that they had entered into a military alliance in violation of the Geneva agreements. The U.S. was criticized because it then had about 5,000 military advisers in South Vietnam. The Geneva accords limited the U.S. military mission to the 684 in Vietnam at the time of the 1954 cease-fire. The U.S. and South Vietnam were also criticized by the ICC for hamstringing the commission's efforts to check on imports of arms in violation of the Geneva accords.

The reader would never guess from the White Paper that the Geneva accords promised that elections would be held in 1956 to reunify the country. The 1961 Blue Book at least mentioned the elections, though somehow managing to make them seem a plot. "It was the Communists' calculation," the Blue Book put it, "that nationwide elections scheduled in the accords for 1956 would turn all of South Vietnam over to them . . . The authorities in South Vietnam refused to fall into this well-laid trap." The White Paper omits mention of the elections altogether and says, "South Vietnam's refusal to fall in with Hanoi's scheme for peaceful takeover came as a heavy blow to the Communists." This is not the most candid and objective presentation. From the Vietminh point of view, the failure to hold the elections promised them when they laid down their arms was the second broken promise of the West. The earlier one was in 1946 when they made an agreement to accept limited autonomy within the French union, and welcomed the returning French troops as comrades of the liberation. Most of the French military did not want to recognize even this limited form of independence, and chose instead the road which led after eight years of war to Dienbienphu.[1]

The most disingenuous part of the White Paper is that in which it discusses the origins of the present war. It pictures the war as an attack from the North, launched in desperation because the "economic miracle" in the South under Diem had destroyed communist hopes of a peaceful takeover from within. Even the strategic hamlets are described as "designed to improve the peasant's livelihood" and we are asked to believe that for the first time in history a guerrilla war spread not

[1] See Jean Sainteny's *Histoire d'une paix manquée* (Paris, 1953) and Ellen Hammer's *The Struggle for Indochina* (Stanford, 1954).

because the people were discontented but because their lot was improving!

The true story is a story of lost opportunities. The communist countries acquiesced in the failure to hold elections. Diem had a chance to make his part of the country a democratic show-case. The year 1956 was a bad one in the North. There was a peasant uprising and widespread resentment among the intellectuals over the Communist Party's heavy-handed thought control. But Diem on the other side of the 17th Parallel was busy erecting a dictatorship of his own. In 1956 he abolished elections even for village councils. In 1957 his mobs smashed the press of the one legal opposition party, the Democratic Bloc, when it dared criticize the government. That was the beginning of a campaign to wipe out every form of opposition. It was this campaign and the oppressive exactions imposed on the peasantry, the fake land reform and the concentration camps Diem set up for political opponents of all kinds, which stirred ever wider rebellion from 1958 onward in the grass roots *before* North Vietnam gave support.[2] It was this which drove oppositionists of all kinds into alliance with the communists in the National Liberation Front.

Long before the North was accused of interference, its government was complaining to the Control Commission of "border and air-space violations by the south and infringements of the Geneva agreement by the introduction of arms and U.S. servicemen."[3] For four years after Geneva, both North Vietnam and China followed the "peaceful co-existence" policy while the U.S. turned South Vietnam into a military base and a military dictatorship. It is in this story the White Paper does not tell, and the popular discontent it does not mention, that the rebellion and the aid from the North had their origins.

MARCH 8, 1965

[2] Philippe Devillers in the *China Quarterly*, January–March 1962.
[3] *Survey of International Affairs 1956–58*, by Geoffrey Barraclough, a publication of Britain's Royal Institute of International Affairs, p. 420.

# STRAINING AT THE GNAT OF A LITTLE "NON-LETHAL" GAS

From one point of view the uproar over the use of "non-lethal" gas in Vietnam is ludicrous. Here we are, a people prepared to incinerate ourselves and the world if our leaders deem it necessary, and we go into a tizzy because a relatively minor disabling gas is used in Vietnam! Our own men, and the forces we arm, have long been burning up villages with napalm; we have begun to use phosphorus shells, also intended to burn alive; we have been trying out "anti-personnel" bombs which scatter sharp razor-like fragments in a wide area and a new type of bullet which "somersaults" on entering the flesh in a way which makes ordinarily minor wounds fatal.

Our military have speculated about the use of nuclear weapons, and—to test public response—indicated that at some stage as we raise the ante of escalation, we may use them. This has created only a minor ripple of momentary revulsion, on the way from the headlines to the more engrossing sports or women's pages. Then along comes the news that we have been supplying the South Vietnamese with a "non-lethal" gas not much worse than tear gas and everyone acts as if the war had reached a new plateau of horror.

*Le Monde* in Paris angrily takes issue with an unidentified U.S. officer in Saigon who said the problem was to accustom the public to the use of this new gas. The officer was quite right. We have accustomed the public mind at home and abroad to accept much worse things. Our policy in Vietnam is based on the view that we have a right to rain fire and death on the whole area (1) because we suspect its people if given a free choice would accept a government in which communists played a leading part and (2) because we think our national interest demands that we maintain an armed presence in Southeast Asia as a forward base against China. The end for us justifies the means, and the public is easily brainwashed by our multitudinous 'information" agencies into accepting both. Every hour the news tickers click out dreadful incidents which register hardly at all on our numbed minds and calloused consciences. Children are killed in a schoolyard because we suspected there might be Viet Cong in the village. Fifteen people were killed and nine others drowned because we bombed a sampan on suspicion only to find that it had legal clearance for its trip and indeed three of the dead were South Vietnamese soldiers. Fifty helicopters and thirty-seven U.S. warplanes douse a whole area of central Vietnam with bombs and gunfire because we thought guerrillas might be there; none were found but there is no mention of what this did to the people living in the area. Respected South Vietnamese who speak up for a cease-fire are separated from their families and deported without trial, though ostensibly the war is being fought to give the Vietnamese the right to determine their own destiny. If our spirits were not so dulled by our own propaganda, we would realize how shamefully our country is acting.

The blueprint we are following is that application of terror by bombardment, of "victory by airpower," which the Italians first tried out over Ethiopia and the Germans over Guernica and elsewhere in the Spanish civil war. A war we have lost on the ground against poorly armed forces a fifth the size of ours is being turned into an air war against a people with few air defenses, no planes in the South and few in the North. Our message to them is surrender or total destruction. Bombardment has expanded from fixed targets to "reconnaissance bombing" in which bombers have begun to go out with orders to shoot up anything they can find. General Maxwell Taylor, on the eve of his return to Washington for another round of consultations, told the Saigon Lions Club there was no limit to the potential escalation of the war. The ill-fed and ill-armed fighters of the National Liberation Front have defeated us with that same devotion under adversity that we once showed at Valley Forge against a foreign power and its mercenaries. If Britain had acted then as we do now it would have threatened to bomb Paris unless the French government shut off its supply line and ordered the colonists to stop the rebellion. For the British were as determined then as we are now to treat the revolt as a subversive plot rather than the product of long-standing grievances.

The military, who think force can solve everything, have taken over the direction of policy. Pressure is being applied to every maker of opinion to go along. We even have a reporter as able as Max Frankel of the *New York Times* talked into writing that escalated bombing is really a form of negotiation! Secretary Rusk, instead of making policy, goes around like a press agent lunching with editors to sell them the Pentagon's point of view. A professor of humanities at Michigan State, Thomas H. Greer, who was co-author of the seven-volume "Army Air Forces of World War II" and therefore knows something of the subject, warns us against this business of following military judgment. In a letter to the *New York Times* last Sunday (March 21) he reminds us how often "total trust in the military" has proven disastrous for great nations: the German general staff in 1939 assured Hitler of a swift military victory; Admiral Yamamoto, commander-in-chief of the Japanese Navy, was as confident; General MacArthur told President Truman the Chinese would not intervene if we escalated the war in Korea. "I could draw a far longer catalog of errors," Professor Greer wrote, "but these examples are enough to dispel the myth of brass-hat infallibility . . . Military problems are seldom strictly military. They are bound to involve matters of politics, economics, legality, psychology and morality—matters which soldiers often find annoying and baffling. Finally, war involves imponderables no mortal can foresee . . . Informed civilians have an inescapable duty to speak out . . . The most insidious crimes of our time have been those of indifference and silence."

It does the heart good to see white men and black marching together in the deep South to end ancient wrong. But when will Americans awaken to bring an end to the crimes against humanity we are committing in Vietnam? No one asked the American people whether gas, lethal or not, could be used. Who knows what new horrors are being prepared behind the curtain of military secrecy while the Pentagon's highest information officer assures us of "complete candor"? The idea of victory in Vietnam by aerial blackmail which General Thomas S. Power of the Strategic Air Command sets forth in his new book as "design for survival" is a design which is bringing our country into universal opprobrium and can easily lead to universal disaster.

MARCH 29, 1965

# A GREAT STORM IS GATHERING

The Vietnamese leadership and people, in Hanoi and Saigon, in the hideouts of the guerrillas and in their exile homes in Paris, had better move quickly. Only the miracle of direct negotiations between them can save their poor country from as treacherous a trio of defenders as ever came to plague a small nation. Vietnam is caught in a triangular Great Power struggle which may or may not end in a world war, but is scorching its earth and decimating its people. The civil war among themselves is the real lever of foreign intervention, and only its end by fraternal talks can save it from enemies and friends equally dangerous no matter whether looked at from the right or the left. It may be that only the Vietnamese themselves can save the rest of us from disaster.

The Chinese talk big but their only contribution so far was

to delay the arrival of air defense missiles from Russia. It must be painful to the Vietnamese to read Chou En-lai's explanation in the April 18 issue of the Algerian weekly, *Jeune Afrique*. When Ben Bella asked him whether it was true that Soviet supplies had been held up. Chou En-lai replied that it was normal for Peking to preserve its rights of sovereignty by subjecting such material to inspection! The real reason for his government's attitude, the Chinese leader went on, was that Russian defense missiles would mean the entry of Russian technicians to man them—"that is to say, Russian troops, and that is something the peoples of Southeast Asia cannot admit or tolerate." This is tantamount to saying that China prefers to leave Hanoi defenseless against air attack.[1]

The Russians are almost paralyzed between their terrible feud with the Chinese and their hope for relaxation of tension with the United States; they cannot abandon North Vietnam without loss of face to the former, nor defend it without risking a nuclear confrontation with the latter. If the issue were not precipitated in a small communist and Asian country, endangering Russian prestige in both the communist and Afro-Asian worlds, they might find a direct clash between China and the U.S. as attractive a way to weaken both rivals as some in the West did the Nazi attack on Russia. China maneuvers to use the Vietnamese crisis as a wedge between Russia and the U.S., while the U.S. maneuvers to use it as a wedge between Russia and China. This would be fascinating if it were only chess, but it is a game in which every move adds to Vietnamese suffering and the danger of a nuclear war. What if, under the growing pressure, the Russian military were to take over from the cautious bureaucrats?

From all indications the tiny handful who make policy in Washington are playing this game with zest. Johnson, like a second husband, anxious to outdo his predecessor, seems to want another eyeball-to-eyeball confrontation like Kennedy's over Cuba. While he woos the peace movement with private

[1] Chou En-lai said he feared a new Cuba, "that is to say, a situation which would end in a Russo-American negotiation" such as the one between Kennedy and Khrushchev which "sacrificed the interests of the Cuban people." But Cuba is better off today than if it had been plunged into war, and Vietnam could do worse than a similar hands-off agreement between the two big powers.

letters and private talks in order to disarm it, he is steadily escalating the war. The moves toward peace are few and faint, just enough to confuse opposition at home and abroad, while the moves toward a wider conflict are swift and covert, but unmistakeable. Large-scale commitment of combat troops is indicated by the statement Senator Stennis, acting chairman of the Senate Armed Services Committee, issued from his home in Dekalb, Mississippi, over the Easter weekend. He recalled that in three Senate speeches he had opposed the sending of U.S. military to Vietnam when the men were first ordered there in 1954. But he said that we now had to face "the hard fact that we are now in a war that is getting bigger." He predicted that more U.S. troops would be sent in, and that the struggle might last ten years! "Warning against paying too high a price for peace," declared the press release his office circulated over the holiday, "Stennis said, 'While we want to end the war as soon as possible, we must be certain we do so on terms acceptable to us.'" This is the authentic measure of Johnson's peace terms.

The conference on in Hawaii as this is written is accompanied by the familiar hints and qualified disavowals which herald a widening of the conflict. "No decision has been made, Pentagon sources say," the AP reported (*Washington Star,* April 19), "to throw American ground troops directly into the war." All sorts of possibilities are being leaked. Both the *Sunday Times* and the *Sunday Telegraph* in London (April 11) reported talk in Saigon of moving South Vietnam's boundary up from the 17th to the 19th parallel; the destruction of roads and bridges leading south from Hanoi would prepare the way for such a move but U.S. ground troops would be necessary to achieve it. This would be moving from aerial bombardment to invasion. The arrival of Soviet SAMs (surface to air missiles) in Hanoi would make attack on the capital too costly; to take a piece of the country would save face. "The sharpening of North Vietnam's air defenses," the *Washington Post* speculated editorially April 17, "may tend to shift American support tactics to ground forces." A straw in the same dreadful wind was provided by a speech Senator Proxmire made in Wisconsin April 19 supporting the war and declaring "This country must be prepared for the possible commitment of tens of thousands of additional American troops and perhaps much more, with a sharp acceleration of American casualties." (Press release from his office). Huge eight-inch howitzers capable of firing atomic shells have been landed at Da Nang. Major General Max S. Johnson (ret.), former planner for the Joint Chiefs of Staff, speculates in *U. S. News & World Report* (April 26), that instead of "a solid cordon of U.S. troops" such weapons could be used to create "a nuclearized zone" against invasion from the North. Such are the trial balloons going up.

There are some indications that the signals are not entirely wasted on the Vietnamese. The most important suggestion in the joint communique issued by the Russians and the North Vietnamese in Moscow was its call for "the formation in South Vietnam of a national democratic coalition government carrying through a policy of independence and neutrality in full conformity with the Geneva agreements of 1954" (text in *Washington Sunday Star*, April 18). This has gone almost unnoticed in our press. Right-wing sources here complain that the Saigon government is being purged of Catholic pro-war elements in favor of generals and civilians favored by the Buddhists who want peace. On his way through Paris a Vice-President of the Saigon regime, Tran Van Tuyen, told *Le Monde* (April 16) it was necessary to stop the war and that a democratic socialism in Saigon would make it possible to integrate the South Vietnamese left and end the rebellion. This was a new note. It should be read in connection with the interview that General Nguyen Chanh Thi, who seems to have become the most powerful of Saigon's generals and is being attacked here by right wing commentators, gave to Richard Critchfield (*Washington Star*, April 14), saying that U.S. aid to South Vietnam had only made the rich richer and the poor poorer. The race may be on between peace tendencies in Saigon and U.S. military plans if necessary to take over the country and the war altogether.

Now, before we slip over the brink, it is urgent that all peace forces in our own country bury their sometimes petty and personal differences and awaken our fellow countrymen to the dangers. The President's cancellation of visits by the leaders of India and Pakistan reflects his headstrong unwillingness to listen to counsels of caution, especially from countries

which reflect Asian sympathy for a small Asian country helpless under U.S. air attack; we would never dare strike this way
against a big country able to retaliate on its own. The student
peace march on Washington last weekend put the biggest
picket line ever outside the White House and brought 20,000
people including a delegation from Mississippi together in a
huge rally at the Washington Monument. Senator Gruening
of Alaska had the honor to be the one member of Congress
with the courage to address the students. His proposal for an
end to the bombing of North Vietnam was echoed a few hours
later by Senator Fulbright. Gruening's call for negotiations
with the Viet Cong was sneered at by the conservative *Washington Star* although a few days earlier (April 12) it had itself
said editorially, "It is very difficult, to say the least, to see how
a settlement can be negotiated without their participation."
The right-wing press attacked the demonstration and as usual
most of the press ignored the Gruening speech. Even the liberal *New York Post* was stampeded by nervous adult peace
leaders into running an editorial before it took place saying
there was "no justification for transforming the march into a
one-sided anti-American show." If it had waited 24 hours, it
would have seen that the "show" was neither one-sided nor
anti-American but a disciplined and sober affair for which the
students deserve the country's deepest thanks.

APRIL 20, 1965

# OUR SECRETARY OF STATE AND
# THE ACADEMIC COMMUNITY

The war to make Southeast Asia safe for democracy is rapidly turning into a war to make the United States unsafe for free discussion of foreign policy. Secretary Rusk picked a meeting of the American Society of International Law to deliver an attack on critics in the academic community. That speech and the follow-up press conferences by Secretary McNamara and the President have the earmarks of a campaign to steamroller criticism. The White House is mobilizing its satellite commentators to make dissent from its war policies seem aid and comfort to the enemy. Instead of welcoming the campus teach-ins as a means of stirring wider participation in the formulation of policy, the Administration is as anxious to shut off debate in the colleges as in the Congress. Secretary Rusk told the International Lawyers he wondered "at the gullibility of educated men" and their "stubborn disregard of plain facts."

Never have plainer facts been more stubbornly disregarded than by Rusk, McNamara and Johnson since Johnson in 1961 called Diem "the Churchill of Asia" and McNamara sponsored the Taylor-Staley counter-insurgency plan that same year as a way to bring the Viet Cong under control in eighteen months! A steady retreat from reality has accompanied the spread of the rebellion. Only two years ago Secretary Rusk (in his April 22, 1963, speech to the Economic Club in New York) was telling us that "the strategic hamlet program is producing excellent results." The statement has since proven ludicrously false. In that same speech, only a few months before an exasperated people poured happily into the streets to celebrate Diem's overthrow, Rusk was still trying to tell us that South Vietnam under the dictator was showing "steady movement toward a constitutional system resting upon popular consent."

It is hard to match Rusk's record for "stubborn disregard of plain facts." He added to it in his speech to the international lawyers. "There is no evidence," he said, "that the Viet Cong has any significant popular following in South Vietnam." This sets a new high in overstatement. We call attention to the two most recent witnesses to the contrary: one is a comprehensive account in *Figaro Litteraire* (March 3), the other is Georges Chaffard's account in the Paris *L'Express* (April 25) of his recent visit to areas under Viet Cong control. When M. Chaffard in the first installment of his series (*L'Express*, April 11) described the serious damage done to guerrilla supply and morale by U.S. bombings, his report was welcomed in our press by Joseph Alsop, among others. But nobody quotes M. Chaffard's description in the third installment (April 25) of the "harmonious" relations he says have long existed between the guerrillas and the people, and of the schools and hospitals they operate in Viet Cong territory. Nor does anyone quote his account of how the rebellion originated in the effort by Diem to take the land back from the peasants and in the persecution by Diem of Vietminh veterans after 1954 in violation of the Geneva accords. "Most of the regular units of the Front," M. Chaffard writes, "are made up today of relatives of the victims of the Diemist repression." [1]

Mr. Rusk's discussion of international law matched his history. "Every small state," he said, "has a right to be unmolested by its neighbors even though it is within reach of a great power." This will add to the Secretary's fame as a humorist in Guatemala and Cuba. In another notable passage, Secretary Rusk said "our assistance" to South Vietnam "now encompasses the bombing of North Vietnam." Never was a more dubious

[1] Nor after the Tonkin Bay reprisal raids did anyone else in this country cite M. Chaffard's account in *Le Monde* (August 7, 1964) of how the U.S. began to train commandoes and infiltrators for attack upon the North in 1957, three years before the rebellion in the South was proclaimed. We challenge M. Chaffard's new admirers to discuss these earlier revelations.

legal proposition more swiftly passed over. Exactly one year ago, when the British, fighting anti-British rebels in Aden, struck across the border into the "privileged sanctuary" in Yemen, Adlai Stevenson told the Security Council the U.S. had repeatedly expressed its emphatic disapproval of "retaliatory raids wherever they occur and by whomever they are committed." Similarly when the French in 1958 struck across the Algerian border into the Tunisian camps where the Algerian rebels rested and trained, Senators Kennedy, Humphrey, Morse and Knowland denounced the reprisal raid as a violation of international law and Eisenhower warned the French we would be unable to defend such action before the Security Council. It is a pity no one arose in that respectable audience of international lawyers to quote back at Rusk the sardonic summation on the subject to be found in Schwarzenberger's *Manual of International Law*. It says "military reprisals are open only to the strong against the weak." If Hanoi had an air fleet and a navy to match ours, we would never dare do what we are doing. This is why we look like a big bully to Asia.

The bombings confessed the failure after four years of our effort to win the war in South Vietnam by counter-insurgency. The McNamara press conference confessed the failure of the bombings in North Vietnam to force Hanoi to "call off" the war (in accordance with our kitchen spigot theory of the rebellion) or at least to stop the flow of men and supplies; McNamara claims infiltration has been stepped up. The Secretary made much of the fact that by destroying bridges and roads we were forcing the Viets to move from rail to road and from road transport to their feet. But it was on their feet that the Vietminh defeated the French as it was on their feet, despite a similar control of the air and a far greater destruction of highways and bridges, that the Chinese "volunteers" forced us back to the 38th parallel in Korea. McNamara's record for clairvoyance is as poor as Rusk's. In October, 1963, he told the country that everything was going so well in South Vietnam that 1,000 American "advisers" would be withdrawn by the end of the year and the war would be brought under control by 1965.

There is nothing left now but to take over the war with our own combat troops, but in this we are encountering unexpected resistance. The government in Saigon seems to be opposing our wish to put U.S. combat troops into the country. Jack Foisie of the *Los Angeles Times* foreign service reported [2] that Ambassador Taylor since his return from the Honolulu conference had been to see Prime Minister Quat twice about the introduction of American ground forces. Dr. Quat is reported to be worried "about the internal reaction to the presence of more and more Americans" and to feel that the sending of infantry units "smacks of permanency, of occupation." Secretaries Rusk and McNamara might fruitfully study the remark Foisie quotes from an American official in Saigon who said, "Washington can't understand Quat's attitude, but we can. He still thinks of this as a civil war—Vietnamese against Vietnamese—and he hates to think of the effect of American involvement since it just adds to the painful hatreds being created between North and South Vietnamese." Dr. Quat is himself a North Vietnamese, though one of the bitterly anti-communist refugees from that area. Beverly Deepe from Saigon the same day (*New York Herald-Tribune*, April 25) reported "some of the Northern-born anti-Communists openly resent their homeland being bombed." She said "Vietnamese of all political colors believe the American military leaders are moving closer and closer to the French colonial position militarily—thus incurring all the disadvantages psychologically of being tabbed as colonialists, but with none of the colonialists' advantages of political control."

This is clearly evident in the troop question. Dr. Quat "is known to feel" Jack Langguth reported from Saigon (to the *New York Times* April 25) that "the landing of a large number of infantrymen would raise unpleasant recollections of the French colonial war." But Langguth added significantly, "his opposition is not believed to rule out further consideration of the matter." In any showdown, the U.S. and not Dr. Quat will make the decision, though at the expense of increased disaffection in Saigon. "Strong combat troops would be introduced into South Vietnam," the *New York Times* reported from Washington that same day on the basis of one of those "deep backgrounders" for the favored few, "to prevent the United States' expulsion from the country." Does this also apply if the Saigon government were to initiate talks with the rebels for a cease-fire and ask the U.S. to leave? A move of this kind seems to be

[2] *Washington Post*, April 25.

feared by Americans and bitter-enders in South Vietnam. Miss Deepe reports them worried about the possibility of pro-neutralist trends in the elections called for the city and provincial capitals May 30. The prospect of free elections seems always to fill the U.S. with anxiety. The Acting Chief of State also appealed last week for election of a National Congress, but it is feared this could "easily be penetrated by pro-communist and pro-neutralist elements," possibly paving the way for peace. This reappearance of democratic institutions in which a popular will for peace may express itself is regarded by our people in Saigon (Miss Deepe writes) as part of an "invisible, unarmed subversive war . . . far more significant than the violent, bloody guerrilla war in the countryside." The self-determination Rusk claims to be defending in South Vietnam is what we most fear. The refugees streaming into the cities from the villages we are destroying in our all-out air warfare against the rebels are hardly likely to favor a further step-up in American intervention. We fear the popular will in Vietnam and we fear it at home.

MAY 3, 1965

# THE FORMS OF DEMOCRACY, BUT
# NO LONGER THE REALITY

The swift and obedient fashion with which Congress rubber stamped Lyndon Johnson's moves toward wider war in two hemispheres recalls those pages in which Gibbon describes how shrewdly Augustus laid the foundations of Imperial rule in Rome. Caesar's heir was scrupulous in maintaining the forms of the Republic. Augustus sat in the Senate and affected merely to be the first among equals. He and his successors "consulted the great national council, and *seemed* to refer to its decision the most important concerns of peace and war." The italics are Gibbon's. It was only later, after the murder of Caligula, that "the dream of liberty" came to an end "and the Senate awoke to all the horrors of inevitable servitude." Then, as the scene darkens, in another parallel we should take to heart, the Caesars woke up to find themselves at the mercy of the Empire's overgrown armies. These began by extinguishing liberty abroad and ended by crushing it at home. A new race of "polished and eloquent" sycophants "inculcated the duty of passive obedience, and descanted on the inevitable mischiefs of freedom." Pick up almost any newspaper and you may read Johnson's little court of columnists preaching the same doctrines today.

The way the President's $700,000,000 appropriation for Vietnam was put through the Congress bore the earmarks of a master manipulator. The money by his own admission was not needed; what he wanted was a blank check of authority to widen the war as he saw fit. He could have asked such authority directly. But then the resolution would have been a naked request for war powers and it would have had to go through the Senate Foreign Relations Committee. Its chairman, Fulbright, and at least eight others of its members have grown critical of the expanding war. The grant of power was wrapped in a request for military funds so it would pass through the less critical Senate Appropriations Committee and because it is difficult to vote against supplies for troops on the firing line. This is a measure the consequence of which may be war with China. Yet it was approved by the House within twenty-four hours after seventy-five minutes of discussion, with less than fifteen minutes allowed to the opposition. In the Senate, the bill was rushed through in the same fashion, with only five hours allowed for debate. The 408–7 vote in the House and the 88–3 vote in the Senate resembled a stampede of steers in Texas. An arrogant, aggressive and compulsively possessive man has put his LBJ brand on the Congress as he has on his family and retainers.

Only three Senators, Morse, Gruening, and Gaylord Nelson

of Wisconsin, voted "no." Many of those who voted "yes" indicated their misgiving. But fear of White House displeasure proved stronger. As we begin the descent into what may become one of history's greatest catastrophes, political cowardice won out over conscience. Even Stennis of Mississippi, who was floor manager for the Administration, admitted after Morse's great speech in opposition that Morse was "brilliant" and had raised "some serious points." Not a single Democrat rose to protest when Morse said Johnson was following Goldwater's course. Four Republicans expressed anxiety. Javits objected to "sneaking in" an authorization for combat troops via an appropriation bill; Cooper of Kentucky and Carlson of Kansas urged more effort at negotiations; Aiken of Vermont opposed the bombing of the North. Gore of Tennessee implied that escalation of the war to the North was planned before the Pleiku bombing in February. Church of Idaho, Pell of Rhode Island and Clark of Pennsylvania indicated that they were voting "yes" with reluctance; Clark urged negotiations with the Viet Cong and a gradual cessation of bombing the North.

The surprise of this lopsided "debate" came in its closing moments when Robert Kennedy of New York for the first time spoke out on foreign policy. He said he was voting for the resolution because Senator Stennis had assured the Senate (but very equivocally) that this was "not a blank check." He said he thought "our efforts for peace should continue with the same intensity as our efforts in the military field" and that we had "erred for some time in regarding Vietnam as purely a military problem." He ended by indicating his disagreement with Johnson, too, on the Dominican Republic. "Our determination to stop communist revolution in the hemisphere must not be construed," Kennedy said, "as opposition to popular uprisings against injustice and oppression just because the targets of such popular uprisings say they are communist-inspired or communist-led, *or even because known communists take part in them.*" The italics are ours. It is not easy to say such things in the present atmosphere. Bobby Kennedy was in the inner circles which ran the Vietnamese war and supported Bosch in the Dominican Republic during his brother's Administration. His criticism is significant. Taken in connection with Teddy Kennedy's leadership in the fight against Johnson on poll taxes, we have here the possible nucleus of a liberal opposition against Johnson. His warmest defenders, notably the Goldwaterite Tower of Texas, came from the Republican side.

But it will take more than a few reservations *sotto voce* to halt the drift toward a big war. Fear of offending the White House was also apparent among those who were silent or absent. Of eight absent Senators, three—Dodd, Smathers and Symington—were recorded in favor of the Johnson resolution. The five others, some of whom have been critical, preferred to go unrecorded. These were Fulbright, Russell, McGovern, Burdick and Metcalf. And Senator Gruening, perhaps to balance off his opposition to Johnson on Vietnam, supported his action in the Dominican Republic. Historians as passionately anti-Castro as Theodore Draper (letter in the *New York Times*, May 12) and Robert J. Alexander (letter in the *New York Times*, May 9) have bitterly rejected Johnson's claim that intervention in Santo Domingo was necessary to prevent a Red take-over. It reflects the nature of the Johnson era that a liberal who has fought all his life against use of the Big Stick in Latin America should feel it politically expedient to endorse it now.

MAY 12, 1965

# THE WHITE HOUSE OUTSMARTED ITSELF AND PUT THE SPOTLIGHT ON THE TEACH-IN . . .

The Washington teach-in was both the dupe and the benefi-
ciary of White House manipulation. In order to obtain Mc-
George Bundy's agreement to debate, the committee in charge
made no less than thirty different changes in program and
panels. Bundy even insisted on vetoing the committee's choice
of who was to debate with him. He declined to match wits with
Professor Hans Morgenthau, perhaps because Bundy would be
unable to treat so respected a senior political scientist with the
crisp condescension which is Bundy's stock in trade. All was
arranged to suit his wishes; this was reflected in Bundy's last-
minute regrets when he said the program was "fair to a fault."
On the other hand, it was because the President's right hand
man on foreign policy was expected to take part that the
teach-in obtained such widespread commercial TV, radio and
press coverage. In this respect the White House outsmarted
itself. It put the spotlight on the meeting and Bundy's failure to
appear made it look as if the Administration was unwilling
to stand up to its critics in a fair debate.

Whether Johnson felt that Bundy simply had to go to Santo
Domingo or seized on this as a last-minute excuse is not something one can determine from the outside. But if the Dominican
emergency was the real reason, some other official could have
come in his place and read his speech for him. Instead all the

White House sent was Bundy's statement of regret. The suspicion that the Administration was only looking for an excuse to back out may easily be countered. All it need do is permit Bundy on his return to accept the university committee's challenge to reschedule the debate. (It never did.)

Whatever the White House does, the teach-in should be extended from the campuses to as many local communities as possible. The organizers should emphasize the difference between the Washington teach-in and the kind of foreign policy seminars the State Department organizes. These, preferably, are semi-private briefings in which (as in the closed party meetings in the Soviet Union) only the official line is expounded. Even the wider public forums on foreign policy which the State Department helps to organize around the country are notable for the absence of any real opposing point of view. The Department prefers these brain-washing operations to genuine debate. In this it fits perfectly with the Johnson Administration.

While some Administration officials of minor rank took part in the evening panels, the only defenders of its point of view in the morning and afternoon sessions were other academicians. There was no one who could speak for the Administration. Even Arthur Schlesinger, Jr., who debated Professor Morgenthau at the morning session, turned out to be not a spokesman for the White House but for the opposition bloc beginning to form around the two Kennedy brothers in the Senate.

The pointed asides of this "defender" must have rankled more with the White House than the attacks he was supposed to be answering. Schlesinger said Johnson's speech the preceding Thursday promising economic aid for Vietnam was merely an echo of Bobby Kennedy's speech in the Senate the day before; that after reading the White Paper he reflected on the gullibility of Secretaries of State; that he did not approve of the bombing of North Vietnam and that "if we took the marines we now have in the Dominican Republic and sent them to South Vietnam, we'd be a good deal better off in both countries." It was clear from Schlesinger's speech that Johnson, in winning Goldwater, had lost the ADA.

Professor Hans Morgenthau charged that instead of a two-party system in foreign policy the Administration sought what it "euphemistically called consensus," and that the "spontaneous movement" represented by the teach-ins was filling the function of a parliamentary opposition. He said that instead of policy being based on facts, facts were being distorted to fit policy. He said he warned Diem in 1955 that if he continued his repressive policies he would finally have no support left outside his own family. He said one of the members of the afternoon panel had located Diem in a monastery in this country "and presented him to the CIA" in 1954.

Isaac Deutscher, the third speaker at the morning session, said he spoke as "an unrepentant Marxist." He said he wanted to put the crisis in perspective by reviewing some of the assumptions underlying the cold war: "As long as we accept them, we will go from crisis to crisis." The principal one was that of a military threat from the communist powers. He said the Truman Doctrine and NATO were based on the myth of a Russian military threat to Europe. "Propaganda pictured two colossi," the biographer of Stalin and Trotzky said, "but if we looked closely one saw a difference. The U.S. had emerged from the war with barely a scratch while Russia was prostrate and bleeding profusely. It had suffered twenty million dead alone and had only thirty-one million men against fifty-three million women. Russia was physically unable to be a military threat to anyone. I have been all my life a critic of Stalin for lack of freedom but he was no menace to the peace of the world. That was a myth inflated to apocalyptic dimensions." Deutscher saw a similar myth about China in the propaganda of the Vietnamese war. Deutscher concluded by saying that the class struggle had degenerated into the morass of power politics, into a struggle of oligarchies, one falsely under the banner of socialism, one falsely under the banner of freedom. He spoke a language Washington has not heard in public since the cold war and the witch hunt began two decades ago.

The afternoon session was a little disappointing. The panel method gave none of the participants adequate time for a full exposition. The discussion tended, as in TV panel shows, to fly off in all directions. I was a "resource person" (horrid phrase) on a panel myself in the evening on the origins of the war and the nature of the Viet Cong. It's difficult to be both a reporter and a participant even on a small scale. It was an inspiring occasion. Those intense and concerned young faces, eager to learn, filled one with new hope. The teach-in movement is making democracy meaningful on the one issue where it has counted least and is needed most. The intellectuals are beginning to do their duty.

MAY 24, 1965

# HALF DOVE, HALF HAWK AND WHOLLY OPPORTUNIST

Eighteen months later, two John F. Kennedy aides have joined the teach-ins against the Vietnamese war, Arthur Schlesinger, Jr., in an article for the *New York Times* Sunday *Magazine* September 18, Richard Goodwin in a speech to the national board of the ADA the day before. They now make their own much of the criticism they disdained at the time of the Washington teach-in in May of last year; what was then heretical has now become obvious and respectable. But both the "middle way out" offered by Schlesinger and the "National Committee Against Widening the War" proposed by Goodwin are opportunistic in design. Goodwin's rhetoric before the ADA was heroic. In pursuit of principle, a man should be ready to stand "if necessary, alone against the multitude." It is "our duty as patriots . . . to oppose any President" whose policy "threatens the grandeur of this nation." But all he opposes is any *further* escalation of the war in the North. His committee "will not be aimed at withdrawal or even a lessening of the war in the South . . . It will neither be against the Administration nor for it . . . Its purpose is to help the President." Its stand "will not end the war in South Vietnam. It may even prolong it . . ." He sounds like a Patrick Henry saying, "Give me liberty or give me death—or give me some compromise so I can stand with the British."

Schlesinger, though far abler, is in much the same position. When he pinch-hit for McGeorge Bundy at the Washington teach-in, defending the Johnson war policy, though with reservations, Schlesinger asked the professors to moderate their criticism. "What this country needs," he quipped, "is a good night's sleep." The *New York Times* article is his awakening from this to a brilliant and passionate attack upon the fallacies of the war. But he differs from Goodwin only in proposing that we "taper off" the bombing of the North "as prudently as we can" and offer the Vietcong amnesty if they lay down their arms, open up their territory and abide "by the ground rules of free elections." This is a lot to ask after the recent farce in Saigon. In the meantime he is prepared like Goodwin for intensification of the war in the South, though with more stress on social reform. This looked promising when John F. Kennedy first broached it in 1961. It is delusion today. So is Schlesinger's notion that the U.S. can draw back and let the South Vietnamese army "take all the initiative it wants." It is clear by now that it has no stomach for battle. Schlesinger is still engaged in the same self-deception he criticizes in the past and he engages in it for the same reason—because it is not politic to face up to the whole truth.

The Goodwin proposal for a new committee nevertheless raises serious political questions. One's attitude toward it will depend on one's assessment of the war. If Johnson is planning an invasion of the North, with all the heightened risk that entails of war with China, then a broad committee based "simply" as Goodwin says on "the victorious slogan of the Democratic party in 1964 . . . No wider war" might be the answer. But if Johnson—as many well-informed observers here believe—is planning not an invasion of the North but a major expansion of the war in the South, then the committee could end up by being as big a trap for the peace forces as was the 1964 campaign.

The Mekong Delta, where the bulk of South Vietnam's

people live, has until now been the scene of little fighting and much tacit agreement between the Viet Cong and the government forces. Richard Fryklund, just back from Saigon, reports in the *Washington Star* (September 15) talk of adding another four or five divisions to the six already in Vietnam so we can take over the war in the Delta, too. In that densely populated area—unlike the jungle highlands—this would be not just another escalation but a new war—a war against the South Vietnamese people. Its human cost in their casualties and ours would be enormous. We dare not acquiesce in such a crime. We ought to be for ending the bombing of the North and de-escalating the war in the South while we offer to negotiate with the Viet Cong as U Thant has proposed. I am convinced that were peace negotiated along these lines both North and South Vietnam would be taking U.S. aid and friendly to the U.S. within a few years.

Either we move toward peace or we continue to move toward catastrophe. No "middle way" is any longer possible. The strategy of limiting the war to the South means a long, painful struggle which will only increase impatience at home for quick and easy bombing solutions. Nixon's campaign to end it without "appeasement" or more ground troops may have a dreadful corollary: the use of the atom bomb as a short-cut. Poor wobbly old Eisenhower was trotted out on educational TV last Monday night to say that he was ready in 1953 to use nuclear weapons to end the Korean war and to imply that we ought to do the same in Vietnam. "We'd have won the war in a week if we had used them," Eisenhower said, like any Air Force Strangelove. Of course, he explained, "no one in a sane moment" would use them against Russia—Russia can hit back—but that doesn't mean that "in sticky situations you couldn't use a proper [sic] kind of nuclear weapon sometime," i.e. against those who can't. Ike didn't "see any difference between gas warfare and this kind of warfare." In his fuzzy logic, if one can be press-agented as humane, why not the other? Eisenhower argued against "the fear of using a weapon that the free world might need in some outlying place where people or life seems to be cheap, and they want to have their way," while we—he of course did not add—want to have ours. The mere suggestion is enough to deepen racial suspicion in Asia.

The Eisenhower interview may prove the beginning of a campaign to sell "proper" kinds of nuclear weapons in "little" wars like Vietnam. Johnson's policy at the moment looks like a lesser evil, as he did beside Goldwater in 1964. But his "middle way" soon turned into exactly that peace-by-quickie bombardment Goldwater had advocated. The Republicans may be the first to talk of nuclear weapons but Johnson may be the first to use them. Something better than opportunism is needed to keep us from this abyss.

SEPTEMBER 26, 1966

# WILL WE DO IN VIETNAM WHAT THE NAZIS DID IN HOLLAND?

Comedy and tragedy rub shoulders as the Vietnamese war widens. In the wake of the second of those B-52 sledge-hammer-against-flea raids by the Strategic Air Command, 2500 troops invade the Zone D jungle thirty miles north of Saigon but find no trace of the elusive enemy. The AP's first complete report derisively notes the haul at the end of this costly operation. Since this seemed to disappear from the morning papers next day, we give it here from the *Washington Evening Star* (July 6): "Three stacks of love letters, tied in a yellow ribbon from a girl to a Viet Cong soldier; seven Japanese water canteens of World War II design; a Viet Cong illustrated magazine; one French artillery shell made in 1932." A few more raids of this kind and our side can establish a Flea Market in Saigon.

In London, the *Daily Mirror*'s Saigon correspondent reports an interview (July 4) in which our new strong man, the playboy Air Force General Ky, now head of the South Vietnamese government, was asked who his heroes were. "I have only one," he replied, "Hitler." This charming interview makes it easier to understand why one of Ky's first acts was to suspend virtually the entire press of his country, an order hastily rescinded when the effect was to boost the circulation of the Viet Cong's underground paper in Saigon (*Washington Star,* July 3). Such are the antics of the Free World's newest Chief of State.

Two days after the London *Mirror* interview was published General Ky announced a *"bac tien"* (march north) movement to "liberate" North Vietnam (*Washington Post* July 7). Though this was frowned upon by the U. S. Embassy, we have extended our own "liberation" campaign. When we hit Nam Dinh July 2, our bombings of the North reached a new stage. The attack on Nam Dinh forty miles southeast of Hanoi was the first on an industrial city in the Hanoi-Haiphong area, the heart of North Vietnamese population and industry. Nam Dinh is a center of light industries, principally textiles. Our objective was the oil storage tanks in the city. "Smoke rose 3,000 meters and was visible 300 kilometers away," *Le Monde* reported (July 4–5), adding "No information was given on losses inflicted upon the population, but it would be astonishing if only oil was burned up." Two military missions were flown the same day, it was announced in Saigon, "against military bases at Dienbienphu" (*New York Times,* July 3). Dienbienphu, according to a story in *Paris Match* last November 15 by the first French journalists allowed to visit the place in ten years, is now a model farm. A leaflet dropped on North Vietnam the same day boasted endearingly that 2,788 aircraft had dropped bombs in 89 strikes from February 7 until April 30 and that "violent attacks" would be continued until "Hanoi and the Chinese Communists stop their invasion of South Vietnam." When the spokesman was asked about this he said he did not believe the Chinese had invaded but the language had been chosen "for its propaganda value" (*New York Times,* July 3). How much propaganda value is there in falsehoods so blatant even we aren't gullible enough to believe them?

The public is being prepared for the bombing of the Hanoi-Haiphong industrial complex. An AP dispatch from Vienna (*Le Monde*, July 4–5) quotes an Albanian labor union official just back from Hanoi who declared with an almost audible sneer that all the Russians had sent there were "some medicines, two hundred bicycles and five accordions." But our military through Hanson Baldwin (*New York Times*, July 4) leak intelligence reports of "huge crates" being unloaded from communist-flag ships at Haiphong with "what are believed to be weapon, ammunition and military supplies" which "may have" included latest model Migs. "Unconfirmed reports" (they have to be pretty "unconfirmed" to rank as such with military intelligence) even say the North Vietnamese "now have, or will eventually be provided with, ground-to-ground ballistic missiles with a range in excess of 1,000 miles." This triggered a flood of similar stories and a State Department statement July 6 estimating that there soon would be four SAM (surface-to-air missile) sites, each with six missiles, outside Hanoi. On July 7, House Republican Leader Gerald Ford had just issued a statement calling for air strikes "before the enemy uses the weapons against the side of freedom." Even slant-wise, these missiles cannot shoot further than forty miles. They are purely defensive, but can shoot down even U2s at altitudes of at least 80,000 feet. In the Cuban crisis we at least had the excuse that IRBMs placed in Cuba could reach much of the U.S. mainland. Here all the SAMs can do is reach our attacking planes.

There may be worse in the offing: bombing of the North Vietnamese dikes. These support the irrigation works of the Red River delta. Bombing the dikes has been discussed several times in the French press but has been blacked out of the American. In its July 4–5 issue *Le Monde* speculates whether the dikes will be our next target. In its July 6 issue it carries an article by the famous agricultural expert, René Dumont, describing the enormous effort put into the irrigation system to meet the needs of overpopulated North Vietnam. The most tempting moment for our military, especially if they meet serious defeats in the South during the summer, will come at the end of the rainy season in August, when the waters are at their height. Blowing up the great dikes to the North of Hanoi would be comparable to an H-bomb in its effect, flooding the entire delta region, wiping out the summer rice crop and drowning from two to three million people. North Vietnam could survive the loss of the industries it has built up since 1954 but to bomb the dikes would mean starvation. Destruction of dikes was one of the war crimes for which Seyss-Inquart, chief of the Nazi occupation in Holland, was hanged in Nuremberg. The Hague Convention years before had made such action a violation of international law but Goering pleaded at the trial, "In a life and death struggle there is no legality." Has this become our viewpoint, too, even though Vietnam is hardly a life and death matter for us? The bombardment of the dikes would be genocide.

JULY 12, 1965

# TIME TO TELL THE TRUTH
# FOR A CHANGE

*We are ready now, as we always have been, to move from the battlefield to the conference table. I have stated publicly, and many times, again and again, America's willingness to begin unconditional discussions with any government at any place at any time. Fifteen efforts have been made to start these discussions with the help of forty nations throughout the world, but there has been no answer.*

—LBJ ANNOUNCING TROOP BUILDUP IN VIETNAM JULY 28

As in the U-2 incident, our government has again been caught in falsehood. It owes the country an honest explanation before more of our sons die in Vietnam. The State Department's admissions in the wake of Eric Sevareid's revelations in *Look* explain a cryptic remark made by UN Secretary General U Thant last February and a mysterious leak at UN headquarters in New York last August. "I have been conducting private discussions on the question of Vietnam for a long time," U Thant told a press conference February 24, "I am sure that the great American people, if only they knew the true facts and the background to the developments in South Vietnam, will agree with me that further bloodshed is unnecessary." Then he added sadly, "As you know in times of war and of hostilities the first casualty is truth." He was slapped down the same day in a curt White House statement.

This brings us to the leak, which now falls into perspective. "In twenty months," Mr. Johnson said in a White House speech August 3, "we have agreed to fifteen different approaches to try to bring peace, and each of them has been turned down by the other side." This was too much for someone at UN headquarters. Someone called in two UN correspondents, Hella Pick of the *Manchester Guardian* and Darius S. Jhabvala of the *New York Herald-Tribune*, and leaked the story which the State Department has now confirmed, that only eleven months earlier, in September 1964, we turned down a chance for secret peace talks U Thant had arranged with the North Vietnamese.[1] It appeared in the *Herald-Tribune* August 8 and in the *Manchester Guardian* August 9. The account in the latter suggests that the source of the story was someone close to Adlai Stevenson and that he told it in such a way as to put the blame on the State Department and avoid direct criticism of Kennedy and Johnson.

The *Manchester Guardian* story said Washington had "cold-shouldered at least two opportunities for contacts with North Vietnam in the last two years. The first was after the fall of Diem in the autumn of 1963, when Hanoi "was willing to discuss the establishment of a coalition neutralist government in Saigon." Note that the reference was to a coalition neutralist government and not to a National Liberation Front govern-

---

[1] An earlier hint of this had appeared the previous April 18 in a dispatch to the *St. Louis Post-Dispatch* from its UN correspondent, Donald Grant.

ment. This throws light on another cryptic remark by U Thant at his press conference last February. "In my view," he then said, "there was a very good possibility in 1963 of arriving at a satisfactory political solution." The second lost opportunity mentioned in the *Manchester Guardian* account was the secret meeting to which Ho Chi Minh had agreed in September, 1964, but which we rejected. The *Guardian* went on to say:

> Details of these peace moves have come from an unimpeachable source. The State Department, however, seems to be dismissing the report of Ho Chi Minh's willingness to talk last year as irrelevant. It says there was no indication that anything would come of it, and hints that President Johnson was not involved in the matter at all. Nor is it clear whether the State Department ever informed President Kennedy that Hanoi was willing to talk after the fall of Diem. *Mr. Adlai Stevenson certainly knew of these moves, and it appears to have been one of his great regrets that Washington did not react positively.* [Emphasis added.] The intermediaries who were involved in the effort to bring about a meeting between Hanoi and Washington believe that the Communist position hardened as a result of Washington's negative attitude.

Sevareid's account of his talk with Stevenson shortly before the latter's death last July adds to the August leak. It reveals that U Thant made two more attempts at peace. The September meeting was rejected for fear that it might leak to the Goldwater forces during the election campaign. "When the election was over," Sevareid relates, "U Thant again pursued the matter; Hanoi was still willing to send its man. But Defense Secretary McNamara, Adlai went on, flatly opposed the attempt." The argument against peace talks was that "the South Vietnamese government would have to be informed and that this would have a demoralizing effect on them; that government was shaky enough as it was." McNamara denied this and the State Department's spokesman last Monday said the Secretary of Defense "did not participate in the U.S. government handling of this matter." But the spokesman did not deny that a second Rangoon meeting with the North Vietnamese was possible after the election. U Thant's next effort was a cease-fire offer on U.S. terms. On this, the spokesman was evasive. He said it was not true that U Thant "at any time said he would accept any formulation concerning a cease-fire that the U.S. might propose—although he did advance his own suggestions." When pressed for clarification, the spokesman would only say, it would be "highly inappropriate to disclose the details." The Department always seems to consider candor inappropriate. Through this bureaucratic fog we can see that the Department dares not deny the second Rangoon meeting it turned down nor the offer of a cease-fire. "Stevenson," Sevareid's account continues, "told me that U Thant was furious over this failure of his patient efforts but said nothing publicly."

Apparently U Thant persevered in his efforts, however. For if one goes back and rereads the transcript of the February 24 press conference one sees that he said he had "presented concrete ideas and proposals" to the principal parties concerned, including the U.S., but that the results "have not been conclusive." Next day UN headquarters reported a message from Hanoi that it was sympathetic to the proposals U Thant had outlined.[2] But the same day at a press conference Secretary Rusk made clear U.S. rejection. He said the U.S. would not enter negotiations to end the Vietnamese war until North Vietnam gave some "indication" that it was "prepared to stop what it is doing and what it knows it is doing to its neighbors." This embodied the view that the war was a simple case of aggression from the North and implied that we would not negotiate until the other side laid down its arms.

What terms was Hanoi thinking of? In the *Weekly* last April 12, "Peace Feelers? Is the Truth about Them Being Withheld?" we reprinted a letter to the *Times* of London April 1 by William Warbey, a British Laborite M.P. back from talks in Hanoi with Ho Chi Minh and Prime Minister Pham Van Dong. Warbey outlined their terms for a settlement as told to him and previously "to others who passed their message on to Washington." This called for a neutralized North and South, with resumption of trade between them, but with autonomous regimes on both sides of the 17th parallel. "The people of the Southern zone" would have the right "to form and support a government which genuinely represents all the major sections of the Southern population" and each zone would have

---

[2] *Facts on File* for 1965, p. 74E3.

the right "to enjoy economic, cultural and 'fraternal' relations with the countries of its choice," i.e. South Vietnam could be linked economically and culturally with the West if it so chose while North Vietnam presumably would remain linked with the Soviet bloc. Warbey wrote that the only precondition on which the North was insisting was the cessation of bombing attacks upon it. Note that these terms did not call for a government based on the National Liberation Front but on "all the major sections of the Southern population," and that it was broad enough to envisage free elections. It was also suggested that eventual reunification might be based on a bi-federal system. This would seem to offer a solution which would be democratic and honorable and a face-saver for the U.S. This may make it easier to understand what U Thant meant when he told a luncheon last Tuesday, the day after the State Department's admissions, "If only bold steps had been taken as late as 1964 I feel that much of today's tragic development could have been avoided."

The day the Warbey letter appeared in the *Times* of London, Mr. Johnson was asked at press conference whether he had "any evidence of a willingness on the part of the Communists to negotiate" in Vietnam. We called attention in that same issue of April 12 to the curious wording of his reply. He said he had "no evidence that they are ready and willing to negotiate *under conditions that would be productive.*" Our italics. Last Monday's press conference at the State Department suggested that what we would consider "productive" would be restoration of an independent South Vietnam under our wing. The Department's spokesman insisted that the Johns Hopkins speech last April 7 did not mark any change in policy when it offered "unconditional discussions." To prove continuity of policy he read the reporters two previous Presidential statements. In one, at an AP lunch, April 20, 1964, Mr. Johnson said "Once war seems hopeless, then peace may be possible. The door is always open to any settlement which assures the independence of South Vietnam and its freedom to seek help for its protection." This implies (1) that peace can only come when the other side realizes war is hopeless and (2) that the settlement to which our door is open is one which assures an independent South Vietnam, which can call on the U.S. and

SEATO for protection. The other quotation offered was from Johnson's message August 5, 1964, assuring Congress "that we shall continue readily to explore any avenues of political solution that will effectively guarantee the removal of Communist subversion."

Any compromise which would give the National Liberation Front some role in a coalition government would seem to be ruled out by that formulation. It implies their surrender or extermination. The fact that the State Department put these two quotations forward as embodiments of our policy foreshadows war to the bitter end rather than negotiation. When a reporter said, "Well, all that does not say that he [Johnson] is willing to have unconditional discussions," the Department's spokesman replied, "Well I think then that we are hung up on semantics." This makes sense only if "unconditional discussions" means something very different from unconditional negotiations. In negotiations we would still insist on winning at the bargaining table what we have yet to win either on the battlefield or in our dealings with the Vietnamese people. When reporters at the press conference tried to elicit what standards the government imposes in determining whether peace feelers are "serious" or "sincere," the spokesman retreated behind a smoke-screen of double-talk. The truth I believe is that we wait for a signal that the other side is ready, not to negotiate, but to surrender.

I hope I am wrong because if this is the policy then it will take a good many years of fighting and a lot of American and Vietnamese lives. It will poison our relations with the Soviet Union and may end the hopes of preventing a new step-up in the arms race. The Soviets, as can be seen in the latest attack from Peking, are under fire for serving U.S. interests in trying to bring about peace. Peking discloses that Kosygin went to Hanoi last February 6 in an attempt to bring about a negotiated settlement. This was also the report carried by the *London Sunday Observer* February 7 from Hong Kong in a dispatch by Stanley Karnow which reflected the judgment of the U.S. intelligence community there. That was the day Johnson, under the impact of the Viet Cong attack on our barracks at Pleiku, ordered the bombing of the North in accordance with contingency plans drawn up months earlier and long urged upon him by the military. To bomb the North while Kosygin was there virtually as our emissary trying to bring about peace, and to continue the bombing indefinitely instead of limiting it to a reprisal raid, may turn out to have been the Big Mistake of the war. It hardly made the search for peace easier. On this, too, the Administration has been deceptive.

NOVEMBER 22, 1965

# WHY SHOULD THEY TRUST JOHNSON
# ANY MORE THAN WE DO?

Goldberg under Johnson is stuck at the UN, as Stevenson so often was under Kennedy, with the task of making black look white, a belligerent policy look peaceful. His speech at the General Assembly is to be read not as diplomacy but as public relations. It will go down in the annals as another of those peace offensives with which his master has prefaced his successive escalations. Even as the dove cooed, the hawks swooped. B-52 raids on the demilitarized zone marked a qualitative escalation, for these had only been used once before in the North, against Mugia pass last April; McNamara announced a 30 per cent increase in warplane production; and in Washington, the White House, the Pentagon and State, in horrified unison, denied reports in New York and London that the U.S. planned to suspend its bombing to give Hanoi more time to consider Goldberg's proposals. To make sure Goldberg was not taken too seriously by the other side, Johnson held a press conference the same day and declined when asked to characterize Goldberg's proposals as either important or new. This was probably the most honest statement Lyndon Johnson ever made. All he would say was, "I think it is good for him to say it," as if this were an exercise in occupational therapy to keep a frustrated UN spokesman from blowing his top.

Goldberg's speech had to fit the crusty old elements of past Johnson and Rusk peace offers into a shiny new case designed to look as much as possible like the real thing—that is, U Thant's Three Points. When the works are opened up, it is easy to see how different Goldberg's is. In the first place, he is still trying to collect a price for Johnson's blackmail bombings of the North. U Thant's Point 1 was the unconditional cessation of these bombings. But Goldberg's is to stop them only if assured "that this step will be answered *promptly* by a *corresponding* and *appropriate* de-escalation from the other side." The italics, which are ours, light up the trap. How fast would we consider prompt and how much withdrawal would we accept as appropriate and corresponding? The North would have to come hat in hand to satisfy us on the price of ending our bombardment, and act under threat of resumption. In effect the first step would be not a time-table of our withdrawal, as de Gaulle suggested, but a time-table of theirs. Until we got our assurance, we would not put into effect this "prior" cessation. The weaker power must submit to the stronger. In addition the North, by bargaining its withdrawal against our bombardment, would have to equate the two morally, to justify Johnson's course since February, 1965, and to admit itself the invading aggressor. It must not only accept the conqueror's terms but wipe clean his bloody hands.

From the North's point of view its armed intervention was only a response to the blackmail bombings. It sees us intervening in a civil war which broke out because of our persistent violations of the Geneva agreements. From a world point of view, we would set a precedent whereby any strong power would be able to bomb any weak power until the weaker accepted its terms. That is the jungle law of reprisal to which we have always objected when practiced by other powers. U Thant asked cessation of the bombings not only as unmistakable evidence of a good faith otherwise all too questionable but as obedience to world law.

In U Thant's view this would set the stage for Point 2, a mutual reduction of military activity in the South to pave the way for a cease-fire and peace talks. But Goldberg's Point 2 is full of tricky pitfalls. He wants "a *supervised, phased* withdrawal of all external forces." What would be left after the withdrawals we had required in return for an end to the bombings? Who would supervise? How could the guerrillas afford to open up their secret bases, their one protection against our savage bombardments, to outside view until assured of a peace satisfactory to them? What would we consider "external forces?" How many would we accept as indigenous? How many would we call Northerners in disguise? These are skillfully hidden mines on the path of negotiation.

The guerrillas cannot be expected to lay down their arms until satisfied that they would have a satisfactory role in the making of the peace and the shaping of their country's future. U Thant's Point 3 called for their participation in the settlement. "Some argue," Goldberg said, referring to a lost intramural battle he and Humphrey are reported to have waged within the White House, "that, regardless of different views on who controls the Viet Cong, it is a combatant force and, as such, should take part in the peace negotiations." But Johnson does not want to admit, by recognizing the Viet Cong at the peace table, that we have been fighting an indigenous rebellion, for this would take the moral grounds from under our intervention and the political grounds from under his effort to restore a safely non-leftist South Vietnam. So all Goldberg was allowed to say is that this, the key question, would not prove "an insurmountable problem." Johnson wouldn't close a deal for a bull on his ranch on such vague terms.

The guerrillas must find no more reassuring Goldberg's vague declaration that we do not "seek to exclude any segment of the South Vietnamese people from peaceful participation in their country's future." In 1954 similar promises, much more explicitly spelled out, guaranteed the Vietminh an amnesty and full political rights. These were broken with our encouragement and they were killed or put into Diem's concentration camps. That is when the rebellion started. How can you expect the rebels to give up in return for the same kind of promises? What we offer must look to them like a one-way ticket to the jails and prison islands the Ky regime has already filled with militant Buddhists.[1] How many Americans really trust Johnson? Why should the Viet Cong?

OCTOBER 3, 1966

# A NEW NAVAL—AND PERHAPS MOVIE —HERO MAKES HIS DEBUT IN WASHINGTON

Lt. (jg) Dieter Dengler, USNR, a handsome young fellow of twenty-eight, in dazzling Navy whites, appeared under TV floodlights before the Senate Armed Services Committee September 16 to tell how he refused under torture to sign a statement condemning the U.S. while a communist prisoner in Laos and how he escaped last June. He was captured in February after his plane was shot down by ground fire while on a bombing mission over the North Vietnamese border. At the close of his story, both the Senators and the audience—for the first time in the memory of reporters present—broke into applause. One felt that a new naval—and perhaps movie—hero was being born.

[1] Robert Shaplen's estimate of the number jailed (*The New Yorker*, August 20) is "four or five thousand."

According to a Pentagon press release, the only documents Dengler was carrying when captured were his ID card and the expired German passport he used when he came to the U.S. in 1957. He is now a U.S. citizen. The news that a pilot with a German passport had been captured created an uproar in Germany where it was cited as evidence that Germans were being recruited for service in Vietnam. The passport has never been satisfactorily explained. It is a violation of regulations to go into combat with anything but one's ID card. Dengler said he carried the passport because it would explain his German accent, an explanation that would more plausibly fit the Battle of the Bulge, where American and German troops were locked in combat, than the jungles of Southeast Asia where natives can't tell one white man from another. Perhaps Dengler thought he might get better treatment by using the passport to prove he was a German rather than an American.

No such questions were raised by the Senators, who treated Dengler with small-boy admiration. The most fervent was Senator Thurmond, who broke into a threnody on the subject of freedom, "the most precious word in the English language next to God," and wanted to know what message Dengler had on the subject for the young people of this country. Dengler seemed vague. His only description of freedom was that it meant being able "to walk down the street, just to go and buy what you want." This sounded more like the Consumers' Union than Jefferson. "And if it means fighting for it," Thurmond pressed him, "it is your opinion that they would be following the part of wisdom to do so, would they not?" "If the government thinks so," Dengler replied, "yes, sir." The answer seemed to fit the accent perfectly.

Senator Smith wanted to know if peace demonstrations at home had encouraged the Viet Cong. "The only thing that I heard," Dengler told her, "was that these Pathet Lao think that the U.S. is going to go broke by the amount of aircraft they shoot down." Senator Byrd asked whether he had seen any evidence of Chinese participation in the war. Dengler, no doubt unaware that the Pentagon press release said he stole a Chinese rifle when he escaped, said "I saw Russian trucks and Russian weapons and I saw U.S. weapons. I did not see any Chinese indication of anything, sir." Perhaps he had better be re-briefed. Senator Russell was disturbed because Dengler's captors wore—as the Pentagon press release said—"U.S. type shirts and trousers, sunglasses and rubber boots" and had U.S. M-1s and carbines. U.S. military aid certainly gets around.

Dengler said the villagers were friendly. No one asked him how they felt about U.S. bombings. In San Diego he was asked whether he expected to be returned to active duty in Vietnam. "I hope not," was the reply, "but if Uncle Sam wants me, I certainly will be on my way." Otherwise he said he'd rather stay in the United States and open "a German-type restaurant."

SEPTEMBER 26, 1966

# BOBBY BAKERISM ON A WORLD SCALE

If Johnson really believes in co-existence, the place to prove it is in Vietnam. "Our task," he told the editorial writers in New York last Friday (October 7), "is to achieve a reconciliation with the East, a shift from the narrow concept of coexistence to the broader vision of peaceful engagement." If that were really his purpose, he could not find more willing collaborators than Ho Chi Minh and the South Vietnamese National Liberation Front. Ho Chi Minh has been trying all his life to find a basis not only for coexistence but for a "broader vision of peaceful engagement" with the West. This is why he negotiated the agreements to stay in the French Union after the war, and why he signed the Geneva pact in 1954, and why time after time he has offered to settle the present conflict on a basis which would give South Vietnam democratic self-government and neutrality in a framework which recognized the principle of Vietnam's essential national unity without insisting on reunification at this time.

A broad vision of peaceful engagement also lies behind the program of the NLF. In calling, from its beginning, for a neutral belt of South Vietnam, Laos and Cambodia, the NLF suggested engaging three different neighboring peoples with different social systems in a common effort to insulate themselves from great Power politics and ideological rivalry. The latest interview given Wilfred Burchett by the head of the NLF also envisages peaceful negotiation within South Vietnam in calling for the broadest kind of coalition government to restore peace and make social reconstruction possible. I am convinced from my talks last spring in Saigon and Cambodia that most Vietnamese on both sides are ready for just such a fraternal re-engagement. The NLF would like American help in reconstruction once American troops have left. The replacement of napalm with aid would be the symbol and the guarantee of just that peaceful engagement Johnson says he wants, but refuses to seek, in the one place where it counts, in the country our bombers have so ravaged North and South a recently returned flier described it as a lunar landscape, cratered and denuded.

We could not achieve a greater moral and political victory over China than to demonstrate, by a peace negotiated with the NLF, that co-existence with the United States is possible, that we do not oppose social change, that we are not the citadel of world counter-revolution. But that is not what Johnson means by coexistence and peaceful engagement. What he seeks is to buy the acquiescence of Moscow and of Eastern Europe in crushing the Vietnamese rebellion and if necessary China should Peking intervene. This is wheeler-dealerism on a world scale, the application to international affairs of those talents for seduction and corruption which have served Lyndon Johnson so well in his climb to power. He has been eager to talk with everybody except the brave men we have been fighting; he has offered concessions not only to Moscow but to Peking and even to Hanoi if they would abandon the South Vietnamese rebels to our merciless military machine. Not "let us reason together" but let us haggle together has been his guiding principle. To the blackmail of the North Vietnamese bombings, he adds the bribery of economic and political favors for East Europe. This is Bobby Bakerism globalized.

Johnson has ruined morally all who deal with him at home and he will ruin all who deal with him abroad. Humphrey and Goldberg have been destroyed by the seductive arts that turned them into his tools, and the same fate awaits the East Europeans who accept his favors while he rains death and destruction worse than any mankind has seen since World War II on a small and poorly defended country. We do not compare Johnson to Hitler nor our country to Nazi Germany but Der Fuehrer at Munich, too, assured Chamberlain there would be peace in our time if only the West recognized the right of the Sudeten Germans to dismember Czechoslovakia in the name of self-determination. Every step of Nazi expansion, down to the Nazi-Soviet pact, was proclaimed as just a step toward peace. If our military machine crushes the Vietnamese rebellion, it will mete out similar punishment wherever subject peoples seek their freedom from corrupt oligarchies linked with American interests. Vietnam is intended to be a lesson to the poor of Brazil and to the disaffected everywhere; a training ground for the Legions of the Pax Americana. If our military win in Vietnam there will be no holding them elsewhere or at home.

The essential issue is the suffering of the Vietnamese people and our unwillingness to bring it to an end unless they surrender to our will. *The threatening precedent is the right of any great power to bomb any small power into submission.* The test of the United Nations is whether it can focus clearly and sharply on this crime and this menace to world order. To offer Eastern Europe more business and better credits if they will shut their eyes to this is not conciliation but corruption. To offer Moscow a non-proliferation treaty for acquiescence in what we are doing is to shelve German nuclear ambitions at the price of a far greater threat to world law and order. What value is to be placed on our hint that we may accept boundaries in Eastern Europe when we violate them in Eastern Asia? How firm will the Oder-Neisse line be when we get through with the boundaries of North Vietnam and Laos and Cambodia and Thailand?

Let us try to see what is happening in a fresh perspective. What if Japan were again a great military power and it was bombing a small country in Latin America allied with the United States? What would we think if our Secretary of State paid a friendly visit to the Prime Minister of Japan under such circumstances and began to negotiate favors from him, like landing rights for a New York to Tokyo airline? Imagine how Latin allies under Japanese bombardment would feel if they saw pictures of their supposed American protector in friendly confabulation with Tokyo? This may help us to see what Johnson has already achieved in his talks with Gromyko. Whatever else comes of them, the moral effect is debasing. Johnson debases the Russians and he debases the American people. He drags us down into moral imbecility as we allow the killings and the burnings and the defoliations and the lying to go on. Johnson speaks of defending "freedom" in South Vietnam but Poland's Deputy Foreign Minister, Winiewicz, spoke the plain truth when he told the UN General Assembly last Monday that "the imposition by force of a military junta" upon the people of South Vietnam was being presented by the U.S. as "an implementation of the principle of self-determination." Compare the Orwellian double-think of Johnson's speech with the anguished description of what we are really doing to South Vietnam in the *New York Times Magazine* October 9 by Neil Sheehan, just back from three years of covering the war.

"I wonder," Sheehan wrote, "when I look at the bombed-out peasant hamlets, the orphans begging and stealing in the streets, and the women and children with napalm burns lying on the hospital cots, whether the United States or any nation has the right to inflict this suffering and degradation on another people for its own ends."

This is the abomination against which the world's conscience must be mobilized. This is the horror we must not let any phony olive branches elsewhere hide from view. This is the crime our country is committing. And this is what we must condemn, lest a later generation ask of us, as they ask of the Germans, who spoke up?

OCTOBER 17, 1966

# WHY *NOT* BRING CHRISTMAS
# UP TO DATE?

One bit of holiday cheer is the news that for years to come we won't need a poverty program for the Pentagon. The December issue of *Air Force,* just in time for Christmas, brings a projection into the 1980s by a Colonel Posvar who is chairman of the Division of Social Sciences at the U. S. Air Force Academy. It shows a globe with the northern section of Richer Nations as white as new-fallen snow while the southern section of Poorer Nations is prettily pockmarked with little red symbols showing various kinds of armed conflict—enough to keep his graduates busy into their old age. He sees (in capitals) "Revolution Rampant in Africa and Latin America" and even touches cheerfully on the "policy dilemmas" which will arise as communists "maneuver us into a choice" between supporting "local elements" with "reasonable social and economic grievances" but "tainted with communism" or "supporting reactionary or racist governments that are resisting change." He leaves the reader to guess—it's not hard—which side our B-52s will bolster.

This is the shape of that *Pax Americana* for which the Pentagon labors. Our military, like Trotskyists in reverse, dream of permanent revolution requiring permanent agencies of suppression. Their in-house literature looks back to the *Pax Romana,* and extols it as having given the world five unparalleled centuries of law and order. The troubles they don't speak about also parallel those of the Romans, the need for a virile fighting ideology to combat a subversive faith. We refer to Christianity, which threatens the *Pax Americana* as it once threatened to undermine the *Pax Romana*. The Romans seem gradually to have solved the problem. At first, as Gibbon ironically describes them, the Christians persisted in "their humane ignorance" and could not "be convinced that it was lawful on any occasion to shed the blood of our fellow creatures." But by the fifth century, as portrayed by Gibbon's continuator, Dean Milman, in his *History of Latin Christianity*, "The Christian God . . . had become a God of battle. The cross . . . glittered on the standards of the legions . . . We find bishops in arms."

Now these Christians seem to be relapsing into their old ways. The Pope, not satisfied with Christmas and New Year truces in Vietnam, is calling for one continuous holiday armistice leading to negotiations. The Protestants are no better than the Catholics. The National Council of Churches wants to stop the bombing of North Vietnam and even asks for more "candor," noxiously implying that our leaders have been telling us less than the truth. How can the military carry out their invigorating tasks if the clergy go around whining for truces? How can they, amid all this pacifistic preachment, bring up a younger generation to the manly virtue of visiting aerial conflagration on obdurate villagers? What could be more hurtful to the morale of our troops than to have the Pope say, as he did on December 8, "How opposed to one another are these two forms, these two events, Christmas and war?" If our sorely tried military had to choose between them, their only way out would be to get rid of Christmas. A less radical course would lead to its modernization. Surely, considering the resources and the willing intellectuals at its disposal, the Pentagon could convert it into a Holiday of Pacification, with Kris Kringle jumping out of a helicopter in a jolly Green Beret, gifts in one hand for the submissive and in the other a little can of instant hell to napalm the wicked.

DECEMBER 19, 1966

# MORE THAN STEEL AND
# CHROME CAN BEAR

At this tense moment, when there is hope everywhere that peace may emerge from the Vietnamese New Year cease-fire, the rest of the world may spare a little time to consider what it is asking of us Americans. If men live by symbols, then all we live by is threatened. This can be seen if we strip away non-essentials and get down to the sensitive and painful layers of the mind, where the decisions are really made. To call off the bombings, to sit down with the rebels, to accept some kind of coalition regime, open or disguised, would be to admit that we had lost the war. And that, the world should recognize, is very hard indeed.

Everything America stands for is at stake. And not just America, but everything the modern world admires. And not just the capitalist world, but all that Lenin and his comrades aspired to ever since the days when *Fordismus* was the magic word of Bolshevism, its gleaming goal, a future of mass production, brought at last to the muddy villages of Mother Russia. It is the Machine, it is the prestige of the machine, that is at stake in Vietnam. It is Boeing and General Electric and Goodyear and General Dynamics. It is the electronic range-finder and the amphibious truck and the night-piercing radar. It is the defoliant, and the herbicide, and the deodorant, and the depilatory. It is the products and the brand names we have been conditioned since childhood to revere. It is the ideal of our young men. This—do not be deceived by the cowboy tall in the saddle smoking Marlboros on TV, as distant a figure from our lives as Tarzan of the Apes—this ideal is to be an Ivy League-suited executive in one of those chrome and glass skyscrapers which are our cathedrals. It is to be a human particle as shiny and antiseptic and replaceable as any machine part, in the world of business. This is more than a drive for money. It is the veneration of efficiency. It is faith in technology, in mechanical solutions for every problem, in the Gadget as God. This is the faith those uncouth guerrillas in Vietnam have placed in jeopardy.

When General LeMay said we could win the war by bombing them back to the Stone Age, he was speaking up from the depths of our deepest horror. What fate could be worse than to put people back in the Stone Age—without refrigerators, supermarkets, even toilets? Now we're frantic because for our purposes these Vietnamese peasants were in the Stone Age already, and had never heard of the comforts we were going to blast away from them. Down there in the jungles, unregenerate, ingenious, tricky, as tiny as a louse or a termite, and as hard to get at, emerged a strange creature whose potency we had almost forgotten—Man. To sit down now and deal with him is to admit that the Machine is lost to Man, that our beautifully computerized war, with the most complicated devices for killing ever assembled and the most overwhelming firepower ever mustered, has failed. To ask us to give up our faith in General Motors is like asking a Joan of Arc to give up her faith in God; we, too, may prefer the fire, for this really shakes the foundations of our security. These are the invisible blows that rain down on Detroit while everybody worries about Hanoi. We ask the world: Dry your tears about those uprooted peasants—if you look closely you will see that *they* are still there. And think of our poor frustrated bulldozers.

FEBRUARY 13, 1967

# X

---

**A**

**VISIT**

**TO**

**VIETNAM**

**AND**

**CAMBODIA**

# WHAT IT'S LIKE TO BE IN SAIGON

What I remember most of Saigon is the heat, the squalor and the despair. I began by being terribly frustrated and ended by being terribly fascinated. The frustration arose from trying to get things done in a country which seems engaged in a giant conspiracy to slow everything down; I'd hate to have to run a war in the vast snafu that is South Vietnam; only an Eagle Scout like Westmoreland could stand it without going off his rocker. Just what the fascination was I don't quite know, perhaps it was the ringside seat Saigon offers on the inexhaustible vitality and folly of the human race.

The heat lay like a suffocating blanket on the city, and it was hard to know which was worse, the sunny days or the cloudy when a blue haze of carbon monoxide lay low over the teeming streets. At night with the windows open in a cheap hotel which charged New York prices, one slept not just naked but with every pore alert for an occasional hint of breeze. After the midnight curfew one is awakened from time to time by the dull thud of mortars like a giant tapping on distant doors. One night the whole hotel shook, the doors went rat-tat-tat, as a huge armada passed overhead and dumped its deadly freight somewhere far off in the darkness. There were three waves of this miniature earthquake and one suddenly realized the meaning of the term privileged sanctuary, for Americans in Vietnam can sleep with the assurance that amid the heavy traffic overhead, there are no enemy planes. Goliath never had it so good.

Even on the quieter nights, sleep begins to be impossible around five. There is a constant roar of heavy trucks from the clogged waterfront nearby. The noise overhead surpasses that in the areas adjoining La Guardia airport, and starts much earlier; the decibel factor alone makes it easy to believe that Saigon's Tan Son Nhut is now the world's busiest airport. The guerrillas have cut the railroads and made the roads impassable everywhere—except for those who pay their fees and are granted passage. For Americans it is safe to travel only in the skies. In the morning one emerges early on streets from which the garbage is no longer carted away. This and the lax currency control on entry are the first signs of disintegration; the government is falling apart. The generals maneuver, no longer so much for power as for some political foothold. Their wives, so it is said, are the brains of the family and devote them to the business of selling export and import licenses. The coolies who used to collect the garbage probably make five times as much now on the docks or in construction, for labor is scarce in the war boom that has seized Saigon. One newspaper article I saw suggested that maybe garbage collection ought to be handed over to free enterprise, a touching testimonial to the spread of the American theology to these lands beyond the sea.

In the mornings, moving from air-conditioned U.S. offices to the hot bake-oven outside, one felt ninety-eight years old by 10 A.M. and ready to collapse in a pre-lunch siesta under an electric fan, those days electricity was available. After lunch, one hastened back to the darkened and sweaty refuge of one's hotel room. The once beautiful and broad avenues of the great city outside are filled with a mad tangle of vehicles. Here a tiny donkey cart carries a rustic family into town; it is loaded down with pots and pans and bags. From the interstices children look out big-eyed with wonder. There a two-seater cyclopus goes by with two soigné matrons, exquisitely kept in their privileged middle age, engaged in shrewd and vivacious conversation. The streets swarm with cyclopuses—the old rickshaw raised to a higher technological level by being wedded to the bicycle, with which the driver pushes from behind. Next in the hierarchy of public transport is the motorized cyclopus, then tiny Renault taxis. They contest the streets with a constant flow of jeeps and military buses. Maneuvering dashingly amid this wildly tooting herd of vehicles is an occasional Vietnamese motorcycle "cowboy" with miniature Stetson and tight Western movie pants. The costume makes the slight, delicate-boned Vietnamese look more mannikin than man, a tiny caricature of a Texan. The scene is dominated from time to time by the passage, often under armed escort, of some Vietnamese VIP in a Peugot, Mercedes-Benz or Cadillac; these testify to how many people do quite well on the war.

Most of the people's daily life seems to be spent in the streets. On the crowded sidewalks, capitalism is in flower. Half the population of Saigon seems to have set itself up in business with items from the American PX. Everywhere there are tiny stalls selling Gillette razor blades, Spearmint chewing gum, Almond Joys, Colgate toothpaste, Chesterfield cigarettes and Hershey bars at a generous markup. So large an outflow from the PX indicates that military service has not stifled the Yankee trader spirit in our troops. Along the curb and under the stalls, mats are spread on which whole families lunch and dine; the food is cooked on a tiny brazier, and delicately served by the mothers. The meals, mostly seafood stews served on rice, are eaten with the gusto of a family picnic. Everybody seems to be having a good time, from the children begging in the streets to the shoeshine boys showing off to an admiring crowd how much they can overcharge the big barbarians from oversea. In the endless pageantry of the streets, I even encountered one patriotic demonstration. Just before 8 A.M. on Nguyen Hué street I was attracted by a crowd standing at attention while the South Vietnamese flag was raised and a loud speaker broadcast the national anthem. When the ceremony was finished the crowd filed into the building. It was the headquarters of the General Confederation of Employers. This evidence of a renaissance in national spirit may give Henry Cabot Lodge a lift.

The crew of the Air Vietnam plane on which I flew from Hong Kong to Saigon was entirely Vietnamese. Lunch was first rate French Asian cuisine with good French wines. The stewardess gave me my first glimpse of how demurely seductive the Vietnamese woman's costume can be: delectably feminine loose flowing pants as the undergarment, usually white, with a kind of split sari over it of contrasting color. It is the direct opposite of the strip tease. The girl is completely covered from throat to feet, not even the ankles are visible. Yet as the girl moves the flowing garments suddenly mold and reveal the figure for a fleeting intimate moment. The moving limbs provide a constant, spontaneous and luminous ballet.

The civilian arrival hall of the airport at Saigon was a huge shed of wood and tin, almost furnace-like in its suffocating heat. When I finally got away in an Air Vietnam bus, the sky was a luscious pale blue with tufts of white cloud but the scene below was hot and dusty. April, before the monsoon rains begin, is Saigon's hottest and driest month. I saw no signs of the mortar attack on the airport a few days earlier. It must have been in a distant corner of that huge airport. There was a big unpainted restaurant with a billboard in French advertising the first dentifrice of the Republic with "fluor." Other billboards as we sped by advertised the Lambretta scooter, GM's Cadillacs and Chevrolets, and Pan Am. We passed villas taken over by the military. Sandbag embankments were visible behind their low white walls. Some of the villas were as big as palaces. We went over a bridge and caught a glimpse of dark unpainted shacks high on stilts along a river bank as far as one could see. Near them, set back from the water, were white and pink stucco villas with gardens behind high white walls. The rich and the poor seemed to live almost side by side in this neighborhood.

At the hot dusty freight shed which is Saigon's air terminus, a taxi driver made a deal with me—the newly arrived sucker—for 200 piastres to the Hotel Caravelle, or ten times the normal price. Then he strode off in lordly satisfaction, leaving me to handle my bags. Several eager urchins seized them despite my effort to explain in French and English that I had no cash. When I got into the minature cab and left them empty handed, I was treated to a pantomime of pained indignation and an outburst of grandiloquent Vietnamese by the budding entrepreneurs until my lordly driver handed out two five-piastre bills to quiet down the demonstration. At the Caravelle, only a few blocks away, I learned that my telegraphic confirmation of a reservation was worthless. I soon discovered that the Caravelle was inhabited by phantoms. I had the names of half a dozen persons to see, all presumably at the Caravelle, and all equally

268 I. F. STONE

unknown to the management. I did not learn until later that every room there was acquired only by intricate bribery; the lucky few who have rooms are forced to treat the management as a pampered mistress; one day asked to bring expensive film from the PX, another day some choice foodstuff. The only exception was A. J. Muste and his CNVA [1] delegation which got a big room, perhaps because it was conveniently wired for sound by the police and they preferred to have the pacifists where they could keep a close watch on their comings and goings. I soon was sent off to what I was assured was a modern air-conditioned hotel. The room at the Federal turned out to have a broken down fan and a shower which never once in my eight day stay had hot water.

Saigon, as I emerged on it that Sunday afternoon, must have been a lovely French Asian capital before the war with its broad tree-lined boulevards, open squares and shady arcades. Now it seemed an Asiatic honky tonk. Though it was siesta time, here and there U.S. soldiers in pairs sauntered dolefully past the many bars looking like Bill Mauldin types in search of an ersatz Mama. Small boys were already out pimping in the hot afternoon, hinting in pidgin English at bizarre pleasures. The immemorial entrepreneurial spirit flourished in the world's oldest commodity, women, but the soldiers seemed too shy to close such deals in broad daylight. Warding off importunate pedicab drivers I made straight for the big white building at Nguyen Hué street and Le Loi boulevard which is the center of journalistic activity in Saigon—JUSPAO, the Joint U. S. Public Affairs Office, on a square adjoining the white walled palace of Saigon's City Hall. JUSPAO is surrounded by a barricade, with a guard house at either end. I got by one of them only to find the main entrance locked. As I walked from one locked door to another, alone behind that white-washed barricade, one lone American in full view of the promenading Sunday crowds, I felt conspicuously alone, an easy tempting target for any potshot from a VC sympathizer. That was my one moment of apprehension. Soon one treats the possibility of being hit by a bomb in Saigon as matter-of-factly as the chance of an auto accident in the States.

Fortunately one locked side door was soon opened for me by

[1] Committee for Nonviolent Action.

a lonesome duty officer. I was greeted inside by a huge picture of Lyndon Johnson, looking in that setting almost Orientally inscrutable. Next to the picture was a sign in English and Vietnamese saying peremptorily, "Clear your weapon before going topside." When I asked the duty officer what clearing one's weapon meant, he said it meant taking any live bullet out before going upstairs but that actually the order had been superseded by a later one simply requiring all weapons to be left below. I was heartened by this sign of progress.

Before being permanently accredited as an American correspondent, one has to obtain a press card from the South Vietnamese government. This is the sole act of deference to Vietnamese sovereignty required of the visiting American. The contrast between the two press HQs reflects the real balance of forces. JUSPAO has taken over a multi-storied elegant white building on one of the town's most important squares. The ARVN press office is housed in a nearby second story loft, dark, grimy and cooled only by an old-fashioned fan. A press card is issued without question, and for most U.S. correspondents that one visit to the loft is all they will make during their tour of duty. A formal military press briefing is held there at 4:30 P.M. each day, a half hour before the daily briefing at JUSPAO, but only a few wire service men, on days when they are hungry for news, turn up. The military briefing officer speaks in Vietnamese but often interrupts his interpreter to correct the latter's sometimes incomprehensible English.

Back across the street, in the air-conditioned realm of JUSPAO, with its snack bar, its PX and—like oases—its clean water fountains, the American finds himself, as the French say, *chez lui*, at home. The newcomer, even if a stray heretic like myself, encounters that unpretentious amiability which is the most attractive and democratic side of our American character. I had failed to bring the required letter from one's editor but after some good-humored joshing from a press officer who told the military I was chief cook and bottle-washer of my own publication, my card was issued. I was also asked to sign a form absolving the U.S. government from liability if anything happened to me while riding in a military plane. During the eight days I was in Saigon I met with nothing but courtesy from U.S. officers, civilian or military. The question in my mind was how so many well-meaning, friendly and intelligent people, with so much in the way of funds and Vietnamese informers at their disposal, could guess so consistently wrong about events in Vietnam. Honolulu, and its aftermath of anti-American riots, were only the latest examples of this incomprehension. I would like to sketch out a tentative answer on the basis of what I saw and heard.

The first thing that strikes one is the extent to which the Americans in Vietnam live in enclaves—not just military but psychological enclaves. JUSPAO, the Embassy, the various AID missions and the military HQs in Saigon are like miniature fortresses in a hostile land. They reminded me strongly of the sand-bagged and barricaded offices of the British in their conflict with Israel's Haganah and the terrorists in the three turbulent years before Britain withdrew from Palestine in 1948. But these fortresses are vulnerable from within; they depend on Vietnamese employes and there is no certain way to distinguish friend from foe. The situation must be apple pie for Viet Cong intelligence. Our press and our soldiers live in a world apart; few speak even such bad French as mine, much less Vietnamese. The mentality we develop is the "compound" complex which has always afflicted foreigners living as traders or soldiers in a foreign land. We bring America with us wherever we go, and live wrapped in a kind of cellophane which separates us from the people of the country. Our relations with them are almost entirely mercenary, and the women, the informers and the soldiers we buy are about as unsatisfactory as bought love is everywhere. They must secretly regard us with amusement or contempt.

To watch the young Ivy Leaguers arriving briskly at the Embassy of a morning is to feel oneself on the eve of the Harvard-Yale game. The team spirit is bursting out all over; it demands optimism; patriotism is equated with euphoria. All is for the best, albeit not in the best of all possible worlds. One day the official spokesman is enthusiastic about the firing of General Thi as a move against "war-lordism." When Thi's removal turns out to be a bad mistake, the same spokesman discovers that these are just the birth pangs in South Vietnam of "federalism," the problem of integrating each region into the national whole. He even touches on the U. S. Civil War until a tart newsman suggests there are enough civil wars going on in South Vietnam without rehashing the problem of the Gray and the Blue. Everything is public relations and public relations is make-believe. Every top official is more concerned with his "image" than with unpleasant realities. To mention these is to get off the team. Bright gimmicks are turned into speeches and proliferate into pamphlets long before anything has been accomplished or even after hopes have collapsed. The word is taken for the deed. As one moves from talking to the men who work in the field to those who work in Saigon and then think of the men in Washington, one sees that the further from the scene the more imaginary the picture we have created. The most confining enclave of all is this enclave in our heads.

Under the supposed benevolence of our policy one soon detects a deep animosity to the Vietnamese and a vast arrogance. We assume the right to remold them, whether they choose to be remolded or not. The war, like the cold war, has developed a vein of zealotry alien to the easy-going American character. An enthusiastic psychological warrior, anxious to impress me, took me out for a drink on the cool veranda of the Continental Palace; one could imagine how the French planters and civil servants must have gathered there in the afternoons for their aperitifs. My new found friend—he claimed to know all about me—told me that in working with captured VC he found that 95 per cent were "recoverable" human beings. It was my first evening and I did not dare repay his hospitality by asking what we did with the other 5 per cent— dispose of them like Kleenex? Directives go down from on high to treat the villagers with some discrimination. But the poor GI's one encounters are too full of rage at the fate which has brought them there. A boy from Mobile told me 50 per cent of the people in Saigon were VC, 45 per cent indifferent and 5 per cent with us; he thought we ought to go all-out to win the war—smash Hanoi—or go home. His buddy from Minnesota said at first he had been afraid all the time. He described the sleepless nights in the jungle, the stink of the water. Now he had become a fatalist; he felt he might get it anywhere, so why worry? Terrorism is hard to take, to see a buddy blown up by a mine or knocked off by a sniper hardly makes one benevolent to the natives. One hears frightful stories of troops in the field setting fire to villages or, on evacuating them, defecating in the cooking utensils, out of sheer hate and resentment.

In Saigon, on R and R (rest and recreation), the bar girls gyp the troops with the skill of their sisters in the clip joints of Greenwich Village. A soldier can spend a month's pay on "Saigon tea" and emerge as virgin as he entered. The soldiers feel that they are taken advantage of on every hand, and they are. I heard a burly sergeant explode one night at the Caravelle when he found, as usual, that advance reservations had been ignored. "We're out there in the jungle trying to hold this country together," he shouted angrily, "and this is what we get for it." There is hardly benevolence in the words one hears so frequently at the daily military briefing—"search and destroy"— as if we were an Old Testament God. In the cool panelled classroom in which the briefings are held, the only theory of the war which seems to emerge is implied by the "kill count" as if we were on an insect extermination mission and could go home when all the termites had been destroyed. It is significant that those like General Lansdale and Colonel John Paul Vann who would approach the Vietnamese as people soon find themselves sidetracked, suspect and frustrated. The machine instinctively reacts against the human, and what we are running, or what is running us, is a bureaucratic war machine.

Americans with cameras search out VC atrocities with indignation, but the use of napalm and saturation bombing is regarded merely as another form of technology. The machine is forgiven atrocities many-fold more terrible than those of the guerrillas. The Vietnamese are expendable. I came across cold warriors who had operated in Germany, in Bolivia, in Brazil and in Santo Domingo and now, in all innocence, commit similar follies in Vietnam. They place a very high value on the purity of their intentions and a very low estimate on the motivations of the Vietnamese. One old acquaintance gave me a briefing on all we were doing for the Vietnamese and then dropped remarks which revealed a very different attitude. The editors in Saigon, who have been asking for freedom of the press, called a one-day general strike to protest an attack on a pro-government editor (the military could hardly object to that) but appended to this a demand for greater press freedom. When I asked my friend about this, he said cynically, "they only wanted to save a day's newsprint." Yet he had been telling me we were there to protect democracy from communism. Every demand for democratic rights is regarded as perverse if not subversive; this is also the basic attitude toward elections. One often feels our people regard the Vietnamese as irrelevant to our worldwide holy war against communism. As my friend said, "After all it's only an accident that this war is being fought here. We have to smash the idea of wars of liberation." If Vietnam and the Vietnamese are badly battered in the process, it's too bad. The growing awareness of this essential indifference to their fate is giving the Vietnamese a common despair that might some day prove stronger even than fratricidal passion.

Our capacity for overlooking the obvious is enormous. Even one of the best and most independent reporters here was shocked by the anti-Americanism of recent demonstrations in Saigon and in Hué and Danang. He shares the naive view that we are there to help the Vietnamese and regards the demonstrations as sheer ingratitude. The simple fact that occupying armies, whether allied or enemy, always become unpopular hardly ever figures in official calculation. It would be too hard to reconcile it with the planned steady increase in the number of troops. This, in a country as fiercely nationalistic as Vietnam, spells more trouble of the same kind but to face the facts might force us to recast our policy. An experienced British correspondent told me that several months ago he raised the question with a U.S. official of the resentment and annoyance created by the influx of foreign troops, with the money to get first choice of everything from women to pedicabs. He predicted that urban unrest might prove worse than the trouble in the villages. He was told he ought to try and be more "constructive."

A group of Buddhist neutralists of whom I shall tell more in my next letter published a volume in French and English called *Dialogue*. In one of them Pham Cong Thien writes, "Here is my Nada prayer: Lead us not into Salvation, but deliver us from Deliverance." This is the true cry of the heart from a country torn apart.

MAY 9, 1966

# WHAT VIETNAMESE SAY
# PRIVATELY IN SAIGON

The strategy of U.S. press relations in South Vietnam is that of the Warm Embrace. It is easier to get away from a bar girl on Nguyen Hué street than from the loving arms of Press Chief Barry Zorthian's bureaucratic octupus for tenderizing (and ultimately digesting) the visiting correspondent. VIPs like Joseph Alsop get a broad view of the war from General Westmoreland's own plane, or a specially prepared memorandum like that given Cyrus Sulzberger to confirm his worst suspicions of the recent protest movement in Hué and Danang. Everything is done to make it comfortable and easy to cover the war through official channels, and the most enterprising visitor soon turns from the exhausting task of penetrating the strange world and the strange tongues outside to the warm womb of the JUSPAO (Joint U. S. Public Affairs Organization) HQ.

The visitor can easily find most of his limited time consumed by official briefings and visits to show-pieces and battle scenes. Every effort is made to enlist the visitor emotionally in the war. I decided to keep away from the offer of field trips. I had no desire to compete with Hanson Baldwin. I wanted to get some idea of civilian politics and for this I wanted to talk with Vietnamese. I decided to stay in Saigon and try my luck on my own. In this installment I want to let a few of the Vietnamese speak for themselves.

My most surprising encounter came early one morning while waiting for an appointment at a U. S. AID Mission compound.

An elderly Vietnamese to whom I smiled asked me in French if I knew any German. I said I knew a little. He brought out a grimy German primer in French and asked how I pronounced a certain word. I have forgotten the word but I cannot forget the conversation. It was so different from the American stereotype of what it should have been. Our conversation turned to politics. When I asked him to what party he belonged, he pulled a cross from under his shirt. He was a refugee from North Vietnam, a former landowner who had lost one of his children, a two-month-old infant on the trek south in 1956 through jungle and over mountains. I expected him to be a bitter-ender. Instead, though employed by the U.S., and speaking in a U.S. mission, he was for peace.

He raised his hand, with the five fingers outstretched. "This," he said in French, "is a war of depopulation. Soon only one Vietnamese in five will be left. This is a war *sans issue*—with no way out. It would take two million soldiers for victory, and that is impossible." He ran his hand expressively down in front of his face. "It's all a question of face," he said. Then, in vivid pantomime, rolling up his pants leg and rubbing an aching stomach, he imitated the ragged and hungry guerrillas the U.S. was up against, but couldn't wipe out. "It's all a question of face," he repeated.

"We must return to Geneva," he said. He was for a cease-fire, for elections to be supervised by a UN force (he dismissed the currently scheduled elections cynically), and for a negotiated peace, to be followed by an American withdrawal. "In the cities," he said, "people don't like the communists but don't want to be soldiers. In the countryside everywhere people are sad and unhappy. But here in Saigon"—and he grimaced—"many people are making money on the war. They are building apartment houses for the Americans. They'd like the Americans to stay for a hundred years." He shrugged his shoulders in a gesture of despair.

Another surprise was an interview with a Vietnamese lawyer, a high official of the country's permanent civil service. I cannot identify him more closely. Like my Catholic friend, he was in despair over what the war was doing to his country. "There is no way out," he said, "except to recognize and negotiate with the National Liberation Front. It controls two-thirds of the territory and almost half of the people. In legal terms, this is physical sovereignty. It's a reality and peace can only be made by dealing with realities. Everyone wants peace but peace cannot be made in Peking or Hanoi. It must be made here. We must invite the NLF to the negotiating table."

We spoke together in one of those comfortably cool upper middle class villas with walled gardens where life goes on in Saigon much as it has for a generation despite the continued warfare. The lawyer was French educated, of wealthy family, a cultivated and witty man, unable to speak publicly—death or deportation is the penalty for peace talk. "It is obvious that the Front has grown stronger not weaker with U.S. intervention. According to your McNamara's own figures only 50,000 of the Front's 270,000 men are from the North. The forces against them outnumber them more than three-to-one yet the Front can withstand them. This is a reality which cannot be ignored."

He was against reunification. "The North is communist. Our life requires a republican and liberal government," he continued. "If the U.S. recognizes the Front, invites it to a conference, and proposes a republican government, I believe the Front will accept this so long as the regime is non-aligned, and represents all political tendencies including the communists. It would take twenty years to rebuild the South to the point where it was strong enough to confront the North in reunification. I would normalize trade and exchanges of all kinds, I would sell them rice and buy their cement and coal. But I would oppose even confederation at this time. If it can't be accomplished in Germany, how can it be accomplished here? The two systems are too different."

When I brought up the question of elections, I found my new friend skeptical. "Where would they be held?" he asked. "Only in the cities, and even in the cities of Saigon, Hué and Danang, the Viet Cong is strong. How can you have elections when three-fourths of the territory is not included?" Then he brought up another fundamental obstacle. "Communist and neutralist candidates are to be barred," he noted. "But who is to decide who is a communist or a neutralist? This means that pro-war and anti-communist candidates will be the only ones allowed to run."

This civil servant relies on two factors to make a successful negotiation possible. "One," he said, "is that the war is impoverishing all of us, North and South. The other is that Ho and most of the Northern leaders like those of the National Liberation Front are Western educated and closer to us in outlook than they are to China. The Front is not entirely communist but a national front, with many genuine nationalists in it. I knew Nguyen Huu Tho, president of the NLF, when we were in the university together. I remember when he began an anti-French movement in 1950. He was a real nationalist, not a Vietminh. The leaders of the Front came out of the same milieu as ourselves. We understand each other. They want a democratic regime, neither communist nor anti-communist. We need a legal and civilian U.S.-backed regime here which can negotiate with the NLF." He envisaged withdrawal of U.S. troops only after negotiations, and he was against retention by the U.S. of its bases in South Vietnam. "You don't need them," he said. "The Seventh Fleet gives you a powerful offshore base."

Off the main streets in Saigon are smaller unpaved alleys lined by miniature houses for this miniature people. On one of them is a three-story structure, again small by our standards, which houses Van Hanh University, a Buddhist school of higher learning. One of the heroes of its students and of the peace movement is a Buddhist bonze who is also a poet, the Venerable Nhat Hanh. Some of his anti-war poems have been set to music and his latest volume of verses sold 4000 copies, enough to call it sharply to the attention of the police. They were given orders to pick up all the copies they could find in the bookstores. I had the pleasure of talking with him in his tiny apartment near the university. He represents not only a neutralist point of view—though this term seems pale and colorless beside his hatred of war and injustice—but of secularism in politics. "I'd rather speak as a Vietnamese than as a Buddhist," he told me. "I have many Catholic friends and we share a distrust of our own religious leaders." The group of intellectuals who gather about Nhat Hanh distrust the militant Buddhist leader Thich Tri Quang, for example. While U.S. sources—always prone to see red in any opposition—regard Tri Quang as a communist, these students think him more wrapped up in a confessional conflict with the Catholics than concerned with peace and national objectives.

Thich Nhat Hanh's personal creed seems to be compounded of Buddhism and existentialism. His group published a little book last year called *Dialogue*. In it, in an open letter to the Rev. Martin Luther King, Nhat Hanh defended those bonzes who had burned themselves to death in the demonstrations which led to the fall of Diem. He wrote that Buddha in one of his former lives "gave himself to a hungry lion which was about to devour her own cubs." He said the self-burnings were not suicide but an act "of highest compassion" in order to call the attention of the world to the sufferings of the Vietnamese people. In his letter to Dr. King, Nhat Hanh wrote "Nobody here wants the war," and ended with a prayer which gives the flavor of his religious and philosophical outlook, "Lord Buddha, help us to be alert to realize that we are not victims of each other. We are victims of our own ignorance and the ignorance of others." He is a slightly built man of forty, who moves in an aura of modesty and serenity. He speaks English, for he studied the philosophy of religion at Princeton in 1961 and was a lecturer on Buddhism at Columbia in 1962–63. The students and younger faculty people who crowd his apartment look on him with reverence.

"Nobody can win this war," he told me. "Vietnam can only lose. The South Vietnamese and U.S. government speak of a social revolution but nothing can be done while the war is going on. The war undermines everything. It is too late for the Americans to realize a social revolution anyway. After seven years of American intervention, the Viet Cong are stronger than ever, and 200,000 American troops mean 200,000 '*bêtises*' [blunders, stupidities] a day, antagonizing people further.

"You cannot distinguish the VC from the peasants. Every day the number of peasants killed is far greater than the number of VC. Every day of war makes more VC. The first essential is a cease-fire, then all else will follow. The VC prefer political to military means. I believe they would accept a cease-fire. They feel that the current peace moves are not genuine. The thing to do is to stop the bombings North and South, stop all offensive military action, and do it sincerely and the other side will reciprocate.

"Our real aspiration is to make Americans our friends not in war but in reconstruction, otherwise it will be very slow. The French built schools as a friendly memorial. You too must leave a good sentiment in Asian hearts."

The monk deplored a moral degeneration on both sides. "It is a shame for us and for all humanity," Nhat Hanh said, "that while war devastates the villages, here in Saigon people make money from the war. A new class of Vietnamese has been created who serve the Americans and profit from the devastation of their own country. They are men without culture or feeling. On the other hand most of the American soldiers here are not well educated, do not understand the Vietnamese and constantly offend. They sell watches to get girls. The people feel their country is being flooded with these foreign troops and controlled by them. This makes a very bad impression and gives VC propaganda its chance. This is why we are losing the war.

"In 1954 when Diem first came in, we had a chance to win. But the Diem government made too many mistakes. The Americans did not realize the psychological struggle and stressed mostly the military. The VC are very clever. They come to the villages in simple dress. They take care of babies, clean the houses and practice austerity. The government agents arrive beautifully dressed. They draw big salaries. They give orders and they withdraw after a few hours.

"The Americans," Nhat Hanh continued, "instead of helping us to stand on our own feet, have made us more dependent, so that now we even have to import rice. On top of that, the intensification of the war and the bombing have made almost a million people homeless. In the refugee camps conditions are beyond belief. The refugees are supposed to get seven piastres a day. A young man needs a kilo of rice a day. This costs fifteen piastres in Saigon, but in the refugee camps because of the cost of transportation the cost of rice may go as high as forty to sixty piastres a kilo. For seven piastres all one can buy is a thin soup.

"It is hard to live with the communists," the monk said. "They will not allow freedom of thought where they take over. But we must not despair, nor be too afraid of them. We have to face up to them and forge our own links with the people."

Nhat Hanh and his group have organized a little Peace Corps of their own to work in the villages. It has established three camps where students work and live among the peasants. "The urban intelligentsia," he said, "must earn the trust of the peasants." He himself was at one of these camps in a nearby area when the recent mortar attack on the airport took place. "We were not afraid of the VC mortars," he recounted, "but we were terrified by the U.S. plane raids which followed. The villages nearby suffered greatly."

He thought the Buddhists deficient when it came to social issues. "We consider ours a school for training youth in social service," he explained. "We follow the ideas of Gandhi and of Vinobha Bhave," the Indian who led a voluntary land redistribution campaign. Nhat Hanh feels that only by such grass roots work can his group hope to compete in peace with the communists. "Remember," he said as our conversation ended, "nobody can win the war. It can have only one end—to destroy all Vietnam." In one of his most famous poems he asked, "If we kill man, with whom shall we live?" Beyond politics and ideology, this is the simpler existentialist vision that moves Nhat Hanh and the young intellectuals gathered around him.

Every visitor tends to seek out the like-minded and therefore to discover what he hoped to find. The views brought back by pro-peace people like myself are therefore as apt to be skewed as those with which the U.S. bureaucracy comforts itself. I want now to report a quite different interview with an outstanding political figure, the famous Dr. Phan Quang Dan, who may yet play a leading, and perhaps unexpected, role in South Vietnam.

Dr. Dan became famous in 1959, when he was the one oppositionist elected to the National Assembly in Saigon in spite of an electoral law designed to return a rubber stamp legislature. He was barred from taking his seat on trumped up charges of violating the electoral laws. His life may serve to illuminate the complexities of Vietnamese politics, and some of the surprises which may lie ahead. Dr. Dan is a Northerner, born in Vinh in 1918, educated in Hanoi. While still studying medicine he began to work in the anti-French underground. He founded an anti-communist and anti-colonialist paper in Hanoi after the war and refused offers of posts in two coalition governments set up by Ho Chi Minh in 1946. Instead after the agreement between Ho and the French he went into exile in China. He established friendly relations with the Kuomintang and became a political adviser to the exiled Emperor Bao Dai but broke with him in 1949 because Dr. Dan felt the independence the French offered was phony. He continued his political and medical career in exile, obtained a medical degree at the Sorbonne in 1949, and a master's in public health at Harvard in 1953. When Diem set up his first government in 1954 he offered Dr. Dan the Secretaryship of Social Welfare but Dr. Dan refused it. He came home next year, however, to organize work in preventive medicine, to set up a clinic for the poor which he still operates, and to organize a legal opposition. Dr. Dan was arrested in 1956 for criticizing the rigged elections for that year's Assembly. The office of his opposition paper was blown up by Diem's secret police and it was finally suppressed in 1958. He was arrested again after the unsuccessful paratroop revolt of 1960. His luster was somewhat dimmed, I was told, when in his 1963 trial he recanted and praised the strategic hamlet program. But if this is true it came after three terrible years of imprisonment while awaiting trial, two of them in solitary confinement in a secret cell under the Saigon Botanical Gardens where he was savagely tortured.

Dr. Dan is one of the heroes of the democratic resistance. But Dr. Dan, as it turned out in my interview, is also an advocate of continuing the war to victory, and of sharply restricting democratic rights in the process. I interviewed him in the rather poverty-stricken clinic he operates off the crowded market place in suburban Gia Dinh. He is small, dynamic, intelligent, dark-eyed and fast talking.

"I was quite surprised," Dr. Dan said, "to read in the papers that the Americans are worried lest the coming Constituent Assembly be dominated by Buddhists or neutralists. I think such an outcome impossible. I believe the elections will return a rightist majority and that the left will be weak, as is natural in time of war against communism. The picture has been distorted by the agitation of a few hundred teen agers in Saigon.

"The difficult problem will be the setting up of valid political organizations which can form a stable and workable majority government. If the Assembly is splintered, if no majority is possible, the elections will turn out to do more harm than good. At present, because of the long years of political repression, beginning with French rule, we have no real political parties. Religious groupings were tolerated because religion was thought not to be dangerous. So we have religious rather than political parties—Buddhists, Catholics, Cao Dai and Hoa Hao.

"The Catholics are a well organized political minority in which the priests serve as cadres. The Buddhists, though a majority—I am myself a Budhist by tradition—are divided into too many factions. The Buddhist Institute, so prominent in the recent demonstrations, is strong in Central Vietnam but not here. Not a single southern province joined their movement. The Southern Buddhists are not active politically. I believe the vote will be fragmented among these diverse religious groups and that if the Catholics, the Cao Dai, the Hoa Hao and the Southern Buddhists can get together they can form a strong anti-Communist regime.

"The elections will provide a legal basis for the South Vietnamese government. Now everyone says there is no legal administration, only a self-appointed junta. After the elections it will be clear that the National Liberation Front represents very little and exercises control only by terrorism. There is nothing to worry about," he said, addressing me as if I were Ambassador Lodge, "the elections will make it much easier for the Americans. People will no longer be able to say this is a government of warlords."

I asked Dr. Dan whether it would be possible to have a free election without a free press. He thought there ought to be freedom of the press but with limitations. He thought the U.S. press printed too much military news. He would restrict this to official Ministry of War communiques. He also thought all pro-Communist propaganda should be barred.

"How to determine what is pro-Communist?" Dr. Dan said in answer to a question. "If someone talks in favor of Hanoi or against the Americans, I would bar that as pro-Communist. The Americans are our most important ally. Few Vietnamese are anti-American because they know the U.S. has no colonial ambitions. I also would allow no candidate to speak for a negotiated peace. That would create confusion. I am not against asking Hanoi to withdraw its troops and then come to the conference table but I am against a cease-fire, for we are not the aggressors.

"The Buddhist Institute is ambiguous on all this. Sometimes it sounds as if it were for peace at any price. The Buddhists should remember what happened to Tibet—the most Buddhist country in the world—under communist domination."

Dr. Dan was more optimistic than any American with whom I spoke or any American of whom I heard. "We are much closer to victory than the Americans think," he said. "Basically our people are immunized against communist propaganda. The inflation is not as serious as some contend. After all we do have full employment. Now if we get a strong administration, and get ahead with pacification, the war can be won in a relatively short time. Peace will come not through negotiations but through military victory."

The French tried operating through a puppet monarch, Bao Dai. We tried operating through a Mandarin dictator and then a series of military regimes. We have yet to play the card represented by Dr. Dan; some Americans are already talking of this as our next move. It could open a fresh period of suffering and disillusion.

MAY 16, 1966

# BEHIND THE FIGHTING
# IN HUÉ AND DANANG

A U. S. Embassy official in Saigon said to me, "Nobody can come out here with an open mind and not have it changed by what he sees." Since most VIPs see only U.S. officials, it is not surprising that their minds are changed in the desired direction. Perhaps mine is closed. Though I listened as sympathetically as I could to officials of quite different views, I must confess that I heard nothing to change it. On the contrary, it seemed to me that the same exercise in self-delusion so many newspapermen have observed in the past was still going on. I cite as example a remark which offers a clue to the current crisis in Hué and Danang. At one of the first backgrounders I attended in Saigon I was startled to hear a briefing officer dismiss the Buddhist student demonstrations. "The students," he said, "don't represent anything."

I thought the remark all the more disturbing because it came from an official who has a reputation for intelligence and candor. It may well be that if you could run the whole population of Saigon through a computer it would turn out few had ever heard of the student protests. Conceivably you might also find that they expressed the most widespread feelings in the country—weariness with the war and antagonism to the presence of so many foreign troops. To dismiss the Buddhist students out of hand as unrepresentative seemed to me very foolish. Students tend to be the most concerned and vocal group in every society. They are the men and women who will soon be gov-

erning the country. To decide that they represent nobody is a
comforting way to dismiss protest, but a sure way to miscalculate political forces. Admittedly there are students of varying
opinion in Saigon: pro-war students and anti-war students,
anti-election students and pro-election students, Catholic students and Buddhist students. It was only the last the briefing
officer was downgrading.

These tranquillizing rationalizations become the premises of
policy. Ever since the Buddhist demonstrations were sparked
by the removal of General Thi, there has been a disposition in
the U. S. Embassy not only to dismiss the demonstrators as "just
a bunch of Buddhist beatniks" but also to hope the military
would disperse them by force. This is the historic delusion that
revolutionary movements can be scattered with a whiff of gunpowder. There was disappointment that Ky did not put down
the Saigon demonstrations by force and that he withdrew his
troops from Danang in April after we flew them there for
a confrontation with anti-government troops. From several
sources I heard not only that Ky was being advised to precipitate a showdown in Danang but also that there were promises
of U.S. funds to rebuild the city if his planes had to bomb out
the rebels. There was a strong current of disapproval when Ky
backed down and promised elections instead.

At one briefing I heard an officer object when a correspondent's question characterized the South Vietnamese
government as a military dictatorship. "There is no military
dictatorship here in the European sense," the briefing officer
said smoothly, "Ky is not a Salazar." He certainly isn't. The
junta of generals which Ky ostensibly heads runs no such firm
regime. The mercurial and clownish Ky is not to be compared
with Europe's oldest and most enduring fascist dictator. But
Portugal's is the kind of clerical authoritarian regime the dominant forces in the U.S. establishment would welcome in South
Vietnam. Our No. 1 fear is of elections. An American of vague
background I suspected was CIA—"you might say I'm in business," he said—told me the U.S. was afraid if elections were
held "the liberals and the uneducated people" might win and
"ask us to leave." The U.S. establishment fears even right-wing
politicians lest they prove responsive to war weariness. Even
those Vietnamese opposed to elections want a more broadly

based government. It seemed to me an indication of Ky's un-importance that not a single Vietnamese with whom I talked about the political future even mentioned him; it was as though Ky were irrelevant. The consensus is that the country does not have a government in any real sense; the differences are about how to create one, whether by elections or by some form of military-civilian coalition, whether to make peace or to make war. What the U.S. establishment fears is that once representative government is launched, it will be hard to control. What our military men desire is a secure base while they carry on the war; they want no disruptive experiments in democracy. It is here that military needs conflict with political aims. To win the people you have to risk letting them express themselves, and that means risking a government which might negotiate peace.

The South Vietnamese are already beginning to "vote with their feet." This is the meaning of the rising rate of desertions from South Vietnam's army. At JUSPAO HQ, a comforting rationalization has been found—the soldiers are not deserting to the enemy, they are only going home to their villages because they are tired of the war! But no one recalls that this is how the Russian Army began to melt away in 1917. They didn't join the Germans; they just began to go home. In South Vietnam as in Russia, the soldiers want peace and the peasants want the land. The CIA comforts itself because there are few if any well-known figures in the National Liberation Front. One Vietnamese with whom I discussed this pointed out that few revolutions have been led by men who were well known before they succeeded. How many Russians in 1917 had ever heard of an obscure fanatic who used the name of Lenin in his Swiss hideout? The handful of little known Bolsheviks were able to take power because they acquiesced in soldier desertions and peasant land seizures. This war and South Vietnam can fall apart and into the hands of the NLF in much the same way.

No one can talk with Vietnamese for any length of time without realizing that no outsider, however well intentioned, can solve their problems. A defeated Japan submissively accepted a thoroughgoing land reform and much beneficient social change at American hands. But the Vietnamese are neither defeated nor submissive; they are as stubborn and fanatically determined as the Irish or the Jews. They'll fight us and themselves to exhaustion. Religious, nationalist and communist passions are contending within them all at once. South Vietnam in one generation is passing through secular, national and social struggles Western Europe was able to spread out over three centuries. And our presence has exacerbated all these tensions. Bitter feeling between Buddhist and Catholic may even now be erupting in a religious civil war. The appointment of General Cao, a Catholic, as the new commander of the First Army Corps, will provoke the Buddhists. It is an indication of how little has changed and how little we have learned that this faithful supporter of the Diem dictatorship should have been until now in charge of psychological warfare. While the Catholic community in South Vietnam, especially in Saigon, has been liberalized and split by the fresh winds blowing through the church ever since Pope John, U.S. policy has allied itself with the bitter-enders who still favor military dictatorship.

Behind the scenes one feels that in Vietnam, as in Laos and elsewhere, the military and the CIA pursue their own policies whatever the conflicting directives and contradictory rhetoric from Washington. I believe U.S. influences had a hand in the anti-election agitation of recent weeks. An indicator of this, in my opinion, was the sudden appearance in the political arena of the normally non-political Vietnamese Confederation of Labor. This is one of the tamest of the world's labor federations; it managed quite well under Diem until his last most paranoid period; it rarely calls strikes. Its long time head, Tran Quoc Buu, has close and friendly relations with the U. S. Embassy, which praises him to visitors as a force for democracy. When this force for democracy led his troops into the streets to demonstrate against elections, some Embassy officials in off-the-record comments to newsmen hailed this as a constructive development and asserted that Ky had overestimated the Buddhist demand for elections and made a mistake in giving in to it. Tran Quoc Buu was earlier a bulwark of Brother Nhu's dreaded Can Lao police organization. The CIA, in Vietnam as in Germany, has tended to take over much of the leftover secret police apparatus. Tran Quoc Buu, who is sensitive about his Can Lao past, may have steered clear of the CIA but I am sure he would not have demonstrated against elections if he thought the U.S. establishment in South Vietnam was for them.

The military situation is almost as frustrating for the U.S. as the political. The optimism the Americans in Saigon exuded last Fall has completely evaporated. Then, visiting newspapermen, European as well as American, were infected by the exuberant confidence of the U.S. establishment and impressed by the swift buildup of U.S. men and bases. The word was that the U.S. war was not to be confused with the French, that our effort was so much greater in quantity as to have become different in quality. The Viet Cong in the path of this steamroller were bound soon to be crushed. Experts as well as novices were taken in, perhaps because they all shared the natural tendency of industrialized peoples to overestimate the material factor in war.

This heady euphoria has vanished. In the U.S. leadership on the spot—civilian and military—there is a sober realization that no quick solutions are in sight and that a long, long war lies ahead. This reflects the failure of the bombings in the North to prevent a steady buildup of the rebel forces in the South, and the success of the Viet Cong in evading the many "search and destroy" operations so flamboyantly launched against them. They have shown a frustrating capacity to evade battle when we seek it and to strike when and where we do not expect it. All our machines, in other words, have failed to convert this from a guerrilla war, with all the advantages that gives the rebel side.

The only optimistic story I have seen since my return, quoting unnamed officials who expect a decisive turn for the better in the war early next year, seemed to emanate from the State Department. On the other hand the Army's Chief of Staff General Harold K. Johnson, in a little noticed speech in St. Louis (UPI in *Washington Daily News*, May 14), said the fighting in South Vietnam would last for ten more years. That is as good as saying forever.

In Saigon there was talk of putting 1,500,000 men into South Vietnam. It was claimed that with this many men we could start at the Camau peninsula in the south and "sweep the country clean" up to the 17th parallel—probably of people as well as Viet Cong. Judging from Korean war experience, putting 1,500,000 men into South Vietnam would require mobilization of 4,500,000. In Saigon one often hears it said that while we can't lose, we also can't win. But I notice that Hanson Baldwin, in arguing the case for mobilization in *The Reporter* (May 19), broaches a more pessimistic possibility than stalemate. He wrote, before the current crisis, that if civil war broke out between Saigon and Hué, or if Ky used force to prevent a Buddhist neutralist government from taking power, the South Vietnamese army might disintegrate. "If this situation were coupled with a strong Vietcong offensive," Baldwin concluded, "U.S. armed forces might well find themselves fighting for their lives."

In a fundamental sense there is really nothing new to report from Saigon. The war continues to be based on two ideas, both old and discredited. The first and older, which aroused the U.S. to a high pitch of war fever when practiced by the Spaniards against the Cuban rebels in the 1890s, is to concentrate the population of contested provinces in urban enclaves and "refugee camps" so that the peasants would "no longer be permitted to fight as rebels one day and appear as peaceable citizens the day after . . . The countryside was then to be cleared of all supplies and the starvation weapon turned against the insurgents." This description of the Spanish "reconcentrado" policy by Walter Millis in *The Martial Spirit,* his study of our war with Spain, applies to our tactics in the Vietnamese war. Henry Cabot Lodge spoke of the "heroic battle of the patriots" against this kind of "cruelty and oppression" but that Lodge was our Ambassador's grandfather and the patriots referred to were Cubans.

The other, newer idea is that of *"la guerre révolutionnaire"* which the defeated French military worked out after Dienbienphu and tried unsuccessfully to apply in Algeria. A mixture of counter-terror, totalitarian organization of the population and promises of a "social revolution" is the formula for winning the people from the insurgents, "pacifying" the countryside and smothering the rebellion. The idea is to apply Marxist and Maoist ideas in reverse. But communism in reverse is fascism—the use of police state methods, thought control and a one-party system to safeguard the status quo. A briefing officer, explaining to me the "social revolution" promised by the Honolulu

Declaration, outlined step by step how the communists take over and organize a village, and then showed step by step how we plan to imitate them. It never seemed to have occurred to him that imitating communist methods, even in reverse, was a strange way to build democracy. Our pacification procedure begins with a "census of grievances." This in practice seems to be a method for recruiting informers by intimidation. CIA teams are to interrogate one villager after another in private to spot and weed out VC sympathizers.

The classic way—at least as old as the Spanish inquisition—to certify one's own orthodoxy in interrogations of this kind is to inform on others. The quality of such information is apt to be so unreliable as to set off a chain reaction of unjust condemnations and intensified resentment. The pacification teams operate under a high-sounding Ministry of Revolutionary Development. Under the surface of the revolutionary verbiage, the formula adds up to McCarthyism plus social welfare measures. It is as if teams of armed McCarthyites with CIA training were sent into the small towns and villages of the United States to weed out Reds, pinkos and peaceniks. A briefing officer explained to me naively that in training the pacification teams we had been using a large proportion of Vietnamese belonging to the ultra-right Dai Viet and Vietnamese Kuomintang parties because we "needed an ideology stronger than democracy" with which to combat communism! He did not seem to realize the full implications of this confession.

No country has been promised social revolution more often. As early as 1950 the French were saying that pacification depended on winning the hearts and minds of the peasants with social reform. Diem promised a social revolution. So did General Khanh. So did Marshal Ky and Lyndon Johnson. No country talks more of revolution than ours, but none is more counterrevolutionary in practice. In Vietnam as in Latin America, we are allied with the forces which oppose social change because they stand to lose by it. We are always shopping around for gimmicks that sound revolutionary without threatening to disturb the status quo. "Somebody had the idea," a briefing officer told me, "of introducing the concept of People's Capitalism into the pacification program. His proposal was to get the villagers to invest their money in municipal and government bonds." The officer added regretfully that "this proved to be too sophisticated and had to be dropped." I half expected to hear that the same genius was going to convert Viet Cong by giving them stock in Texas Gulf Sulphur.

MAY 23, 1966

# WHERE COMMUNISM HAS REALLY BEEN CONTAINED

Peace lies like a benediction on Cambodia. To go from Saigon to Pnom Penh is to go from the Inferno of Southeast Asia to its Paradiso. Despite the war, the break-off in diplomatic relations and the constant border incidents, Air Vietnam and Royal Air Cambodge still fly on alternate days between the two capitals. Nowhere else in the world could an hour's flight provide so sharp a contrast. To land in the capital of Cambodia after eight days amid the squalor and apprehension of Saigon is fully to savor the blessings of a neutralist policy in Southeast Asia. On the one side a dark, dirty crowded airport, where travellers are subject to interminable delays while tired and sheepish GI's pour in. On the other side, a white, clean and relaxed airport, with hardly a uniform in sight except for one police control official.

On the ride into Pnom Penh, I was struck by the absence of check-points and barricades, the cleanliness of the broad boulevards leading into Prince Sihanouk's capital, the modern apartment houses around the city, the well-kept lawns. The city, with its many parks and wide streets, delights the eye after the uncollected refuse of Saigon. At the bougainvillea-covered Hotel Royale, with its palms and its swimming pool, its wide halls and air-conditioned rooms, I got a palatial bedroom at only $8 a night with—luxury of luxuries—a hot bath.

In a cyclopus from the hotel into town for dinner, the night was like velvet. There were no planes overhead, no mortar or howitzer shells exploding on the outskirts. On a stroll after dinner, it looked as if everybody was out on the sidewalk after the heat of the day. The shops are open, the movies do a brisk business mostly with Italian-style spectaculars made in Hong Kong. Children play on the sidewalks but they don't beg as they do in Saigon. No one clutches at your sleeve to sell his sister. There are no importunate cyclopus drivers. The bars are few. The huge open air market in the center of town sells everything from flowers to comic books in French and Khmer. A white visitor walking amid this short, slight people, darker than the Viets, feels no apprehension. I felt much safer walking back to the hotel through the dimly lit residential areas and the dark parks than I would have felt in Washington.

In my three days in Cambodia I was charmed and delighted by the successful mixture of the traditional and the modern characteristic of Prince Sihanouk's regime. At the huge Royal Palace compound, a miniature Asian Versailles, the Queen Mother preserves the country's links with its ancient monarchy. In a guided tour through its buildings of exquisitely gilded wood and intricate yellow-blue tiles, the visitor sees the coronation sword which dates back to the seventh century, the high coronation throne under the seven-tiered sacred parasol, the two-storied pavillion from which the monarchs mounted the royal elephants, several twelfth-century cannons and a small fortune in the dynasty's gems under glass. Everywhere are images of Naga, the seven-headed sacred serpent of Vishnu, and of Buddha in that mixture of Brahman and Buddhist faith brought there three centuries ago by India's traders and missionaries. From a palace in one corner of the grounds, the gongs and xylophones of the Royal ballet school were going full blast at morning rehearsal, off limits, like an Oriental seraglio to visitors.

Not more than a mile away, on the banks of the broad and

leisurely flowing Mekong, there is a sight of quite a different sort. An exposition hall built on clean modern lines displays the results of ten years' development (1955–65) under the Popular Socialist movement established by Prince Sihanouk. Graphic colored charts show no tractors in 1955, and 1030 in 1965. Here the regime boasts that illiteracy is now only 20 per cent and that in one year, thanks to a volunteer teaching campaign (it recalls Castro's Cuba) there will be none. Popular Socialism seems to have stimulated private enterprise. The charts show an impressive expansion in private and mixed enterprises; the publicly owned sector is more recent and confined largely to banking and the export-import business, which has more than doubled. The United States is conspicuously absent from the countries shown as having trade accords with Cambodia. China and the Soviet bloc are there, so is Japan. The country has trade accords with both West and East Germany, as with South and North Korea, a demonstration of neutralism in trade as well as politics.

Much taken for granted elsewhere seems novel after a week in South Vietnam. It is a pleasure to be able to drive thirty kilometers out into the countryside without armed escort and with no fear of mines or snipers. In a model village a squad of officials in black trousers, white shirts and black ties were waiting to receive us. High green-tipped sugar palms against a blue sky with cotton tufts of clouds provided the backdrop. Children played with the pump handle of a new village well and roamed with the geese and chickens under the thatched houses built on stilts. Birds and flowers were everywhere. We were proudly shown outdoor toilets, a clean though rudimentary hospital and dispensary, and a training school for midwives attended by bright-eyed nurses in starched white uniforms. We inspected a new school with a children's playground. Then we drove out of the village past an Esso station and two bonzes walking along the road in orange robes under white parasols. We inspected a dam being built to make possible two rice crops a year, a novel departure in an easy-going country, underpopulated by Asian standards, where a favorite saying has been "If it grows," i.e. wild, "why bother to plant it?" On our way back that evening in Pnom Ponh we visited a lovely pagoda, lit up like a Christmas tree with bright red and green lights. A rather pompous bonze inside wanted to know how many Buddhists there were in the United States and lost all interest in further conversation when told very few. The tiny temple bells tinkling sweetly in the evening breeze in the darkening garden outside were unforgettable.

The ruler of this Oklahoma-sized kingdom with its five million people has had to make up for its military weakness with political guile. In steering a course amid international rivalries and revolutionary pressure, Prince Sihanouk has far outdistanced LBJ as a wheeler-dealer. The Prince ascended the throne at the age of eighteen in 1941 at the beginning of the most turbulent period in its history. He wrested independence from the French before the Geneva conference, forced the withdrawal of the invading Viet Minh and by a five-hour "sit-down strike" at Geneva delayed the signing of the Geneva accords until Molotov and Chou En-lai gave way on his demand that Cambodia, unlike Vietnam, not be neutralized. It was left free to import arms and to make defensive alliances. Cambodia was then considered the most pro-Western of the new regimes in Indochina. Since then, Prince Sihanouk has shown extraordinary agility. He checked republican sentiment by resigning the throne in 1955 in favor of his father, thus freeing himself for that active participation in politics which was not allowed him so long as he was king. He outmaneuvered the local communists by joining the neutralist camp at Bandung, in return for promises of "non-interference" by Communist China and North Vietnam. A month later he signed his first agreement for direct military aid from the U.S. Later that year his Popular Socialist Party won 80 per cent of the votes and all of the ninety-one seats in the National Assembly.

Sihanouk could, if he were not so clever, truly say *"L'etat c'est moi."* It is as if he were a Louis XIV, a Tito and a Harry Truman rolled into one. No one has been more skillful at getting aid from all sides. At home, "Monseigneur" has managed to reconcile monarchy with a democratic facade, Five Year Plans, and enough "socialism" to make Cambodia seem fraternal if confusing in Moscow and Peking. In his spare time, he writes first-rate editorials for his French language press and composes popular songs. There's been nothing quite like him in all the annals of statecraft. He's genuinely popular. His country unlike Laos and South Vietnam is troubled by no communist guerrillas. Indeed it is the only regime in Southeast Asia where the communists have been contained. This is what makes consistent U.S. hostility to him seem so irrational. The Communist Chinese have treated Sihanouk with a social and political "correctness" intended to demonstrate their readiness to co-exist with different social regimes on their borders. But the U.S. has allied itself with Cambodia's ancient enemies—the Thais and the Viets—and sought through the CIA to overthrow him. A "Free Serei" movement aimed at Sihanouk serves as guide and tool for our Special Forces. Sihanouk, like Cambodians generally, fears the Viet, whether communist or anticommunist. As late as March 6, 1964, he accused Hanoi of being as "vague as the Anglo-Saxons" in replying to his request for a guarantee of his borders. But Prince Sihanouk has come to believe the Viet Cong will win and that his country's safety lies in cultivating good relations with the rebels and with Hanoi. "Our American friends are remarkable organizers, brilliant technicians and excellent soldiers," the Prince wrote three years ago. "But their incontestable realism stops short of the realm of politics, where the attitude of the ostrich seems to them to conform to their best interests."

The Cambodian attitude toward the Vietnamese war was reflected while I was there in the April 22 issue of *Réalités Cambodgiennes,* an unofficial mouthpiece. It carried an interview with a second lieutenant, Tram Minh Bach of the South Vietnamese Air Force, who had fled for refuge to Cambodia. He defected after he was upbraided in brutal and insulting fashion by his American "adviser" in front of his own men. He said, "The Americans act like bosses and treat us like 'boys' "—the word "boy" as thus used in French is an echo of colonialism. When he was asked if he might join the Viet Cong, the lieutenant replied that he opposed both communist and American domination of his country. "The nationalist and independent policy of Prince Sihanouk is basically the best for this region," he said. "He defends his country and nothing more and he makes it progress in peace. That is an example all Vietnamese patriots ought to meditate."

An unsigned editorial in the same issue put forward a subtler neutralist view. It dealt with the nationalist demonstrations against Ky in Hué and Saigon as led by the Buddhists under Thich Tri Quang. It derided the idea of free elections in a country "where the government only controls a fifth of the territory and a quarter of the population." It said that while the nationalists were tired of the war, disgusted with American domination and hostile to the military junta in Saigon, they were so compromised by their own political pasts as to fear NLF reprisals if the Americans left. "In fact, all the nationalists of Hué, Danang and Saigon want," the editorial continued, "is that the U.S. allow them to replace the team presently in power while the U.S. continues to 'protect them against the Viet Cong.'" It advises true nationalists to join the National Liberation Front "so that they can counterbalance the communist influence there and preserve the future." It draws a parallel with the French resistance where Gaullists fought side by side with communists. This allowed the non-communists after liberation "to bring into being a government in which the communists had a place—but no more than that." It said the time had come for joint action between nationalists and communists to establish a provisional government which would ask for American withdrawal. "We sincerely believe," the editorial concluded, "that the Americans, no longer having a juridical excuse to justify their presence, would acquiesce in this demand—and would not be so displeased, in reality, to put an end to an adventure which, carried to its conclusion, as they are already sufficiently aware, would result inevitably in a disaster for them." In the Cambodian view, only joint action against the U.S. can prevent a communist takeover in Vietnam and make possible a neutralist solution. This reflects Prince Sihanouk's own wily record, in which he has outmaneuvered communists not by fighting them but by taking them into camp.

I had hoped while in Cambodia to speak with some representative of the NLF or at least with Wilfred Burchett, who has been covering the war from the rebel side. Burchett was in Hanoi, but from another source in close touch with the Front and recently returned from Viet Cong territory I was given a summary of its views.

"It is not true that Peking forbids Hanoi to talk peace or that Hanoi forbids the NLF to do so," my informant said. "The

Front is free to negotiate. Washington must understand that the Front is not a tool of Peking. The Front claims to be the sole representative of the South Vietnamese people in the sense that there is no other organized force with which to deal. Any group can join the Front if it is sincerely for independence and the end of American intervention. The door is open."

My informant said this was why the Front had never set up a provisional government, though it has a parallel administration everywhere in South Vietnam. It wants as broadly based a government as possible for the final take-over. It has no faith in elections. It doubts that they will be held and feels sure that if they are held, they will be as phony as were those under Diem. "It is wrong to think," my informant told me, "that the Front is strong only in the villages. In every mission, in every part of the government, the Front has its people. When a South Vietnamese soldier gets a fifteen-day pass to go home and visit his native village, he goes to an office of the Front and gets it stamped to assure him a safe conduct. When trucks go out of Saigon to Mytho they obtain a *laissez-passer* from the South Vietnamese government. But on top of this, outside Saigon, there is stamped an authorization of the Front.

"The Front collects taxes in every city, including Saigon. It is already planning for the maintenance of law and order in Saigon when the government falls apart and it takes over. The Front realizes there will be a serious problem to prevent looting and killing. The day Saigon is liberated the only protection the Americans will have will be the Front. Protection will not be easy in a city of 2,000,000 seething with hatred. The problem is made the more serious because Saigon has become a city from which law and morals have disappeared. The day authority is finally transferred to the Front will be a critical one and the Front has several dozens of armed cadres trained and ready to take over control and maintain law and order.

"U.S. emissaries," he continued, "want to negotiate some way to stay in South Vietnam. They are wrong. They have to leave just as the French did. Only then can they have an embassy, negotiate trade relations and discuss economic aid. But first, all traces of occupation must be ended.

"The Front wants a neutral foreign policy. It sees reunification as a thing of the distant future. Too many differences and difficulties make it impossible at this time. The internal policy will be socialist, but not like China or North Vietnam; it will be another of those forms of Asian socialism of which some variant may be found everywhere in this region. The U.S. must realize that this is a struggle for independence, not a war of aggression. The Front regards Thich Tri Quang as a man of the Middle Ages who wants some way to keep U.S. troops in South Vietnam. The Front wants a truly independent South Vietnam. Even Ho Chi Minh's idea of a bi-federal union is something for the future."

The NLF sees the Indonesian People's Conference as the possible germ of a larger neutralist confederation that might some day unite South Vietnam, Laos and Cambodia. So does Prince Sihanouk. The Conference last year brought together neutralist and communist Front representatives from North and South Vietnam and from Laos with those of Cambodia. South Vietnamese neutralist exiles from Paris were also in attendance. The Conference is soon to open a permanent office in Pnom Penh which might someday play a part in peace talks. The little publicized recent visit to Moscow by the King of Laos and his Prime Minister, Prince Souvanna Phouma (*Le Monde*, May 19), indicate that they are still thinking along neutralist lines, too. Cambodia's ruler believes that only by peace and politics can communism be contained. For twelve years the United States has tried to contain it by military dictatorship, repression and war. The Viet Cong is far stronger today than when it started. After twelve years, Cambodia's success and our failure, Cambodia's progress and Vietnam's suffering, should be enough to show which is the wiser course.

MAY 30, 1966

# XI

---

**WE
ALWAYS
SEEM
TO
GUESS
WRONG**

# MACK SENNETT IN LAOS

The story of the U.S. intervention in Laos, of which Arthur J. Dommen's book *Conflict in Laos* is the first full-length study, recalls one of those early Mack Sennetts in which the hero is chased over and over again through the same revolving door. Three times forces financed by the United States have overthrown its neutralist Prime Minister, Prince Souvanna Phouma. Three times he has been restored to power, once by elite paratroopers we trained only to have them turn against us, the second time by an international conference we convoked to save our rightist protegés from complete defeat, the third time, earlier this year, by angry orders from Washington, which seemed at last to be getting tired of the comedy. The Laotian Royal Army, which fared so ludicrously in each of these episodes, is the only one in the world wholly on the U.S. payroll. It is also the highest paid in Asia, though the U. S. Comptroller General complained to a Congressional investigating committee that he had no way of knowing how much actually reached the troops and how much stuck to the fingers of its generals. Each time this army has risen against Souvanna Phouma, it has proved unable to defeat neutralist or leftist forces it far outnumbered. After each of these escapades, the left has emerged stronger than before. The virtue of Dommen's book is that it argues the case for learning something from this ignominious series of military debacles and reconciling ourselves to neutralism not only in Laos but in the rest of Indochina.

Dommen was bureau manager and roving Southeast Asian correspondent for United Press International in Saigon and Hongkong from 1959 to 1963. Indochina was his beat. But his book is not a journalistic quickie. The country and the people come alive in his pages. His up-to-date account of the intermittent Lilliputian civil wars in Laos and their relation to the bigger one in Vietnam could hardly be more timely since Indochina is the place where the new Johnson Administration may most easily stumble into full-scale war after pledging itself in the election campaign to peace. Two main skeins help us unravel the tangled story. The first is that we have gone on regarding neutralism as inherently wicked in Southeast Asia, long after we have accepted it elsewhere. The other thread in the story of Indochina is that the U.S. has come to have two different policies for dealing with communist states. In Eastern Europe we no longer regard the Soviet bloc as a monolith. We recognize diversity and encourage it. But in Asia we treat China, and its two communist neighbors, North Korea and North Vietnam, as a faceless mass to be dealt with as we did the Russian Revolution from 1917 to 1933, by non-recognition, economic blockade, and exclusion from the world community. Dommen's book on Laos dares recognize the wisdom of de Gaulle's view that the advent of the Sino-Soviet split makes it worthwhile in Asia, too, to deal with the individual communist states and resistance movements as distinct national entities with divergent interests which could be exploited to make the neutralization of the area a viable solution.

Such a policy was hinted at last June 9 in a report by a member of the CIA's Board of National Estimates which was leaked out to the press. It looked toward "some kind of negotiated settlement based upon neutralization" to end the war in Vietnam. Dommen's book is in line with that policy. If we actually adopt it, we will show the same capacity as the French for learning our lessons the costly way.

When the smoke of villages being napalmed for "freedom" clears away, it will be seen that we lost two great opportunities in Indochina. The first was after the war, when the leftists we have been fighting in both Vietnam and Laos had close relaitons with the OSS, and appealed to us for aid on the basis of FDR's Atlantic Charter which had inspired them with its

promise of liberation from colonialism. With the onset of the
cold war, we rejected their appeals and supported the French
effort to reimpose their rules. The second opportunity was in
1954, with the Geneva settlement. The neutralization we are
beginning to consider now we could have had then. What
Dommen fails to make clear, partly because the story gets lost
in the details, partly because he is too respectful of the State
Department, is that this first attempt at neutralization failed
because John Foster Dulles opposed it and set out instead to
bring Laos, South Vietnam, and Cambodia into the American
sphere of influence. Dulles stopped talking about a rollback
of communism in Europe after the 1952 campaign, but that
seems to have remained a catchword of policy in the Far East.
As recently as last May 4, William P. Bundy, Assistant Secretary of State for Far Eastern Affairs, told the House Appropriations Committee that our military and economic aid to Laos
and South Vietnam along with Formosa, South Korea, Thailand, and the Philippines was intended "to produce a situation
of strength from which we may in time see a rollback of communist power."

It is the idea of building a series of advanced bases around
Communist China which explains the course of events from
1954 onward. Cambodia became the stepchild of U.S. policy
because it insisted on remaining neutral, as the Geneva pact
provided. That pact seemed to provide our favorite formula—
free elections—for reuniting the divided countries of Vietnam
and Laos. But here East and West switched sides. Our formula
for reuniting Korea and Germany, where we were sure we
would win, was free elections. The communists rejected them
there, where they knew they would lose, but pressed for fulfillment of the election pledge in Vietnam. The U.S. soon indicated (*China Quarterly*, January-March, 1962) that it "would
not sit by quietly if faced with the prospect that South Vietnam
might go Communist, even as a result of free election." So on
our side, too, end justified means. We backed Diem not only
in blocking the elections but in rejecting every appeal from
North Vietnam for trade and better relations. East and West
Germany, despite their bitter differences, trade with each other
on a substantial scale. But we made the 17th parallel between
North and South Vietnam one of the tightest Iron Curtains in

the world. In Laos we tried our best to prevent the elections but failed. When they were finally held in 1958, the country reunited, and a coalition Cabinet established under the neutralist Prince Souvanna Phouma, we cut off aid to help the rightists overturn it and set up a dictatorship instead. This split the country wide open again.

No country could be easier to split. The enormous complexity of its politics is in inverse ratio to its size. A majority of its people are not Lao at all. To climb from the broad, fertile valley bottoms where the Lao dwell into the mountain jungles is to enter the realm of primitive tribes of Meo, Kha, and Thai, whose lands often straddle unmarked borders between Laos and Vietnam to which they are wholly indifferent. The loyalties of these ethnic groups, as Dommen writes, "transcend all ideological groupings and are of a more permanent character." The relatively advanced Lao live in a medieval-style kingdom whose semi-independent fiefdoms have both used, and been used by, the great Powers in their cold war. Three figures have dominated the Laotian political landscape since 1954. Their exotic names sound as if they came out of Gilbert and Sullivan. In the view of Dommen and almost every journalist who has visited the area, two are idealists: Prince Souvanna Phouma and his half-brother, Prince Souphanouvong. The third, General Phoumi Nosavan, is a sharpie. It should not be hard to guess which one ended up on our payroll. The two Princes stem from the vice-regal branch of the Laotian royal family. Both were educated in France and came home as engineers to work in the civil service. Both joined the resistance movement after the war, were driven into exile in Thailand and appealed in vain for U.S. aid in their liberation struggle. Souvanna Phouma, the elder and more moderate of the two, finally returned home to become Prime Minister of Laos in the closing years of French rule. Souphanouvong, a brilliant scholar who spent one term in jail in Vientiane reading classical Greek, turned left in the same period, and became head of the Pathet Lao. At the time of the French collapse in 1954 this leftist guerrilla movement, with aid from Ho Chi Minh, had obtained control of the two Northwestern provinces adjacent to China and North Vietnam. General Nosavan was once in this guerrilla movement under Souphanouvong, but defected to the

French who rewarded him with rapid promotion in their territorial army. Later he was picked by the CIA as our favorite "strong man" for Laos.[1]

The whole story of Laos under our influence stinks of money. We debauched this lovely, sparsely inhabited mountain jungle country, a lotus-eater land where food is plentiful and the problems, like the ideologies, are mostly imported. The State Department under Dulles insisted, over the objections of the Joint Chiefs of Staff, in establishing a 25,000 man Royal Army in Laos. To train it, we sent in something called a Programs Evaluation Office, made up of U. S. Army officers in civilian clothes. These disguises were required because the Geneva agreement of 1954 allowed only a small French military mission. The establishment of this huge army for a country of 2 million created a sharp inflation. The cost of living doubled. To sop up the inflation we poured in all kinds of luxury goods. According to Dommen the leftist party of Prince Souphanou-vong showed "little or no concern" with teaching Marxism-Leninism to the villages. "Instead of analyzing the struggle against 'imperialism,' their propaganda," Dommen tells us, "pointed to the American aid program as evidence of a scheme to exploit Laos for foreign purposes. Potential converts were sent from their villages on trips to Vientiane so that they could get an eyeful of the luxurious homes and cars that Lao government officials had bought with money meant to help Laos become economically independent."

No country in Southeast Asia has more money per capita pumped into it than Laos and in none has less reached the ordinary villager. The U. S. Embassy once claimed in its own defense that it had imported "only" three Cadillacs and thirty Buicks, "all lowest priced models," into this almost roadless country!

The Royal Army has grown from 25,000 to 70,000. It had five generals when the French left. Now it has 121, probably the highest ratio of generals to troops in the world; the U.S. still

[1] Phoumi Nosavan is an enterprising man. He became worried last year that U.S. funds might be shut off. So according to Le Monde (May 24–25, 1964) he opened a gambling house in Vientiane for the benefit of his general staff and then the world's only "legal" opium den. Dommen confirmed this story in a telephone conversation with me.

has no way of knowing how much pay and allowance is pocketed by the generals. The one certain fact about this gravy train army is that it can't fight. Its near collapse in Phoumi Nosavan's 1960–61 revolt against Souvanna Phouma led the U.S. back to Geneva in 1962, where it negotiated a new pact with Communist China and North Vietnam for the neutralization of Laos. A new coalition was set up, representing right, left, and neutralist forces. But instead of a true coalition, we created a *troika*, Khrushchev style. The restored Prime Minister, Souvanna Phouma, instead of being made the head of a united government, merely presided over a triple-headed monster, each head of which was supported by a different set of great Powers. Prince Souphanouvong's Pathet Lao drew their support from North Vietnam and beyond that first from Russia and later from China. The rightist Royal Army was securely in the hands of our man, General Phoumi Nosavan, and the funds for its support went directly from the Pentagon to him. The Prime Minister and his handful of neutralist troops under Kong Le were precariously dependent on the State Department and, oddly enough, limited Russian aid.

The setup might be termed a triple *troika*. The Pentagon backed the right. North Vietnam and China backed the Left. The neutralist center—and this brings us to the third level—was dependent on the State Department. The U.S. government itself was split three ways. In Laos, as Dommen explains, policy has been bedeviled because the U. S. Embassy, the U.S. military, and the CIA have each had independent sources of funds and independent channels of communication to Washington. The conflicts among them have added to instability. The military and the CIA have disliked the coalition from the start and welcomed the coup d'état upsetting it last April. Washington insisted on putting Souvanna Phouma back as Premier but the unsteady structure of the government laid the neutralist forces wide open to intrigue from right and left. When fighting broke out again after the coup the neutralist forces split in a little civil war of their own, one wing joining the Pathet Lao while the other, with Kong Le and the Prime Minister, became prisoners of the right. The result, as Bernard B. Fall notes in a new and enlarged edition of his *Street Without Joy*, is that Laos seemed to be headed "toward the kind of 'polarization' into Right and Left which had gotten it into deep trouble twice before."

The sharp-eyed Fall notes that on the eve of the coup last April which overthrew Souvanna Phouma's neutralist coalition, a secret meeting took place between General Phoumi Nosavan and his fellow "strong man" from South Vietnam, General Khanh. Such a meeting and cooperation between them was bound to increase North Vietnamese suspicion. The military in both countries might have hoped, Dr. Fall writes, "that a Communist reaction against *both* countries might bring about large-scale American help to what would be in effect an Indochina war at 1953 level," i.e., a total U.S. military involvement and an extension of the war. This has long been Khanh's one hope of saving himself.

Dommen concludes, as did Dr. Fall last year in his brilliant *The Two Viet-Nams,* that the only safe way out is neutralization and that North Vietnam is prepared to accept an independent South Vietnam linked in a neutral belt with Cambodia and Laos, as the Vietnamese National Liberation Front and Prince Sihanouk have long proposed. The remedy may seem risky, but less so than a widened war. There is no reason why a firm system of international guarantees could not be worked out for such a settlement. The best guarantee would be the mutual interests it served. In the Pentagon, State, and CIA there are men who hope for such a solution now that the elections are out of the way. Another, perhaps more powerful group, would rather widen the war than recognize that it is lost.

DECEMBER 17, 1964

# VIETNAM: AN EXERCISE
# IN SELF-DELUSION

The morning I sat down to write this review,[1] the *Washington Post* (March 25) carried the news that Malcolm W. Browne had been arrested and held for two hours by South Vietnamese Air Air Force officers at the big U.S. air and missile base at Da Nang. The incident is symbol and symptom of the steady degeneration in the conduct of the Vietnamese war. These two books by two newspapermen who won Pulitzer Prizes last year for their coverage of the war, Browne for the Associated Press, David Halberstam for the *New York Times*, record the agony of trying to report the war truthfully against the opposition of the higher-ups, military and civilian. The books appear just as the war is entering a new stage when honest reporting is more essential than ever, but now restriction and censorship are applied to black it out. Da Nang, the main base from which the war is being escalated to the North, was officially declared "off limits" the day before Browne's arrest and newsmen were told they could not enter without a pass obtainable only in Saigon, 385 miles to the south. "Newsmen," the dispatch on Browne's arrest said, "doubted such a pass existed." The incident occurred only a few days after the highest information officer at the Pentagon claimed that its policy on coverage of the war was "complete candor."

What makes these books so timely, their message so urgent,

[1] Of *The New Face of War* by Malcolm W. Browne and *The Making of a Quagmire* by David Halberstam.

is that they show the Vietnamese war in that aspect which is most fundamental for our own people—as a challenge to freedom of information and therefore freedom of decision. They appear at a time when all the errors on which they throw light are being intensified. Instead of correcting policy in the light of the record, the light itself is being shut down. Access to news sources in Vietnam and in Washington is being limited, censorship in the field is becoming more severe. Diem is dead but what might be termed Diemism has become the basic policy of the American government. For years our best advisers, military and civilian, tried desperately to make him understand that the war was a political problem which could only be solved in South Vietnam. Three years ago the head of the U. S. Mission spoke of the war as a battle for the "hearts and minds" of the people, and primarily the villagers, whose disaffection had made the rebellion possible against superior forces and equipment. To win that battle it was then proposed to spend $200,000,000 to bolster the Vietnamese economy and raise living standards. Though much of this money seems to have been frittered away, it was at least recognized that the military effort was only one aspect of the problem. Now we have adopted Diem's simple-minded theory that the war is merely a product of communist conspiracy, that it is purely an invasion and not a rebellion or a civil war, and that all would be well—in Secretary Rusk's fatuous phrase—if only the North let its neighbors alone. This is the theory of the White Paper and this is the excuse for bombing North Vietnam.

While the war expands, the theory on which it proceeds has narrowed. Washington's "party line" on the war has been shrunk to rid it of those annoying complexities imposed by contact with reality. The change becomes evident if one compares the White Paper of 1965 with the Blue Book of 1961. The Blue Book was issued by the Kennedy Administration to explain its decision to step up the scale of our aid and the number of our "military advisers" in South Vietnam. The White Paper was issued by the Johnson Administration to prepare the public mind to accept its decision to bomb the North and risk a wider war. The change of policy required that rewriting of history we find so amusing when we watch it being done on the other side.

Four years ago the Blue Book told us that the basic pattern of Viet Cong activity was "not new, of course." It said this followed the tactics applied and the theories worked out by Mao Tse-tung in China. It said much the same methods were used "in Malaya, in Greece, in the Philippines, in Cuba and in Laos." If there is "anything peculiar to the Viet-Nam situation," the Blue Book said, "it is that the country is divided and one-half provides a safe sanctuary from which subversion in the other half is supported with both personnel and materiel." This implied a conflict which was doubly a civil war, first between the two halves of a divided country and then between the government and communist-led guerrillas in one-half of that country.

The White Paper disagrees. It abandons complexity to make possible simple-minded slogans and policy. It declares the conflict "a new kind of war . . . a totally new brand of aggression . . . *not* another Greece . . . *not* another Malaya . . . *not* another Philippines . . . Above all . . . *not* a spontaneous and local rebellion against the established government." (Italics in the original.) The "fundamental difference," the White Paper says, is that in Vietnam "a Communist government has set out deliberately to conquer a sovereign people in a neighboring state." This implies that there is no popular discontent in the South to be allayed, no need to negotiate with the rebels. The war is merely a case of international aggression and the aggressor is to be punished by bombardment until he agrees to call off the invasion. The rebellion can be shut off, all this implies, as if by spigot from Hanoi. The truth about the war has been tailored to suit the Air Force faith in "victory by airpower." This was Goldwater's theory and this has become Johnson's policy.

Browne's book sheds some sharp light on the White Paper's thesis. The White Paper says the war is "inspired, directed, supplied and controlled" by Hanoi. But Browne reports that "intelligence experts feel less than 10 per cent and probably more like 2 per cent of the Viet Cong's stock of modern weapons is Communist made." He also reports that "only a small part of Viet Cong increase in strength has resulted from infiltration of North Vietnamese Communist troops into South Vietnam." Browne also tells us that "Western intelligence experts

believe the proportion of Communists [in the National Liberation Front] is probably extremely small." He describes it as
"a true 'front' organization appealing for the support of every
social class." Browne declares the Front a "creature" of the
Vietnamese Communist Party and says it has "strong but subtle
ties" to the Hanoi regime. For many Vietnamese, nevertheless,
"the Front is exactly what it purports to be—the people's
struggle for independence." This is what our best advisers tried
to tell Diem. This is what our bureaucracy now refuses to see
rather than admit past error and defeat. It prefers to gamble
on a wider war.

The really terrible message in these books is not that the
bureaucrats have tried to deceive the public but that they have
insisted on deceiving themselves. The Vietnamese war has been
an exercise in self-delusion. David Halberstam tells us in *The
Making of a Quagmire* that when the first Buddhist burned
himself to death, Ngo Dinh Diem was convinced that this act
had been staged by an American television team. The Buddhist
crisis, as Halberstam describes it, "was to encompass all the
problems of the Government: its inability to rule its own people; the failure of the American mission to influence Diem . . .
Observing the government during those four months was like
watching a government trying to commit suicide." The stubborn insistence of the South Vietnamese dictator on insulating
himself from reality spread into our own government. The most
important revelation these two books make is the unwillingness
of the higher-ups in Saigon and Washington to hear the truth
from their subordinates in the field.

South Vietnam swarmed with spies, but apparently they
were only listened to when they reported what their paymasters wanted to hear. Halberstam says that at one time Diem
had thirteen different secret police organizations. Browne provides a vivid picture of how our own intelligence agencies
proliferated. The CIA, Special Forces, the AID Mission, the
Army, the Provost Marshal, the Navy, and the U. S. Embassy
each had its own operatives. But they were not, in Browne's
words, "one big happy family." On the contrary they "very
often closely concealed" their findings from other agencies "because of the danger that the competitors may pirate the material and report it to headquarters first, getting the credit."

All this fierce application of free enterprise to the collection of information seems to have been of little use because of a top level political decision. "Ever since Vietnamese independence" (i.e., 1954), Browne reveals, "American intelligence officials had relied on the Vietnamese intelligence system for most of their information." This was "because of Diem's touchiness about American spooks wandering around on their own." In the interest of preserving harmony, "somehow the intelligence reports always had it that the war was going well." We circulated faithfully in orbit around our own satellite. Diem's men told him what he wanted to hear, and ours passed on what he wanted us to believe. Halberstam confirms this. In those final months before Diem's overthrow, "CIA agents were telling me that their superiors in Vietnam were still so optimistic that they were not taking the turmoil and unrest very seriously." John Richardson, then CIA chief in Vietnam, displayed a kind of infatuation with Diem's brother Nhu and his wife. Halberstam describes a lunch with Richardson in 1962, shortly after the *New York Times* sent him to Saigon, in which the CIA chief dismissed Nhu's notorious anti-American remarks as simply those of "a proud Asian." As for the tigerish Mme. Nhu, Richardson thought her "sometimes a little emotional, but that was typical of women who entered politics—look at Mrs. Roosevelt!"

A persistent Panglossism marked our entire bureaucracy up to and including the White House. General Harkins, our military commander in South Vietnam, said "I am an optimist and I am not going to allow my staff to be pessimistic." Halberstam describes a briefing at his command post after the battle of Ap Bac in January, 1963, the kind of set-piece battle for which our military had long hoped and which they first described as a victory though it turned out to be a disastrous defeat. With "the government troops so completely disorganized that they would not even carry out their own dead," "a province chief shelling his own men" and "the enemy long gone," General Harkins told the press a trap was about to be sprung on the enemy!

The enemy was the press. When the facts about Ap Bac could no longer be concealed, headquarters became angry "not with the system" that brought defeat, Halberstam writes, **nor** with the Vietnamese commanders responsible for it "but with the American reporters who wrote about it." Admiral Harry Felt, commander of all U.S. forces in the Pacific, gave classic expression to the bureaucratic attitude toward the press when he was angered by a question from Browne. "Why don't you get on the team?" the Admiral demanded.

When Halberstam, Browne, and Neil Sheehan,[2] then with the UPI, visited the Mekong Delta in the summer of 1963 and saw for themselves deterioration of the war, their reward for reporting it was a campaign of denigration. Rusk criticized Halberstam at a press conference. President Kennedy suggested to the publisher of the *New York Times* that Halberstam be transferred to some other assignment, a suggestion Mr. Arthur Hays Sulzberger, to his credit, rejected. The bureaucracy counter-attacked through Joe Alsop, who insidiously compared the reporters on the scene to those who a generation earlier had called the Chinese communists "agrarian reformers." The *New York Journal-American* wrote that Halberstam was soft on communism. A friend in the State Department told Halberstam, "It's a damn good thing you never belonged to any left wing groups or anything like that because they were really looking for stuff like that." Victor Krulak, the Pentagon's top specialist on guerrilla warfare, was vehement in his criticism of the press: "Richard Tregaskis and Maggie Higgins had found that the war was being won, but a bunch of young cubs who kept writing about the political side were defeatists." The official attitude was epitomized by Lyndon Johnson, then Vice President, on his way back from Saigon in 1961. He had laid the flattery on with a shovel, calling Diem "the Churchill of Asia." Halberstam reports that when a reporter on the plane tried to tell Johnson something of Diem's faults, Johnson responded, "Don't tell me about Diem. He's all we've got out there." A brink is a dangerous place on which to prefer not to see where you're going.

The hostile attitude toward honest reporting is made the more shocking because reporters like Halberstam and Browne, as their conclusions reveal, were critics not of the war itself but only of the ineffective way in which it was conducted. The

[2] See the vivid account in his preface to Jules Roy's agonized and eloquent *The Battle of Dienbienphu.*

forces for which they spoke, the sources on which they depended, were not dissident Vietnamese but junior American officers. Their books disclose little contact with the Vietnamese. The battle between the press and the bureaucracy arose because the newspapermen refused to report that the war was being won, but there was not too much reporting of why it was being lost.

For Halberstam the war was a lark, a wonderful assignment for a young reporter; his pages reflect his zest and are full of graphic reportage, though also marked by some egregious errors, such as locating Dienbienphu in Laos and attributing the origin of the *agrovilles* to the French whereas they really sprang from Nhu's mystical authoritarianism. For Browne the war was less romantic. The life of a wire service reporter on call twenty-four hours a day in so tense a situation is no picnic. His book is written in flat agency prose. Both men acquitted themselves honorably, in the best tradition of American journalism, which is always to be skeptical of any official statement. But both books are marked by a characteristic intentness on the moment. The idea that the past may help explain the present appears only rarely. There is no time for study, and American editors do not encourage that type of journalism in depth which distinguishes *Le Monde* or the *Neue Züricher Zeitung*.

This defect is most damaging in reporting on the origins of the revolt against Diem. The average American newspaper reader got the impression that this was brought about by esoteric and long-distance means, by communist plotters activated from Hanoi to engage in that mysterious process referred to in our press as "subversion." This is the closest modern equivalent to witchcraft. Halberstam's account of the origins is better than Browne's, but the real roots of discontent are touched on only peripherally. We get a glimpse of them in Halberstam's report that General Taylor after his first mission in 1960 recommended "broadening the base of the government, taking non-Ngo anti-Communist elements into the Government; making the National Assembly more than a rubber stamp; easing some of the tight restrictions on the local press." The prescription was for a little of that democracy we were supposed to be defending, but Diem would not take the medicine. The accumulation of grievances, the establishment of concentration camps for political opponents of all kinds, the exploitation and abuse of the villages, the oppression of the intellectuals, the appeal of the eighteen Notables in 1960, and the attempted military coup that year, "the long standing abuses" which finally led to the revolt, are not spelled out as they should be [3] and would be if U.S. reporters had more contact with the Vietnamese. In a flash of insight Halberstam writes:

> Also, though we knew more about Vietnam and the aspirations of the Vietnamese than most official Americans, we were to some degree limited by our nationality. We were there, after all, to cover the war; this was our primary focus and inevitably we judged events through the war's progress or lack of it. We entered the pagodas only after the Buddhist crisis had broken out; we wrote of Nguyen Tuong Tam, the country's most distinguished writer and novelist, only after he had committed suicide—and then only because his death had political connotations; we were aware of the aspirations of the peasants because they were the barometer of the Government's failure and the war's progress, not because we were on the side of the population and against their rulers.

This accounts for how poorly these reporters understood the central problem of land reform, how few realized that from the standpoint of the peasants, particularly in the Delta, Diem's land reform policy like his hated "*agrovilles*" and our equally unpopular "strategic hamlets" seemed to be mechanisms for reinstating the rights of the landlords who had fled during the long war against the French. Diem's downfall, and the rebellion's success, were largely due to the fact that he tried to do what even the Bourbons in France after the Revolution were too wise to attempt. He tried to turn back the clock of the revolutionary land seizures. In the name of "land reform" many peasants found themselves being asked to pay rent or compensation for land they had long considered their own.

This lack of contact with the Vietnamese people, and this fellow feeling for the junior officers who were sure they could win the war if only HQ were different, also accounts for the weak way both books fizzle out when the authors try to supply

[3] The best account is by the French historian Philippe Devillers in *North Vietnam Today*, edited by P. J. Honey.

some conclusions. Both oppose negotiation and neutralization. Halberstam is indignant with the indifference to Vietnam he encountered on his return home. He believes Vietnam "a legitimate part" of "our global commitment." He feels "we cannot abandon our efforts to help these people no matter how ungrateful they may seem." For the "ungrateful" majority, the American presence has only succeeded in polarizing the politics of the country between authoritarian communists and authoritarian anti-communists; the former at least have the virtue of being supported by native forces. The anticommunist minority was grateful, of course, and feared that with American withdrawal they would be treated as mercilessly by the National Liberation Front as Diem had treated veterans of Vietminh after 1954, although a specific provision of the Geneva agreement forbade persecution of those who had fought against the French. The files of the International Control Commission from 1955 onwards were full of complaints that ex-Vietminh had been thrown into concentration camps or executed without charge or trial. In any eventual settlement in Vietnam, the future of minorities must certainly be a matter for concern, but the notion that we have a mandate from Heaven to impose on an unwilling people what we think is good for them will strike few Asians or Africans as an object lesson in democracy.

The feeble ending of Browne's book is even worse than Halberstam's. "Perhaps in the end," he writes, echoing the clichés of the counter-insurgency experts at Fort Bragg, "America will find it can put Marx, Lenin, Mao and Giap to work for it, without embracing Communism itself." To apply communist methods in reverse, the favorite formula of our counter-insurgency experts, does not make them any less unpalatable or dangerous to a free society. The basic tactic confuses the effect with the cause. To see "wars of liberation," the Pentagon's dominant nightmare, simply as a reflection of conspiracy, to overlook the social and economic roots which make them possible, to prescribe counter-conspiracy as the cure, is not only likely to ensure failure but it tends to shut off debate on peaceful alternatives. Here the growing tendency of the Johnson Administration to make it seem disloyal to question the omni-competence of the Presidency is reinforced by the natural tendency of the

Pentagon to see doubts about resort to force as unpatriotic. There is the danger here of a new McCarthyism as the Administration and the military move toward wider war rather than admit earlier mistakes.

APRIL 22, 1965

# AN OFFICIAL TURNS STATE'S EVIDENCE

The most important battle in South Vietnam was the fight to let the American people know what was going on. Two reporters who shared Pulitzer Prizes for their part in it, David Halberstam of the *New York Times* and Malcolm W. Browne of the Associated Press, have published their accounts of this battle between bureaucracy and press.

Now, in *Mission in Torment,* we have the story as seen from the other side. John Mecklin, a *Time* staff man, took leave of absence to serve as Public Affairs Officer of the U. S. Embassy in Saigon from May, 1962, to January, 1964. The story he has to tell is not peculiar to Saigon. The same struggle goes on in Washington. Covering the Pentagon, the State Department and the White House is a continual rassle between reporters trying to get the news and press officers putting out the government's "party line." If the latter had their way we would all sound like American equivalents of *Pravda* and *Izvestia;* too many do. "In Saigon in 1963," Mecklin writes, "the newsmen were regarded as enemies not only by local authorities but also by the American Mission." In this, Washington often seems to differ only in degree from Saigon.

Mecklin charges that the newsmen were rude, self-righteous and humorless, but he substantially confirms their indictment. Where Halberstam and Browne complain of a constant effort to mislead the press, Mecklin pleads in extenuation that the higher-ups believed their own falsehoods. "The root of the problem," he says, "was the fact that much of what the newsmen took to be lies was exactly what the Mission genuinely believed, and was reporting to Washington. Events were to prove that the Mission itself was unaware of how badly the war was going, operating in a world of illusion. Our feud with the newsmen was an angry symptom of bureaucratic sickness." The defense is more damning than the newsmen's accusations. All governments lie, but disaster lies in wait for countries whose officials smoke the same hashish they give out.

Mecklin lets us see that even this was not the whole story. There were falsehoods the officials believed and falsehoods they told deliberately. "To the best of my knowledge," Mecklin writes, "no responsible U.S. official in Saigon ever told a newsman a really big falsehood. Instead there were endless little ones." When the newsmen didn't fall for them, Washington complained. "There was a patronizing holier-than-thou tone in the official attitude toward the press," Mecklin relates. "We repeatedly received cables from Washington using expressions like 'tell the correspondents' to do so and so or 'explain how they were wrong' to write such and such. This was like trying to tell a New York taxi driver how to shift gears." This also goes on in Washington where Johnson sometimes seems to think the Constitution made him not only commander-in-chief of the nation's armed forces but editor-in-chief of its newspapers.

In one of his last dispatches as a *Time* correspondent in Saigon in 1955 after Diem had been in office nine months, Mecklin quoted an unnamed "prominent American journalist" as saying after his first interview with Diem, "Sort of a screwball, isn't he? His eyes don't even focus." By the time Mecklin got back to Saigon seven years later, U.S. information policy was designed to make sure that nobody else's eyes focussed properly on Vietnam either. Mecklin's book reveals that the notorious State Department Cable No. 1006 of February 21, 1962, which the Moss subcommittee of the House on government information policies later exposed, was regarded within the bureaucracy as liberalizing press relations! This basic directive was drafted jointly by Arthur Sylvester at Defense and Robert Manning at State; it reflects the animosity to a free press characteristic of both departments. "It was 'liberal'," Mecklin comments wryly, "in the sense that it recognized the right of American newsmen to cover the war in Vietnam, but it was otherwise little more than codification of the errors the Mission was already committing." Conveniently, the text was classified but the Moss subcommittee was allowed to reveal that newsmen were to be advised against "trifling criticism of the Diem government" and not to be taken along on military activities likely to result in "undesirable stories."

This is not ancient history. The old habits march on. *Mis*information is still the hallmark of the government's information policy. Two examples may be cited, one minor, one major. The minor one concerns the replacement of General Harkins by his deputy, General Westmoreland. Every few months, it would seem, Harkins would issue a statement saying the victory "is just months away"—this was his prediction, Mecklin recalls, the very day Diem was overthrown. When Westmoreland stepped into his old commander's shoes, the tired Army mimeograph machines ground out the same old tripe. "Like Harkins two years earlier," Mecklin notes, "Westmoreland's press notices described him as a 'no-nonsense' officer."

A major example concerns the State Department's recent White Paper. The Mecklin book, like Browne's, rebuts its central thesis. "Like everything else in Vietnam," Mecklin writes, "statistics on infiltrated matériel and personnel from the North were highly debatable. There was no question that significant Chinese and North Vietnamese supplies had been smuggled . . . But the vast bulk of Viet Cong weapons and equipment were American." Mecklin also has "no doubt that several thousand Viet Cong officers and other trained personnel had infiltrated from the North" but he adds that "the overwhelming majority of their forces were recruited locally." The White Paper was intended to prepare public opinion for the bombing of the North. Mecklin says that by destruction of factories and training camps in the North "the Viet Cong would be weakened, but probably not much more than the efficiency of the Pentagon would be reduced if the air conditioning were shut off." For Mecklin the talk of bombing supply routes "made even less sense" because most of the smuggled supplies were moved on foot or in sampan. In a graphic simile Mecklin writes, "As the French discovered so disastrously at Dienbienphu, air attack on coolie jungle supply routes is like trying to shoot a mouse hiding in a wheatfield from an airplane with a rifle."

Two hitherto undisclosed scenes stand out in the Mecklin book. One was an interview with Kennedy on April 29, 1963, when the President asked him, "Why are we having so much trouble with the reporters out there?" Mecklin thought there would be less trouble if officials were more candid. He wanted Kennedy to put a stop to "excessively optimistic public statements" in Washington and Saigon and the habit of "complaining" to editors and publishers "about unfavorable stories" from reporters in the field. Mecklin says he found Kennedy "skeptical but willing to try."

One wonders whether Mecklin was not naive. We know from Halberstam's book that Kennedy himself tried to persuade the publisher of the *New York Times* to transfer him out of Saigon. Six months later Kennedy was to issue the biggest optimistic whopperoo of the war—the McNamara-Taylor statement at the White House October 2, 1963, that all was going so well in Vietnam we could withdraw 1,000 men by the end of the year and complete "the major part of the U.S. military task" by the end of 1965!

Another White House scene on which Mecklin lifts the curtain for the first time was a special meeting of the National Security Council on September 10, 1963, when the Buddhist crisis was about to bring down Diem. The Bay of Pigs made Kennedy aware of how wrong the Joint Chiefs of Staff and the CIA could be. Had he lived longer, he might soon have come to feel the same way about their advice on Vietnam. Mecklin was invited to be present to hear a report from a special two-man mission Kennedy had hurriedly sent out to Saigon for a fresh look at the state of the war and of popular support for Diem. The mission was composed, Mecklin relates, of a Penta-

gon General and a senior Foreign Service officer, "both relatively unknown, though experienced Vietnam hands." Each
reported separately. Their reports turned out to be so different
that when they finished, President Kennedy asked, with that
dry wit which made him so winning, "Were you two gentlemen
in the same country?"

Mecklin writes that security regulations prohibit him from
reporting anything further about the meeting. He does say
that while every other agency thought the time had come to
reform, or get rid of, the Diem regime, "the Pentagon, unper-
suaded that the war had been affected by the Buddhist up-
heaval, continued to agitate for no real action at all," while the
CIA "was more or less of the same opinion." This should be
read with Halberstam's and Browne's accounts of how stubbornly deaf General Harkins and the top CIA man in Saigon,
Richardson, remained until the very end when their junior
officers in the field tried to tell them what was going on. The
lack of congressional or popular control over these huge military and intelligence bureaucracies allows them to go on being
wrong with impunity. Each "mistake" leads on to a bigger one.

Yet Mecklin would drag us further into the Asian morass. He
advocates the use of combat troops to take over the war in
South Vietnam, he believes the national interest requires it and
he thinks the war can be won in no other way, though it may
take many years and many men. At one point he talks of the
need for an army of 1,000,000 men. I wonder how he reconciles
this with his observation that we have been losing because we
have not won the peasant over to our side. The peasant, Mecklin says, in the most perceptive passage in his book, is aware "if
only intuitively" that the U.S. is in Vietnam for "global strategic considerations, not because of sympathy for the Vietnamese people." To step up the bombings North and South as
we have been doing, and to follow this with combat troops
as we have begun to do, means to burn up much of Vietnam
for those global strategic considerations. This is unlikely to
endear us to the least intuitive peasant in Vietnam or anywhere
else.

MAY 29, 1965

# WHY WE FAIL AS REVOLUTIONARIES

Some things cannot be learned. A man cannot learn *not* to breathe. There are limits on the adaptation of societies, as of organisms. An established order cannot run a social revolution. Nicholas I was so impressed with the Decembrists who tried to otherthrow him that he ordered a summary of their criticisms to be drawn up for the guidance of his government, though only after they had been exiled or executed. "It is necessary," this document said, "to improve the condition of the farmers, to end the humiliating sale of human beings." Nothing came of these proposed reforms. Instead the regime established, in the dreaded Third Section, a new type of political police. This is the inescapable pattern of counter-revolution when it tries—in the currently fashionable phrase—to win the hearts of the people. The regime may be aware of the need for social reform, but is unable by nature to bring it about. The failure of the Decembrists was the high water mark of the Holy Alliance, which sought to police Europe against the dangers of liberalism, as the U.S. since the Truman Doctrine has sought to police the world against the dangers of communism. Without over-stressing historical parallels, it is instructive to go back and notice that the Holy Alliance, in intent, was not as bleakly reactionary as it was in practice. It, too, sought to combine progress with repression, as we do in Vietnam. Metternich's famous secret memorandum to Alexander I envisaged a stability which "will in no wise exclude the development of what is good, for stability is not immobility." A new pamphlet from Mr. McNamara's Defense Department, arguing the case for military assistance, uses almost identical phrases. It quotes with approval a study of the military in underdeveloped countries which says "The military . . . may be able to play a key role in promoting mobility while maintaining stability." The military dictators we supply nevertheless do turn out to be immobile, as did the Holy Alliance before them, though it too was not without social insight. The reactionary Catholic theologian Baader who helped frame the Holy Alliance "maintained," long before McNamara's computers came up with the same revelation at Montreal, "that revolutionary sentiments are due . . . to the poverty of the masses." These are distant branches of the same family tree which gave us the Honolulu Declaration.

This perspective is necessary if we are to understand why we have failed in twelve years to bring about the social revolution so often promised in Vietnam. Four Americans who took part in this effort record their experiences in a new book, *Men Without Guns: American Civilians in Rural Vietnam*. The editor, George K. Tanham, went to Vietnam in 1964 as Director of Provincial Operations for AID and is at present deputy to the Vice-President of the RAND Corporation. He was writing the book's concluding chapter when the Honolulu Declaration was made public. "It should be noted," he comments somberly, "that similar high-sounding declarations in the past have accomplished little. However," he concludes, with an obvious effort to sound a bit hopeful, "with the full backing of the Saigon government and with such high level American support, this new rural-development effort may succeed." Considering Mr. Tanham's experience and position, that is not a very hearty testimonial, though events since Honolulu already make it look too optimistic.

Mr. Tanham's three collaborators have each provided a close-up from firsthand experience of the AID program in three different types of provinces. Robert Warne covers Vinh Binh in the Mekong Delta. Earl Young tells of his work in Phu Boh, in the Central Highlands. William Nighswonger describes his work in the coastal province where the U.S. air base at Da-nang is located. Like so many Americans who have worked at the grass roots in Vietnam, their reports have an honesty and sobriety very different from the glossy version of events which figures in Saigon's pamphlets and Washington's speeches. But at a certain point even these men stop short, as if at a wall they dare not climb.

How often can intelligent and well-meaning Americans see glamorous "revolutionary" programs collapse into the same old repression without noticing there is something fundamentally wrong? In his preface, Mr. Tanham makes the familiar point that while the Viet Cong have exploited rural dissatisfaction, "the governments of South Vietnam from Diem to the present have not met this challenge . . . and shown the way toward real economic and social progress. In spite of frequent high-sounding government declarations, there has been no real revolutionary effort." Why should this be surprising? Mr. Tanham has long been one of the government's experts in studying communist revolutionary warfare. These experts pore through communist literature but seem to miss the elementary and essential points, perhaps because to speak plainly in terms of class interests is regarded today as slightly subversive if not politically pornographic. How can you expect revolutionary changes from a government based on the possessing classes? We have been supporting a series of dictatorial regimes based on absentee landlords, military men and urban business types who can no more think in revolutionary terms than a horse can fly.

In a chapter on "Challenge and Response," Mr. Tanham demonstrates his own lack of adequate response to this challenge. The lack is characteristic of the U.S. counter-insurgency establishment. He writes of the Viet Cong, "Land is taken from the landowners, many of whom are in Saigon or other large cities, and redistributed to the peasants." Naturally the peasants like this. Why don't we do the same? Because the government we support is based on the landlords. Mr. Tanham does not ask the question nor provide the answer. Both are obvious, but this is the kind of obvious that counter-revolutionary movements are incapable by their nature of recognizing. A related example is provided by Mr. Warne's account of Vinh Binh province. He relates that "land ownership in Vinh Binh is confused since most of the land records were destroyed by the Vietminh. It is estimated that 60 per cent of the farmers do not have title to the land they farm. Only about a third of these now pay rent, because in the insecure areas the landowners are unable to

collect rents." This is revealing, but Mr. Warne seems to miss
its significance. If 60 per cent of the farmers do not have title
to the land, 60 per cent of the farmers stand to lose the land
they till if Saigon re-establishes control. If two-thirds of these
farmers now pay no rent because these areas are "insecure,"
then the return of security means the return of the rent col-
lector. From the peasant point of view the "pacification" drive
thus looks like an attempt by the landlords to regain control
of the land. It would be quite a feat to take a peasant's land
and win his heart at the same time.

The most revealing thing about this book is that it says so
little about land reform. Mr. Warne, who worked in the Mekong Delta, where this is a crucial problem, gives us only a
passing glimpse of the land ownership situation. "Through the
government's Land Reform Service," Mr. Warne writes, "some
tenant farmers are making installment payments to purchase
land confiscated from the French and from large Vietnamese
landowners. However, the majority of these installment contracts are in arrears at present." The land reform forced many
peasants to pay for land they had seized when the landlords
fled during the French war. Wherever the area is "insecure,"
peasants take advantage of the fact to forget about the install-
ments due.

"In 1958, as a land reform measure," Mr. Warne writes, "the
government disallowed holdings in excess of 240 acres, but this
regulation has not been well enforced." As a matter of fact, as
I learned in talking with U.S. farm experts in Saigon only a
few weeks ago, these maximums have been easily and widely
evaded though they are fantastically high when compared with
the land reforms in Japan (ten acres rice-land, family maximum) or Formosa (seven acres). Though an American farm
adviser as early as 1955 began pressing for agrarian reform to
"save the day in the coming battle for Vietnam," the reform
when Diem finally enacted it was limited, belated and tricky.
In a peasant country like Vietnam, this was politically fatal.
Yet the whole subject gets only a few passing remarks in *Men
Without Guns*.

The record shows more pressure for land reform in Vietnam
during the Eisenhower Administration than since; as our military intervention has grown, our capacity for political maneuver

has shrunk. In the Johnson years the subject has been soft-pedalled, though it still appears in our political litany about Vietnam and Latin America. There are several reasons for muffling talk of land reform. One is that in Vietnam, as in Brazil, it alienates the local upper classes with which we are allied. Another arises from the contrast between our preaching and our practice. Where U.S. lands have been seized for agrarian reform, we have either overthrown the government and forced return of the land, as in Guatemala, or tried by every means, fair or foul, to bring down the offending regime, as in Cuba. A third reason, apparent in congressional appropriation hearings, is the instinctive hostility of Southern Senators and Congressmen, often themselves *latifundistas,* to talk of breaking up big estates for the sake of the landless. Eastland, who so admired Trujillo, may fear this lest it give *nigras* bad ideas in his own delta. The main reason we drop the subject so easily is that our real concern in Vietnam, as in Latin America, is not with the people but with our anxiety to demonstrate that we can contain communism. This inevitably degenerates into a military operation. The military may indeed carry on some "civic action." This is no new departure. Our marines in Nicaragua and the Dominican Republic built wells and improved sanitation during the occupation of the 1920s. Then we handed these countries over to dictators we had trained. Our concern was to make them safe for the United Fruit Company. Somoza and Trujillo were our products in the twenties and thirties like Diem and Ky in the fifties and sixties. Though everybody from LBJ down constantly talks of social revolution, the record shows our real concern is with putting it down, not bringing it about. We like to talk about revolution, but we rush in helicopters and napalm when it threatens to break out. This is the real face of the *Pax Americana* we are trying to impose.

JULY 30, 1966

# XII

---

## RELUCTANT OPPOSITIONIST: FULBRIGHT OF ARKANSAS

# AN AMERICAN ANTHONY EDEN

This first biography of Senator Fulbright [1] is panegyric almost to the point of caricature. Within the first few pages, Tris Coffin calls him "a modern Prometheus . . . a public philosopher . . . an investigator to rank with Pecora and Walsh . . . a social critic of the American scene to compare with de Tocqueville and Mark Twain." This is advertising copy, not serious writing. It is difficult to appraise Fulbright justly because he does not fit the easy stereotypes of American politics. He is not a rebel, a dissenter, a crusader, or a fighting liberal. He is not a liberal at all. In Britain this young heir of Fayetteville, Arkansas's First Family would have been easily placed. There he would have been recognized at once as a well-educated young country squire of minor but inherited and ample wealth, with a taste not so much for politics as for public life. There he would naturally have joined the Conservative Party, and soon found himself on its rebel wing among those who wanted a more thoughtful foreign policy. He would also have been allied with those Tories who have a feeling for social reform as long as it is neither too sweeping nor too hasty. This is the landed civilized gentleman type, not unknown even today in New England and the South but foreign to the American egalitarian tradition. We are willing to extend equal treatment in politics even to Rockefellers—after all they are only trying to make a bigger bang with a bigger buck—but the country gentleman is as alien to our tastes as hereditary monarchy. (We prefer *elected*

[1] *Senator Fulbright: Portrait of a Public Philosopher* by Tristram Coffin.

Caesars.) In England Fulbright might conveniently be described as an American Anthony Eden. Here the average American would be puzzled by the comparison. None of us finds it easy to place J. William Fulbright in our rather rough-and-ready political categories.

Now that Fulbright has become a hero on the left and to the peaceniks, a saga has grown up around him. One of its best known episodes is the lone vote he cast in the Senate in February, 1954, against a $214,000 appropriation to continue the work of Joe McCarthy's investigations subcommittee. One would therefore expect to find a passion for civil liberties in Fulbright's record. But he is not a passionate man, even when it comes to the First Amendment. One would never guess it from this biography, but Fulbright's voting record on the basic political freedoms in those terrifying years of McCarthyism was a poor one, not so different from that of his fellow Senator from Arkansas, McClellan, who also helped to do McCarthy in. As one veteran Arkansas politician told me, "Bill [Fulbright] always sounds more liberal than he is while McClellan is less reactionary than he sounds." Both voted in 1950 to override Truman's veto of the Mundt-Nixon Internal Security Act, which for the first time in American history set up a regulatory body, the Subversive Activities Control Board, to determine and label dangerous ideas and associations, on the model of the Pure Food and Drug Act. Both voted two years later to override Truman's veto of the McCarran-Walter Immigration and Naturalization Act, which was framed in the same repressive spirit. Those veto messages were eloquently in the Jeffersonian tradition, but Fulbright did not respond to their music.

Though Fulbright once taught constitutional law, it never seems to have permeated his marrow. In 1954, when John Sherman Cooper and the late Estes Kefauver had the honor to be lone Senate voices against the Anti-Communist Control Act, another panicky product of the McCarthy era, Fulbright, like McClellan, voted for it. In one key vote during the same period Fulbright turned up on the right of McClellan. That was the vote in 1953 on McCarran's Compulsory Testimony Act, designed to circumvent the Fifth Amendment and "make Communists talk." Such conservatives as George of Georgia and Hoey of North Carolina attacked it as a breach in the Bill of

Rights. Among the ten Senators who had the pluck to go on record against this bill in that dangerous time was Stennis of Mississippi and McClellan of Arkansas. Fulbright was not among them. Even in 1958, four years after McCarthy had been destroyed by censure, Fulbright was with McClellan and the right-wingers in backing a bill to overrule the Supreme Court's decision reversing the state sedition conviction of the communist Steve Nelson. Many conservative lawyers opposed the bill as disruptive of state-federal relations in many fields of the law; liberals opposed it as giving free rein to backwoods inquisitors. Fortunately the Senate managed by a one-vote liberal majority to bury it. This was another example of Fulbright's queasy reluctance to appear ready for co-existence with communists at home though he might advocate co-existence with them abroad. It was McCarthy's disruptive effect on foreign relations rather than the pall he cast at home which seems to have moved Fulbright into active opposition. Yet in March, 1954, he had the nerve to challenge a witch-hunter more powerful and enduring than McCarthy—J. Edgar Hoover, the No. 1 Sacred Cow of American politics. Fulbright told the Associated Press he would no longer give security information to the FBI because McCarthy was getting any information he wanted from FBI files "whether authenticated or not." Hoover's effusive admiration for McCarthy is a subject few have dared mention, then or since.

Fulbright's attitude toward the snoopers-after-subversion often seems more a matter of aristocratic disdain than libertarian fire. In a speech on The Higher Patriotism last April, he said with his characteristic dry wit, "In the abstract we celebrate freedom of opinion as a vital part of our patriotic liturgy. It is only when some Americans exercise the right that other Americans are shocked." He often seems more the Whig than the liberal. Fulbright felt so little like a liberal during the witch hunt years that he was exempt from the panic that several times swept liberals into proving they were not communist by sponsoring some of the worst legislation of that period, much of it still avaiable on the statute books for use in our next period of hysteria. One example is the detention camp section they added to the Internal Security Act in 1950. Another is the communist outlawry section of the Communist Control Act in

1954. This was so loosely drawn that its frightened liberal sponsors (Humphrey, Morse, Douglas, and Kennedy) could have been proscribed as communists by their own definitions. Fulbright never felt it necessary to prove his political purity by such self-defeating antics. These shadings are absent from Coffin's portrait, as is Fulbright's greatest single contribution to American freedoms—the 1957 Senate Foreign Relations Committee hearings at which he exposed the State Department's bill to restrict foreign travel in all its bureaucratic and totalitarian nakedness. The Department has not ventured actively to push another measure since.

Fulbright is the most civilized and urbane man in the U. S. Senate and can easily survive an honest and realistic portrait. Coffin's biography is conspicuous for its protective *lacunae*. You would never gather from it that in domestic matters—except federal aid to education, public housing, and generally (but not always) rural electrification—Fulbright's record is not so different from any other Senator from a gas and oil state. Coffin does not mention Fulbright's position in two scandalous episodes of the 1950s. He was for the Dixon-Yates contract by which the power interests hoped to get a hold on the TVA, and he sponsored the bill by which natural gas producers hoped to reverse the Supreme Court's decision in the Phillips Petroleum case and free themselves from federal regulation. Eisenhower regretfully vetoed the bill after a Republican Senator created a national uproar by revealing that a lawyer-lobbyist for the bill had left a $2500 "campaign contribution" with one of that Senator's friends.

Not the slightest whisper of any such transaction attaches to Fulbright. He is a man jealous of his personal integrity. Old friends engaged in the most above-board and honorable lobbying complain of his inaccessibility even for those harmless favors which are the coin of normal politics. But his record does reflect political necessities and expediencies.

Some of his intimates say he was more liberal in the Thirties when he was a young lawyer in the Justice Department. Fulbright's evolution toward a more conservative position may be said to follow the topography of Arkansas, a state divided between the Populistic and poor hill country of the north and west, and the "deep South" plantation country of its rich

Mississippi delta lands in the south and east. The division is much like that which separates aristocratic tidewater from the poor white uplands in the Eastern-seaboard South, where the conflict of classes since colonial times has also been a function of geographic maldistribution. In Arkansas the hill country has rarely produced its Governors and Senators but when it does they move to the right in order to placate their wealthier constituents in the plantation country. The Populistic Faubus, a man from the hills, wooed the delta country with highways and swung it behind him by a racism not native to his own and Fulbright's "country" in the north and west. There Negroes are few and men wear the Stetsons and boots of the cow country. Fulbright found his own common denominator with the "Southerners" by virtue of wealth, education, family, and breeding.

He was a Rhodes Scholar who became the youngest college president in the country as head of the University of Arkansas. No one could be more different from the rednecks whom the real or pseudo aristocrats of the South despise. Faubus, by comparison, is a poor white radical, like Wallace of Alabama. But to preserve these gentlemanly ties with the delta, Fulbright's record on labor, as on race, has been as irreproachably correct as that of any conventional Southern Democrat, however liberal he might be on issues affecting distant heathen lands and continents. Fulbright voted, for example, in favor of the Taft-Hartley Labor Act and against minimum wage legislation. On Negro issues over the years—whether the poll tax, the Fair Employment Practices Commission, anti-lynch legislation, or civil rights bills—he has been as Southern as mint julep. His record in defense of the filibuster is also without stain. Nor was he with the tiny handful of Southern Congressmen who risked the political wilderness by refusing to sign the Southern Manifesto. In August 1958 he took the unusual step of filing a brief *amicus curiae* with the Supreme Court as a token of regional loyalty in the Little Rock case. This brief, characteristically, was no racist document, but the distinguished exposition of a pessimistic view of human nature like that expressed by disillusioned anti-democratic thinkers in the years after the terrible storms of the French Revolution had subsided. To read it is to see why Fulbright is best described as a highly literate if not always enlightened conservative; that is, in the true and

British use of the term, and not as it has come to be applied in this country as a euphemism for crypto-Fascists or Texas oil men with a screw loose.

Tris Coffin's hero-worshipping portrait achieves its highest level of unrecognizability in calling Fulbright a modern Prometheus. Fulbright would never have had done anything so irregular as stealing fire for Man. He would have sent Zeus a carefully prepared but private memorandum suggesting that it would be better to give man fire than risk the tumultuous uprisings sure to be provoked by cold meats on a rumbling stomach. Fulbright's favorite mode of procedure is to operate within official privacy by sending the President a memorandum. His famous investigation of the Reconstruction Finance Corporation in 1950, when he was chairman of the Senate Finance Committee, came only after President Truman had failed to heed his private remonstrances for a cleanup. Fulbright so little likes the role of party maverick that he is sensitive to this day about the charge that the "mink coat and deep freeze" revelations of that inquiry helped the Republicans defeat the Democrats when they ran his friend Adlai Stevenson in 1952. His next exploit of renown, his attack on the "strategy for survival" conferences under U.S. military auspices, was accomplished entirely intra-murally, in a 1961 memorandum for President Kennedy and Secretary McNamara. This was only made public on the angry insistence of Senator Strom Thurmond, himself a Major General in the U. S. Army Reserves. Senator Thurmond may not have meant it that way, but he thereby performed a public service. He wanted, of course, to expose Fulbright but only succeeded in exposing the military by forcing publication. The issues Fulbright raised were fundamental and the danger to which he called the incoming Kennedy Administration's attention real and continuous—the danger of a military-rightist effort to brainwash the country. The widest possible publicity was called for. To settle the matter privately, "between gentlemen," as it were, saved Fulbright from appearing to be picking a fight with his own party's incoming Administration. But it overlooked the need for making the public aware of the danger.

This must also be said of his third major attempt at reform by private memorandum—his effort in 1961 to head off the projected Cuban invasion. The Bay of Pigs affair illustrated the

weaknesses of the Senate Foreign Relations Committee. It
tends to lag behind the press and to be less well-informed
than the better newspapers. The fact that Cuban exiles were
being trained by the CIA in a secret hideout in Guatemala for
an invasion of Cuba was first exposed by the newspaper
*La Hora* in Guatemala City October 31, 1960. The story was
published in this country by Ronald Hilton in the November,
1960, issue of his now defunct *Hispanic American Review* at
Stanford, picked up thence by *The Nation,* and independently
verified by the *New York Times* in January, 1961. A vigilant
Foreign Relations Committee, prepared to play a watchdog
role, could have sent its own investigators down there, held
public hearings, and alerted the country to the danger. Fulbright's intervention was a case of belated happenstance. The
fullest account, by Sidney Hyman in *The New Republic* a year
later, said Fulbright happened to speak with the President late
in March. Mr. Kennedy heard the Senator was planning to
leave for Florida on the thirtieth. Since the President himself
was preparing to fly down to Palm Beach the same day, he
invited Fulbright to join him on the plane. Fulbright saw in
this a chance to discuss the invasion reports appearing in the
press. He asked Pat Holt, a Foreign Relations Committee staff
member, to draft a memorandum outlining Fulbright's reasons
for judging any such invasion plans unsound. The memorandum itself did not become public until after the decision was
made and the Bay of Pigs invasion attempted. It was printed
two years later in 1963 in the volume of Fulbright papers
edited by Karl Meyer: *Fulbright of Arkansas: The Public Positions of A Private Thinker*. The circumstances make the sub-
title seem pretentious. For the Cuban memorandum was the
private position of a Senator, and Senators are supposed to do
their thinking in public. How can the Senate fulfil its constitutional duties in foreign affairs if the Chairman of the Senate
Foreign Relations Committee expresses his opposition on so
grave a matter only *in camera?* Fulbright's influence at that
now famous but then secret White House conference, when he
was the only opponent of the plan to invade Cuba, would have
been stronger if there had been an aroused and informed public
opinion behind him. To create it should have been the job of

the Foreign Relations Committee; but such militancy was not then at least Fulbright's style.

The memorandum itself shows how belated and limited was Fulbright's own awakening on Latin American policies. In suggesting constructive alternatives to U.S. military intervention below the border. Fulbright proposed that we offer the Central American countries "tax incentives for real land reform." This overlooked the fact that the main obstacle to land reform in Central America, as in the Caribbean and parts of northern South America, has been the United States. Castro's insistence on land reform at the expense of the American sugar and cattle companies ended his chances of peaceful coexistence with the United States. The precedent for the CIA's plot to overthrow him was its successful overthrow seven years earlier of the Arbenz regime in Guatemala after it dared take some of United Fruit Company's idle acreage for land reform. Lyndon Johnson as majority leader then backstopped that CIA operation with a hard-line "Monroe Doctrine" resolution which Fulbright and every other Senator except Langer supported. The naive unawareness of these realities in the Cuban Memorandum must make Latin Americans despair. It is true that the attack on Guatemala was excused as an effort to prevent the establishment of "a Communist bridgehead in the Americas" but once Arbenz had been driven out, not only the land reform but Guatemala's first income tax—another supposed goal of enlightened North American policy—was repealed without a word of protest from Fulbright, or even from Morse and Lehman, then the chief critics of the Dulles foreign policy elsewhere in the world.

There was another reason why Fulbright kept his opposition private in the Bay of Pigs affair. It is only recently that Fulbright has begun appealing to public opinion as a means of marshalling opposition in foreign policy. His views on the proper relationship between the Senate and the White House have changed considerably in the last year or so, though you would hardly guess it from the Coffin biography. Five years ago Fulbright favored Senatorial acquiescence in Presidential leadership in making foreign policy. In a speech at Charlottesville in April 1961 he defended Lyndon Johnson's support as Majority Leader of the Eisenhower-Dulles foreign policy because "failure to support the President . . . could easily have led to political warfare between the parties over foreign policy." This is the conventional view, and its acceptance tends to free the military, intelligence, and State Department bureaucracies from criticism, and to withdraw from political debate the basic issues of war and peace. Fulbright would be even less likely to agree today with another passage in that same speech in which he said the Senate could not "substitute its judgment" for that of the President "without confusing the image and purpose of this country in the eyes of others." Something close to Senatorial abdication was the burden of a speech a month later at Cornell when Fulbright wondered "whether the time has not arrived, or indeed already passed, when we must give the executive a measure of power in the conduct of our foreign affairs that we have hitherto jealously withheld." In those first months of Kennedy's Presidency, Fulbright saw the Senate's function as a subordinate member of the Administration team. Its function as he then saw it was not to appeal to the people over the head of the President but to win their support for the policies the White House initiated. "As the fate of the nation depends upon the people," Fulbright said in concluding his Charlottesville speech,

> it is obviously dependent upon their understanding of the reasons for their burdens and their tolerance to bear them. It is in this role that I see the primary obligations of the Senate. That is, constantly to explain and rationalize the burden which the people bear, to help them to that degree of understanding which will compel their agreement.

This assumes that our Presidential Caesars know best, and that it is the Senate's duty to be their loyal advocate.

If the Bay of Pigs affair began to give Kennedy a healthy skepticism about the reliability of his military, intelligence, and foreign policy apparatus, it may also have begun to wean Fulbright away from his readiness to rely on the leadership of the White House. A diametrically opposite view of the Senatorial function was expressed by Fulbright in his Johns Hopkins speech on The Higher Patriotism last April. There he urged the Senate "to revive and strengthen the deliberative function which it has permitted to atrophy in the course of twenty-five years of crisis." He wanted the Senate to act "on the premise that dissent is not disloyalty, that a true consensus is shaped by airing our differences rather than suppressing them." He wanted the Senate to "become, as it used to be, an institution in which the great issues of American politics are contested with thoroughness, energy and candor." He called on the Senate no longer to be swayed "by executive pleas for urgency and unanimity, or by allegations of aid and comfort to the enemies of the United States" and warned that such appeals may be "made by officials whose concern is heightened by a distaste for criticism."

This about-face in Fulbright's conception of the Senate's function was the result of an about-face on concrete questions of foreign policy, above all on the war in Vietnam, which Fulbright had hitherto supported, even to the point—as few people realize—of being ready to go along with an expansion of the war to the north.

DECEMBER 29, 1966

# FROM HAWK TO DOVE

Like most of his Senate colleagues, Fulbright was slow to become a critic of our involvement in Indochina. In 1954, when Nixon was canvassing the Senate privately for intervention, the only Senator to speak up against "sending American GIs into the mud and muck of Indochina" was former Senator Ed Johnson of Colorado. One question some future biographer of Fulbright should try to answer is why so informed and enlightened a Senator was so slow to recognize what was really happening. This slow start is hidden from view in Tristram Coffin's overly flattering and protective biography. Fulbright did not oppose intervention when Eisenhower almost embarked upon it in 1954, nor when Kennedy began it in 1961. Fulbright's Senate speech in June of that year combined standard liberal precepts about the need for social reform with equally standard support for military aid in the anti-guerrilla struggle. He blamed Diem for the rise in guerrilla activity but at the same time thought Diem's critics unfairly harsh. He sounded as balanced as a party platform:

> The regime . . . can point to a record of steady accomplishment. Yet [it] has lacked something in benevolence . . . Opposition, including that of anti-Communist elements, has been vigorously suppressed. It is a regime that of necessity has been authoritarian, but one that also has been perhaps unnecessarily severe. On balance, however, it must be said that the accomplishments of this regime are overlooked by many observers and commentators, who all too frequently have accepted uncritically the most abusive gossip and propaganda about President Diem and his administration.[1]

As recently as the spring of 1964 Fulbright was still far from ready to translate liberal generalities into concrete dissent on foreign policy. In his famous speech in March 1964 [2] on "Old Myths and New Realities"—a speech which owes more to its title than its content—Fulbright said the country must "dare to think unthinkable thoughts." But on the central issues of Cuba, China, and Vietnam, his conclusions, as distinct from his liberal sentiments, would not have startled a *Reader's Digest* editor. He thought the U.S. should maintain its political and economic boycott of the Castro regime; that we should not recognize Communist China or even "acquiesce in her admission to the

---

[1] Compare Robert Guillian, probably then the best informed Far Eastern correspondent in the world, writing from Saigon two months earlier that year in *Le Monde* (April 6) where he described "the muzzled press, the abolition of all liberty, the farce of a false parliamentary regime, the paralyzing dictatorship" and said South Vietnam under Diem "by a strange and fascinating mimicry" was transforming itself into "a bad copy of a communist totalitarian regime."

[2] Reprinted in the appendix to Coffin's biography but with the date erroneously given as March 1966.

United Nations under present circumstances"; and that we should continue and if necessary intensify our military efforts in Vietnam.

To reread that speech now is to understand why Johnson seems to be more bitter about Fulbright than he does about the more consistent and radical opposition to the war by Morse and Gruening. For Fulbright's position on Vietnam in the spring of 1964 was indistinguishable from Johnson's. Fulbright thought that until we had improved our military position "there can be little prospect of a negotiated settlement which would assure the *independence* of a *non-Communist* Vietnam." The italics are ours, to emphasize Fulbright's formulation of the very conditions Johnson would soon use to hedge his offer of "unconditional negotiations." Fulbright then thought that we had "no choice but to support the South Vietnamese government and army" in order to defend our "vital interests" in Vietnam.

What were those vital interests? Fulbright did not say. But his over-all view of Southeast Asia strikingly resembled that which Johnson was later to unveil at the Manila Conference. Fulbright said, as Johnson often does, that "our purpose is to uphold and strengthen" the Geneva agreement, though he had just finished calling for an "independent" and "non-Communist" South Vietnam and the agreement called for elections to let its people decide whether they wished to be independent and non-communist. This contradiction is characteristic of American official policy. Then Fulbright went on to say that we seek only "to establish viable, independent states in Indochina and elsewhere in Southeast Asia, which will be free of and secure from the domination of Communist China and Communist North Vietnam." He continued, in a passage that deserves close study:

> I emphasize that we wish these nations to be *free of and secure from* [italics in original] domination by Peking and Hanoi, but not necessarily hostile to these regimes. Our objective is *not* [italics in original]—and in this I believe I am accurately expressing the official view of the United States Government as well as my own—to establish our own military power in Indochina or in any way to bring the Indochinese peninsula under our own domination or even to bring them into an American "sphere of influence."

This, too, like official policy is shot through with contradictions. Isn't an American sphere of influence implicit in the terms? How else could we be sure these states remained "free of and secure from" Hanoi and Peking? Who would draw the line between policies "not necessarily hostile to" Peking and Hanoi and policies we would regard as too un-hostile or too friendly? Our record of animosity toward Cambodia illustrates how we draw the line and how we make our displeasure felt when we feel it has been crossed. Is this not comparable to our Monroe Doctrine in Latin America? Is it not the germ of the Johnson Doctrine sketched out at Manila for Southeast Asia? To see it objectively we need only imagine our reaction if Peking were to announce that while it did not wish to establish a sphere of influence in Central America and the Caribbean, it would seek a system of states independent of Washington, though not necessarily hostile to it! To draw such a parallel was still too unthinkable for Fulbright in March 1964.

From Johnson's point of view, the policies Fulbright now criticizes were the same policies Fulbright had himself sketched out the year before Johnson adopted them as his own. In that speech Fulbright said he was prepared to go along with "whatever strategic decisions are found necessary," whether we decide "to continue or intensify our present support for the South Vietnamese government without expanding the scale of the operation, whether we seek a general negotiation without first trying to alter the military situation, *or whether the war is carried to the territory of North Vietnam with a view to negotiating a reasonable settlement."* [3] The italics are added. This means that in March 1964 Fulbright viewed with equanimity the prospect of extending the war to the North in order to soften it up for a settlement we would regard as "reasonable." This was the very policy Johnson was to put into effect the following February. It was not expressed in a bloodthirsty way but it was otherwise not essentially different from the policy advocated by Goldwater and the Air Force hawks, though the fact was kept hidden, of course, during the 1964 campaign.

But the future historian and biographer must not rest content with cynically noticing this unspoken agreement. He must dig

[3] Quoted from the speech as printed in Fulbright's book, *Old Myths and New Realities,* which went to press in May, 1964.

deeper. To decide on wider war as a way of forcing Hanoi to accept our terms, required three forms of preparation. There had to be an incident, to arouse the country's emotions. There had to be a Congressional blank check to the President for a wider war. And there had to be the deployment of air, naval, and combat units for the escalation. The Tonkin Gulf affair in August 1964, provided for all three. Fulbright's role was to put the blank check resolution through Congress for Johnson. Could he have been as innocent of what was really happening as he and his first biographer claim that he was? "It was an aberration . . . I just don't understand what happened," Fulbright now says, and Tris Coffin comments, "This is a painful honesty few would essay." But neither admit that the Tonkin Gulf resolution made possible in August what Fulbright himself had outlined in March as one way to a "reasonable settlement" of the Vietnamese wᵃr.

Three pieces of the puzzle are available now that may not have been available to Mr. Coffin when he wrote his biography. One is the revelation by Tom Wicker, Washington Bureau chief of the *New York Times*, in an *Esquire* article on Johnson (November 1965), that Johnson had been carrying the Tonkin Gulf resolution "around in his pocket for weeks waiting for the moment" when it could most favorably be presented to Congress. The second is a story in the July 23, 1964, issue of the *Saigon Post*, which only recently came into my hands. This reveals that the "moment" for which Johnson was waiting was bound soon to happen because there had been a sharp step-up, beginning in July 10, 1964, of commando raids upon the North. These increased the probability of a clash with the U.S. since American naval forces were then standing by off North Vietnam, whether to direct and cover the raids, as the North Vietnamese charged, or, as we claim, merely to observe what was happening. (The probability of an incident was increased by the fact that South Vietnam's navy was made up of former U.S. naval vessels. Their silhouette on enemy radar would be indistinguishable from our own.)

It is a pity that Mr. Coffin did not question Senator Fulbright about these commando raids, or notice that just such raids were proposed by the Senator in his March 1964 speech as it was originally delivered and is now reprinted in the appendix to Coffin's biography. The original language suggesting expansion of the war to the North differs curiously from the version published in Fulbright's own book, from which I quoted above. The original phrasing was:

> . . . and finally the expansion of the scale of the war, either by the direct commitment of large numbers of American troops or by equipping the South Vietnamese army to attack North Vietnamese territory, possibly by means of commando-type operations from the sea or the air.

Not only Morse and Gruening, the two who voted against the Tonkin Bay resolution, but Senators as different as Russell, McGovern, Nelson, and Scott were concerned by indications that the Tonkin Gulf incidents might have been provoked by just such commando raids on North Vietnam. The Administration was so anxious to bury all such possibilities from public view that last November 24, when it finally released the text of the hearing held by the Senate Foreign Relations Committee on the Tonkin Gulf resolution August 6, 1964, it blacked out not only its answers but even Morse's questions on this sensitive point.[4]

Now I come back to that *Saigon Post* story of July 23, 1964, which throws new light on the Tonkin Bay incidents. It appeared less than two weeks before these incidents occurred. It was an interview with Ky, then Air Commander, saying that there had been a 40 per cent increase "in air operations aimed at sending Special Forces teams in[to] North Vietnam." The *Post* said, "The official admission came as unconfirmed reports by Vietnamese sources told of widespread explosions rocking industrial centers and harbor areas in North Vietnam since July 10." These sources said "key industrial and harbor targets had been destroyed."

These were exactly the kind of operations Fulbright had originally proposed only a few months earlier in March. Could he have been in ignorance of what was going on? It is true that the U.S. press did not carry the *Saigon Post* interview with Ky, perhaps because our military have done their best to keep com-

---

[4] The substance of this interrogation may easily be reconstructed, however, by comparing the clumsily censored transcript with Morse's speeches in the Senate August 5 and 6, 1964, in the *Congressional Record* which is, happily, still free from censorship by the Pentagon or State.

mando raids on the North out of our papers ever since they began sporadically in the mid-Fifties. But Fulbright did not have to look any further than the *New York Times* of August 4, 1964, two days after the first Tonkin Gulf incident, to read that according to military sources "destroyers on patrol have sometimes collaborated with South Vietnamese hit-and-run raids on North Vietnamese cities, though the destroyers themselves stay in international waters."

Yet Fulbright in response to Morse's questions on the Senate floor lent his prestige to the official cover story: "the best information" he had from official sources was "that our boats did not convoy or back up any South Vietnamese naval vessels that were engaged in such attacks." When Senators Nelson and Scott asked about reports that our vessels were operating within the twelve-mile limit claimed by North Vietnam, Fulbright answered querulously. "Why should the U.S. be so careful about the sensitivities of North Vietnam? We were there for the purpose of observation of what went on in that area, because our people felt it necessary as part of our activities in protecting and helping to protect South Vietnam . . ." Even Mr. Coffin for once is led at this point to smile derisively at his hero. "For those with long memories," he writes, "there was strong irony here. Fulbright might have been 'Ole Tawm' Connally or Walter George growling at that damn young nuisance from Arkansas." Fulbright, as Coffin recognizes, covered up the peculiar background of the Tonkin Gulf incidents and this made it possible to push through authority for a wider war.

Recently another piece of the puzzle surfaced into public view. Escalation of the war into the North also required extensive deployment of additional military forces. In the transcript of the closed Senate committee hearings of August 1964—which was not released until last November 24—there is the text of a statement submitted to the Foreign Relations Committee by Secretary McNamara, which disclosed for the first time that large-scale deployment of forces to the Far East was already under way.[5] Among six major military steps being taken

[5] The transcript was finally cleared by the State Department for publication last July 12. It seems strange that it was not made public by the Foreign Relations Committee until four months later, after Congress had

were the "movement of fighter bomber aircraft into Thailand," from which the bombing of North Vietnam was to begin in February; and "the alerting and readying of selected Army and Marine forces" with which, once the election was over, we were to abandon the fiction of advisory role and plunge into combat operations. A major expansion of the war was in the works but there was no hint of this in the Senate debate. When the Senators voted a blank check for an enlarged war, few knew that Johnson had already begun to cash it, even before it was signed. But the transcript of that hearing behind closed doors shows that Fulbright and the Foreign Relations Committee did know that a major escalation of the war was in the works.

These newly released McNamara disclosures have scarcely been noticed. They make Mr. Coffin's apologetics for Fulbright hard to accept. Mr. Coffin writes that Fulbright put the Tonkin Gulf resolution through the Senate because "he accepted the Administration theory that this would keep the war from widening." Now we can see, from McNamara's detailed account of the military deployments the Administration had set in motion, that the resolution legalized secret preparations to widen the war.

These new revelations call for a fuller explanation from Fulbright than the apology he offered in his memorable speech last April on "The Higher Patriotism" when he had at last moved into open opposition to the war in Vietnam. It is a speech so eloquent that it makes much that went before forgiveable, but it still leaves much unexplained.

The Senator said he first began to express his doubts about the escalation policy in a memorandum to Johnson in April, 1965. That was two months after the bombing of the North began. The Coffin biography reveals that he then went to see the President on June 14. Here Coffin adds to our knowledge of what happened with a vivid picture of "Fulbright sitting quiet and restless while the President lectured him at a machine gun clip, words tumbling over each other in that peculiarly flat drawl," as Johnson pulled memoranda from every pocket. "Let me show you how many times we have offered to talk to

---

adjourned; and that the release date fell on Thanksgiving Day, an ideal day for the publication of news one wants as few people as possible to read.

them . . . they have spit in our eyes. How do you negotiate with folk like that?" (The words are presumably Coffin's paraphrase of Fulbright's account.)

When the Senator finally had a chance to speak, Coffin relates, he "said he was going to oppose, publicly, a further escalation of the war." But we still do not know the full story of Fulbright's evolution from a quiet hawk to an outspoken dove. What we do know is that when he shifted from a supporter to a critic of Administration foreign policy, as he did on the Dominican Republic as well as Vietnam, the weakness of the Senate Foreign Relations Committee as an independent check on the Presidency became evident. The years of cozy bi-partisanship in foreign policy had long rendered it almost moribund.

JANUARY 12, 1967

# A DROWSY WATCHDOG

Fulbright's effectiveness as a brake on the widening war in the crucial months ahead will depend on the effectiveness of the Senate Foreign Relations Committee, its staff and his capacity as chairman. Fulbright is talking about the possibility of more Vietnam hearings this year, but the record in the past is not encouraging. Though the committee contains some of the ablest and most liberal members of the Senate—Aiken of Vermont and Case of New Jersey on the Republican side; Mansfield, Morse, Gore, Church, Clark, and McCarthy on the Democratic side—most of them seem to be cloakroom crusaders, brave in private, cautious in public, fitfully aroused and poorly informed. Judging by the record, the staff seems to be lethargic; either it does a poor job of briefing the members before a hearing or the Senators then ignore the questions and memoranda prepared for them. I and other newspapermen blushed at their clumsy performance in interrogating Arthur Sylvester, Assistant Secretary of Defense "for Public Affairs," i.e., propaganda, last August 31, when their blunderbuss methods enabled this skillful newsman-turned-bureaucrat to evade the real issues in Pentagon efforts to manage the news.

The three best informed members of the committee are Fulbright, Mansfield, and Morse. Morse alone operates from outside the gentlemen's club inhibitions of the Senate Establishment. Mansfield from time to time, in special reports and speeches, lets fresh air in on stale situations, but at the decisive moments he usually subordinates his own better judgment to the compulsions of his post as Majority Leader, which means Presidential lieutenant. Even more than Fulbright, he tries to mold policy by private influence within the Administration; events have shown this does not amount to much. Fulbright, like Mansfield, is at his best in his thoughtful speeches. Both men are far wiser than Lyndon Johnson, but he is smarter than they are and is continually taking them back into camp. Fulbright as Chairman of Senate Foreign Relations lacks that tireless passion for searching out the jugular fact which makes a first-rate investigator. He is a reflective rather than a combative man, easy-going by temperament and drawn to the Establishment by birth and natural bent. It is an index of the deepening crisis in foreign policy, and a tribute to the man, that he should have moved as far as he has into the uncongenial role of oppositionist, but those who see him intimately note that he is depressed rather than exhilarated by it. He does not have the heretic's zest for standing alone, and often succumbs to the temptation of returning to the fold.

Those aware of this weakness did not miss its skillful exploitation by Vice-President Humphrey when he brought Fulbright along to join in the welcome to the President on his return from Manila that rainswept night at Dulles Airport just two months ago, nor the President's own masterly histrionics. First Johnson appeared coldly to ignore the prodigal's return, then rewarded him with a warm embrace. Next day the President gave Fulbright an hour's private briefing, and instructed Rusk to continue it over lunch. The result was a statement by Fulbright unexpectedly hailing the result of the Manila conference. While Fulbright expressed the opinion that a cessation of the bombing "might be useful," he had come around to the Johnson view that "the North Vietnamese certainly ought to indicate their willingness to respond to such an initiative on our part."

This lack of consistency makes it hazardous to count on Fulbright's independence. His first break with the Johnson Administration's belligerent policies abroad was over the Dominican Republic rather than Vietnam. Not since Borah forty years ago has a Chairman of the Senate Foreign Relations Committee challenged a President of his own party as Fulbright did Johnson when he attacked the Dominican intervention. The counterpart was Borah's attack on Coolidge's military intervention in Nicaragua in 1927. The circumstances were so alike as to be a useful reminder of the stale choreography with which the State Department handles our Latin American relations. "The first landing of troops," one standard historian has written,[1] "was declared to be solely for the protection of American lives and property, but there was little evidence that American lives and property were in jeopardy . . . The spectre of Russian Bolshevist activity in Latin America was conjured but refused to walk." Yet even in the midst of an attack as scathing as Borah's, Fulbright left his door open to the White House by absolving Johnson from blame for the Dominican intervention. He was careful to say that Johnson could not have acted differently on the basis of the "faulty advice" given him "by his representatives in the Dominican Republic," though Fulbright must know this is a polite falsehood; the Big Stick policy is instinctive with Johnson. Fulbright even added that he was sure "as I know President Johnson and indeed most U.S. citizens are sure, that our country is not and will not become the enemy of social revolution in Latin America." This is the language of the courtier, for whom untruth seems justified if it may flatter the monarch into a better course.

There is an even more serious warning in the Dominican

[1] Graham H. Stuart: *Latin America and the United States.*

affair for those who hope, as indeed I do, for national leadership from Fulbright. Those two speeches on the Dominican intervention provided a brilliant autopsy, but the patient might not have been dead if Fulbright had been more alert or courageous at the decisive moment. Tris Coffin lifts the curtain on this in his biography, though without assessing its significance. He provides an inside account of that White House conference with Congressional leaders which Johnson called in 1963 to discuss recognition of the military junta which had overthrown Juan Bosch as President of the Dominican Republic. This was one of Johnson's first moves as President and his first break with the Latin American policies of Kennedy. Kennedy had cut off economic aid and withdrawn recognition in protest against the coup and in the hope that this would force the military out of power. Now Johnson assembled Congressional leaders to hear Under-Secretary George Ball report that the military junta would fall unless aid were resumed and relations restored.

Three members of Senate Foreign Relations, Fulbright, Mansfield, and Morse, were among those invited to that White House conference. Johnson, as Mr. Coffin reveals, turned eagerly to Fulbright after the State Department presentation and asked, "What do you think, Bill?" That was the moment— and not almost two years later—when Fulbright should have spoken up. The fall of the junta would have opened the way to the restoration of Bosch, the Dominican Republic's first elected President in more than a generation, and heartened every democratic regime in the hemisphere. They are all haunted by well-founded fears of collusion between their military and ours. Mr. Coffin writes that Fulbright did not like the decision to recognize the junta. But instead of opposing it he replied, "In a case like this, when the Congress has no information of its own, and the State Department presumably has the facts, we have no alternative but to support the Department." Mr. Coffin relates that Mansfield also gave his "reluctant assent" and that "the only outright refusal" came from Morse.[2] Morse asked Johnson first to consult with the Presidents of Venezuela

[2] Later, so I have heard, Johnson shrewdly told Morse, "You know two of those fellows [meaning Fulbright and Mansfield] voted against their consciences." This was said, of course, to flatter Morse. The wily Texan never misses a trick.

and Chile. Both had opposed the military coup and feared the contagion of its example. They would certainly have advised Johnson to maintain the Kennedy policy, especially when it seemed on the verge of succeeding.

What were the facts in the State Department's presentation which so impressed and inhibited Fulbright? Mr. Coffin does not tell us. But the main argument trundled out, as I have learned elsewhere, was the same superannuated scarecrow, the oldest employee in the Department's Latin American division—not to support the military might open the door to a communist takeover. The Department too often thinks democracy risky. But it was two years before Fulbright made the retort he should have made then. "Obviously if we based all our policies on the mere possibility of communism," Fulbright told the Senate in his first speech on Dominican policy, September 15, 1965, "then we would have to set ourselves against just about every progressive political movement in the world, because almost all such movements are subject at least to the theoretical danger of communist take-over."

It was a question of judgment, not of facts. To let the State Department make the judgment by supplying the supposed facts is to make the Foreign Relations Committee its prisoner. The most disquieting point in the record of the committee is that it seems so rarely to go after the facts on its own. Fulbright has been on the committee since 1945 and its chairman since 1958. In all that time it has much too often seemed dependent for its facts on official briefings, and whatever could be elicited from them by hit-or-miss interrogation. Though these briefings notoriously give the Senators information little different from, and often considerably less than, they can read in the newspapers, they are usually held in executive session. The effect is to hide from better informed critics outside just how floozy is the inside dope given the committee.

Fulbright recently told the Associated Press that he was going to investigate Vietnam further in the new year. This will mean very little, however, if confined to the usual questioning at the annual review given the Senate Foreign Relations Committee in secret sessions at the beginning of each year by the Secretary of State. At the very least, Rusk should be required to do what McNamara does in his survey of military posture and policy before the Appropriations and Armed Service Committees of both houses. McNamara releases the text of his annual review to the press and then makes public a censored version of the hearings.

A prime example of the committee's failure to do its homework was Rusk's own confirmation hearing. This episode ranks high in the untold tales of this drowsy watchdog. Rusk was Assistant Secretary of State for Far Eastern Affairs in 1951 during the clash between Truman and MacArthur. The ultracautious Rusk then committed the one incautious act of his life. Three days after General Bradley made his famous declaration that MacArthur's plan to expand the Korean war into a war on China would be "the wrong war, at the wrong place, at the wrong time, and with the wrong enemy," Rusk turned up in the camp of the MacArthurites. Rusk was persuaded by John Foster Dulles to speak at a China Institute dinner arranged by Henry Luce. The other two speakers were Dulles and Senator Paul Douglas, both strong supporters of MacArthur against Truman. At this dinner Truman's young Assistant Secretary of State for Far Eastern Affairs delivered himself of a speech which overnight made him the hero of *Life, Time,* Senator Taft, David Lawrence, and the rightist press. The *Washington Post* reported that Secretary of State Acheson was "hopping mad" and that Rusk had not cleared the speech in advance with the State Department. Acheson held a press conference disavowing the implication that the Rusk speech signaled a shift in policy away from limited war in Korea. Even Arthur Krock joined Lowell Mellett, Marquis Childs, and Walter Lippmann in taking Rusk to task. Dean Rusk would have committed the American government not just to the containment or even the isolation of the Peking government but to its overthrow. "Such an objective," Lippmann wrote in a column "Bradley vs. Rusk" (May 22, 1951), "excludes a negotiated settlement in Korea and is just another way of announcing our terms are once again unconditional surrender." Later that year Rusk was eased out of the Department. Dulles, at that time Chairman of the Rockefeller Foundation, then got Rusk the job of being its President at a salary the *New York Times* said was between $50,000 and $75,000 a year, no mean consolation.

Who would have dreamt that nine years later this darling of

the Republicans would turn up as Secretary of State on Kennedy's New Frontier when the Democrats returned to power? Yet except for a few half-hearted questions from Aiken, no hint of this record appeared in the Rusk confirmation hearing before Senate Foreign Relations (nor in the press [3]). The staff only had to check back in newspaper files to dig it up. It is unbelievable that Fulbright did not recall it, for when that Rusk speech was made Fulbright was actively supporting the Truman position as a member of the Senate Foreign Relations Committee in the famous MacArthur hearings. The speech was memorable for the sentence in which Rusk called Communist China "a colonial Russian government—a Slavic Manchukuo on a larger scale." Manchukuo is what the Japanese named the regime they established in Manchuria in the 1930s under the puppet Emperor Pu Yi, last of the Manchus. Events since have richly demonstrated that Rusk's characterization of Communist China as a mere puppet of Moscow was one of the most splendid prat falls in the annals of prophecy. There were of course all sorts of practical political reasons for keeping Rusk's record out of sight, but all of them derive from that acquiescence in sham which is the price of membership in the nation's elite. The banker Robert Lovett, the most stratospheric of all the high mandarins in the New York foreign policy establishment, had turned down the job as Secretary of State and recommended Rusk to Kennedy instead. So Fulbright and his colleagues were silent as an Administration pledged to get the country moving again saddled itself with a Secretary of State more rigid, if anything, than John Foster Dulles himself.

In all the years of our involvement in Indochina, back to the two billion dollars we squandered on the French war, Senate Foreign Relations never held public hearings on it until last year. An example of what an energetic Foreign Relations Committee might have done was provided by the Porter Hardy subcommittee of House Government Operations in 1959 when it exposed the bribery, perjury, and wasted millions which marked our foreign aid program in Laos. Its 984 pages of hearings, though censored, still provide the most thorough insight into our policies in the Indochinese states. J. Graham Parsons presided over this mess as U. S. Ambassador to Laos and

[3] Except for my *Weekly*.

was severely criticized by the House committee for helping to hide it from public view. But Senate Foreign Relations unanimously confirmed him that same year for promotion to Assistant Secretary of State for Far Eastern Affairs. Parsons was not corrupt; he was just outstanding even in the Foreign Service for his rich endowment of complacency. Within a few weeks of his confirmation, he was appearing as a star witness before the House Foreign Affairs Committee to pillory Albert M. Colegrove and the Scripps Howard press for the first major attempt in U.S. journalism to expose the Diem dictatorship. All that Parsons then denied has proven all too true. It is incredible that Fulbright and his colleagues failed to see through him.

Fulbright and his colleagues performed a service when they held their first public hearings on Vietnam last winter. They, and the television companies by covering them fully, finally opened a public debate on issues which had too long been settled by drift and default. But the hearings also demonstrated limitations to be corrected if future hearings are to be more effective. There is no substitute for preliminary staff investigation in the field; a committee must know the answers in advance if it is not to be "snowed" by slick official witnesses. Lower level officials are more productive witnesses than those of Cabinet rank; the former know more about actual operations. Often, as reporters know, they are anxious to expose what their superiors would rather cover up. There is no reason why experienced newsmen, who have actually covered the war, should not be summoned as witnesses; events amply testify that some newsmen have been better judges of this war than the officials. Last winter's hearings were too heavily weighted with top officialdom, though their subjection to public interrogation provided some interesting fireworks and gave the country a chance to see just how smug they tend to be. The only two non-official witnesses, George Kennan and General James M. Gavin (retired), made a real contribution, but suffered from the inhibitions which a lifetime in the bureaucracy imposes, a fear of being "too far out" and a timidity which led them to take back much of what they had said as soon as hostile questions were asked from the pro-war side.

Above all, the hearings showed that after all these years the committee still lacks expertise in Indochinese affairs. The fundamental issue in Vietnam, in any effort to win the people, as American experts have often said, is land reform. It is both a clue to the failures of the past and to negotiation in the future: the National Liberation Front, in promising private ownership, seeks to allay peasant fears of losing their land to the same kind of savage and sectarian land reform that stirred a peasant revolt in the North in 1956. Not to keep an eye on this issue is to miss what concerns the peasants most. Future hearings, for example, should focus attention on the alarming fact that when Dr. Dan recently proposed in the Constituent Assembly that the new constitution guarantee the peasants the land they actually till, the proposal got only three votes in an Assembly heavily weighted with landlords. He also got no support from the U. S. Embassy in Vietnam, though we are presumably pledged by the Honolulu and Manila declarations to land reform and "social revolution."

It is revealing that land reform is not even listed in the index to last year's hearings and was mentioned only a few times in passing. The best discussion of the land problem is a series of articles by Richard Critchfield in the *Washington Star* last January, which Senator Clark inserted in the record. These are by far the most valuable part of the whole 743-page transcript. It is a pity they were never discussed before the TV audience, since they reveal that 3,000 rich Saigon families can earn as much as $40,000 a year on their *legal* rents and holdings, much less the higher rents and larger holdings they often get away with. As American troops move into the costly task of subduing the Mekong Delta, the resistance they encounter will be severe because, as Critchfield wrote, "The crux of the problem has yet to be tackled . . . the redistribution from big to small owners of more than 2 million acres." To move in before, and without, land reform is to reconquer the Delta for the big landowners with American lives. This is the truth of which the country has not yet been made aware.

The Foreign Relations Committee missed an opportunity when General Maxwell D. Taylor appeared before it. Taylor's first report to Kennedy in 1961 advised extensive social and political reform if South Vietnam were to be saved. Diem succeeded by a bitter campaign in getting American aid without those reforms. Taylor should have been asked to tell the committee that whole story. Here the committee and its staff were again asleep at the switch. Even Morse asked Taylor legalistic questions about the SEATO pact instead of focusing on the aborted social and economic reforms Taylor once recommended. The failure to institute them cost Diem's life and is costing many American lives. They will never be instituted either by a military junta made up from the landlord class nor by a Constituent Assembly in which the peasantry, the bulk of the people, is conspicuously unrepresented. Only a government which includes their spokesmen can negotiate peace and end a quarter-century of instability. These are the issues on which the country needs to be educated and these are the issues Fulbright and his colleagues have yet to explore.

Establishment liberals avert their eyes from this record. But it's just as well to be clear-sighted about it, as a hedge against disappointment and to bring pressure on him and his committee. They are going to have to do a lot better in the future than they have in the past if they are to help bring the country back to peace.

JANUARY 26, 1967

# XIII

## THE
## YOUNGER
## GENERATION

# A TRIUMPH OF YOUTH, NOT OF
# ELECTRONIC HARDWARE

When Colonel Glenn finally went into orbit, it was a feat of mechanical technology, a stunt in a competition for world prestige. No new dimensions were added to the human spirit. The only new dimension promised was for the game—and curse—of war, which moves toward outer space. Gagarin, Titov and Glenn are triumphs neither of socialism nor democracy, but of the same machine type civilization; both sides manage to organize their energies best when the challenge is linked to wreaking murder, out of self defense and for the highest motives of course, upon the other. The man in the sky is still the man in the cave.[1]

In the four thousand students who came to Washington last week-end we salute a different youth, achieving a different and more difficult orbit. After the dreary McCarthy years, in which fear of non-conformity lay like a pall on the campus, this marked the launching within "Turn Toward Peace" of a new student movement. No lucrative industry, like that of aerospace, stood by to focus all its public relations apparatus on this feat; no powerful bureaucracy, like that of the Pentagon,

[1] At press time there came word of an exchange of messages on peaceful cooperation in space between Khrushchev, who has already pointed out reassuringly that the vehicles which carried Gagarin and Titov could deposit nuclear bombs upon any point on earth, and Kennedy, who is racing so hard for peace that he had to increase the Eisenhower military budget by almost 25 per cent.

provided them with million dollar vehicles in which to set out. As they boarded buses for Washington, no corps of scientists stood by to measure the slightest reactions of heart and spleen to the gravitational pulls of indifference, hostility, suspicion and apathy. They made it on their own.

Friday, when the first students began to arrive, was a miserable day of sleet and fog. By noon of Saturday, when the sun came out like a benediction and all the neighboring church bells rang, the students had ringed Lafayette Square and packed the sidewalks in front of the White House and the old rococo State Department building next door. It was the biggest peace demonstration Washington has ever seen, and the biggest demonstration of any kind here since Negro organizations held their famous Prayer Meeting some years ago before the Lincoln Memorial. Just as the Negroes had picked the symbolism of the Memorial in their prayer for a new liberation, so the students marched off at twelve-thirty to the tomb of the Unknown Soldier across the river; there high up above the city and the Potomac, without speeches or banners, they laid a wreath. In this silent pantomime was a plea no hateful propaganda could distort.

For the sophisticated observer, there had also been an unmistakable message in the bright young faces and the banners of the immense picket line. These were no longer the beatniks of the fifties nor the party-liners of the forties. Both a new courage and a new maturity were visible. There was a fresh spontaneity in the hand-painted signs they carried. This was a Third Camp demonstration, aware of the dreadful similarity in the military logic and nation state lawlessness on both sides. One banner quoted Camus, "Neither Victims Nor Executioners" and another Thoreau, "Unjust Law Exists." The leftist heretic and the New England anarchist were alike congenial to this new youth, searching for perspectives more human than any divisive ideology and expressing a secular conscience far different from the ersatz Godliness of the Pentagon. "Make the World Safe for Humanity" said one banner, and another "The Deeper the Shelter the Bigger the Bomb." A third protested "Man Isn't a Mole" and another, "I'd Rather BE." One said, "Soviet Students We Criticize Our Government. You Must Criticize Yours. Both Sides Are to Blame." Another suggested

"Men Who Want to Be Soldiers—Why Not Astronauts?" Here their orbit crossed Colonel Glenn's.

The young President, when he looked from the windows, must have been touched by the number of these youthful pickets who quoted his own words. One said, "Neither Dead Nor Slave But Alive and Free—JFK"; another, "Let's Call A Truce to Terror"; a third "Let Us Never Fear to Negotiate— JFK" but a fourth, the most numerous, was impatient. It said "Mr. President, We Support the Peace Race. Let's Begin." The sober, admirably drafted policy statement circulated by the students was critical. It protested the "first strike" note creeping into the Administration's military planning. It questioned the morality and the logic of renewed testing. It attacked the civil defense program, saying "By creating the illusion of public safety, civil defense encourages public support for the kind of 'hard' foreign policy being urged by extremists." It might have added, had it known, that the same hard policy was being urged that day in Chicago by Secretary McNamara.

On Friday and Saturday, smaller contingents fanned out to lobby in the White House, on Capitol Hill, in the State Department and at the Soviet Embassy. These visits, like some unexpected difficulties, were an education. The White House was the one place where they found both sympathy and an ability to establish communication; the hot coffee the President sent out to the pickets was a gesture of friendliness, and there was respect in the high level of the advisers assigned to meet the student delegates: McGeorge Bundy, Jerome Wiesner, Ted Sorenson and Mark Raskin. The students felt understood; one Presidential adviser even suggested they should have picketed the Pentagon instead of the White House. What the students found less encouraging there was the concern with the easily possible, with making no move which was not sure of success in Congress—the caution, the conservatism. This combination of competence and conventionality is indeed the hallmark of the Kennedy Administration.

Elsewhere the students did not fare as well. At the Soviet Embassy they met affability but were unable to break through Soviet clichés. The State Department was worse; there they encountered "party line" without the affability. Some members of the delegation left in anger when they were treated to what they described as a series of pompous lectures on U.S. policy, and told they were hurting their country by not presenting a united front to the world! On Capitol Hill, except in the offices of such friendly members as Mrs. Edith Green of Oregon and William Fitts Ryan of New York, the reception accorded the students was described as often rude. The worst was Chet Holifield of California, who sneered that someone had "filled the students full of baloney," an odd comment from a once liberal Congressman grown so inflated on Pentagon and AEC ozone as to be unrecognizable to his old friends.

The most disquieting revelation was how frightened non-official Washington still remains. All Souls Unitarian turned students away when they asked a place to sleep. Metropolitan A.M.E. wouldn't let them use its premises because they were to be addressed by Norman Thomas and many of its members were government employes afraid of so subversive an association! Even Union M.E., which allowed its use as headquarters, forced the last contingent out onto the sidewalk in the cold night to wait for their buses. The National Press Club and both Howard University and George Washington refused to let them hold their final rally in their auditoriums—"too controversial." Norman Thomas—that evergreen of the peace movement—and Emil Mazey of the Auto Workers had to deliver the moving addresses with which the demonstration ended in the open and the cold near the Washington Monument.

FEBRUARY 26, 1962

# SNCC'S MIGHTY HANDFUL

There is nothing wrong with our younger generation when it can produce a movement like SNCC. Not since the great pre-revolutionary generation in Russia, its assorted Narodniks, SRs,[1] Marxists and Tolstoyans, has any great power produced as devoted a group of youngsters as the four hundred or so Negro and white young men and women of the Student Non-Violent Coordinating Committee, which held its fourth annual conference here in Washington at Howard University the weekend of November 29.

I have had the privilege over the past few years of getting to know a few of them. They are an impressive lot. Purity is the only word for their intrinsic quality—the absence of self-seeking or of vanity. They are the stuff of saints. They are determined to change our country, and for them the most fundamental change of all is to win by non-violent means, to answer hate with love. They stand in a line that runs back from Gandhi to Tolstoy to Thoreau to St. Francis to Jesus. I regard them with reverence.

To be with them was a moving experience. They draw sustenance, the whites as well as the blacks, from Negro roots. Most of them are not religious in any conventional sense, but the whole movement is steeped in Negro religiosity at its best. On one side of their nature, they are sophisticated intellectuals; on the other, they feel akin to the Negro racial past. "We have a mandate," said their chairman, John Lewis, "from our fore-fathers who were slaves." One moment they were talking of

[1] Social Revolutionaries.

the need for a planned economy and the next they were singing, "Like Christ, they died for you and me." They are ragged and ill-fed but their eyes shine. Against just such a consecrated few, powers more formidable than the lily-white South have fallen in the past, Czars and Caesars.

Cattle prods will not help, any more than it once helped to feed them to the lions. The South has a right to be terrified. Robert P. Moses, the director of SNCC's voter registration drive, used an unforgettable metaphor when he spoke of SNCC's work as an "annealing process." This young ex-school teacher from New York, with his round, brown African face, told the conference, "Only when metal has been brought to white heat, can it be shaped and molded; this is the annealing process. This is what we intend to do to the South and the country, bring them to white heat and then remold them."

The vision which provides a pattern for that remolding is beyond race; it seeks the emancipation of Man from his own suicidal divisions. Bob Moses is a sober seer, and does not fool himself. "The problem of the Negro is not the same as that of the European immigrant," he told the conference. "He could be accepted gradually as part of a broader European community. Our country and the world have not yet grappled with the problem of creating a community broad enough to encompass the Negro and the African." When it comes, it will have to be big enough to hold all mankind.

The Mexican, the Puerto Rican, the white unemployed, were not forgotten at this conference. James Baldwin and Bayard Rustin, like Lewis and Moses, saw the Negro's problem in broad human terms; to emancipate himself, he must emancipate the rest of us, from unemployment, from prejudice and from war. Baldwin spoke with the fury of a Hebrew prophet; Rustin with the objectivity of a still youthful Negro elder statesman, who believes as a lifelong pacifist and Socialist that only in a broader movement can the Negro hope to win jobs and freedom, and make a revolution "in a serious sense."

SNCC originated in the Fall of 1960 out of the sit-in student movement which began in Raleigh, N.C., in the spring of that year. Never have so few managed to make a bigger impact in a smaller space of time. They cheered when Lewis in his closing speech said, "We'll march through the heart of the

South as Sherman did." Though an unarmed few, they have already set a whole region trembling; the earth shakes again as always under the footsteps of faith.

DECEMBER 9, 1963

# THE SOUTH'S REBEL KLANSMEN AND THE STUDENT REBEL LEFT

In the sciences, fresh insights are often obtained by putting familiar facts in a fresh frame of reference. The nature of the Klans in the South, and the repeated acquittal of its killers, may usefully be looked at in terms of experience in the colonial world. In Palestine, in Cyprus, in Algeria and in South Vietnam, we have seen the power of a relatively few terrorists or guerrillas to disrupt law and order. The handful can succeed only if they have the sympathy and the support, passive at least, of the general population. The people of whom the terrorists are an extremist wing may themselves abhor bloodshed, yet they will acquiesce in the means because they agree so strongly on the end. The Klans, in this perspective, are the Eoka, the Irgun, the Viet Cong, of the white South. They terrorize and murder in defense of a system in which the white majority in the South believes.

In Cyprus, in Palestine, in Vietnam, sympathizers hid terrorists from the police. In the South white juries refuse to convict Klansmen; white forces of law and order often sympathize with, or secretly join, them. The Klans, now as during Reconstruction, are the white South's way of fighting the white North in defense of its peculiar institutions. This differs from—indeed it is the exact reverse of—the colonial struggle in that it seeks to perpetuate a colonialism of our own. Colonialism degrades one people in order to allow another people to enjoy the benefits of cheap labor in semi-serfdom. This is the colonial relationship the Klans are trying to perpetuate in the South. This is white supremacy as it is known in Rhodesia and South Africa as well as Alabama and Georgia.

Here, as there, the whites are so intent on maintaining their domination of the blacks that they are prepared to give up their own liberties and accept coercive systems to repress not only rebellious blacks but sympathetic whites. So white men in our South who dare disagree with white supremacy find themselves forced out of business by boycott, threat and ostracism. The Klans are the secular arm of the South's drive against racial heresy. This is what makes the investigation by the House Un-American Activities Committee, with its emphasis on petty stealing by Klan leaders, so ludicrously wide of the mark. And this is what makes proposals for new criminal legislation seem so futile because they all break down on the same rock of refusal to convict. Though limited and covert, we are confronted here with a kind of rebellion—a rebellion of the white South—and rebellions are not put down by legal means.

Those who would understand the student revolt against the war in Vietnam must widen their field of vision to see that by and large the student minority so deeply involved in this Southern struggle is the same student minority which feels so intensely opposed to the war in Vietnam. These students compare the one rebellion with the other and are doubly revolted. In the first place, they cannot help but contrast the overwhelming force mustered to put down the rebellion 9,000 miles from home while they have difficulty even in obtaining a full contingent of federal registrars for the South, much less the federal marshals or soldiers necessary to protect the registrars and those who wish to register with them. In one place we have 150,000 soldiers; in the other we do not have 150—or one-tenth of one per cent—as many registrars, indeed we do not have fifty. The students have seen their friends and comrades in the integration struggle beaten or killed, and the killers acquitted, while this same government claims to be helpless here but asks them to go fight against a rebellion there. In the second place, these students see the struggle in the South and the struggle in Vietnam as parts of the same world-wide struggle, the struggle of colored races to shake off white domination. The leadership of the struggle in Vietnam may be communist and dictatorial, but it is the same leadership which has been struggling since the last World War against foreign armies and their puppets. The students who have shown their willingness to face death in the South are not willing to face it in Vietnam. The latter, emotionally and philosophically, is not their war. That is how they feel.

What is the wise national policy for dealing with this student revolt, even from the standpoint of those who see the Vietnamese war as a test of national prestige in a larger world contest with two communist rivals, Russia and China? The wise national policy, it seems to me, is to let those who prefer to fight in the South do so. Unthinking enthusiasm, blind devotion, anti-communist fervor and herdlike conformity may be counted on to produce enough troops for Vietnam. It takes far more guts to fight the civil rights struggle in the South. It is lonelier, it is more exposed, and its chosen weapons are not napalm and bombers but non-violence and love.

Those few youngsters who are willing to engage in this task are a rare national asset, the real heroes of our time. It is because of them that our country looks very different in the eyes of the world from Rhodesia or South Africa. They are the ones who have stirred the Southern Negro from a century of submissive slumber. They have helped force the pace of civil rights legislation and enforcement. They have given the world a spectacle whose value is beyond price in a world festering with racial hatred—the spectacle of young white people from privileged homes going out to risk their lives on behalf of underprivileged blacks. They have made it possible for us to boast that our country is doing more to eradicate racism than any other country on earth, white or black. The kids of SNCC and CORE have served their country well on its most difficult and honorable battlefield. It is understandable that the Stennises and Eastlands would like to root them out and send them off to Vietnam instead. But let not the rest of us be deceived. This is not a test of their patriotism but of our good sense.

A substantial portion of our press is off like a lynch mob in full hue and cry against the student rebels. Their numbers, their views, their actions are being exaggerated and distorted; we invite you to read for yourself the actual statement of their aims issued by the leadership of the Students for a Democratic Society. It is an eloquent one. This majority of the rebel minority is seeking the right to opt for national service, in the slums, in the South, in the Peace Corps. They ask that those who object to the war in Vietnam be allowed to serve on these other fronts. We believe nothing could be more creditable to our country and more useful to its future than to accept their offer and their challenge. This idealistic youth is the same youth already serving in Peace Corps abroad and poverty program at home. They are the seed corn of a better future. They embody that strain of idealism which in every generation has written the brightest chapters in our American history. They are the spiritual sons of the Jeffersonians and the abolitionists. They have already proven their mettle, besieged as they are by the ignorant rich of Birchism on one side and the ignorant poor of the KKK on the other. There could be no greater folly than for the government to be drawn into a frontal conflict with the best youngsters of our time. Instead of alienating them further, we ought to take up their offer to enlist in their own way.

NOVEMBER 1, 1965

# A WIDENING GULF AND
# A DEEPENING DESPAIR

A terrible gulf is opening in our country. The victory of Maddox over Arnall in the Georgia Democratic primary is only the latest evidence that leadership is slipping to the poor white know-nothings in the South. Those who talk so scornfully about middle class liberals and want a working class third party might reflect on the fact that in the North as well as the South the bitterest resistance to the Negro's struggle comes from the white working class. And those who are making a slogan of "the unrepresented people" might notice that the racists of Grenada and Cicero also feel unrepresented by the Congresses which have passed so much civil rights legislation. Maddox's ax handles are as emotionally satisfying a symbol to these whites as Carmichael's black panther is to many Negroes. Both symbols point in the same direction, to racial war. We fight a civil war abroad while one grows up at home.

A new kind of secession is in the air. Not the simple territorial division, relatively easy to heal, which created the Confederacy but a less tangible secession more dangerous to the social fabric. There are an increasing number on right and left, among white and black, who would like to opt out—just where they do not know, but *out*. There is not only a readiness to tear down the pillars of society if they cannot obtain satisfaction, but even a perverse hope that all will fail. Behind the cry of black power, for all its smoother exposition for white sympathizers, lies an emotional urge to *separate*. The savagery in

Grenada and Cicero reflects a readiness to get rid of blacks al-together if they try to come out from behind their ghetto walls. All the bestial hate that created the crematorium can be read in the face of white mobsters. I shuddered to hear a sociologist say at the opening of an NBC show last Sunday night on the race troubles of Chicago and Cleveland that we must either make the huge effort required to give the Negro real equality or exterminate him. He meant this as an impossible and unbelievable alternative. But anything can happen if demagogues, black and white, preach hate long enough.

To the secessionists of race must be added the secessionists of politics. Much of the New Left politics is an attempt in disillusion to secede from the American political system. The New Left convention in Los Angeles last weekend is a warning of what may happen nationally in two years' time. From a distance the observer is appalled at the notion of what Reagan's defeat of Brown for the Governorship could do to American politics. But California liberals and leftists are as disgusted with Brown as most of us in the country are with Lyndon Johnson. To read the brilliant and exhaustive indictment of Brown in the October *Ramparts* is to understand the furious sense of being sold out that made the New Left wash its hands of Brown even though this may mean a rightist victory. This is the mood in which many people are going to sit out the 1968 campaign. It's going to be hard to sell them Lyndon Johnson again as a lesser evil even if the Republicans—as now appears—run on a platform calling for A-bombs in Vietnam and more police clubs at home.

Only peace in Vietnam can reunite the ranks left-of-center and leave our energies free to close the racial gulf at home. Only peace can end the fearful alienation of so many of our best intellectuals, black and white, men who could do so much in the urgent tasks of social reconstruction if once recalled from the wilderness of their own self-exile in revulsion against Johnson's barbarous war.

OCTOBER 10, 1966

# XIV

---

**SOME**

**EPITAPHS**

**ON**

**NOBLE**

**TOMBS**

# HENRY A. WALLACE

Henry Wallace was an exasperating cross between a saint and a village innocent. He never gave to his work as political leader or editor the kind of hard grappling with fact that he applied to corn breeding. In the 1948 campaign, he often read second-rate scripts prepared by third-rate Communist Party liners. He could be a most woolly-minded man, and some of his offhand remarks (like that on the communist takeover of Czechoslovakia) could make the hair even of devoted followers stand on end. But of all the political leaders of the New Deal generation none has proved a truer visionary. All the major ideas he espoused, and for which he was savagely ridiculed, have since become accepted parts of governmental thinking and policy: the ideas of the "ever-normal granary," of food for peace (derided as a proposal to give a quart of milk to every Hottentot), and of full employment were Wallace's. So was the idea that the postwar world, in the decline of imperialism, would be "the century of the common man." The most hostile storm of all was stirred by his anti-cold war campaign for the Presidency in 1948. But two decades, and many billions of armament dollars later, we and the Russians have come around to accepting the idea he espoused of peaceful co-existence, as some day we will with the Chinese. He applied to world politics the best strain of his native evangelical Middle Western idealism. We followed him with love in what we knew would be a lost battle in 1948. But what he stood for no longer looks lost today.

NOVEMBER 29, 1965

# ALEXANDER MEIKLEJOHN

We record with sorrow the death at ninety-two of Alexander Meiklejohn, one of the great Americans of our time. As an educator, his influence was not limited to Brown, Amherst and Wisconsin. He taught us all by his presence and example. Few men have combined such deep conviction with such courtesy towards opposing points of view, such foreboding about man's fate with so sweet a serenity and so ever-fresh a joy. He was a philosopher in the ancient sense; his concerns were the good life and the good society. For him as an American, the First Amendment was the essence of all that is best in our country and he spoke up for it when many were afraid to speak. Fittingly, his last message was a letter protesting the contempt action brought by the House Un-American Activities Committee against Dagmar Wilson, Donna Allen and Russ Nixon. His was never "a fugitive and cloistered virtue." We will always remember him with love.

JANUARY 11, 1965

# CLARENCE E. PICKETT

To know Dr. Clarence Evan Pickett was to know what the Friends mean by the inner light. It shone from this most unassuming man. It did not dazzle but it warmed and it was unforgettable. Those whom the world forgot the Friends Service Committee under his direction remembered: textile strikers during the great depression, the homeless fleeing the Spanish Civil War, Jews seeking a refuge from Nazi Germany, the armies of the uprooted after World War II, Negro victims of police brutality. When the Service Committee and Dr. Pickett were awarded a Nobel Peace Prize in 1947, the Norse spokesman said, "It is the silent help from the nameless to the nameless which is their [the Quaker] contribution to the promotion of brotherhood among nations." Dr. Pickett liked the phrase. He carried the torch of kindness from one generation to another, a saintly figure in a ravaged world.

MARCH 29, 1965

---

# ESTES KEFAUVER

---

No sooner had Estes Kefauver been elected to the House in
1940 than he became one of the few Southern Congressmen to
fight for repeal of the poll tax. His maiden speech in the Senate
nine years later was against the filibuster. He was the only
Southern Senator to support the Supreme Court's school desegregation decision; the only one who did not sign the Southern Manifesto. He believed in democracy with a small d: in the
Senate, he antagonized the oligarchy by trying to break the
dead hand of raw seniority precedence and to institute election
of committee chairmen by the committees themselves. In the
Democratic Party, he challenged the bosses; they never forgave
his exposure of the links between the big machines and crime.
They took Stevenson as a lesser evil in 1952. Still, a poor man
in politics, with the professionals against him, Kefauver got as
far as the vice presidential nomination in 1956. His finest epi-
taph was the sign somebody hastily scrawled over his headquarters in 1952 when the machine politicians barely stopped
him, "Nobody wants Estes but the people." Not since Norris
and La Follette has anybody in the Senate been so consistently—to use old-fashioned language—for "the people" and
against "the interests" as Estes Kefauver.
    The language is old fashioned because acquiescence in the
domination of American life by giant corporations is the mark
of our time; they rule by sharing power with the big wheels of
the labor movement and by comfortable adjustment to the demands of the welfare state. Big business, big labor and big
politics enjoy an Era of Good Feeling, in which each shows a

fraternal concern for the others' racket. Kefauver seemed a Don Quixote amid (if this be the right expression) the Cool Cats. Several obit writers referred to him as a tilter against windmills. But the windmills of Cervantes were imaginary monsters. Those against which Kefauver tilted were real: the effort in the Dixon-Yates scandal to let the private power crowd take over TVA; the gross overcharges of the steel giants and the uneconomic nonsense of the automobile industry; the ugly greed with which the drug companies market their often dangerously untried nostrums and exploit the aged and the sick. He died in the midst of a fight to expose the efforts of the big drug companies to prevent the sale of lower priced drugs in Latin America. In this area Kefauver left behind the first two major reforms of their kind since 1914: the Kefauver-Celler Act of 1950 tightening up the anti-trust laws and last year's Kefauver-Harris bill tightening up the pure food and drug laws. Nobody ever achieved more against greater odds. His administered price hearings are an eye-opener to our economic realities, and paid off richly in curbing steel and drug prices. Behind the scenes, a mere inquiry from his anti-trust subcommittee was often enough to stop a corporate steal. Kefauver in this sense was indeed a tribune of the people, wielding a one-man veto made possible by his integrity, industry and courage.

This last of the Southern Populists affected the manners of a mountain rustic, but he was one of the few really sophisticated intellectuals in the Senate. Some of Wall Street's best corporation minds came off second best in his deft cross-examinations. With all this went a devotion to traditional American freedoms few have shown in the past two haunted decades. He voted several times against the House Un-American Activities Committee in the House; he was one of the ten Senators who voted to uphold Truman's veto of the Internal Security Act's thought controls in 1950; he was the only Senator to vote against outlawry of the Communist Party in 1954. In 1955, in the fight over the Formosa resolution, Kefauver was one of the few who tried to keep the doors open in the Far East for a United Nations settlement of the dispute over both Formosa and the offshore islands. His speeches then showed the same bold non-conformity and insight that marked his entire career. We salute his passing with sorrow and grateful reverence.

SEPTEMBER 2, 1963

---

# ELIZABETH GURLEY FLYNN

---

In one sense Elizabeth Gurley Flynn died a failure but in another she died a success. The Communist Party of which she was chairman had lost almost all influence and respect; younger, more independent-minded members drifted away when it failed to recognize the implications of the 20th Congress and remained an uninspiring echo of Moscow. Its leadership became a kind of left-wing Old Folks Home, clinging to the conspiratorial and bureaucratic habits of the past. It was a strange position for her latter years, as the stuffy atmosphere of Moscow's hierarchy was a strange place for her to die. The fiery young Irish labor agitator, most passionate and eloquent of America's now vanished IWWs, the long-time mate in free love of her fellow anarchist, the wonderful Carlo Tresca, deserved a better end. The pity of it is that so few will realize how much Elizabeth did in her long and devoted lifetime for the betterment of the American working class. The great strikes she led on the eve of World War I were part of the epic struggle of U.S. labor to win its rights. The American Civil Liberties Union she helped organize is our oldest sentinel of basic liberties. A jail term under the Smith Act and isolation were the rewards of her old age, but some day, in a quieter atmosphere, her services to her country will be remembered. Because of her and other radicals like her, American workers are no longer the helpless victims of exploitation to be found elsewhere in this hemisphere. This was her success.

SEPTEMBER 14, 1964

---

# A. J. MUSTE

---

A. J. Muste was a wanderer on the face of the earth, a Witness in the ancient sense, driven by an impossible compulsion, to fulfill a truly Christian mission. Every minister at all worthy of his calling knows the daily agony of compromise. Muste refused to compromise. He resigned his first pastorate out of opposition to World War I, declaring simply that wars were not in the spirit of Christ. He left the church for the labor movement. Like that carpenter's Son, he was a life-long agitator, a radical pacifist. He once estimated that in fifty years he had been arrested thirty times. He was a friend of Gandhi's and he brought back the tactics that flowered in the students' non-violent campaign against segregation in the South, the most successful application in the Western world of non-violence. He lived a life of poverty, and in the Middle Ages would have been recognized as a saint. His latest pilgrimage for peace was to Hanoi. "The world needs a revolution," he once wrote, "in feeling, in sensitivity, in orientation, in the spirit of man." He was the kind of racist we desperately need— his concern was the race of man. It is a measure of his worth, and of his place in the peace movement, that though he died at 82, he leaves so sharp a sense of loss, a gap in the leadership there is no one to fill.

FEBRUARY 20, 1967

# XV

---

# IN
# JEFFERSON'S
# FOOTSTEPS

# THE BOND DECISION UPHOLDS
# OPPOSITION TO THE WAR AS
# FREE SPEECH

The Julian Bond suit was the first free speech case to reach our highest court involving opposition to the Vietnamese war. It was also the first time that the Supreme Court passed on the right of state legislatures to determine the qualifications of their own members. The State of Georgia, in arguing the right of its legislature to exclude Bond because he supported SNCC in opposing the war, relied on the principles of federalism and of the separation of powers between legislature and judiciary. Georgia argued that its legislature had a right to be the final judge of the qualifications of its members.

The Court, in rejecting these arguments, relied on the views of Madison in the framing of the Constitution. He successfully opposed a proposal to give Congress power to establish qualifications for its members. He cited British Parliamentary experience to show how easily this could be abused to bar new members whose views the majority disliked. The Court held that for Georgia's legislature to exclude Bond because of his views on the war would be a violation of the First Amendment and his freedom of speech.

This unanimous decision, by Chief Justice Warren, reflects a half-century's progress in civil liberties. In World War I, the only Socialist in Congress, Victor Berger of Milwaukee, was expelled for opposing the war. In the period of anti-red hysteria which followed, five Socialists were expelled from the New York State legislature. Charles Evans Hughes, soon to become a Republican Chief Justice of the Supreme Court, defended their rights in vain. Earl Warren, another Republican Chief Justice, has in a similar situation forced the Georgia legislature to seat Julian Bond.

There are few countries where free traditions are deep enough to allow in wartime the kind of criticism SNCC voiced and Bond endorsed. SNCC said the U.S. had been deceptive in its "concern for freedom of the Vietnamese people, just as the government has been deceptive in claiming concern for the freedom of colored people in such other countries as the Dominican Republic, the Congo, South Africa, Rhodesia and in the U.S. itself." It also said, "We recoil with horror at the inconsistency of a supposedly 'free' society where responsibility for freedom is equated with the responsibility to lend oneself to military aggression." This was no mild murmur of disagreement.

The Georgia House voted 184 to 12 that any man holding such views could not honestly take the oath to uphold the Constitution. The Supreme Court ruled that the power to exact the oath could not be used "to restrict the right of legislators to dissent from national or state policy under the guise of judging their loyalty to the Constitution." In a world where most of the newly "liberated" countries of Asia and Africa allow no dissent whatever, and the European Soviet states are barely beginning to allow a little feeble disagreement, this is a decision to make Americans proud. Jefferson isn't dead yet, despite our dirty little war and our huge military bureaucracy. We can still spit in its eye.

DECEMBER 12, 1966

# ONE MAN'S SEDITION MAY BE ANOTHER MAN'S LOYAL GOOD SENSE

The day before the Supreme Court last Monday handed down its decision on the New York State anti-subversive laws there was an unusual event in Moscow. Fifty young Russians unfurled hand-painted banners near Pushkin's monument and held a demonstration. They demanded the repeal of Article 70 of the Russian Federal Criminal Code as "unconstitutional." This is the law which provides up to 10 years in jail for "anti-Soviet agitation and propaganda," and was used to send the writers Sinyavsky and Daniel to prison.

We link this with the Supreme Court decision because they have a common background—the use of alarming but vague phrases in the law to cover the persecution of non-conformist opinion. Under Stalin, an ill-defined law against "counter-revolutionary" crime was used to put suspected critics in labor camps; the equally vague law about "anti-Soviet agitation and propaganda" is being used today against writers who do not toe the party line. The Supreme Court in its decision was striking at a similar evil in our own country.

Here the target of the majority were laws designed to keep "subversives" out of state employment, to punish teachers or other state employees for "any treasonable or seditious word or words" or for advocating "criminal anarchy." The Court struck them down as unconstitutional for a vagueness dangerous to fundamental liberty. This is what the Russian youth also meant by "unconstitutional."

One of the New York State laws invalidated goes back to the anti-radical hysteria in World War I. The others are the products of the anti-red hysteria during the late forties and during the Korean war. Some of the "loyalty oath" regulations involved have already been rescinded in New York but this decision will invalidate the use of similar devices in other states. The cases arose when four college teachers and a librarian refused on principle to sign certificates under oath that they had never taught revolutionary doctrine or belonged to any party which did. These oaths were part of a program for keeping teachers under surveillance.

Just fifteen years ago the Supreme Court in the Adler case upheld this system of regulation 6–3 under the so-called Feinberg law. Black, Douglas and Frankfurter dissented. Last Monday Black and Douglas were in a new majority of five which reversed that old decision. Clark, the last survivor of the six who then upheld it, wrote the minority dissent, with Harlan, Stewart and White. The Adler decision reflected the McCarthyite climate of that time and upheld the right to protect schools from the bogey of "infiltration."

Mr. Justice Clark based his dissent on the government's right to "self-preservation." This is close kin to the arguments used by Soviet jurists like Vishinsky for their repressive legislation against "counter-revolutionaries." Mr. Justice Brennan for the majority spoke more wisely when he said "Our experience under the Sedition Act of 1798 taught us that dangers fatal to First Amendment freedoms inhere in the word 'seditious.' And the word 'treasonable' if left undefined is no less dangerously uncertain."

In a joint dissent twelve years ago Justices Douglas and Black said the New York law "inevitably turns the school system into a spying project . . . Ears are cocked for tell-tale signs of disloyalty . . . Why was the history teacher so openly hostile to Franco Spain? . . . What was behind the praise of Soviet metallurgy in the chemistry class? . . . What happens under this law is typical of what happens in a police state . . . Fear stalks the classroom . . . A deadening dogma takes the place of free inquiry."

Soviet readers who come across that quotation will be startled by its aptness to their own lives. A state which sets out to
"preserve itself" by forbidding thoughts it considers dangerous
ends by casting a pall over all free discussion. This is universal
experience in every form of society.

JANUARY 24, 1966

# HISTORIC VICTORY

Only those who lived, and fought through, the postwar witch
hunt of the late forties will be able fully to savor the Supreme
Court's unanimous opinion last Monday striking down the registration provisions of the Internal Security Act as unconstitutional. The Act originated in the Mundt-Nixon bill in 1948, a
product of the atmosphere created by the Hiss-Chambers case.
It came out of the House Un-American Activities Committee,
and it was the pride and joy of that up-and-coming young
Congressman Richard Nixon. Some of the country's most conservative lawyers, led by John W. Davis, opposed the bill. Mr.
Justice Tom Clark was then Attorney General and proudly recalled in his concurring opinion Monday that he, too, opposed it.
The Court's decision is a triumph for Harry Truman. Just fifteen
years ago as President he vetoed the Act in an eloquent defense
of civil liberties only to have it passed over his veto. He said
its provision for a Subversive Activities Control Board would
put the government into "the thought control business." The
decision was also a triumph for Warren, Black, Douglas and
Brennan. Four years ago they dissented when the Court upheld

the registration provisions but declined to pass on the question of whether they were enforceable under the Fifth Amendment. Black's dissent will live as one of the finest defenses of First Amendment rights ever handed down from our highest bench. Mr. Justice Brennan's decision Monday limited itself to holding the registration provisions contrary to the privilege against self-incrimination. Never was an historic issue decided in a drabber opinion. But it does finally bury the idea that the government can police ideas as it does pure food and drugs, forcing suspected communist organizations or fronts to register and to label their publications and radio-TV broadcasts as communistic. Since the judgments of the Subversive Activities Control Board rested on parallels between positions taken by Moscow and those taken by domestic organizations, and since communists also espouse many progressive ideas, the way was open to proscribe radical and liberal organizations of many kinds as communistic. The Southern atmosphere, where the whole civil rights movement is regarded as a communist plot, enables one to understand the use that could be made of such a statute. So do the current attacks on the peace movement. From time to time we are accused of optimism and of undue faith in free American institutions. Such splendid victories may help explain these failings. To John Abt and Joseph Forer, the Communist Party's lawyers in the long fight against this Act, our congratulations.

NOVEMBER 22, 1965

# ON THE KLAN, THE REDS
# AND THE UN-AMERICANS

It is characteristic of all human societies to take effects for causes. This provides scapegoats by which people evade their responsibilities. An example is the uproar over the Klan in the murder of Mrs. Viola Gregg Liuzzo. Klansmen may have pulled the trigger, but the bullet, the gun and the hate were supplied by the South. In a fundamental sense the South is guilty: its century of lawless resistance to full emancipation, its maintenance of *mores* that prescribe the humiliation and degradation of the Negro, its elevation of racial purity and supremacy to a regional religion, all these have fostered that sexual sickness which made the killers feel they were carrying out a sacred duty to the white race. *Mrs. Liuzzo was executed in her car because there was a Negro on the front seat with her:* this is the truth about the murder people shy away from. Killing is encouraged by the general feeling in the South, among its "good" people as well as its bad, whenever civil rights workers are slain—that they somehow got what they asked for, that they had no right to "butt in" on the South's affairs. The Klan and the murder are the result. To focus on the Klan is to enable the respectables who know better to put their guilt on "rednecks" who don't. To propagate racial ethics is to foster racial murder.

On top of this regional sickness is a national sickness—that when anything goes wrong it must be due to communists. A paranoid corollary is that only firm anti-communists are above suspicion. This underlies the Administration's pressure to have the Klan investigated by the House Un-American Activities Committee. "This is because its chairman, Mr. Willis, is a Southerner," Tom Wicker disclosed in the *New York Times* March 30, "and because the committee's reputation would make it immune to charges of leftist influence." Does it take an investigation to prove that an organization which preaches Anglo-Saxon white Protestant supremacy is un-American? Could so obvious a proposition be regarded as "leftism"? "The possibility that the Klan might also be treated as a subversive group," Mr. Wicker reports White House reasoning, "probably would have to await the outcome of a Congressional investigation." Is study required to realize that organizations which preach hatred of Negroes, Jews and Catholics and contempt for Americans of "non Anglo-Saxon" origin are profoundly disruptive in a nation like ours? This was the strategy of Nazi propaganda before the war—to set Americans against each other by anti-Semitism and racism. To ask so discredited a bunch of witch-hunting old dodoes as the House Un-American Activities Committee to investigate the Klan is to demonstrate how shaky is our own commitment to our supposed national ideals. It is also to reveal the vulgar opportunism in the White House.

To hear Speaker McCormack joining in is to despair of people ever learning from the past. The Un-American Activities Committee originated in the Dickstein-McCormack resolution of 1934. The "un-American" propaganda it was supposed to investigate was the racist propaganda by the Nazis with assistance from native groups like the Klan. But very soon, under the chairmanship of another Southerner, Dies of Texas, the committee behind the smokescreen of anti-communism was attacking the New Deal and defeating such great Americans as Frank Murphy, then a pro-labor Governor of Michigan, later a Justice of the Supreme Court. In thirty years of existence, the committee has only on rare and fleeting occasions ever touched on any menace from the right. Its staff, like that of its counterpart in the Senate, Eastland's Internal Security Committee, is full of superannuated FBI men conditioned to nothing but anti-communism and of ex-communists who bring to the hunt an exaggerated notion of their old party's importance and the fanatic's readiness to twist the truth. It is characteristic that the "dean" of the crowd is a former business manager of *The Daily Worker*. Add the fact that McCarthyism never died out in the South, that perjurers and psychotics long discredited in Washington still perform before "little un-American committees" in the legislatures of the deep South, and that the whole area is convinced the Southern Negro would still be getting off the sidewalks if it weren't for a communist plot. This assures that any Klan investigation by the un-Americans will soon turn into a circus designed to smear the civil rights movement.

There is a warning here for those inside civil rights organizations who have been leaking "red" smears against CORE and SNCC. Columnists like Joe Alsop, David Lawrence, and Evans and Novak have become their sounding boards. The youngsters in CORE and SNCC have antagonized their elders by their brashness and conceit. But they have also brought fresh vigor to the fight. The kind of passionate devotion that makes youngsters ready to risk their lives in the South is not apt to be accompanied by sage moderation; if it were, they would have stayed at home. Only the sensitive, the rebellious, the extremist could or would do what these often exasperating but wonderful youngsters have done. There are neither ties nor resemblances between them and the sedate elderly people who run the Communist Party in this country. They reflect, espouse and develop a whole range of radical ideas, social and racial, some of them wacky with despair. But every movement of liberation requires its fringe of zealots and wilder men; otherwise the moderates would have no way to scare the other side into compromise. I saw the process at work in the Jewish struggle against the British in Palestine where a handful of direct actionists, there men of the right, gave the moderates leverage. This is the normal dynamics of a liberation struggle, not a plot. The plot is the plot to split the movement and rid it of the indispensable zealots by imposing some kind of "loyalty" oath and exposing it to defamation and discredit by the un-Americans.

APRIL 5, 1965

# XVI

---

OUR

LESS

THAN

FREE

PRESS

# WHEN THE GOVERNMENT LIES,
# MUST THE PRESS FIB?

As a boy in small town America, February 22 was made memorable for us small fry by red-white-and-blue cardboard hatchets and candied cherries, symbols of the Father of Our Country, who could not tell a lie, even if the consequence were a painful loss of prestige in the paternal woodshed. Now it seems the Parson Weems story about the cherry tree may no longer be regarded as quite the right upbringing for American youth. Now it seems that no truly patriotic American, especially if a newspaperman, is supposed to tell the truth once our government has decided that it is more advantageous to tell a lie. This is the real meaning of President Kennedy's appeal to the American Newspaper Publishers Association for self-censorship in the handling of the news. Mr. Kennedy put it more tactfully. He asked editors to ask themselves not only "Is it news?" but "Is it in the national interest?" But the national interest in a free society is supposed to lie in the fullest dissemination of the facts so that popular judgment may be truly informed. It is the mark of a closed or closing society to assume that the rulers decide how much the vulgar herd shall be told.

The President's real meaning was clearer to those who attended the two-day secret mass briefing, or official brainwashing, for the press at the State Department earlier in the week. There Assistant Secretary of State for Public Affairs Roger Tubby seemed to be implying that the Cuban invasion might have worked if the press had not printed so much about it in advance. He wanted newspaper editors to ask themselves whether a particular bit of news might help the enemy, and to call the State Department and ask if they were in doubt. One newspaperman present who had the spirit to challenge this was Richard Dudman of the St. Louis Post-Dispatch who objected that Tubby assumed the only thing wrong with the Cuban invasion was that it didn't work. Assuming, Dudman asked, that it was poorly conceived whether it worked or not, wouldn't it have been better to have had more information and more public discussion? This elicited only a polite mumble from Tubby, an old State Department hand now back in service who shares its ineradicable view that Papa Knows Best. This was not just post mortem since Mr. Kennedy himself told the briefing that there would be other situations, not similar he hoped, when our preparations would have to be made in secret. (I see no reason why American readers should not be allowed to know this since Soviet bloc reporters present were allowed to hear it and since I was not invited I am not bound to secrecy.) This opens the wider prospect of more adventures in which we make war without declaring it and brings us to the incident over which officials at the briefing expressed the greatest irritation.

This incident illustrates the dangers of hastily sweeping the Cuban affair under the rug without a full investigation.[1] The incident was the bombing of Camp Libertad, the military airport near Havana on April 14, just before the invasion began. This bombing was "covered" not only by a false story but by a false plane landing in Miami. The false story, quickly scented by several newspapers, was that the bombing was done by defecting Castro airmen stationed on the field. The false plane landing story was fully told in Time magazine April 28. It said the operation against Cuba started "with a surprise attack by B-26 light bombers on Cuban airports" to destroy Castro's air force. "To lend credence to a cover story that the bombings were by pilots defecting from Castro's air force,"

[1] Eisenhower who managed to go through the years of McCarthyism without ever uttering the term "witch hunt," suddenly discovers this term and advises against a "witch hunt" into the Cuban debacle. Obviously a full inquiry would also open up the story of the Guatemalan affair during his Administration.

*Time* reported, "a few .30-caliber bullets were fired into an old Cuban B-26. A pilot took off in the crate and landed it at Miami . . . A reporter noted that dust and undisturbed grease covered bomb-bay fittings . . . guns were uncorked and unfired. The planes that actually did the bombing never were seen." Officials at the briefing sessions made it clear they think the newspapers should not have exposed the falsity of this story. This goes beyond the standard of asking editors to ask themselves whether a story is in the national interest. It asks them to print as true whatever the government may think expedient in a given situation. It says that when the government lies, the press should fib. This is how *Izvestia* and *Pravda* are edited, but it hardly fits Jefferson's idea of a free press.

This incident calls for further examination. A B-26 raid on Cuba's military airports is quite an operation. We still don't know the full story. Was it by Cuban or American pilots? Where did the planes come from and where did they land afterwards? Were U.S. facilities used? These are the questions Cuba could raise if the incident were ever brought before an international tribunal. We are constantly talking of the "infamy" of Pearl Harbor, but here we had a hand in a sneak attack without a declaration of war on a neighboring country with which we are still legally at peace. The false story which covered it could not hide the truth from the Cubans; they knew they had not been bombed by planes from their own airfields. The false story—*and this is the important point*—was designed to hide the truth from the American press and the American public. It was not the enemy, it was our own people, this story was intended to deceive. Was it in the national interest to let the government deceive the American people? Is it ever in the national interest to let a government deceive, not a supposed enemy, but ourselves?

What if this sneak attack were on a larger country than Cuba, with a big air force of its own, able to return to bomb our cities? What if Castro had retaliated by bombing Miami? To raise these questions is to see the danger of allowing such agencies as CIA secretly to make war on its own, in violation of law, treaty and Constitution. To raise them is to see how indispensable it is to preserve some check upon them through a free press. To raise them is also to see on how dangerous and slippery a road we are proceeding.

The danger will not be met by the currently fashionable proposal to take cloak-and-dagger activities out of the CIA and put them in the Pentagon. The danger will be worse if authorization for secret war-making shenanigans is put in the hands of the military, with the far greater resources at its disposal; in any case the Cuban affair was a joint enterprise of CIA and the armed forces. The danger lies in these "para-military" activities themselves on which Mr. Kennedy suddenly sets so much store. To embark on secret warlike activities against peoples whose governments we dislike, is to set out on a course destructive of free government and of peace.

MAY 3, 1961

# WHAT JOHN F. KENNEDY NEVER
# UNDERSTOOD ABOUT FREEDOM
# OF THE PRESS

Pierre Salinger's book *With Kennedy* shows how deeply resentful Kennedy was of press criticism, and how eager he was for some way to put restraints on the press. He opened his first press conference after the Bay of Pigs by shutting off all questions on it. "I do not think," he said, "any useful national purpose would be served by my going into the Cuban question this morning." The morning papers next day were critical of his refusal to discuss the subject. "He was still burning when I saw him in mid-morning," Salinger relates and then discloses Kennedy's outburst—

> "What could I have said that would have helped the situation at all? That we took the beating of our lives? That the CIA and the Pentagon are stupid? What purpose do they think it would serve to put that on the record?" He shook his head. "We're going to have to straighten all this out, and soon. The publishers have to understand that we're never more than a miscalculation away from war and that there are things we are doing that we just can't talk about."

This passage makes it easier to understand why Kennedy was such a James Bond fan; the words reflect that kind of a universe, of constant conspiracy and imminent destruction. The conclusions to be drawn are the opposite of Kennedy's. If we are "never more than a miscalculation away from war" then it certainly does serve a national purpose to put on the record that the Pentagon and the CIA are stupid. For the greatest danger of miscalculation arises from the secret operations of this huge military-intelligence apparatus. The safety of the country demands more, not less, knowledge of its operations. But Kennedy's reaction was his famous speech to the American Newspaper Publishers' Association six days later, asking in effect for self-censorship in reporting clandestine operations like the attack on Cuba. Yet he himself, as we now know, told Turner Catledge of the *New York Times* months later that he wished that paper had published more about the Cuban preparations because it might have saved the country and himself from what proved to be a disaster.

At one moment the naive Salinger talks of keeping secret "things better for the enemy not to know about." But a more urgent concern becomes plain in his discussion of Kennedy's animosity to the reporting out of Vietnam in 1961–63. "Stories began appearing with increasing regularity," Salinger writes, "describing heavy involvement of U.S. forces in Vietnamese operations . . . they presented the American people with a picture of widening war in Southeast Asia—and it was this picture which . . . the Administration did not want to present."

Salinger quotes with approval a silly *Detroit News* editorial which backed Kennedy's drive for more "restraint" in reporting. It said the First Amendment did not intend "that a nation shall commit suicide rather than keep a secret." The real intent of the First Amendment was to *prevent* national suicide by making it difficult for the government to operate in secret, free from the scrutiny of a watchful press.

That "monolithic and ruthless conspiracy" Kennedy conjured up before the newspaper publishers as the enemy may prove less dangerous than the monolithic and ruthless conspiracy of cold warriors which operates through the Pentagon and the CIA. The Bay of Pigs showed it could make the President himself a prisoner of its melodramatic stupidities. Vietnam is a daily reminder of its mendacity and incompetence. We need more disclosure, not less, if we are to protect the country from it. But Johnson continues the efforts at "news management" Kennedy began.

OCTOBER 3, 1966

# HARRISON SALISBURY'S DASTARDLY WAR CRIME

The animosity in Washington to the *New York Times* and Harrison Salisbury is more than resentment that they added to the dimensions of the credibility gap. The deeper reason is that they put a spoke in the wheels of the Pentagon's plans for intensifying the air war. A week before the *New York Times* published Salisbury's first dispatch from Hanoi, the military were already worried by acceptance in the Western world and at the Vatican of Hanoi's charge that residential areas had been hit and civilians killed in our air raids of December 13 and 14. These were the heaviest on the North Vietnamese capital since its oil facilities were bombed last June 29. Henry L. Trewhitt reported to the *Baltimore Sun* from Washington (December 20) that the Pentagon feared the effect of the worldwide outcry on the White House "where targeting is approved." The military had been hoping, Mr. Trewhitt wrote, to expand the list of approved targets to include "more of North Vietnam's industrial potential" and of its electric generating plants although these were "in many cases surrounded by relatively dense population." The military feared the worldwide outcry had put the White House "on the defensive" and made approval of these targets less likely. To have these charges confirmed by an executive of America's No. 1 newspaper, himself a reporter of long experience, made it impossible to downgrade criticism abroad as enemy propaganda or anti-American prejudice.

Thus this feat of free journalism is to be measured not by the exposure of civilian deaths in the past but by the possible saving of civilian lives in the future. The myth that we have been bombing the North with surgical precision is dead. Any stepup in the air war can only be taken now against a general recognition that it will carry us further along the path toward a war of extermination. Hanson Baldwin's efforts in the *New York Times* December 30 to counter the effects of the Salisbury dispatches ("Bombing of the North: U. S. Officers Call It Effective and Limited") only made matters worse for the Pentagon. It disclosed that in our little limited war we were dumping a half million tons of bombs *per year* on Vietnam North and South. This, Baldwin admitted, is "somewhat more" than those expended against Japan in the entire Pacific area during the four years of World War II. He did not add that South Vietnam is not supposed to be an enemy but an allied country. The sheer tonnage we dispense may make other countries with guerrilla problems decide American aid is worse than the disease. It looks as if the U. S. Air Force remedy for an aching head is to shoot it off.

The disturbing aspect of the Salisbury trip is the reaction

of the Washington press corps. That America's foremost paper could send a correspondent to an enemy capital in the middle of a war and expose the misleading character of our own government's pronouncements was extraordinary. It has few parallels in history and it should make Americans proud of our free institutions and their continued vitality. This was something one would expect every newspaperman to boast about, no matter how he felt about the war itself. This was freedom of the press in the best Jeffersonian tradition. But the Salisbury exploit instead of being greeted by applause has evoked as mean, petty and unworthy a reaction as I have ever seen in the press corps. Part of it, no doubt, is jealousy, for Salisbury's passport was validated for North Vietnam last year along with several dozen other newspapermen but only he obtained a North Vietnamese visa. Part of it is something worse; the State Department, we may be sure, did not pass the word along to so many of its favored correspondents that they could go to North Vietnam in the hope that they would turn in any such report on what our bombers had been doing.

So a barrage of slander has been laid down. *Time* (January 6), which can always be counted on for well-rounded views, attacks Salisbury's reports as "uncritical, one-dimensional." *Newsweek* (January 9) said of Salisbury's observation that "American bombing has been inflicting considerable civilian casualties in Hanoi"—"To American eyes, it read like the line from Tass or Hsinsha" [misspelling in the original]. The *Washington Post,* which had hitherto kept its fervent support of the war to its editorial columns, was frenetic. Two days after the first Salisbury dispatch appeared, its main page-one story with a four-column headline was "Hanoi Seen Exploiting Its Civilian Casualties." Since the civilian casualties could no longer be denied, since the Pentagon itself was admitting them, Hanoi was now accused of "exploiting" them—a clear violation of the rules of war: apparently civilian casualties should be quietly buried in unmarked graves. The story, by Murray Marder, said "North Vietnam will admit more Western newsmen in an evident attempt to undermine the Johnson Administration's claims that its policy is to avoid bombing civilians." This was a double twist which would have delighted Goebbels.

Another bit of frenzied journalism followed on New Year's

Day when the *Washington Post*'s Pentagon correspondent, George C. Wilson, turned up with a communist pamphlet issued last November on the bombings of Nam-dinh. He said "intelligence sources here . . . have copies of it." After somehow obtaining a copy, Mr. Wilson checked (1) with "intelligence sources" which "said it was authentic" and then (2) asked Arthur Sylvester, the Pentagon's top press officer, "if the pamphlet was indeed an authentic one." Sylvester replied, "Yes, so far as I know." After this passionate exercise in verification, Mr. Wilson then proceeded to discover that figures in the pamphlet were the same as the figures given Mr. Salisbury in Nam-dinh. "It is probable, but not certain," Mr. Wilson hinted darkly, "that President Johnson has been told about the relationship between the casualty figures in the *Times* and the pamphlet." Maybe he'll cancel his subscription. The climax of the *Washington Post*'s impotent fury was a story next day, "Ho Tries a New Propaganda Weapon" by Chalmers Roberts, which was so turgidly slanderous it may properly be characterized as ponji-stick journalism—like the dung-tipped spears in Viet Cong booby traps. Even this was topped by Crosby Noyes in the *Washington Star* January 4, where this ordinarily civilized journalist seemed to have gone completely off his rocker. He said this was the first U.S. government in history to permit "the systematic subversion" of its military commitment abroad. He attacked "an important segment of the press" for its "utter lack of identification . . . with what the government defines as the national interest." He thought it strange if not sinister for the government to allow any visits to Hanoi at all. Poor Joe McCarthy! He died too soon.

JANUARY 9, 1967

# XVII

A

GIANT

IN

CONVULSION

# IN THE NAME OF MARX AS ONCE
# IN THE NAME OF JESUS

The end of the Sino-Soviet conference and the happy beginning of the Khrushchev-Harriman talks has distracted attention
from another momentous meeting in Moscow. The mission from
Peking and the mission from Washington overshadowed a
mission from the Vatican, the arrival of two papal envoys to
attend the golden jubilee of the Patriarch Alexis, "the first
time," the Associated Press reported, "that the Vatican has
assigned clergymen to attend a major ceremony of the Russian
Church since the great schism of 1054" which occurred after
"Catholic missionaries in Russia were imprisoned and murdered." Nine centuries ago the East-West split was between
Rome and Moscow; the bitterness was between Christians, as
we see it now between Marxist-Leninists; the doctrinal differences between the Eastern and Western Churches were as
subtly hair-splitting and as difficult for the innocent heathen to
understand as is the doctrinal dispute between the Muscovite
and the Chinese Marxists. Blood was shed in the name of Jesus,
as it may some day be shed in the name of Marx; in both cases,
behind the dogma the sophisticated will scent the clash of rival
bureaucracies, then of priests, now of commissars, seeking to
consolidate and extend their power in mutual fear and suspicion. It is not by enlistment in such ancient forms of power
struggle that intellectuals can help mankind find its way to
safety in the thermonuclear age.

Power and not dogma is at stake. For Mao to rehabilitate

Stalin is nonsense; if Mao had obeyed Stalin, Chiang would still be in power. For Stalin like Khrushchev put Russian state interests ahead of revolution elsewhere. Equally nonsensical is Mao's claim to be the more perfect Leninist. Under Lenin revolutionary workers seized power in the cities, and then worker armies fastened their power on the countryside. Under Mao revolutionary peasants seized power in the countryside and then peasant armies captured the cities. In both countries a monolithic hierarchic party ruled from above wields power; in both the dictatorship of the proletariat is a myth. The "cult of personality" is one of the topics in dispute between them but in one country there is a cult of Khrushchev and in the other a cult of Mao. In 1956 Mao was the "liberal" and Khrushchev was saying Stalin-style that the Hungarian revolt might have been avoided "if a couple of writers had been shot in time." Then Mao, in his exhortation to "let a hundred flowers blossom, let a hundred schools of thought contend," seemed to be wedding John Stuart Mill to Karl Marx—until the experiment showed such wide resentment in China against power-corrupted communists and stultifying thought controls, that the lid had to be clamped on again. The two rivals feel for each other's weak points. Mao's aborted "great leap forward" and largely abandoned communes threaten his internal prestige, as does the failure of Khrushchev's efforts peacefully to solidify the East German regime. Mao and Khrushchev, like Pope and Patriarch almost a thousand years ago, move toward schism. Like warring Christians before them, warring Marxist-Leninists would sooner co-exist with the heathen than with each other. While Moscow reaches westward for agreement, so does Peking; the Chinese have been trying for months to replace Soviet ties with new trade arrangements in London, Ottawa and Paris.

The growing split between Moscow and Peking has its good and its bad side. The good side is that with the split, as with the split that brought Protestantism to birth, the existence of rival power centers and rival dogmas in the communist camp must end thought control. It is true that Moscow and Peking each has its own system of thought control, as Luther and Calvin had their own in the struggle with the Papacy. But the existence of so many rival "one and only" true interpretations of Gospel became an object lesson in pluralism and opened the door to the right to think for oneself. We may hope for a similar development in the stuffy communist world. To read the Russian statement is to see how Khrushchev is pushed, for popularity, further along the pathway to destalinization. There is no doubt that Khrushchev has the better side of the argument, both internally and internationally; the Russians want more freedom at home and they want peace abroad. The weakest point ideologically in the Chinese latest blast at Moscow is its attempt to prove the need for a continued hard-line dictatorship. The Chinese contend that dictatorship is required because "class contradictions" still exist. But the classes they specify are hoodlums, idlers and such. These are not classes at all in a Marxist sense, and the excuse recalls Stalin's similar rationalization for terror in the thirties and forties long after landlord and *bourgeois* had been wiped out. The "class enemies" he killed were often the most devoted of his own party comrades.

The bad side of the split is that in a world of growing race tension, the split between Moscow and Peking will seem to millions only another variant of an omnipresent struggle between rich whites (in this case Russians) and underprivileged colored peoples (in this case Chinese). There is evidence that Peking is already exploiting this, and playing on a White Man's Peril to the colored man's revolutionary struggle, as some Americans once spoke, and some Russians may again, of a Yellow Peril. This is a poisonous half truth. It is not by eliminating the white man, whether "imperialist" American or "revisionist" Russian, that the "revolution" can be made secure. The revolution man needs runs deeper than that. The struggle of Negro and Indian in British Guiana; of Negro and Indian in Africa; of Malay and Chinese all over Southeast Asia; of "brown" India and "yellow" China shows that the worse parts of man's nature are not packaged only in white. Internecine hates and tribal rivalries will survive the white race. The Chinese thesis that there can be no peace until "imperialism" is destroyed is only another variant of the familiar "just-one-more-war-to-make-the-world-safe-for-something-or-other." In every major war of history, men have been mobilized by the false hope that just one more big bloody mess and all would be well. Mao comes in where Woodrow Wilson went out, and just in time to have the H-bomb punctuate this folly.

On the international plane, the Sino-Soviet split is not to be welcomed even if it leads to a limited nuclear test ban agreement between Washington and Moscow. Peace between U.S. and U.S.S.R. is not real peace if it merely reflects the beginnings of a bigger struggle between Russia and China. We believe our government should seize the opportunity to make a nuclear test ban agreement, and match Moscow's declaration in its latest blast at Peking that it would never use nuclear weapons first. But if we are wise, we will supplement a Russian agreement with a Chinese agreement on a nuclear free zone for the Pacific *while there is still time*. We are for a reconciliation with Russia *and* a reconciliation with China. To substitute one kind of East-West struggle for another, to move toward an entente with Russia in preparation for an even more cataclysmic future struggle against China is not progress. Reconciliation is mankind's need, and we who drove Peking to extremes by our hateful policies of embargo and isolation, should be the ones to make the first move. It is by magnanimity, and not by missiles, that man's future may be made secure.

JULY 16, 1963

# WHY CHINA BUILDS BOMBS AT THE EXPENSE OF BREAD

Those whom the gods would destroy they first render complacent. China's giant strides to nuclear power represent the most important political and military development of our time. But both the great capitals challenged are doing their best to pretend nothing has happened. *Pravda,* in the prize journalistic underplay of the century, gave sixteen words at the bottom of page five to the news that China had successfully tested a guided missile with a nuclear warhead. In Washington the *Daily News* hit the streets with a banner headline which should be preserved for the wry amusement of posterity. It said, "Red China's Missile Test Doesn't Scare Pentagon." If we had been editing that paper we would have put a second line under it, "But Pentagon's Smugness Scares Us."

Secretary Rusk, seven days after the first Chinese nuclear explosion in 1964, assured the country that it would be "a very considerable number of years before there is anything there" i.e. in China "that would impose any serious problem." In their fourth nuclear test in two years, the Chinese have shown that they could (1) build an operational intermediate ballistic missile, (2) perform the difficult feat of miniaturizing a nuclear warhead for it and (3) perfect the safety factor to the point where they could detonate it over their own territory. These were no small achievements. They were enough to make *Le Figaro* (October 28) say that China had overtaken both England and France in the field of nuclear missiles (neither has yet tested a missile with live nuclear warhead) and must now be regarded as the No. 3 nuclear power.

Chinese nuclear capacity has been even more underestimated than was the Soviet Union's. In a Senate speech October 18, just before the latest Chinese blast, Senator Jackson (D., Wash.) expressed surprise at "the weapons sophistication displayed" in the first three Chinese tests. The surprise in the first was the use of enriched uranium-235 instead of plutonium, which meant that the Chinese could build up a stockpile faster than expected. The surprise in the third, last May, was the use of "thermonuclear materials," which indicated that they could build H-bombs of an advanced type. The new feat, requiring a high degree of engineering competence, was accomplished faster than Secretary McNamara expected in the predictions he made last December to the NATO Council. His forecast of a Chinese ICBM by 1975 may be an underestimate. "Considering the progress made in developing a nuclear missile system with an operational warhead," the famous nuclear physicist Ralph Lapp told the *Weekly*, "it would not be surprising if the Chinese could test an ICBM in two years." Senator Jackson, who is chairman of an atomic military applications subcommittee, believes China might put nuclear missiles on those of its submarines which are outfitted with tubes for surface launching of missiles. This would be enough to threaten our coastal ports. The Chinese may be able to deter us from an atomic attack on them earlier than we expected. The mere prospect will change the politics of Asia and the world.

The Chinese announcement of their nuclear missile test is too quickly being dismissed as propaganda. Much can be learned by a thoughtful reading. When they say that "at no time and in no circumstances will China be the first to use nuclear weapons," this is no more than a recognition of our nuclear superiority. All they can hope to do for many years to come is to have enough missiles to be able to inflict unacceptable damage on us if we make a nuclear attack on them. If they can hold two major cities like San Francisco or New York hostage in this way, that may be enough. This is also the logic of the French *force de frappe*. The idea of the French force was born when Moscow, in the Suez crisis, threatened London and Paris with nuclear missiles. The French would never dare attack Russia with their inferior nuclear force but they believe the threat that they might be able to "take out" Moscow and Kiev would be enough to deter Russia from making a nuclear attack on France. The Chinese are talking sober nuclear strategy when they say their weapons are "entirely for defense." If they can build enough nuclear strength to neutralize ours, we could only wage conventional war against them. There they have the advantage of their huge manpower and their readiness to fall back on a guerrilla "people's war." These are assets which can be used on the defensive only, but the combination would make China impregnable to successful attack. This is the strategic meaning of the Chinese missile and this is what makes it irrelevant for President Johnson to warn the Chinese as he did in Malaysia October 30 that any nuclear potential they may acquire will be counterbalanced by our superior power. The Chinese do not need to match us to deter us.

The lesson of the Chinese missile is that to stop the proliferation of nuclear weapons is a political, not a technological problem. When a nation as poor as China can develop the nuclear missile so quickly, it should be clear that they are no longer available only to large rich nations. To stop the spread of nuclear weapons requires some means of guaranteeing the smaller powers security without them. Now is the time to recall those occasions in the late fifties and sixties when China appealed to us in vain for a nuclear-free Pacific, and for a pledge that nuclear weapons would not be used against non-nuclear powers. That was the time to stop the Chinese nuclear missile.

The Chinese demand then is the same demand being made now by some forty non-nuclear powers in the current debate over non-proliferation at the UN General Assembly. They are unwilling to renounce nuclear weapons unless the nuclear powers, in the words of the resolution, "give an assurance that they will not use, or threaten to use, nuclear weapons against non-nuclear weapon states." Neither the Warsaw Pact powers nor the NATO powers are supporting this resolution. This is why the Ambassador of India was so bitter in his speech at the UN October 31. India is not disposed to sign a non-proliferation treaty unless the big powers agree to stop expanding the vast nuclear arsenals at their disposal. India wants nuclear arms and their delivery vehicles reduced and then eliminated. It wants nuclear renunciation to be mutual, and not for smaller powers only. Even if nuclear "umbrellas" are offered the smaller powers, it would be at the price of lost independence and the risk of deals made over their heads. It must seem hypocritical to the smaller powers for Johnson to say, as he did in Malaysia, that they would be making bombs at the expense of bread. To them this may seem the price of survival in the nuclear jungle. Our bombing of North Vietnam gives them a taste of what the defenceless may expect.

NOVEMBER 7, 1966

# THE ESSENCE OF WHAT IS HAPPENING IN CHINA

We do not claim to understand what is happening in China, nor to know which faction in its titanic struggle is right. But looked at within its own Marxist frame of reference, Mao seems to have reversed Marx as Marx reversed Hegel. For Hegel the dialectic of history was the unfolding of an immanent Idea. Marx turned Hegel upside down and found the ultimate cause in material circumstance. As Engels said in his essay on Feuerbach, Hegel asserted "the primacy of spirit to nature" while Marx "regarded nature as primary." The very metaphors of Maoism are a return to idealism. Thus the basic impact of "the Great Proletarian Cultural Revolution" as explained in the document which launched it officially, the decision of the Central Committee of the Chinese Communist Party last August 8, is that it "touches people to their very souls." This is the language of theology; it is mystical and evangelical. It is a kind of Marxist Methodism. Its aim, as the Central Committee then said, "is to revolutionize people's ideology" and "as a consequence to achieve greater, faster, better and more economical results in all fields of work."

This gives ideology primacy over material circumstance. It is in contradiction to Marx. "It is not the consciousness of men that determines their existence," Marx wrote in his *Critique of Political Economy*, "but on the contrary it is their social existence that determines their consciousness." The Maoists are aware of this contradiction. One of the documents being sent out by Peking is a *People's Daily* editorial of June 2, 1966. In it Mao is quoted as saying—

> . . . while we recognize that in the general development of history the material determines the mental and social being determines social consciousness, we also—and indeed must—recognize the reaction of mental on material-things . . .

In emphasizing "the reaction of mental on material things," Mao is returning to the primacy of the Idea.

In this new Marxist system it is not strange that the main enemy is "economism." The "reactionaries" are accused of offering the peasants more economic incentives and the workers—horror of horrors!—higher wages. It is no accident that the main reliance of Mao is on students and intellectuals—on those who can be moved by ideas and ideals (though these often merely disguise a desire for power) as against the peasants and workers who want a higher return for their labor. Marx wanted to utilize economic motivations to transform society. Mao wants to eliminate them *in order to transform man himself*. This is the tremendous dream of his old age. It is in keeping with this that the main Maoist "Gospels" read like early Christian homilies. The oldest, "In Memory of Norman Bethune," urges Mao's follower to learn "the spirit of absolute selflessness" from this Canadian surgeon who served the Loyalists in Spain and then the communist guerrillas in China. The latest, "The Foolish Old Man," says again that faith can move mountains. Mao's belief is that if he could mobilize China's industrious and gifted people to work together for more than self, under the impulse of revolutionary fervor, they could make a Great Leap Forward and eradicate backwardness overnight.

To stimulate this fervor, Mao has made another break with Marxism. Hegel, a truckler to the powers-that-be, saw the Prussian State as the final product of the Dialectic, its ultimate resolution and perfect embodiment. The Marxists saw the fulfillment of the dialectic in the communist state, which would be classless, without exploitation of man by man, and therefore in no need of coercion by police or soldiers; the state itself would thus "wither away." There would be no more "contradictions." But Mao, in the words of that same *Peking Daily* editorial, affirms that even in socialist society "there will still be contradictions after 1,000 or 10,000 or even 100 million years." It says struggle alone "can constantly propel our socialist cause forward." The psychological truth hidden here is that only an enemy, something to hate as well as something to love, can energize the younger generation and the people to greater effort. Hence they must be supplied with "monsters" to slay. This epic conflict is to provide greater satisfaction than any mere material reward. For man cannot live by bread alone; he needs drama.

To miss all this is to miss the essence of what is happening, and its appeal to the best youth of China. It is that same call to struggle and sacrifice that has recruited the first followers of all great religions and revolutions. To his exasperated opponents, trying to keep a huge country together with baling wire, Mao's call for supermen must seem, like Nietzsche's, genius streaked with lunacy. It will probably prove as impracticable as the Sermon on the Mount. If Mao fails, as all his great predecessors have failed, it is because man, still half-monkey, cannot live at so high a pitch, and when the bugles die down prefers a quiet scratch in the warm sun.

JANUARY 30, 1967

# XVIII

---

## FRUSTRATING

## OUR

## LATIN

## NEIGHBORS

# HOW *DO* YOU CRUSH AN INSPIRATION?

At the close of a TV program last Sunday, September 23, Senator Keating of New York, one of the worst of the Republican war hawks, asked General Lucius D. Clay a cute question. "As a military man," Senator Keating said, "do you recognize that the weapons that they have in Cuba could be used either offensively or defensively?" The question was designed to undercut the President's assurances that the arms in Cuba were defensive. General Clay might have replied tartly that only a civilian could ask such a question. Obviously a shotgun can be used "offensively" even against an H-bomb installation if anybody with a shotgun could get close enough, but that doesn't make the H-bomb a defensive nor the shotgun an offensive weapon when one confronts the other. Instead General Clay gave an answer which goes to the heart of the Cuban problem. "I'm not too concerned," he disappointed Keating by replying, "about the Cuban situation as an offensive threat against the United States. But the possibility that it could become the base for the inspiration of revolutions in other parts of Central and South America is very real and one that cannot be discounted."

So the question is: how *do* you crush an inspiration? The Joint Resolution passed by the Senate does indeed empower the President "to prevent by whatever means necessary, including the use of arms, the Marxist-Leninist regime in Cuba from extending, by force or the threat of force, its aggressive or subversive activities to any part of this hemisphere." But what if Cuba is not so foolish as to challenge a giant neighbor's overwhelming power by using force or threat of force? What if it operates, as General Clay fears, by "inspiration"? How do you crush an inspiration? Do you use the marines? Or the Strategic Air Command? We could destroy Cuba—utterly—within an hour. But how destroy its memory in the hearts of Latin America's kindred millions? Cuba, left alone, *really left alone* honorably to work out its destiny, may prove disappointing to their hopes; it may disillusion the rest of the hemisphere; it may shift back, if we allow it, to friendly relations and a mixed rather than a communist society. But crushed by American power, its inspiration would live on in the most idealized form among the Latin hungry and oppressed, the legend of Castro, the Latin American David who defied the Yankee Goliath, who took the sugar lands to give his people bread and dared seize the oil refineries when their foreign masters refused to obey Cuba's laws.

We are, let us remember, the rich man in a huge hemispheric slum. There never was a greater challenge to our capacity to think quietly and step warily than in this Cuban affair. Against this background, what happened in the Senate looks like the attempt of a cautious President to throw sops to an unthinking mob in the hope of controlling it. The Cuban resolution and the 150,000 reservists called up in the Berlin crisis may be seen as gestures to appease a mindless clamor for *action*, to buy time for wiser policies. But when will braver men in the Senate speak out for them?

The only way to combat an inspiration is with another inspiration. But to the inspiration of Castro's daring we counterpose only the spectacle of a deep weakness and a dangerous drift. Only an America prepared to subordinate its private big business interests to the welfare of the hemisphere, determined to abide by its treaty commitments of non-intervention, under leadership strong enough to make peace with Cuba, could provide an inspiration vital enough to counter the one General Clay fears.

OCTOBER 1, 1962

# WHAT JUAN BOSCH TRIED TO DO

Just east of Cuba in the incomparably blue Caribbean lies the island of Hispaniola. Its western one-third, just across the Windward Passage from Cuba, is occupied by Haiti; its eastern two-thirds by the Dominican Republic, barely half the size of Cuba in area and population. It is there that a real answer to Castroism may be given. I have just spent a week in its capital, Santo Domingo, oldest city in the New World, where its first democratic government in more than thirty years has now been inaugurated under President Juan Bosch.

The Dominican Republic has known only two short periods of free government in its history, both in this century, the more recent in 1924–29. From 1930 until his assassination in May, 1961, it was ruled by one of the cruelest and greediest dictators Latin America has known, and the world's oldest, antedating Salazar's in Portugal by two years. By the time he was killed, he had obtained control of two-thirds to three-fourths of the Republic's sugar mills and its industries. Its best pastures and farm lands, about 10 per cent of the productive area of the country, had been vested in the Trujillos. If Stalin built social-ism in one country, Trujillo in a sense built it in one family. With the flight of his heirs and retainers, the Dominican Re-public found itself the owner of a major part of the country's productive facilities. No other government in Latin America is in so fortunate a position. It can plan its economy and push agrarian reform without the need at the very outset to expro-priate private holdings, foreign or domestic. The circumstances were never more propitious for an experiment in democratic socialist development, without terror, class war or dictatorship. Here, if anywhere, the Alliance for Progress and the Kennedy Administration may provide a democratic answer to Castroism. If Cuba is to be a showcase of communism, the Dominican Republic can be a showcase of democratic socialism. Bosch's inauguration on February 27 was also, in this sense, the inauguration of a competition in the Caribbean.

The Kennedy Administration seems to be fully aware of the opportunity and the challenge. Santo Domingo's two luxury hotels, the Embajador and the Jaragua, are full of American experts. A small army of Americans, volunteer and official, have invaded the island. I caught a glimpse of Mr. Justice Douglas, an old friend of President Bosch's, who had been invited to advise the Constituent Assembly now writing the Republic's new Constitution. The Dominicans have a passion for Constitutions; this will be their twenty-fourth since 1821, a record equalled only by Venezuela in a hemisphere where the number of constitutions seems to be in inverse ratio to the amount of constitutional government. The veranda of the luxurious Embajador is full of Americans, military advisers, banking experts, special emissaries of the White House, military men training the army, and no doubt a full contingent of CIA and FBI men. A favorite joke is that the telephone book of the American Embassy is thicker than that of the capital city. There must be close to 500 Americans in the Republic, and I must say that from the Ambassador down they seem a much more sympathetic and intelligent crowd than is usually marshalled by our foreign service. The Ambassador, John Bartlow Martin, a *Saturday Evening Post* writer and a first rate journalist, who published the first exposé of Trujillo in an American magazine back in 1938, is no conventional diplomat. He and his wife are very *simpatico*. They seem to have an excellent staff around them. In his first speech a year ago the Ambassador could say, "when I speak of the danger from the left, I am not talking about reformers, or liberals, or even non-Soviet Marxists. I am talking about men who take orders from Moscow or Peking or Havana . . ." That reference to "non-Soviet Marxists" must represent a high water mark in daring sophistication for the U.S. foreign service.

Yet a certain wariness exists between the U. S. Embassy and

the new Bosch regime, like that of a blushing bride who knows too much about her aged Lothario bridegroom to trust his apparent change of heart. The record of the U.S. in the Dominican Republic inspires as little confidence as did our record in Cuba. No Latin dictator had warmer U.S. support than Trujillo. The Truman Administration courted him, Eastland praised him in a speech to his puppet Congress, Smathers and Speaker McCormick were his friends, Cardinal Spellman blessed him at his Congress of Catholic Culture in 1956; Standard Oil (N.J.), Alcoa and Pan Am were in his claque. All this during the years when he murdered and robbed his people. When Castro and Betancourt jointly supported an invasion to overthrow Trujillo in June, 1959, and a few of the patriots escaped to the hills, the U.S. threw a naval cordon around the island to prevent reinforcements from reaching the anti-Trujillo forces. It is true that Trujillo's downfall seems to have been the result of the U.S. policy—he was the victim of a deal with Betancourt, in which we opposed the Dominican dictator after he tried to kill the Venezuelan leader. In return, Betancourt joined us against Castro.

But after Trujillo was killed, our first response was to support what looked like Trujilloism without Trujillo: the regime established by his retainer, Balaguer, and his son, Ramfis. When popular revulsion made this politically impossible, we shifted grounds, prevented a Trujillo restoration rather than see a revolution, and insisted on the free elections which brought Bosch to power. But few Dominicans can feel sure we may not again support a military strong man. Korean experience is only the latest reminder of what Latins know so well—how easily we reconcile ourselves to military dictatorships.

Bosch's first steps in power seem designed to disengage himself from Washington. His speech February 19 on returning from his trip to the U.S. and Europe emphasized the latter rather than the former as the source of new development contracts. Indeed several days later Angel Miolan, the head of Bosch's Dominican Revolutionary Party (PRD) said Bosch "got four times as much in practical results"—in the shape of credits and technical aid—during his month long tour in Western Europe as he did in his visit to the U.S. Soon after the inauguration Bosch announced the signing of a fifteen-year $150,000,000 agreement with a Swiss consortium (including the Bank of America) to build two dams for irrigation and hydroelectric power, and for an aqueduct to supply fresh water to the capital. Bosch admitted he might have had better terms and lower interest rates if he had financed the projects from international organizations but argued that it would take a year or two for those banks to make preliminary studies and come to decisions and that work was needed urgently to cope with unemployment and hunger. But one wonders whether another motive in dealing with this international consortium was not to lessen his dependence on Washington, which plays the major role in such international institutions as the World Bank and the Inter-American Development Bank. Bosch also touched a tender nerve when he complained that the Council of State which ruled the country before the elections had secretly concluded a contract with Standard Oil for a refinery on terms unfavorable to the Dominican Republic. Bosch said he had received better offers in Europe and had warned Standard Oil that the contract would be reviewed as soon as he took office. Bosch said he did so although he knew "my attitude would be used in spreading throughout the world the report that I am hostile to foreign private investments in this country, that I am a communist, that I am a Fidelista, or that I am something else still more radical." The President-elect's prediction proved correct. Though little has appeared in the U.S. press about the Standard Oil contract, a campaign to picture Bosch as somehow linked to communists has already begun, though he and his entourage are—like most socialists elsewhere—passionately anti-communist and anti-Castro.

But Bosch and his group do not wish to jeopardize their chances for a moderate and peaceful social reform by polarizing Dominican politics between left and right. They see the necessity for private capital in Dominican development—the country, like Cuba, is short of technicians and has no domestic source of capital and capital goods. Castro got his from the Soviet bloc. They must obtain theirs from the West. A revolutionary solution for the Republic's problems is politically impossible; the U.S. would reply with an instant blockade, the Russians are in no position to take on another Cuba; the Chinese could only supply inflammatory pamphlets. The Bosch group would not turn East even if they could—they are far more deeply and philosophically anti-totalitarian than their detractors; one of them is a graduate of a communist as well as a Nazi concentration camp. But they hope to avoid the dangers of reliance on private capital by diversifying its sources, by reducing dependence on the U.S. and particularly by avoiding the appearance of being simply a U.S. satellite.

I gather that there are politically sophisticated American officials who realize that the real U.S. interest in the Dominican Republic is not to have Juan Bosch salute the anti-communist flag every few days in response to attacks in the *Chicago Tribune,* but simply to make a success of his program. If this is done in part with European capital all the better. The U.S. does not need another satellite. It needs a demonstration in Latin America that peaceful reform is possible, and that U.S. aid can be obtained without a demeaning subordination. But whether this magnanimous spirit can survive the more conventional views in Congress, the press and much of the foreign service remains to be seen. The American community felt chilled when Bosch in his inaugural speech failed to praise the Alliance for Progress or to make an attack on Castroism, the two current hallmarks of loyalty to the U.S. party line. But neither would have been politically wise.

The Alliance for Progress has been oversold to its own detriment, and is now being widely attacked for failure to undo, in two years, four and a half centuries of exploitation, misery and ignorance. It would be a rather mangy flag to unfurl at the start of a new and hopeful Latin administration. Within a fortnight of Bosch's inaugural moderate labor leaders from eleven Latin countries complained in Mexico City that labor was being denied its benefits and the Bank for Inter-American Development reported that the peasants were worse off than before. The oligarchy is still hoping by exploiting U.S. obsessions about Castroism and Communism to divert the Alliance into another global handout of dollars the rich can salt away abroad. Bosch resisted pressure to make an attack on Castroism because he feared it would split the country between right and left on an extraneous issue, and make him a prisoner of the right and the Army. Bosch defeated the Union Civica Nacional, the party of the conservative oligarchy, two-to-one; a last minute attempt by the Church to smear him as a red redounded in his favor with both the middle class and the workers; he won more than 60 per cent of the votes.

The campaign can best be understood in Roman terms. Trujillo was not a modern totalitarian dictator, though his control was total; even a social club could not be formed without making El Benefactor its honorary president. Trujillo was like one of the Caesars in the degenerate days described by Tacitus. His power rested on a pampered Army, and a network of informers. He was all but deified, and he hated particularly the old oligarchy which looked down its nose on him as a mixed-blood. The Union Civica Nacional was a patrician republican oligarchic opposition, again like its Roman counterpart. Its candidates for President and Vice President, Fiallo and Baquero, were men of integrity. They managed, perhaps because they were physicians, to walk through the valley of the shadow and earn their bread without ever collaborating with the dictatorship. Their clean record was an affront to weaker folk, who had to knuckle under.

At the same time Fiallo and Baquero had only the vaguest slogans as substitute for a program with appeal to the plebeian masses. These were outside their aristrocratic field of vision. They alienated part of the middle class by emphasizing a fierce de-Trujillo-ization; Fiallo even visited Germany to study de-Nazification there. But Hitler had an enthusiastic following, a party, a philosophy. Trujillo's one party was built only on fear. Except for a small circle of murderers and grafters, he had no base. Almost everybody at one time or another had to bend his neck before the dictator. Bosch campaigned for national reconciliation; he pledged himself to root out Trujilloism in the economic and social sphere, not to stage a giant purge. This won him friends on the moderate right and in the center while his promise to restore democratic liberties, his idealism, his magnetic eloquence, his gift for parable (he is a talented writer) and his program made it impossible for the badly splintered left to put a candidate in the field against him even if it had been able to do so.

There are two Moscow-oriented tiny communist parties, both with their base among well-to-do intellectuals. They are referred to disparagingly by fiery student leaders as "the parties of peace." They were illegalized under the Council of State, as was the Fidelista MPD whose base, also miniscule, is among the *lumpenproletariat* in the terrible shanty towns which ring that side of Santa Domingo which faces away from its dulcet ocean breezes. It is tainted by the fact that at least one of its leaders was "imported" by Trujillo in his latter days to frighten the U.S. with the spectre of a deal with Castroism. The legal moderate left, the June 14 Movement, named for the unsuccessful landings in 1959, is split between a more and a less Fidelista wing. The entire left and part of Bosch's own just-to-left-of-center party would be antagonized by an attack on Castro. If this hot issue is left alone, then Bosch can hold the support of the moderate left. Success for his program would isolate the extremists. This is not so different from the strategy Kennedy himself seems to have been pursuing. Bosch utilized the Betancourt visit and the San Jose conference to emphasize the need for domestic reform and sidestep the demand for military action against Castro. As one intelligent law student told me, "If we have to choose between Union Civica (the right) and the PSP (the orthodox communists), we'll go with the PSP. If we have a chance to choose between Bosch (democratic reform) and Fidel (revolutionary action), we'll choose Bosch." The U.S. had better choose him, too.

But Bosch is up against a redoubtable foe. While the Union Civica has been demoralized by his landslide, the party which finished a poor third, the Partido Social Christiano, is out to destroy him. As a Catholic party, it has strong U.S. connections. In the trade unions and in the university, it out-demagogues the most demagogic elements of the left; the Social Christians have already pulled one short lived minority strike in publicly owned sugar mills where wages have doubled since Trujillo fell. The Social Christians are playing on the communist phobia of the U.S. press and the native oligarchy. It has already spread reports which the Venezuelan government has formally denied that on the eve of the inaugural Bosch refused to join in an anti-Castro declaration with Betancourt, Orlich of Costa Rica and Villeda Morales of Honduras. In a speech of March 19, Bosch nailed this as a lie and also claimed that the Social Christians had the aid of "a great number of Cuban exiles in the United States, particularly in Miami, people who have little to do but write for little papers and for radio stations—to portray us as communists."

Free elections and the hopes aroused by Bosch have exercised a beneficent influence in the Dominican Republic. But under the surface, should he fail, are volcanic forces. Slow hunger walks the streets; every person with a job supports a horde of cousins from the country. The villas on the ocean side of town are almost as luxurious as Miami; the shanty-town on the other side breeds disease and despair. In Bosch's speeches there breathes a moving love for his people and a deep devotion. The cynical oligarchy easily ignores the verdict of the election and has already picked its candidate for a new military dictatorship. In the coffee houses, among the students, one finds a promising generation; intelligence and idealism shine in their brown faces, they are eager to learn. Given ten years of peace and education, this rich little island republic will have its own technicians and engineers and can really be the master of its destiny. We can earn their gratitude or deserve their contempt.

APRIL 1, 1963

# WHAT CHILE NEEDS IS AN OPENING TO THE LEFT

While the center of gravity in U.S. politics is moving toward the right, the center of gravity elsewhere in the hemisphere is moving left. Here a broad national front has been formed behind a Texas conservative to defeat the danger of fascistic influence in the White House. In Chile a broad national front was formed behind a Catholic leftist to defeat a Popular Front candidate with Communist Party support. This divergence in development forecasts trouble unless the time the U.S. gained by the Chilean victory is put to good use. The first essential is to understand better what happened in Chile and what might have happened in the U.S. The election of a communist-supported socialist in Chile, pledged to nationalize U.S. copper and nitrate properties, would have pushed U.S. politics further rightward. The prospect of another Castro in the hemisphere, this time in one of South America's Big Three, would have let loose a burst of hysteria worse than that we have seen over Cuba. It would have given the Goldwaterites a boost in this election, impelled Johnson to new demonstrations of toughness, this time in Latin America, set back the fragile beginnings of peaceful understanding with Moscow and the hope after the election of negotiating an end to the Indochinese war with Peking. When a power as big as the U.S. has fits, the whole world shakes, and fits we would have had if the left had won in Chile.

If we are to use the reprieve wisely, it is important to realize that Frei Montalva's victory in Chile was not a victory for democracy or free enterprise as they are defined in the simple-minded U.S. lexicon. Chile is barely beginning to be a democracy in our sense of the word; it is a nation in which a landed aristocracy has played the game of parliamentary musical chairs much as it was played in England before the Nineteenth Century Reform Bills gave lower class Englishmen the right to vote. It is only in recent decades that pressure from below has forced Chile's oligarchy to utilize one makeshift after another to protect its privileges. The latest was to support a Catholic leftist as a lesser evil. This oligarchy is anti-democratic and anti-capitalistic. The paradox in Chile, as elsewhere in Latin America, is that U.S. capitalist interests allied themselves with the big landowners in policies designed to *prevent* industrial and capitalist development. U.S. copper and nitrate companies have been interested in getting raw materials out of Chile as cheaply as possible, not in developing native industry. For landowners and copper magnates alike this would mean higher labor costs. The biggest push toward industrialism and capitalism in Chile came from its first Popular Front government, which was elected in 1938 and launched the Chilean Development Corporation, the first of its kind in Latin America. It initiated a wide variety of public, semi-public and private enterprises, giving Chile its first steel plant, its first oil industry and its first public power company. The most important measure required for peaceful relations with Latin America and peaceful reform there is to educate the U.S. to the need for such governmental planning and direction if development is to get off the ground in time to match the population explosion and popular aspiration.

U.S. public opinion will also have to accept the fact that this new regime will not "stand firmly with the West" if that means isolating Cuba and embargoing trade with the communist countries. Even Frei's conservative predecessor had begun making copper deals with Moscow, Prague and Peking. Frei deplored the break with Cuba and in a press conference after his election expressed the hope that Cuba could be brought back within the hemispheric fold on the basis of the principles of self-determination after the U.S. elections. U.S. public opinion must also be prepared for domestic measures in Chile more drastic than those proposed by Bosch in the Dominican Republic, Villeda Morales in Honduras and Goulart in Brazil before U.S. interests encouraged their overthrow by the military.

The first necessity of the new Chilean regime is to stop Latin America's second worst inflation (after Bolivia), a bonanza for landowners and primary producers but a savage capital levy on its working class. This requires effective taxes on large incomes and properties. The second necessity is swift land reform. Only about one-fourth of its best arable land is under cultivation, forcing Chile to import food. With 600,000 landless peasants and most of the land in the hands of a few great families indifferent to its wise use, the big estates must be broken up. On top of this, Frei Montalva's Christian Democrats, while on record for the ultimate nationalization of the big copper mines, want immediate control of the industry to expand refining at home and marketing abroad. Here there may be a frontal conflict with U.S. interests.

The inner weakness of the Christian Democratic majority will make itself felt as soon as these conflicts begin. For in

Chile, as in Western Europe after the war, all kinds of reactionary interests jumped on the Christian Democratic bandwagon because they had nowhere else to go. Only anticommunism put together the big majority in Chile. As soon as Frei moves to implement his program in the Chilean Congress, to which elections are scheduled in March, his coalition may begin to fall apart. He may be reduced to a minority regime unless he can, like the Christian Democrats in Italy, achieve an "opening to the left" and form an alliance with those elements of the Popular Front which favor peaceful reform rather than revolution. Here Frei's friendship with Allende and the latter's own socialist background should prove fruitful. It should also be facilitated by the shift in the position of the Chilean Catholic hierarchy in recent years from support of feudalism to support of social reform. Only a new alliance of this kind can give Chile the social reform it needs if major convulsion and perhaps war are to be avoided. But can U.S. public opinion be educated to understand this? Or will we back a military coup if the Chilean oligarchy and the U.S. copper companies cannot corrupt a Frei regime? Last January the *Engineering and Mining Journal*, welcoming the appointment of Thomas Mann as Johnson's policy "czar" for Latin America, expressed satisfaction with his "tough, no nonsense approach" and said Chile would be his first test. In Chile the U.S. can easily destroy the last bulwark to what it fears.

SEPTEMBER 14, 1964

# THE DOMINICAN REPUBLIC AS LYNDON JOHNSON'S HUNGARY

The parallels between U.S. action in the Dominican Republic and the Soviet Union's in Hungary are obvious. Our Monroe Doctrine is like the Russian insistence on "friendly neighbors." The existence of fringe elements—fascist in Hungary, communist in the Dominican Republic—were used to smear both revolutions as extremist, though both were motivated by a desire for democratization. Nagy's appeal to the UN, like that of the Bosch forces, was opposed on the excuse that the matter should be handled by regional organizations: in one case the Warsaw Pact, in the other the OAS, each securely dominated by its respective masters, Russian or American. Both great Powers explained their conduct in the same way: the U.S.S.R. by fear of a Western base, the U.S. by fear of a new communist base, on its doorstep. In both cases the presumed strategic need of the big power was the excuse for riding roughshod over the wishes of the smaller neighbor, and in neither were these exaggerated fears submitted to impartial scrutiny by some international authority.

A less noticed parallel, now unfolding, is the naive and self-righteous arrogance with which Washington and Moscow respectively took it on themselves to decide just what kind of a government to allow their small neighbor. Both great Powers claimed to be avoiding "extremist" solutions. Khrushchev and Mikoyan, themselves engaged in de-Stalinizing the Soviet Union, did not want to put the Stalinists back into power in

Hungary. On the other hand, they did not want the pendulum
of freedom to swing so far that in their opinion it might become "bourgeois," i.e. a regime of basic rights for the individual instead of a milder variety of bureaucratic communism.
They hauled poor Kadar out of prison and once they had used
him to crush the revolution, they did slowly allow him to ease
up the terror and permit a little intellectual freedom on the
edges. Similarly Johnson is busy running the Dominican Republic by remote but unmistakable control: a new government
is being hand-picked from Washington. Its members are even
subjected to FBI clearance. We want, the All-Highest in the
White House says, neither a dictatorship of the right nor of
the left. It cannot be too authoritarian because that would embarrass us in our democratic pretensions. And it cannot be too
democratic, because that might hurt U.S. investors.

This is the bitterest part of the spectacle for Latin Americans. Here we are beginning to play out again some of the
most painful scenes of the Cuban and Mexican revolutions.
When the Cubans, with belated and equivocal help from us,
overthrew the Spanish yoke, the price they had to pay for getting rid of an American occupation was to allow foreign ownership of land: this intensified concentration of ownership in
huge sugar holdings. It fastened on Cuba that monoculture
which impoverished its countryside and which José Marti and
the revolutionaries were pledged to eradicate. In Mexico we
waged a similar struggle against Article 27 of the revolutionary
Constitution of 1917 which sought to recover mineral rights
and peasant lands the dictator Diaz had given away to foreign,
mostly American, interests. We withheld the recognition Mexico needed so badly for international credit reasons. Not until
1923, after private assurances that Article 27 would be interpreted laxly, did we recognize the Mexican Republic. Now we
are doing something similar in the Dominican Republic.
Though we claim to be waging a world-wide struggle for self-
determination and to allow diversity in the world (such is the
language of our propaganda), the Dominican Constitution is
being revised over long-distance telephone to suit Johnson's
ideas.

Dan Kurzman of the *Washington Post* has the distinction
of being the first American reporter to call attention to this

development. The 1963 Constitution was the first ever to be
framed and adopted by the Dominican people through wholly
democratic processes. Mr. Justice Douglas was one of those
who acted as consultant in its framing. It was to be a model
for the hemisphere in establishing a secular state, with provisions for agrarian reform. Kurzman disclosed that in the negotiations for a new government, pressure is being applied to
revise the Constitution. One target is Article 19 which gives
workers a right to profit-sharing in both industrial and agricultural enterprises. Another is Article 23 which prohibits large
landholdings. A third is Article 25 which restricts the right of
foreigners to acquire Dominican land. Another is Article 28,
which requires landholders to sell that portion of their lands
above the maximum fixed by law; the excess holdings would
be resold to the landless peasantry. This is the agrarian reform
we *say* we want in the hemisphere. It turns out that, as in
Guatemala and in Cuba and in Mexico, we oppose it when it
is enacted. An amendment is being proposed, Kurzman reports,
to exempt owners of sugar plantations and cattle ranges. Central Romana, a subsidiary of the American-owned South Porto
Rico Sugar Company, holds thousands of acres of the country's
best sugar and cattle lands (see Selden Rodman's sympathetic
history of the Dominican Republic, *Quisqueya*). Such are the
conditions for American approval. And such is the reality behind our claim to be saving the hemisphere from communism.

In the past half century at home, one basic social reform
after another has been assailed as communistic by the masters
of our big business enterprises; the Square Deal of Teddy
Roosevelt, the New Freedom of Woodrow Wilson, the New
Deal of Franklin D. Roosevelt all were opposed as undermin-
ing property and free enterprise. At home we have defeated
these reactionary forces, though far from completely. But
abroad they continue unchallenged to mold our policy. Our
Latin American neighbors have been forced by military power,
our own or local forces we armed, to bow to the will of Standard Oil and United Fruit and Anaconda Copper and Hanna
Mining and any number of great North American enterprises.
What they have been unable to block at home by invoking the
Red Menace, they have succeeded in doing among our Latin
neighbors. This is why the new Christian Democratic regime

in Chile, fresh from a victory over a domestic Popular Front, is yet so deeply hostile to what we are doing in the Dominican Republic. This is why the OAS force we are trying to muster as our mercenaries is made up entirely (except for 20 policemen from Costa Rica) of forces supplied by the military dictatorships we helped install in Brazil, Honduras and Nicaragua. The Johnson Doctrine aims by force to make Latin America safe for U.S. investment at whatever cost to the democratic wishes of its people or our own often asserted desire for social reform. This is why it will breed a whole new generation of revolutionaries in the hemisphere, driving the youth to despair of peaceful change and contempt for the Alliance for Progress. This is how we create what we fear.

MAY 31, 1965

# A GLOBAL GENDARME

Two *Saturday Evening Post* writers have just come back from the mountains of Guatemala. "You think you have a big problem in Vietnam," a guerrilla leader who calls himself Tito told them, "Wait until the marines come to Guatemala." [1] In two more years the guerrillas expect to be ready. "We think your government will intervene here just as they did in 1954," Tito said. "But we will win because all the peasants are with us." There are guerrillas who talk this way in Peru and Colombia, where we already supply helicopters and napalm for use

[1] "The Undeclared War in Guatemala," *Saturday Evening Post,* June 18.

against them. The poverty-stricken Northeast of Brazil is among the other places in the hemisphere where guerrilla uprisings may some day make their appearance. What are we going to do about them? Are we automatically to go to war against them? How many Vietnams can we fight at once? "We must find an alternative to wars of attrition," says an editorial in *Air Force/Space Digest* for June, "if we are to be able to cope with a succession of Vietnams in various parts of the globe, conceivably more than one at a time." Or it is we who will be worn down.

Much of what the *Post* writers report from Guatemala sounds familiar after Vietnam. They visited a mountain hamlet raided by the Guatemalan army. The soldiers killed fourteen hostages and "left their bodies to rot" in the mountains. "The army told the government that those killed were guerrillas," explained Turcios [another guerrilla leader]. "They didn't kill any guerrillas, but instead they made everybody here a guerrilla." This mistreatment of the peasants is how it all began under Diem. Since the CIA engineered the revolt that overthrew Arbenz in Guatemala in 1954 and replaced him with a military dictatorship, we have given Guatemala $170,000,000 in economic aid and we have been spending almost $2,000,000 a year on its army. A rigged election under a rigged Constitution has now restored a semblance of democracy weak enough to satisfy the army. But a U.S. official there told the *Post* writers the situation was "the most critical in the hemisphere."

We'd like to supplement the *SEP* story with some background. So long as Guatemala was ruled by a military dictator who played ball with U.S. interests, we didn't care what else he did. General Ubico, who stayed in power from 1931 to 1944, was the Batista of Guatemala. When a democratically elected successor, a military man named Colonel Arbenz, moved to take some of the idle lands of United Fruit in a moderate agrarian reform program, he ran into trouble. John Foster Dulles raised a red scare against Arbenz, and mobilized some of the same cast of characters now operating on Vietnam. Henry Cabot Lodge was then our Ambassador to the United Nations and manfully fought off Guatemala's attempt to appeal to the UN. Lyndon B. Johnson, then minority leader, put the Democrats behind Dulles and the CIA with a Senate resolution "affirming

the Monroe Doctrine." After Arbenz was overthrown, the new
government restored the United Fruit Company land, and rescinded the agrarian reform. Thus the hemisphere was made
for free enterprise again.

The bill coming due for the CIA's success may be a heavy
one. Its triumph merely smothered discontent. Now it is bursting out again. "We are going to start the fight," the *Post* writers
heard a guerrilla leader tell a village audience, "by taking the
land from the rich landholders, and we are going to give you
the land to cultivate." A similar appeal has made the Mekong
Delta a stronghold of Vietnamese rebellion for a quarter century against French and U.S. troops alike.

In a pamphlet defending the military assistance program,
ostensibly for the use of high school debaters, the Defense Department argues that military assistance enables us "to communicate to the military sector in developing nations a clear
concept of the part it can and should play in a democratic society." Like Castelo Branco in Brazil, for example? Or Ky? The
Pentagon pamphlet says military assistance enables us to bring
10,000 foreign military students here a year, "the coming leaders of their nation." Some may look to their own people like
U.S. trained oppressors. Others may turn against us; the two
leaders of the Guatemalan guerrillas are military men who
went through the U. S. Infantry School at Ft. Benning, Georgia.
Or the people at home may not like the gifts we send back
with them. When a plane appeared overhead and the *Post*
writers failed quickly to hide, a guerrilla jeered at them, "You
wanna get cooked by your own napalm." There is a limit to the
triumphs of technology. Even Canutes armed with napalm may
not forever quench the tides.

We wish Secretary McNamara would take time off from
improving his image by quoting St. Augustine and T. S. Eliot
and give us the benefit of his thinking on these problems. In
his speech at Montreal he opposed the idea of having the U.S.
act as "a global gendarme" but that has been the spirit of our
policy ever since the Truman Doctrine. Indeed the Defense
Department quotes Truman as the ultimate source for the military assistance program under which (it boasts) we have given
arms to eighty nations—no less! The Pentagon's clinching argument for military assistance in high school debates is that in

the absence of these satellite foreign armies we would have to police the world ourselves and that "would prevent many high school students from going on to college!" McNamara said at Montreal that "the decisive factor for a nation already adequately armed is the character of its relationship to the world." It is this relationship which needs changing. Must we put down popular rebellions wherever they occur? If it takes a million men to win the Vietnamese war, how many more will we need if the bell rings in Guatemala or Brazil? The one concrete proposal to appear amid the soothing liberal generalizations in McNamara's Montreal speech was a call for universal military service. We'll need it if the present policy continues. Even a wholly militarized America will not prove strong enough in the long run to impose its will on a rising sea of discontent.

JUNE 20, 1966

# XIX

---

# TRIBALISM'S TOLL: GERMANS, JEWS, ARABS

# WHAT SOME PEOPLE HAVE FORGOTTEN ABOUT GOD'S "DEPUTY"

One of the elements missing in Rolf Hochhuth's play *The Deputy* and in comment upon it is recognition of the crucial role played by the Vatican in the rise of fascism. The Vatican opposed modern liberalism from its very inception. It denounced Marxism, whether democratic or totalitarian. But everywhere it welcomed fascism—in Italy, in Germany, in Spain, in Austria, in Slovakia and in Hungary. Many commentators have contrasted Pius XII, the central figure in Hochhuth's play, with his predecessor, Pius XI. But Pius XII, in being friendly to Hitler, was only following in the footsteps of Pius XI. Mussolini's seizure of power in Italy could have been blocked if the powerful Catholic Popular Party, and its priestly leader, Don Luigi Sturzo, had been allowed to follow the policy now being applied by Italy's Christian Democrats. An "opening to the left" which united the Popular Party with the socialists and the liberals against *Fascismo,* would have choked off this pestilence at the start.

But Pius XI decided otherwise. He disliked Don Luigi and his party, which had won a following among the peasantry by its advocacy of land reform. He joined the industrialists and the army officers who, like their counterparts a decade later in Germany, saw fascism as a protection for property rights against the clamor for social reform. The Popular Party was dissolved and Don Luigi driven into exile. In Italy, as in Germany, Catholic anti-fascists were sacrificed for a concordat with the dictatorships. These pacts with the devil lent first Il Duce and then Der Fuehrer a cloak of Catholic approval when they most needed it. The March on Rome which Pius XI facilitated was the first step toward Auschwitz which Pius XII never condemned. The louts and paranoids Mussolini marshalled for his coup were the same type who later stoked the human furnaces for Hitler with Jews, gypsies and Slavs too weak to work for Krupp and I. G. Farben. More than the sin of silence lies on the consciences of God's "deputies." They were accessories in the creation of these criminal regimes.

A second element has to do with Allied policy. While the Allies were pressing Pius XII to condemn Nazi atrocities against the Jews for its propaganda value, they were far from whole-hearted about saving the victims. I remember as a young newspaperman the coldness one encountered in the State Department on the subject of refugees and the inhumanity with which the British turned away from Palestine boatloads of Jews fleeing from Hitler's ovens; two, the *Struma* and the *Patria*, sank with their human cargoes. Last October 12, the State Department released a volume of diplomatic papers from the year 1943 (Vol. I: General) in which two painful stories are disclosed. One is a British Embassy memorandum expressing fear lest the Germans "change over from the policy of extermination to one of extrusion, and aim as they did before the war at embarrassing other countries by flooding them with alien immigrants." Milton Friedman of *Jewish Telegraphic Agency*, the only Washington correspondent who paid attention to these documents, commented "It would appear the concern existed twenty years ago in some high places that too many Jews might escape from Hitler and burden the democracies with their presence."

His Majesty's Government in the same memorandum said it was ready to take 4500 Jewish children and 300 women from Bulgaria but could not accept adult males from enemy occupied countries in Palestine owing to "the acute security problem" and the White Paper of 1939, which severely restricted Jewish immigration to the Holy Land lest this antagonize the Arabs. The British were not alone in this kind of thinking. The same volume contains a memorandum from the U. S. Chiefs of Staff objecting to a plan to move 4500 refugees from Spain to camps in North Africa lest this "cause resentment on the part of the Arab population." From a Jewish point of view, it was not the Pope alone who failed the test of conscience. Neither the Gospel of Jesus nor the Gospel of Marx prevented their highest respective spokesmen from making pacts with Hitler. In all the great capitals, political expediency came before humanity. The whole bitter story still feeds Jewish nationalism. When our people were thrown to the furnaces, few really cared.

It helps to heal our hearts that a young German should have written *The Deputy*. It is also a good sign that the play should have aroused such animosity—like a painful memory dragged unwillingly from the subconscious of a whole generation. The protest and the shame indicate that under the hypocrisy and the cant there lives on a concern for human and moral values. The crematoriums should not be forgotten. That one set of human beings could do this to another set condemns our whole species. There are savages within us against whom we must be on guard. The excuses of race and statecraft that are used to justify murder, and silence about it, now threaten the entire human race with a "final solution."

For the play as presented in New York, Herman Shumlin deserves a high mark for courage, a lesser one for artistry. His version is an oversimplified and sometimes vulgarized shadow of the original. Gerstein, Jacobson and Fontana are all debased from Hochhuth's original conception. In the original, the SS man, Gerstein, who tried to help the Jews, was not a hysteric. Jacobson, the Jew hiding out in his apartment, was not the vulgar creature in Jerome Rothenberg's adaption. Fontana, the young Jesuit who goes to Auschwitz in protest, is also diminished in the New York version. But Emlyn Williams is magnificent as the Pope. Severely shortened, the play as produced also focuses too narrowly on the moral responsibility of the Pope while Hochhuth's original brings the German people into the full orbit of guilt. But to see the play is still an experience we recommend as a moral and political duty, though the play in book form (excellently translated by Richard and Clara Winston for Grove Press) is essential to grasp the author's full design and memorable intention. It is Hochhuth's achievement so painfully to have twisted the conscience of the Church and the world.

MARCH 9, 1964

# THE RACIST CHALLENGE IN ISRAEL

To see Israel again after eight years is to be struck at every turn by the triumphant evidence of progress. The flood of new immigrants, which has more than tripled its population since the achievement of independence eighteen years ago, is reflected in a continuous building boom. The dismal acres of shanty towns (*ma'abarôth*) hastily erected for new immigrants were still distressingly visible in 1956. Today they have given way (except for a hard-core of 3,000 which still clings to the old hovels) before whole new neighborhoods—and cities—of towering apartment houses. The roads have widened, the traffic jams grown worse. The country throbs with expansive vitality. Israel has become an affluent society. Even in the once Spartan kibbutzim, the outhouse and the cold outside shower have been replaced by private lavatories and running hot water, provided by individual solar heaters. Everywhere there are flowers. Even in Tel Aviv the whole new northern extension of that rather grubby city has become downright pretty with tree-lined boulevards and flower gardens. Not all the changes are to the taste of those who loved the old Palestine. The Dan Hotel in Tel Aviv has become as oversumptuous as its counterparts in Miami. The Desert Inn outside Beer Sheva, no longer a sleepy Bedouin town, might be in luxurious Palm Springs, except for the *mezuzoth* beside every door and the Arab-with-camel on duty at the entrance. The *dolce vita* has arrived, as the old-timers complain, complete with juvenile delinquents and call girls.

The other big change since the spring of 1956 is in the sense of security. Then infiltrating *fedayeen* from Egyptian training centers in the Gaza strip and Sinai were shooting up settlements at night and making travel after dark hazardous. The Sinai campaign later that year may have been a humiliating setback for England and France, but for Israel it put a stop to these terrorist raids, smashed Czech and Soviet arms dumps across the Egyptian border and established a UN force at the narrow straits where Elath's access to the Red Sea had been shut off by Nasser. This much was accomplished, whatever the wisdom of the retaliatory spiral which led up to the Sinai campaign, and its cost in the alienation of Afro-Asian sympathy from Israel.[1] Today one can travel everywhere with assurance. Unusually heavy rains had turned the country greener and lovelier than we had ever seen it in seven previous trips. Our visit was a succession of unforgettable scenes: Haifa's gleaming harbor from the top of Mt. Carmel, the wide lawns of Mishmar Ha-Emek, the rich green vistas of the once malarial Valley of Israel, the holy places of Nazareth, Tiberius and Safad, lunch on the eastern shores of Lake Galilee at Ein Gev within the shadow of the Syrian border, the mauve hills at twilight which look down on the fertile collectives in that narrow "finger" of Israel which stretches northward between Lebanon and Syria. Later we saw Ashdod, Israel's biggest seaport rising on the dunes where the Philistines once dwelt, and Kiryat Dan, a new complex of factories and farms to the north of Beer Sheva. We saw old friends in kibbutzim like Shoval and Hatzor nearby which were once lonely military outposts and are now thriving centers of rural industry as well as agriculture. Since 1959 the industrial byproducts of the collective settlements equal or surpass their agricultural output. The climax was our climb up those venerable hills to Jerusalem.

[1] See Michael Bar-Zohar's *Suez: Ultra Secret,* newly published in Paris, and Simha Flapan's critical article on it in the May issue of *The New Outlook,* a Middle East monthly devoted to Arab-Jewish reconciliation.

There one can still step backward in time, and savor ways of life centuries apart. A fashionable crowd takes tea on the veranda of the King David overlooking the walls of the Old City and a few blocks away little boys in ear curls and suspenders rock back and forth over their pious schoolbooks in the back-alley yeshivahs of Mea Shearim, keeping alive a medieval universe of orthodox Jewry.

Beneath the prosperous and picturesque surface there are problems grave enough to threaten Israel's future. But for those who have seen the crises of its earlier years it is impossible not to be optimistic. I first saw Palestine November 2, 1945, the day the Haganah began the war against the British by blowing up the watch towers from which they laid in wait for illegal immigrant ships; it seemed hopeless for so small a force to challenge so great an empire. In the spring of 1946 I traveled from Poland to Palestine through the British blockade with illegal immigrants on one of these Jewish Mayflowers. In 1947 I saw the British impose martial law on Tel Aviv in an effort to wipe out the terrorist campaign against them. In 1948 I was a witness to the joint attack of the Arab States on what was then an ill-prepared tiny community of 650,000 Jews.[2] In 1949 and 1950 I saw the lack of food and the letdown in morale which followed the war and the onset of the Arab blockade. To have seen such odds overcome makes it hard to take too pessimistically the problems of the dynamic, confident and expanding Israel of today.

They are nonetheless serious. The first is fiscal: Israel is living beyond its means. Its rate of economic growth is topped only by Japan's and few countries can match its steep rate of increase in exports. But in 1963 its adverse surplus of imports over exports was still $420 million and in the first quarter of 1964 its trade deficit rose to three times that in the first quarter of 1963. Capital imports have been running ahead of the trade deficit so that the government's cash reserves have been growing. But of total capital imports in 1963 of $500 million, $162 million was in German reparations and restitution payments which will now decline sharply. Israel will soon have to meet

[2] In *Underground to Palestine* (1946) I told the story of the illegal trip and in *This Is Israel* (1948) the story of how Israel won its war of independence.

the challenge of austerity and better distribution of income. Its affluent society, like America's, has little-seen but wide fringes of poverty. An ostentatious luxury by the rich does not make this more bearable. And there, as in America, the problem of poverty is intensified by color and "race." Israel has a double "Negro" problem. The darker Jews from the Orient and North Africa, as well as the Arab minority, suffer from prejudice.

The usual Jewish attitude toward the Arabs is one of contemptuous superiority. Our driver northward was a Jew who had fled from the Nazi advance into Hungary but that did not save him from racist habits. When I suggested that we give a boy a lift, he refused, saying the boy was an Arab. When I asked what was the difference, he said Arabs smelled bad. I said that is what anti-Semites said of us Jews in the outside world but this made no impression. His attitude, it is painful to report, is typical. Israel is a country not only of full employment but of labor shortages. Thousands of Arabs do the menial tasks of Tel Aviv. They find it as hard to obtain decent lodgings as Negroes do in America and for the same reasons; many "pass" as Jews to circumvent prejudice. In Haifa I visited the only secondary school attended by both Jews and Arabs but even there the classes turned out to be separate. The State of Israel has done much in a material way for the Arabs but the sense of humiliation outweighs any improvement. The spectacle fills one with despair. For if Jews, after all their experience of suffering, prove no better once in the majority than the rest of mankind, what hope for a world as torn apart as ours is by tribalism and hate?

More progress is being made in dealing with Israel's other integration problem—that of the Jews from the Orient and Africa. For these—unlike the Arabs—are people Israel wants. That does not save them from being looked down upon. Half the people of Israel are now from countries where Yiddish is unknown. In Israel, for the first time, the tender language of East European ghettoes has become an upper class tongue. The Ashkenazi, the Yiddish-speaking Jews, hold the commanding positions in the community. The Sephardi, or Oriental Jews, speaking Arabic, French or the Old Castilian of the Spain from which they were driven five centuries ago, are the hewers of wood and drawers of water. They make up half the population but their children are only 15 per cent of those in secondary schools and only 5 per cent of those in the university. Their cultural level is lower. They cannot afford to send their children to the higher schools. Discrimination has given them solidarity. "Communal" tickets have begun to appear in local elections, pitting Sephardi against Ashkenazi. The right wing parties are making demagogic appeals to the Oriental Jews. On the other side one Yiddish speaking *meshuganah* has just published a book to prove that the Yiddish-speaking from the West are the only true Jews! The government is trying its best to give preferences to the Orientals where equally qualified. It fears lest Israel run into a situation like that of Belgium where after 150 years the conflict between Walloon and Fleming divides the nation. Fortunately the common language of Hebrew, and the melting pot of school and Army, are available to ease Israel's divisions. Education is seen as the key to amalgamation but education costs money and here we come to Israel's other big headache, that of defense.

The amount spent on defense is a secret but some notion of its magnitude may be gathered from a veiled figure in the budget. This shows that about a third goes for an item called "Security, special budget and reserve." This has been rising. It was less than $300 million or 28.3 per cent of the 1963/64 budget and close to $400 million or 30.9 per cent of the 1964/65 budget. The next largest item was education, but this is less than 8 per cent of the budget. Were the arms race in the Middle East to end, Israel could afford to make secondary education free, too, as elementary education is now. Nothing could do more to develop her human resources and end the rankling inferiority of Oriental Jew and Arab. Another way to measure the impact of the arms race is to notice that "security, special budget and reserve" amounts to more than German reparations, UJA, private gifts and donations of food surpluses put together. If Israel enjoyed real peace, she would no longer be dependent on the bread of charity.

However one looks at it, peace is Israel's overriding problem. It's hard for a poor country to keep up with the Joneses in armament. "In the war for independence," said one of those tireless old-timers who make Israel the dynamic community that it is, "a Spitfire was hot stuff. We could buy one second-hand for £2,000. Now the Mystère costs us $750,000; the Mirage, $1,000,000; the super-Mirage, $1,250,000. But planes and tanks are given to Egypt by the Russians for very little. They gave Nasser fifteen submarines and a flotilla of Komars, swift mosquito boats armed with missiles which can shoot from thirty kilometers offshore. Now we're afraid Egypt may get enriched uranium from Moscow, too." Between Russian aid and German scientists there is a real fear that Egypt may some day be the instrument for a second go at Hitler's "final solution." Khrushchev's visit stirred deep anxiety. "The Government of Israel regrets," Prime Minister Eshkol told the Knesset pointedly May 20, "that in spite of the Egyptian ruler's aggressive declarations against Israel he receives political support and supplies of arms from sources that generally advocate peace and co-existence." It is tragic that Israel could not have joined its neighbor in rejoicing over so fruitful and historic an achievement as the Aswan Dam. And it was mischief-making demagogy for Khrushchev to join the Arab States in stigmatizing as an imperialist plot the beginnings of the Jordan water scheme which could benefit the whole area. It does no more than put to use millions of precious gallons otherwise wasted in the Dead Sea.

To inflame the Arab-Israeli quarrel is to risk no small conflagration. Eshkol's statement on the eve of his visit to the United States reiterated previous denials that atomic development in Israel was designed for other than peaceful purposes. But doubts persist. There are circles in Israel which see nuclear arms as a necessity for survival. They fear that neo-Nazi German scientists are using Egypt as a proving ground for "unconventional" weapons. The arms race between Egypt and Israel can become the next hot spot in the proliferation of nuclear arms. A committee of distinguished scholars and scientists in Israel have began to agitate for a denuclearized Arab-Israeli area but there is no echo from Egypt, where a police state represses free opinion. Behind the quarrel which is dividing Israel's ruling party, the Mapai—the quarrel between Ben-Gurion and Eshkol over the irrepressible Lavon affair—is a struggle between younger military men who put their faith in force and an Old Guard which wishes to steer a course of moderation away from the apocalyptic adventurism of Ben-Gurion. The Suez affair showed that B.G. and the military were able to carry on secretly behind the back of civilian government. They might do so again. Now is the time to prevent Egypt and Israel from wasting their substance and endangering the world in the blind alley of a nuclear arms race.

JUNE 1, 1964

# THE HARDER BATTLE
# AND THE NOBLER VICTORY

Israel's swift and brilliant military victory only makes its reconciliation with the Arabs more urgent. Its future and world peace call for a general and final settlement now of the Palestine problem. The cornerstone of that settlement must be to find new homes for the Arab refugees, some within Israel, some outside it, all with compensation for their lost lands and properties. The world Jewish community, already girding itself for a huge financial effort to aid Israel, should be thankful that its victory has come with so little loss of life or damage to either side. The same funds may now be diverted to a constructive and human cause. It was a moral tragedy—to which no Jew worthy of our best Prophetic tradition could be insensitive—that a kindred people was made homeless in the task of finding new homes for the remnants of the Hitler holocaust. Now is the time to right that wrong, to show magnanimity in victory, and to lay the foundations of a new order in the Middle East in which Israeli and Arab can live in peace.

This alone can make Israel secure. This is the third Israeli-Arab war in twenty years. In the absence of a general settlement, war will recur at regular intervals. The Arabs will thirst for revenge. The Israeli will be tempted again to wage preventive war, as in 1956 and now again. The Israeli borders are so precarious, the communications between Jerusalem and the coast, on the coast between Tel Aviv and Haifa, and up the finger of Eastern Galilee, are so narrow, so easily cut, as to be untenable in static defensive warfare. A surprise attack would cut Israel into half a dozen parts. A long war would be suicidal for a community of not much more than 2,000,000 Jews in a sea of 50,000,000 Arabs. Only total mobilization can defend it, and total mobilization is impossible for any extended term in Israel since it brings the wheels of the economy to a crawl. The strategic and demographic circumstances dictate blitzkrieg, and blitzkrieg is a dangerous gamble. To be forced to keep that weapon in reserve is ruinous.

It is ruinous financially and it is ruinous morally. It imposes a huge armament burden. It feeds an ever more intense and costly arms race, as each side seeks frantically for ever newer and more complex weapons. It brings with it a spiral of fear and hate. It creates within Israel the atmosphere of a besieged community, ringed by hostile neighbors, its back to the sea, skeptical with good reason of the world community, relying only on its own military strength, turning every man and woman into a soldier, regarding every Arab within it distrustfully as a potential Fifth Columnist, and glorying in its military strength. Chauvinism and militarism are the inescapable fruits. They can turn Israel into an Ishmael. They can create a minuscule Prussia, not the beneficent Zion for which the Prophets hoped and of which the Zionists once dreamed. The East will not be redeemed by turning it into a new Wild West, where Israel can rely only on a quick draw with a six-shooter.

In justice to Israel no one can forget the terrible history that has turned the Jewish State into a fighting community. Events still fresh in living memory illustrate how little reliance may be placed on the conscience of mankind. Long before the crematoria were built, in the six years of Nazi rule before World War II, refugees met a cold shoulder. Our State Department like the British Foreign Office distinguished itself in those years by its anemic indifference to the oppressed and its covert undertone of admiration for the Axis; our few anti-Fascist ambassadors, like Dodd in Berlin and Bowers in Madrid, were treated miserably by the Department. The welcome signs in the civilized world were few, and even now if events were reversed and Israel were overrun it could expect little more than a few hand-wringing resolutions. Both sides would play up to the Arabs for their oil and their numbers. If the upshot of this new struggle is the expropriation of Western Europe's oil sources in the Middle East, it will only seem to history a giant retribution for the moral failure that forced the survivors of Hitlerism to seek a refuge in the inhospitable deserts, drawn by a pitiful mirage that pictured them as an ancestral home.

The precedent of the cease-fire resolution at the UN *is* a most disturbing one. It accepts preventive war and allows the one which launched it to keep the fruits of aggression as a bargaining card. But Israel has a right to ask what the UN was prepared to do if Nasser had been able to carry out his threats of total war and the complete destruction of Israel. Who would have intervened in time? Who would take the survivors? These are the bitter thoughts which explain Israel's belief that it can rely on itself alone. But to understand this is not to accept it. The challenge to the world is the creation of a better order and first of all to remove the Middle East from the arena of great power rivalry; this alone can keep it from becoming sooner or later the starting point of another world war. The challenge to Israel is to conquer something more bleak and forbidding even than the Negev or Sinai, and that is the hearts of its Arab neighbors. This would be greater and more permanent than any military victory. Abba Eban exultantly called the sweep of Israel's armies "the finest day in Israel's modern history." The finest day will be the day it achieves reconciliation with the Arabs.

To achieve it will require an act of sympathy worthy of the best in Jewry's Biblical heritage. It is to understand and forgive an enemy, and thus convert him into a friend. A certain obtuseness was unfortunately evident in Abba Eban's brilliant presentation of Israel's cause to the Security Council. To rest a case on Jewish homelessness and refuse at the same time to see the Arabs who have been made homeless is only another illustration of that tribal blindness which plagues the human race and plunges it constantly into bloodshed. The first step toward reconciliation is to recognize that Arab bitterness has real and deep roots. The refugees lost their farms, their villages, their offices, their cities and their country. It is human to prefer not to look at the truth, but only in facing the problem in all its three-dimensional, frightful reality is there any hope of solving it without new tragedy.

Just as Jews everywhere sympathize with their people, so Arabs everywhere sympathize and identify with theirs. They feel that anti-Semitic Europe solved its Jewish problem at Arab expense. To a rankling sense of injustice is now added a third episode in military humiliation. Zionist propaganda always spoke of the role that the Jews could play in helping to modernize the Arab world. Unless firm steps are taken now to a general and generous settlement, this will become true in a sense never intended. The repercussions of the 1948 war set off seismic tremors that brought a wave of nationalist revolutions in Egypt, Syria and Iraq. The repercussions of this new defeat will lead a new generation of Arabs to modernize and mobilize for revenge, inspired (as are the Jews) by memories of past glory.

Considering their numbers and resources and the general rise of all the colonial people in this period, the Arabs must eventually prevail. Those who shudder to think that Israel, with all it cost in devotion and all it won honorably in marsh and desert, might be destroyed after a short life as were the Maccabean and Crusader kingdoms before it, all who want it to live and grow in peace, must seek to avoid such a solution. Israel cannot live very long in a hostile Arab sea. It cannot set its face against that renaissance of Arabic unity and civilization which began to stir a generation ago. It cannot remain a Western outpost in an Afro-Asian world casting off Western domination. It cannot repeat on a bigger scale the mistakes it made in Algeria, where Israel and Zionism were allies of Soustelle and Massu and the French rightists. It must join the Third World if it is to survive. No quickie military victories should blind it to the inescapable—in the long run it cannot defeat the Arabs. It must join them. The Jews played a great role in Arabic civilization in the Middle Ages. A Jewish State can play a similar role in a new Semitic renaissance. This is the perspective of safety, of honor, and of fraternity.

One crucial step in this direction is, in the very hour of victory, to heal wounded Arab pride as much as possible, and in particular to reach a new understanding with Nasser. Both American policy and Israeli policy have sacrificed long-range wisdom to short-sighted advantage in dealing with the Egyptian leader. He is a military dictator, he wages his own Vietnam in Yemen, he uses poison gas there against his own people, he runs a police state. But he is also the first Egyptian ruler to give Egypt's downtrodden *fellahin* a break. It is fascinating to recall that Egypt has been ruled by foreigners almost since the days when David and Solomon ruled in Israel. Not until Nasser's time, and the eviction of the British and French at Suez, have the Egyptians at long last become the master in their own ancient house. Nasser's program has given Egypt its first taste of reform, on the land, in the factory, in health and educational services. His accomplishments certainly surpass those of a comparable military figure, Ayub in Pakistan. The U.S. oil interests, Johnson's animosity and Israel's ill-will have been united in recent years in efforts to get rid of him. They have all favored feudal monarchs like Saudi Arabia's whose day is done. It is Nasser who represents the future and who can create the internal stability so necessary to peace. The alternative, if he is overthrown, will ultimately be some far more fanatical and less constructive force like the Moslem Brotherhood. If war makes sense only as an extension of politics by other means, then Israel's victory will make political sense only if it leads to a new era of friendly relations with Nasser. This is the biggest challenge of all to objectivity and insight in both Washington and Jerusalem.

The bigger picture as we write is ominous. The price of bogging down American military power in a peripheral and irrelevant theater like Vietnam is a huge shift in the balance of power in Europe and the Middle East. If the Arabs go through with nationalization of oil resources, the effect on the pound sterling will be catastrophic. This will be another giant step in the disintegration of West European empire. Western Europe in a sense has already lost the third world war. To avert its outbreak, steps are needed as quickly as possible to reduce world tension. The U.S. could contribute mightily by calling off our barbarous and futile bombing of North Vietnam and making peace in South Vietnam. One crisis at a time is enough, indeed too much. The superpowers have taken a first step in the UN cease-fire resolution to damp down the dangers of a wider war in the Middle East, at least temporarily. Can't the same initiative be widened to the Far East?

JUNE 12, 1967

# FOR A UNIVERSAL DAY
# OF ATONEMENT

Walking around East Berlin in 1959, I wandered into a theatre where a movie was playing called *Sterne* (Stars). The stars were the stars of David the Jews wore in the Hitler period. It was a Bulgarian-East German film about a Jewish concentration camp girl with whom a Wehrmacht officer falls in love. Later he joins the Partisans after she is packed into the freight cars for Auschwitz. When I heard that the Eichmann verdict had finally been handed down in Jerusalem, I remembered a scene in that film when the concentration camp inmates first heard rumors that the Germans were burning up people in crematoriums. They went to their leader, an old Jewish doctor, and he reassured them saying, *"Aber die Deutschen sind auch Menschen,"* i.e., "The Germans are also human." He feels no human being could possibly do anything so wicked; the rumors couldn't be true.

In that darkened movie house, amid all those Germans, I cried, remembering the survivors with whom I travelled as a reporter from Poland to Palestine in the spring of 1946, and the stories they told me. I haven't had the heart to follow the Eichmann trial. This one man in the dock is too trivial beside the mountainous toll of humiliation and death he symbolized. Whether sincerely or not, the picture he drew of himself was a picture likely to appeal to many Germans as guilty as he— the picture of the fussy bureaucrat who only did his duty, a cog in a machine. How easily the Germans excuse themselves.

But we learn nothing by blaming them. Events since the war have prepared greater crematoriums. Everywhere men excuse themselves the same way. We dropped "little" bombs on the innocent in Hiroshima and Nagasaki. Now we and the Russians together are prepared to drop bigger ones. The issues have become blurred. And these dreadful truths have become stale and futile commonplaces we all ignore.

I don't know what the verdict will be on Eichmann. I don't care. But it would honor world Jewry if the judges were to refuse even in his case, with all it implies, to impose the death penalty Israel abolished. It would be a noble rebuke to an un-Christian Christian world and to a still brutal Russian communist world of death sentences for minor offenses—to two worlds which share the poison of anti-Semitism still despite the Gospels they respectively proclaim and the horror to which Hitler showed it could lead. Let Eichmann live on like Cain, with the Mark upon him.

It is more important to recognize that the Mark is on all of us. What good is it for Moscow to accuse Heusinger of war crime when Khrushchev himself threatens it on a greater scale, and we do likewise? Would an extra-terrestrial tribunal after a new war distinguish between Russians and Americans and Germans? Is mass murder justified for any reason whatsoever? Is not every national leader a war criminal if he does not recognize that no dispute justifies risking the future of our common human species?

I would proclaim a day of meditation on the crematoriums, a universal Day of Atonement. I would remember that we all marched with Eichmann to the prison or the gallows. Whether it was the human incinerator or the H-bomb, we built it. To be human is to be guilty. No other message has the dimensions to match what Eichmann's trial recalled.

DECEMBER 18, 1961

# *INDEX*

## About the Author

Born in 1907, I. F. Stone has been a working newspaperman since the age of fourteen when, during his sophomore year at a small-town high school, he launched a monthly, *The Progress*, which supported — among other causes — the League of Nations and Gandhi's first efforts at freedom for India.

While at school and college, he worked for daily newspapers in Camden, New Jersey, Philadelphia, and New York.

Since 1940 he has served in succession as a Washington correspondent and commentator for *The Nation*, the newspaper *PM*, the *New York Post*, and the *Daily Compass*. In 1953 he launched *I. F. Stone's Weekly*, a legendary venture in independent, one-man journalism, which he edited and published for nineteen years. He has written extensively for the *New York Review of Books* and long served as a contributing editor. He writes a Washington column at irregular intervals for *The Nation* and many daily papers at home and abroad, including the *Philadelphia Inquirer*, on which he worked while he was in college.

In semiretirement Mr. Stone returned to the philosophy and classical history he had studied in college. He taught himself ancient Greek and wrote *The Trial of Socrates*, a controversial probe of the most famous free-speech case of all time, widely acclaimed on publication in 1988.

Mr. Stone and his wife, Esther, live in Washington. They have three married children.